The Liberatory Thought of Martin Luther King Jr.

The Liberatory Thought of Martin Luther King Jr.

Critical Essays on the Philosopher King

Edited by Robert E. Birt

LEXINGTON BOOKS
Lanham • Boulder • New York • Toronto • Plymouth, UK

Published by Lexington Books
A wholly owned subsidiary of Rowman & Littlefield
4501 Forbes Boulevard, Suite 200, Lanham, Maryland 20706
www.rowman.com

10 Thornbury Road, Plymouth PL6 7PP, United Kingdom

British Library Cataloguing in Publication Information Available

Library of Congress Cataloging-in-Publication Data
The hardback edition of this book was previously cataloged by the Library of Congress as
follows:

Birt, Robert E.
The liberatory thought of Martin Luther King Jr.: critical essays on the philosopher King
/ edited by Robert E. Birt.
p. cm.
Includes bibliographical references and index.
1. King, Martin Luther, Jr., 1929–1968—Philosophy. 2. Nonviolence—United States. 3.
African Americans—Social conditions—20th century. 4. African Americans—Civil
rights. I. Birt, Robert E., 1952–
E185.97.K5L47 2012
323.092—dc23
2012020032

ISBN : 978-0-7391-6552-2 (cloth : alk. paper)
ISBN : 978-0-7391-9780-6 (pbk : alk. paper)
ISBN : 978-0-7391-6554-6 (electronic)

Printed in the United States of America

Contents

Acknowledgments

Every intellectual work, even when done in relative personal isolation, is a social creation. This is especially true of a collaborative work like this philosophical anthology, involving many contributing scholars. So, I especially want to commend all sixteen of my contributing fellow philosophers and scholars whose excellent work made this anthology possible. Your creative efforts have contributed to the formation of a work which, I believe, constitutes a philosophical expression of the Kingian aspiration toward the Beloved Community. I have worked with some of you on previous projects, and look forward to our collaboration on many others. I must also thank Bowie State University, my home institution, and Dr. M. Sammye Miller (my departmental chair) for the financial assistance that helped bring this volume to fruition. We might have encountered a serious hurdle on the way to fruition without that assistance.

As for friends and colleagues who have aided and inspired me in this work, you are too many to number or mention by name. Indeed those who have inspired this work go beyond the limited boundaries of academia and the charmed circle of fellow scholars, philosophers, and intellectuals. They include teachers, preachers, and community activists who were imbued with Dr. King's passion for social justice. They include my mother, Mrs. Hattie Birt, from whom I first learned of the struggles of my people and our family. It was from her that I first learned of the courage of Rosa Parks, the legacy of Dr. King, and the meaning of the Movement that was reshaping the nation during the formative years of my childhood and adolescence. Moreover, it was her teachings in the tradition of what Rufus Burrows calls homespun African American Social Gospelism that first awakened my social conscience, a conscience that remains awakened even though in a more secular form. I owe much inspiration to elder scholars like the late Richard I. McKinney, founder of the philosophy department of Morgan State University, and a contemporary (reportedly associate) of Drs. Benjamin Mays and Mordecai Johnson. And I owe an immense debt to the late Dr. Martin Luther King Jr. himself whose "Letter from Birmingham Jail" was the first piece of philosophical literature I read while still an adolescent, and whose leadership contributed immensely to a Movement without which my life would be far more constrained and less rich than it is. And I am inspired by numerous contemporary movements, both in practical and intellectual realms, that are still committed to the quest for social justice and a beloved commu-

ix

nity free of racism, economic injustice, and all social practices that violate the dignity of the human personality. To the legacy of Dr. Martin Luther King Jr. and to all those thinkers, activists, individuals, and movements still seeking to bring to fruition his quest for a more just society, I hereby dedicate this work as contribution to a common effort.

Introduction

Robert E. Birt

> Too often do educated ministers leave the people lost in a fog of theological abstraction. . . . It is my conviction that the minister must somehow take profound theological and philosophical views and place them in a concrete framework.
>
> —Martin Luther King Jr.

> The philosophers have only *interpreted* the world in various ways; the point is, to *change* it.
>
> —Karl Marx

How do we assess Dr. Martin Luther King as a *thinker*? How do we evaluate his intellectual legacy? The world well knows Dr. King as the pre-eminent leader of the 1960s' Civil Rights Movement. It knows less of him as a philosopher. Yet Dr. King was a thinker before he became an activist, a man of ideas deeply learned in Philosophy and Theology by long years of academic study. This volume of philosophical essays concerns itself with Dr. King as a thinker whose *thought* merits serious engagement. The seventeen scholars who contribute essays to this anthology do not deny King's world historical importance as a human rights *activist*. We do not mean to diminish the activist by engaging the thinker. Indeed the activist informs the kind of thinker King was. But the thinker also informs the activist. And it is probably in the dialectical synthesis of thinker and activist, and his unifying practice of ideation and action, that we find the clearest and most insightful perspective from which to understand the true character of the philosopher, King.

King was not a systematic philosopher; not an academic or professional philosopher. Consequently, some professional philosophers would doubt that he was a philosopher at all. "In what university did King teach philosophy?" skeptics might ask. "In what refereed journals in the field did he publish?" One can imagine the skepticism with which they would greet the claim made by Charles R. Johnson (a philosophically educated man of letters) that King was "our most prominent moral philosopher of the second half of the Twentieth Century."[1] Yet there are few issues more debated in the history of philosophy than the nature of philosophy (or the philosopher) itself. At least since the time of Plato the question "What is Philosophy?" has been a perennial issue of philosophical disputation.

1

The Western philosophical tradition alone often includes such nonacademic thinkers as Socrates, Seneca, Cicero, Montaigne, Pascal, Voltaire, Emerson, Nietzsche, and Camus. Like King, these thinkers were not academicians or systematic philosophers. Like King, many expressed their philosophical vision through letters, essays, and public addresses.[2] One may describe King as a *philosophical man of action*, whose intellectual work grows out of, and takes shape from, his chosen way of being as an insurgent philosopher-activist.

To the extent that one can identify King's thought with some traditional branch of philosophy, it would probably be ethics and social philosophy. For the most part King is a moral and social philosopher whose thought shapes and is shaped by the movement for freedom and social justice. King's thinking also leans toward philosophical anthropology, for example, in his public address "What Is Man?"[3] One can find metaphysical reflections as well that reveal King's intellectual roots in religion as well as in a tradition of philosophical idealism informed by Plato, Kant, Hegel, and Personalism. This is also evident from his criticisms of the materialism of Karl Marx in *Stride toward Freedom*.

But it is not primarily metaphysical reflections that occupy King. Rufus Burrow Jr. rightly notes that "For King philosophical study meant nothing if it could not be applied to eradicate the conditions that demeaned the worth of his people."[4] Contrary to Marx's famous criticism of philosophers, King is more concerned with changing than merely interpreting the world. As Professors Maria del Guadalupe and Scott Davidson note in chapter 9 of this volume, King does not disvalue contemplative life, but rather insists "that the value of all religious and philosophical ideas be rooted in praxis, or in other words, a *way of life*." King's primary emphasis is ethical and rooted in a deep moral concern for social justice—a concern focused on but not limited to civil rights for American Blacks, and also directed to issues of economic justice for the poor, ending class oppression, the quest for peace and opposition to militarism and imperialism. As leader of a liberation movement whose aim is to enlighten the masses and inspire them to liberating self-activity, the form of Dr. King's discourse is not the abstruse treatise but short articles, essays, public addresses, and letters.[5] His classic "Letter from Birmingham Jail" and two public addresses collected in the *The Measure of a Man* are exemplary expressions of Kingian philosophical discourse. Moreover, King's eloquent, deeply philosophical "Letter" was occasioned by his practical involvement and leadership in the famous Birmingham campaign. A classic of his dialectical synthesis of ideation and action, it almost certainly would never have been written had the 1963 Birmingham campaign not happened.

But King's education precedes his activism. His philosophical Odyssey at Morehouse, Crozer, and Boston University prepares him to become a "social movement intellectual." At Morehouse King discovers

Thoreau's "Essay on *Civil Disobedience*," which he describes as his "first intellectual contact with the theory of nonviolent resistance."[6] At Crozer King begins a serious philosophical quest "for a method to eliminate social evil," which leads him to the social gospel theology of Walter Rauschenbusch and an extensive study of the classical philosophical canon from Plato to contemporary existentialists. At Boston University King begins an intensive study of Hegel (his "favorite" philosopher) and Personalism, his "basic philosophical position."[7] He is also inspired by lectures of Mordecai Johnson (Black scholar and Howard University president) to deepen his knowledge of Gandhi and his philosophical commitment to nonviolence. King's pre-Movement philosophical development shapes the kind of activist he becomes. His study of Hegel begins his commitment to dialectical thinking which will inform his conception of history, his conception of the Movement, and his tactics and strategies as a movement leader. King's Personalism, which holds that personality is the metaphysically ultimate reality, affords him metaphysical grounding for the idea of a personal God, and justification for the idea of the dignity of all human personality. Ethical concern for human dignity will become the moral grounds for his opposition to racism, war, economic injustice, and various other social wrongs. It will reinforce his commitment to nonviolence and to the ethical ideal of the beloved community.

Thus, the fundamental principles of King's philosophy take shape before his emergence as a movement leader. Without his youthful philosophical *pris de conscience*, he could never have become the kind of leader that he eventually became. In this respect, he parallels Frederick Douglass who had to attain (illegally) intellectual enlightenment as a slave *before* he could become America's foremost Black abolitionist. But like Douglass, King pursues knowledge for the *purpose* of advancing freedom and liberation.[8] While at Boston University, he and fellow Black graduate students formed the "Dialectical Society," a club "mainly interested in certain philosophical and theological ideas and applied them to the black situation."[9] That they seek to apply ideas to the black situation is again evidence of a practical *emancipatory* impetus behind the most rarefied discourse. Even before Montgomery, while he and fellow students wrestled with perplexities of Hegel, Kierkegaard, and Personalism, moral issues of social justice are uppermost in King's philosophical conscience. King's developing philosophy is *already* a philosophy of praxis—a philosophy of *liberation*. And from Montgomery in 1955 to Memphis in 1968, King's activism would become the social practice of that philosophy of liberation.

It is precisely this deeply ethical and emancipatory emphasis in Dr. King's thought that most deeply engages the philosophical interests of the contributors to this anthology. This seems to be true of those who write on more expressly *theoretical* issues (like Stephen C. Ferguson II on King's conception of dialectics), as well as those whose focus seems more "topical" (like Gail M. Presbey's reflections on the relevance of King's opposition to the Vietnam War to the present American occupation of Iraq). It is King (or the ideas of King) as an *engaged* thinker that is the common philosophical concern of each writer. Of course, the topical focus and points of emphases vary, and these varied emphases result in different perspectives on King. The design of this text has been shaped by these different points of emphasis and thematic focus. Themes do overlap across different perspectives. Some writers situate King within certain philosophical traditions, and evaluate his contributions to those traditions. Some explore King's work from the standpoint of social philosophy or from the standpoint of his contributions to ethics. Some of our writers focus on the philosophical import of King's praxis as a thinker-activist. And there are writers who explore the philosophical and religious theme of hope in Kingian thought. Accordingly, this volume is organized into four parts: 1) "King within Philosophical Traditions," 2) "King as Engaged Social and Political Philosopher," 3) "King's Ethics of Nonviolence," and 4) "Hope Resurgent or Dream Deferred: Perspectives on King's Philosophical Optimism." In exploration of these themes let us now turn to a summary of our writers' probing inquiries of the thought of the philosopher, King.

KING WITHIN PHILOSOPHICAL TRADITIONS

Philosophers, thinkers, and intellectuals of all kinds necessarily inherit intellectual traditions and cultural legacies which deeply inform the shape of their own thinking. Such was also the case with Martin Luther King Jr. Yet many studies of Dr. King's philosophical and theological thought, though fully cognizant of the influences of Plato, Immanuel Kant, Georg Hegel, Paul Tillich, Reinhold Niebuhr, Walter Rauschenbusch, Mohandas Gandhi, and the Boston Personalists, take little note of African American thought and thinkers in the forming of King's philosophical outlook.

Chapter 1 opens this anthology with an essay by John H. McClendon III titled "Is Our Belief That Martin Luther King Jr. Is a Black Philosopher Justified?" It is a refreshing departure from those philosophical studies of King's thought that overlook or give short shrift to King's connectedness to African American thinkers like George D. Kelsey, Benjamin Mays, Mordecai W. Johnson, and Howard Thurman.[10] But McClendon emphasizes the complexity of King as a thinker, and insists that the complexity arises from the fact that King belongs to *several* traditions and that the character of his work doesn't derive from a strictly academic undertaking. As an activist King brings philosophical insight to bear on his practical concerns, and McClendon explores the ways in which this activist commitment informs the shape of King's philosophy. McClendon's es-

say, in its discussion of the question of whether King was a philosopher—and a *Black* philosopher—revisits with new insights issues of the
nature of philosophy itself, and the implicit notions of racial identity
suggested by the moniker "Black philosopher." Concluding that King
was a philosopher as well as activist, McClendon explores the question of
what kind of philosopher King was, and what shape was assumed by
King's philosophical praxis.

George Yancy's "Dr. King's Philosophy of Religion: A Theology of
Somebodiness," which forms the second chapter of this volume, is divided into three sections that mimic important themes in liberation: Context, Reflection, and Praxis. Yancy takes it as an exegetical necessity to
link King's philosophy of religion with his life-world. Hence, Yancy demonstrates the importance of exploring King's early familiar and communal religious influences as formative to King's critical reflections on and
acceptance of the philosophy of Personalism and how this philosophy
was already nascent in King's life experiences. Yancy also shows how
King's conception of racism was existentially rooted in King's early life.
In this way, Yancy demonstrates how King's understanding of the nature
of racism did not grow out of a form of armchair philosophical reflection,
but was experienced by King throughout his life. For King, according to
Yancy, white racism is anti-Christian and theologically profane. Yancy's
chapter speaks to the organic unity of King's lived context, philosophical
and theological reflection, and theological and political praxis. Yancy
argues that King's philosophy of religion, as a theology of somebodiness,
is an expression of a species of liberation theology that is committed to
the liberation of Black people in particular, and to the liberation of all
those who suffer from political and existential disinheritance.

In his essay "Dr. King as Liberation Theologian and Existential Philosopher," James B. Haile II offers another critical perspective on King as a
black liberation theologian, and also as an existential philosopher. Em-
ploying ideas of James Cone, Haile tries to situate King in the discourse
of a Black theology of liberation. He argues that Black theology is not
solely concerned with the ontology of oppression, but with reconciliation
and putting back together of a human community ruptured by racism.
And it is these latter concerns that link the theology of Cone with King's
theology of liberation that seeks reconciliation in the "beloved community." But whereas Yancy emphasizes the importance of Personalism in
King's thought, Haile emphasizes existentialism. Haile describes King as
an "existential philosopher," and Black theology as an "aspect" of Black
existentialism.

Stephen C. Ferguson II, who regards Personalism and Existentialism
as forms of subjective idealism, focuses on King as a dialectical thinker in
an essay entitled "Dr. King as Philosopher: An examination of the Influences of Hegelian Dialectics on King's Political Thought and Practice."
He emphasizes the importance of making a critical *reconstruction* of

King's *philosophical worldview*. Ferguson is concerned both with King's intellectual comprehension of dialectics and his employment of dialectical thought in his social practice as Movement leader. Foundational to this analysis is the social or material context, as a process of objective development, which shapes and directs King's thinking as a dialectician. In exploring stages in the development of King's dialectical thought, Ferguson argues that contrary to what is often assumed—and even what King himself believed—King's early conception of dialectics is *not* Hegelian, but rather reflexive in nature. This is due to precisely the influence of Personalism and Existentialism discerned in King's thought by Yancy and Haile. In fact, Ferguson notes that King actually makes a Kierkegaardian critique of Hegel. King's early adoption of a dialectics of *synthesis* finds its ground in consensus, conciliation, and compromise. But in the post-1965 period, King as a dialectician becomes more Hegelian, approximating a dialectics of *negation* in the practice of a more radical opposition to the status quo.

We can see that a significant part of the efforts of Professors McClendon, Yancy, and Ferguson situates King as a thinker within varied philosophical traditions. But can the engaged social philosopher *form* new traditions of thought or knowledge through the very practice of social activism? Reflection on that possibility is the primary concern of Maurice St. Pierre's "Martin Luther King Jr. as a Social Movement Intellectual: Trailblazer or Torchbear?" This essay explores the ways in which King's work as a thinker-activist reveals him as an exemplar of the "movement intellectual," an *engaged intellectual* whose social praxis is at once both the *creation of knowledge* and the transformation of society. Indeed, one may speak of the creation of knowledge through the transformation of society. The author especially draws upon the theoretical resources of sociology of knowledge and Gramscian theory of culture and the organic intellectual to show how King and the Civil Rights movement created space for themselves in the political fabric of society, and how in the process a new body of knowledge emerged from the Movement's practical and theoretical activity. This analysis of King's praxis of knowledge creation is done against the background of an analysis of "intellectualism" and the intellectual as a social type. St. Pierre's Gramscian analysis implicitly reinforces Ferguson's emphasis on social struggle and the historical-social context in shaping King's thinking as a dialectician.

KING AS ENGAGED SOCIAL AND POLITICAL PHILOSOPHER

King's dialectical thought was mainly directed at understanding and transforming social reality. Hence it is his social and political thought, especially as regarding the themes of community and democracy that is explored by Richard Jones, Tim Lake, and me in the second part of this volume.

Richard A. Jones opens this section with "The Struggle for Loving Communities: Martin Luther King's Agape and World House." Jones views King as a prescient thinker, and sees his vision of beloved community as especially pertinent to the social and ethical issues of our time. King understood that the social, political, and personal fragmentation (now called the "postmodern condition") could only be overcome by a transvaluation of values in community imbued with *agape*. Agape love is one that transcends love of self, family, tribe, race, class, or nation. It is rooted in a philosophical vision of the organic interconnectedness of all life. This conception of the interconnectedness of life, and interrelatedness of the universe, largely informs King's understanding that poverty, racism, and war are related ("tripled headed monster") as direct results of exploitative economic and political interests. While many academic philosophers do not appreciate King as a philosopher, Jones argues that King's philosophical legacy, with his vision of universal human community as World House, is becoming more important as the world continues to shrink due to globalization. And maybe more important than the reasons he is celebrated as a civil rights leader. .

My essay "King's Radical Vision of Community" explores King's vision of community as part of his implicitly *radical* critique of the social order. I argue that King's vision of freedom and social justice is inseparable from his vision of community, and that this social vision entails a radical transcendence not only of racism, but of the entire socioeconomic order that breeds racism, economic injustice, acquisitiveness, imperialism, and war. Community is shown to be the philosophical locus of King's social radicalism. Integral to community is the primacy of the human person, the unalienable *dignity* of *every* human being, but also the idea that the human person as a unique individual can only exist as "person-in-community"—and not as a disconnected atom of aggressive self-interest revered by the tradition of "rugged individualism." Personhood and Community, inseparable ideas in King's moral and social philosophy, constitute the moral basis of King's critique of racial caste, economic exploitation, militarism, and the corrosive obsessions of a consumerist culture that values possessions over persons. King's ethical ideal of community also forms the basis for his commitment to nonviolence and his call for a "revolution of values" to transform our "thing-oriented" profiteering society into a "person-oriented" *cooperative society*. King's radical critique, I argue, is grounded in the prophetic moral tradition within the Judeo-Christian legacy (especially in homespun social gospel of southern Black culture) as well as humanistic strains in Western philosophical idealism.

Professor Tim Lake closes the second section of the anthology with his essay "Martin Luther King Jr.: Toward a Democratic Theory." This essay more specifically looks at King's value for political philosophy. Lake underscores the democratic theory located within the work of Dr. King. Special attention is given to King's conception of human psychology, Christian identity, and appreciation for Marxist social analysis. The conclusion is that King understood the *expansion* of democratic practices to be the best hope for humanity. That is, democratic values and procedures, at their best, are a moral corrective and institutional safeguard against the human propensity for evil.

KING'S ETHICS OF NONVIOLENCE

Our discussion of King's vision of community and democracy clearly indicates that in social questions and politics, King's thinking is primarily that of a moral philosopher. Ethical considerations are his primary concern. Thus it seems quite appropriate that our section on Kingian ethics — his ethics of nonviolence — is opened by Professors Maria del Guadalupe Davidson and Scott C. Davidson's "Ethics as First Philosophy: King, Levinas, and the Future of Peace." This essay examines Dr. King and Levinas as parallel moral philosophers whose thought emerges from the catastrophic violence of the twentieth century. While suffering violence from the dominant culture, both thinkers put forth moral philosophies that resist the temptations of retaliatory violence. Both realize the best hope for humanity is through peace. For both thinkers ethics takes on central importance. For both King and Levinas ethics assumes the status of *First Philosophy*, thus taking the place traditionally attributed to Metaphysics since the time of Aristotle. Through an analysis of King's and Levinas's respective accounts of the ethical relation to the *other*, Professors Davidson argues that both thinkers understand the ethical relation to be rooted in a prior peace. Their analysis of the politics of King and Levinas leads them to conclude that while Levinas's understanding of the political allows violence, King's politics does not. The essay concludes with an exploration of the implications of King's *ethics as praxis* for opening a future of peace.

Yet such a nonviolent ethics of peace must eventually confront the violent *reality* of war. While the Civil Rights Movement was the primary arena in which Dr. King espoused and practiced his philosophy of nonviolence, his most controversial application of his principles of nonviolence was in his opposition to the Vietnam War. King's critique of the Vietnam War is of special relevance today as America involves herself in two more imperial wars. It is with this in mind that Professor Gail M. Presbey offers her essay "Martin Luther King Jr. on Vietnam: King's Message Applied to the U.S. Occupation of Iraq and Afghanistan."

Presbey notes that King's critique of the Vietnam War was at once a moral critique of militarism generally, and of American neocolonialism in particular. The chapter begins with King's early years when he was reluctant to speak out against the war, and explores the factors and reasons that led him to become its outspoken critic. Two topics receive special attention in this chapter. The first is King's message to Americans that there was a "crisis of values," and that Americans needed to rethink their entire order of values as well as their practices regarding war and militarism. (Related to this is King's challenge to America to get on the right side of the worldwide revolution of the oppressed and dispossessed). Secondly, the essay explores the parallels between King's message to Americans during the Vietnam War, and the current context of America's war and occupation of Iraq. Recalling King's critique of the geopolitical and corporate market-driven profiteering interests as motives behind militarism, as well as his call for a revolution of values that would transform a materialistic, consumer-oriented society into a peaceful person-centered community, Presbey shows the contemporary relevance of this moral critique in her examination of the current crisis in the Middle East.

Kathryn T. Gines reflects on the challenge presented to Dr. King's ethics of nonviolence by Black movement thinkers and activists who advocated violent insurgency. Her "Martin Luther King and Frantz Fanon: Reflections on the Politics and Ethics of Violence and Nonviolence" offers an analysis of the ethics and politics of nonviolence advocated by Dr. King, and liberatory violence advocated by Dr. Frantz Fanon, which interfaces the thought of two radically opposed Africana thinkers. Gines notes that in King's *Where Do We Go From Here*, which critiques the revolutionary violence advocated in Fanon's *The Wretched of the Earth*, King opposes violence both *on principle* and on grounds that it is *impractical*. Taking into account the distinction between *principle* (an ethical question) and *impracticality* (a political question), Gines argues that King (and the Civil Rights Movement) and Fanon (and the Black Power Movement) had different political and ethical ends and different means to achieve these ends. Given that difference, Gines reasons that King's critique of Fanon is misguided. Yet she thinks that history has proven King correct (about the politics, if not the ethics of nonviolence) in his assertion that "there is no colored nation, including China, that shows even a potential of leading a violent revolution of color in any international proportions."

Greg Moses, who has published a book on King, also ponders both the efficacy and rightness of nonviolence and violence in his essay "A Shocking Gap Made Visible: King's Pacifist Materialism and the Method of Nonviolent Change." Moses notes that when deciding between violence and nonviolence as means, one cannot but think about ends. Recalling Malcolm X's claim that people have a right to any means necessary in pursuit of freedom and justice, Moses ponders the ethical reasons why violence is rejected by pacifist devotees of liberation like Dr. King. Interestingly enough, Moses argues that King *does not* renounce a people's right to violence (that right being inalienable). Yet in circumstances where that right to violence arises, the method of nonviolent change re-nounces violence. Moses finds two justifications of this renunciation: the first derives from an absolute *duty* that is commonly grounded in faith; the second justification is *strategic* and falsifiable, involving a renuncia-tion of violence as an effective means to bring the movement into surer control of its own future liberation. We might surmise that Moses offers another, different analysis of the distinction between principle and practi-cality that is also addressed in the essay by Gines.

Yet King's commitment to nonviolence is fundamentally a moral com-mitment, a commitment on grounds of ethical principle. In both his ideas and his practice of nonviolent activism, he may be said to embody a philosophical and prophetic vocation as *teacher*. This vision of King's vocation and thought is articulated in Benjamin O. Arah's essay "Socra-tes, Gandhi, and King: Politics of Civil Disobedience and the Ethics of Nonviolent Action." Professor Arah situates King in a tradition of moral witness and sacrifice, and in a tradition of moral dissent and social cri-tique historically represented by such figures as Socrates, Christ, and Gandhi. Not merely a celebration of King's unique legacy as dissident thinker and moral witness, this essay examines the connection between Socrates, Gandhi, and King in a manner that attempts to highlight how the philosophy of nonviolence rooted in ethical idealism was critical to the politics of deliberate civil disobedience that exposed the ills of society. In his exemplary civil dissent King appears as one of the moral educators of humankind.

HOPE RESURGENT OR DREAM DEFERRED: PERPLEXITIES OF KING'S PHILOSOPHICAL OPTIMISM

Thinkers like King who are leaders of a liberation movement cannot pre-vail without hope, and hope is unsurprisingly a persistent theme in the thought of Dr. King. For "when all seems hopeless," Dr. King reasons, "men know that without hope they cannot really live, and in agonizing desperation they cry for the bread of hope."[11] Without hope King could hardly have continued his work as prophetic thinker-activist. In his fight against racial caste, his opposition to war, his struggles for justice for the poor, and his pursuit of the Beloved Community, King and the Move-ment sought (in his words) to "carve out of the mountain of despair a stone of hope." But is that hope real or illusory? And ought not the theme of hope in Dr. King's thought to receive the kind of scholarly treatment that has been given to his thinking on nonviolence, justice, and Agapic love? These are among the questions concerning Kingian hope that are addressed by Professors Floyd W. Hayes III, Bill E. Lawson, and Clanton C. W. Dawson Jr. in the final part of *The Philosopher, King*.

Hayes's essay "Hope and Disappointment in Martin Luther King's Political Theology: Eclipse of the Liberal Spirit" sees King's thought as rooted in a philosophical optimism, liberal theology, and a philosophy of liberal hope. He argues that King opposes white supremacy from within the framework of liberal visions of freedom, equality, and democracy. Hayes offers critical challenges to King's intellectual responses to Black Power and other movements that rejected his philosophical optimism and the ideological liberalism of the mainstream Civil Rights Movement. Hayes is deeply critical of King's liberal philosophy of hope. He argues that liberalism, as a political formula for self-consciously organizing society, is fatally bound to the continuance of a modern understanding of life that simultaneously and cynically excludes and includes Black humanity. Hayes's essay attempts to flesh out an alternative philosophical perspective in which resentment and liberation constitute an injunction to combat oppression.

In "The Aporia of Hope: King and Bell on Ending Racism" Lawson also critically questions King's philosophical optimism. He critically reads King in juxtaposition to Derrick Bell, whose *Faces at the Bottom of the Well* expresses acute skepticism toward the prospects of overcoming American racism and social injustice. Lawson is skeptical of a Kingian optimism rooted in liberal humanist and Christian universalist ideals of brotherhood. He clearly leans toward Bell's view that racism is a permanent feature of American life. King and Bell were both distrustful of the ability of liberal theory to solve the race problem in the United States. This distrust gave rise to differing understanding about the ability of white Americans to recognize the humanity of Blacks. The election of President Barack Obama seems to shift the argument to King's position, but Lawson thinks that current white American attitudes toward the black masses tend to give support to Bell's position..

Dawson seems to affirm the importance and value of hope in Kingian thought. His essay "The Concept of Hope in the Thinking of Martin Luther King Jr." also seeks to help remedy a lack in King scholarship. Dawson sees a lack of scholarly attention to hope in King's philosophical theology compared to the great attention paid to his concepts of love and justice. He argues that hope is fundamental to King's thought and work, and his essay focuses on three key aspects of hope in King's thought. First, it shows how the concept of hope is foundational to King's concept of God. Second, it shows how hope motivated King's sociopolitical thought regarding the possibility of social justice in America. Finally, it examines the role of hope in King's conceptualization of the beloved community. Dawson concludes by inferring that while Kingian hope is plagued with some problematic conclusions, his conceptual framework of hope demonstrates his dexterity as a thinker and is worthy of contemporary reflection.

Perhaps it is only right that a book devoted to the thought of Dr. King should conclude on the theme of hope. King was certainly a philosopher and theologian of hope in the prophetic tradition. Quite appropriately, his last public address on April 3, 1968, spoken to impoverished sanitation workers on strike in Memphis, was essentially a message of encouragement and hope.[12] Hope is as essential as freedom, love, justice, and nonviolence to the philosophical worldview of King. It may well be one of the most important dimensions of his legacy bequeathed to us. And I can certainly say, on a personal note, that my own sense of hope (partly inspired by King, though not grounded in his idealist or theistic ethics or metaphysics) is largely what has inspired me to undertake this project. It is my wish—my *hope*—that this work of my sixteen colleagues and me can contribute in some small way to advancing the quest for social justice to which Dr. King devoted his life.

There is perhaps one concern that I should address before closing. The literature on Dr. King, both popular and scholarly, has grown so voluminous that readers might wonder, "Why *another* book on King?" First, it can be said that King's writings and speeches are an intellectual gold mine that richly rewards frequent philosophical explorations with valuable new insights. It is not without reason that the American Philosophical Association includes a *Gandhi-King Society* among its many learned societies. Philosophers concerned about violence and war, continued racial inequalities, the sufferings of the poor, the atomizing of human bonds by the consumerist ethos of contemporary global capitalism, are likely to find much of value in King's varied critiques of these same evils—evils that have grown significantly in the forty years since King's death.

Furthermore, it should be noted that most of the vast literature on King is not of a philosophical kind, nor are they studies of King's philosophical thought. There are a few fine philosophical studies of King, such as *Search for the Beloved Community* by Kenneth L. Smith and Ira Zepp, John Ansbro's *Martin Luther King, Jr.: The Making of a Mind*, Rufus Burrow's *God and Human Dignity: The Personalism, Theology and Ethics of Martin Luther King Jr.*, and *The Revolution of Conscience* by Greg Moses, a contributor to this volume. I have found the reading of them quite enriching. But probably most works on King are biographical and historical. The *The Liberatory Thought of Martin Luther King Jr.* is a *philosophical* dialogue on King as a thinker. It differs from the single authored volumes in being a *forum* in which we as a *community* of thinkers engage in a conversation about the value, meaning, and continued relevance of King's legacy. And it is intended to encourage a community of dialogue among students, scholars, activists, and socially conscious people in our society at large. If my book contributes to this goal in even a small way, it will happily become (even if only on a modest scale) a philosophical expression of the Beloved Community.

NOTES

1. Charles R. Johnson, "The King We Need: Teachings for a Nation in Search of Itself," *Shambhala Sun* (January 2005), p. 42.

2. King's public addresses often took the form of a philosophical sermon, not unlike some of the addresses of St. Augustine. His "Letter from Birmingham Jail," which invokes the example of the apostle Paul, might well be considered a philosophical epistle, akin to the philosophical letters of Greek and Roman antiquity.

3. Martin Luther King Jr., *The Measure of a Man* (Philadelphia: Fortress Press, 1988), pp. 7–33.

4. Rufus Burrow Jr., *God and Human Dignity: The Personalism, Theology and Ethics of Martin Luther King, Jr.* (Notre Dame, IN: University of Notre Dame Press, 2006), p. 69.

5. Of course, King also authored numerous books that are deeply imbued with his Personalist and Hegelian philosophical outlook. However, these are not systematic treatises, but work geared toward a general public. And while he does explicitly discuss his philosophical positions on occasion, for the most part his philosophical position is subtly implied.

6. Martin Luther King Jr., *Stride Toward Freedom* (San Francisco: HarperCollins Publishers, 1986), p. 91.

7. Ibid., 100.

8. But we must keep in mind that, as many King scholars point out, King was predisposed toward a social consciousness by his upbringing in an activist Black church, and by a father who was an activist minister who would have imbued Dr. King as a child with a prophetic "homespun" social gospel and a "homespun Personalism."

9. Stephen Ferguson II is to be credited for bringing to our attention in this volume the involvement of King and others in this philosophical club. I believe it is also mentioned by Taylor Branch in a biography of King titled *Parting the Waters*.

10. George Kelsey and Benjamin Mays were King's professors of philosophy and religion at Morehouse College. At least the beginnings of King's formal schooling in philosophies of nonviolence and social gospel theology would have occurred while studying with them. And, of course, there's an entire African American intellectual tradition of which King was much aware.

11. Martin Luther King Jr., *Strength to Love* (New York: Walker and Company, 1984), p. 97.

12. King's famous "I've seen the Promised Land" speech can be found in an anthology of his writings and speeches, quite appropriately entitled *A Testament of Hope*.

1

King within Philosophical Traditions

ONE

Is Our Belief That Martin Luther King Jr. Is a Black Philosopher Justified?

*Introductory Concerns about King and
Philosophical Cartography*

John H. McClendon III

At first glance it may seem that the topic of my chapter "Is Our Belief That Martin Luther King Jr. Is a Black Philosopher Justified?" is not in keeping with an anthology devoted to King as a philosopher. The overriding thesis and theme of this anthology is that Dr. King is a philosopher of some kind. I contend and will demonstrate that far from standing outside of the corpus of works that make up this anthology, the very question with respect to the justification of King's status, as black philosopher, is pivotal to such a collective project.

Regarding King's status as philosopher, most discussions on Martin Luther King have involved mapping his place within given philosophical schools of thought. The King cartographers have identified him within the personalist camp; the philosophy of nonviolence, Hegelian school of dialectics, as a Marxist/socialist, and one observer compares King's philosophy with Kantian ethics and another with contractarianism. We have scholars that even contend King's philosophical position is not to be found in any formal (white) school of philosophical thought. Instead King's philosophical perspective grew out of his early family life as well as from the adjoining experiences of the black church and African American community. At the most extreme end of this spectrum, pertaining to the rejection of white philosophical influences, we have Keith Miller's argument that King was not really a philosopher at all; rather he was a simply a preacher located within the African American homiletic tradition. Consequently, King's efforts at waxing philosophically were no more than the attempt of a black preacher to gain intellectual approval from a white audience.[1]

With the exception of Miller's complete dismissal of King as a philosopher, the thrust of this last group seems to center on the problem of how the justification of King as a black philosopher must be made. This group insists that King's credibility as black philosopher is undermined when the scholarly focus of attention is primarily on the white philosophers and theologians, which King formally studied as an undergraduate and graduate student of philosophy and theology. They insist that the genesis of King's philosophical evolution owes more to the childhood influences of family, church, and the African American community at large. Furthermore, these primordial influences are not merely the starting point for King; they actually make up the core of his philosophical outlook. Definitively, in the case of Martin Luther King, the essence behind the meaning of black philosopher adheres in the primordial influences of family, church, and black community.[2]

How King is to be located within a philosophical school, in my estimation, is predicated on the presumptions about the nature of philosophy as an intellectual enterprise. Where one is located on the map actually has a lot to do about the kind of philosophical map that is employed. Furthermore, the justification of King's status as philosopher is not merely a matter with the boundary lines contained within the philosophical map (specified schools of thought) but also is very much about the boundaries that demarcate the map of philosophy from other disciplines, such as theology. The objective of this essay is to explore how various possible mappings can direct us toward the goal of determining if we are justified in the belief that Martin Luther King Jr. is a black philosopher.

One of the foremost tasks of philosophy is to interrogate our basic presumptions and assumptions. In posing the question about King's justification, we are compelled to engage in philosophical discourse about the very subject matter under review, namely the definition of philosophy and its relevance to how we should position Martin Luther King in terms of philosophy generally and particularly within African American philosophical tradition. How we define philosophy is precisely the kind of background activity needed to ground the manner in which we determine if King occupies the space of black philosopher.

Prima facie the act of defining philosophy seems quite innocuous and facile. Yet with due effort and consideration, we can only conclude that such simplicity is only an apparent ruse and we must be cognizant of an essential complexity beyond all simplistic appearances. After all, whenever we undertake work in the area of metaphilosophy, the very definition of philosophy becomes a philosophical problem. The tension embodied in the paradox of metaphilosophy (the philosophy of philosophy) results from the requirement to interrogate all presumptions without limit, and this includes posing the very question, what does it mean to undertake philosophical inquiry?

Given our objective, the justification of King as black philosopher, we cannot overlook the ancillary problem attached to the question of what is philosophy, namely the philosophical puzzle of blackness itself, which is crucial to any definition of black philosophy/philosopher. African American philosophers are not in unanimous agreement on the definition of blackness and in fact this has remained a contested philosophical concept. Therefore, black philosophy/philosopher cannot be presented as an unexamined given, when we attempt to situate King in terms of black philosopher. I think William R. Jones provides us with viable means and methods for tackling the issue of what is black philosophy and how we might determine Martin Luther King's status of black philosopher.[3]

WILLIAM R. JONES, METAPHILOSOPHY, AND THE LEGITIMACY OF BLACK PHILOSOPHY

When we pursue the issue of metaphilosophy, we confront the very particular question of what is black philosophy and hence the question what it means to be a black philosopher. Philosopher William R. Jones in his pioneering essay "The Legitimacy and Necessity of black Philosophy: Some Preliminary Considerations" perceptively explains,

> If I self-consciously denominate a work as a black philosophy-that is "black" is an essential part of the title or sub-title-the intent appears to be one or more of the following: to identify that the author is black—that is, a member of a particular ethnic community, that is his primary, but not exclusive, audience is the black community, that the point of departure for his philosophizing or the tradition from which he speaks or the worldview he seeks to articulate can be called in some sense the black experience.[4]

Jones's notion of black philosophy/philosopher, however, is not a clarion call for some form of a racialist philosophy. Jones makes abundantly clear, "A black philosophy is no way obliged to make race its organizing principle." Jones is not claiming we can have some unique form of black logic or black epistemology. Jones designates that what is meant by "black" philosopher is a matter of "author, audience, ancestry, accent, and/or antagonists."[5]

For Jones the appellation "black" is an ethnic designator, which is social and not ontological in substance. He argues that a considerable amount of Western philosophy is indeed grounded on ethnicity as an organizing principle. Witness how in the history of philosophy we have the conventional references to Plato and Aristotle as "Greek" philosophers or Kant and Hegel's as contributors to "German" idealism.

I contend that Jones's ethnic approach for grounding the definition of black philosophy presents a viable metaphilosophical response to critics that argue that black philosophy amounts to no more than a form of racialized metaphysics far removed from the discipline of philosophy. First, in Jones's view, blackness is not a racial designator; rather it is an ethnic identifier, which as a social category, functions as an organizing principle. Second, Jones argues that philosophy's claim of universality has always been mediated via particularity. The universal principles of philosophy are instantiated by means of particular cultural experiences. Third, Jones discloses that the presumption that particularity is often bound with ethnicity is not an aberration from the general practice of doing philosophy within the Western philosophical tradition. Actually it has served as an organizing principle in Western philosophy for some time. All things considered perhaps Jones has presented us with a framework from which we can consider the status of King as philosopher. Did King, the philosopher, have the black community as his primary audience? Did his philosophical worldview derive from the tackling problems associated with the black community? Who were the antagonists to King's efforts at formulating a philosophy of black liberation?[6]

Rather than answer Jones's applied questions as this point, let us employ them as a heuristic device and guideline for developing the focus of our discussion. Jones's questions offer us a conceptual structure for situating the problem of King's location. With the questions derived from Jones's formula, we need not jump all over the map in a mad scramble to make declarations about finding the undiscovered philosopher/King.

E. FRANKLIN FRAZIER AND THE QUEST FOR THE BLACK PHILOSOPHER

In concert with Jones's observation, sociologist Franklin Frazier in his penetrating essay "The Failure of the Negro Intellectual" argues that if we were to have, with respect to African Americans, any meaningful notion of philosopher, it could not be detached from the requisite that the black philosopher must actually address the philosophical problems, which are adjoined to the context of African American life and its myriad of experiences. Frazier accents that in the case of the black philosopher there is a methodological obligation; namely that methodologically speaking the black experience must be the standpoint for doing philosophy. If we ignore this imperative, in Frazier's estimation, then in effect black people have no real philosophers to speak of when it comes to having a respectable standing in the intellectual community at large. Frazier elaborates,

We have no philosophers or thinkers who command the respect of the intellectual community at large. I'm not talking about the few teachers of philosophy who have read Hegel or Kant or James and memorize their thoughts. I'm talking about men who have reflected upon the fundamental problems which have always concerned philosophers such as the nature of human knowledge and the meanings or lack of meaning of human existence. We have no philosophers who have dealt with these and other problems from the standpoint of the Negro's unique experience in the world.[7]

Now without challenging the empirical veracity of this claim, the actual history of black philosophical tradition, concerning philosophizing about the black experience, I contend that Frazier's injunction merits our attention. It merits our attention because it supplies a possible grid for how we can attempt to place Martin Luther King Jr. as a black philosopher.[8]

Frazier's insights help structure another possibility for how we can confront the issue of King's justification with the formulation of following questions: Was King a philosopher who addressed the fundamental problems that have always concerned philosophers such as the nature of human knowledge and the meanings or lack of meaning of human existence? In other words, does King provide us with a perspective on epistemology and a viewpoint about philosophical anthropology? Furthermore, were such considerations from the standpoint of the black experience? Before we answer these questions, let us further explore the theoretical and methodological implications of Frazier's thesis.

It is important to note that Frazier does not dismiss the need for addressing the traditionally conceived "fundamental" problems of philosophy. Frazier's project is not a call for nihilism, but rather it is a project that affirms the "Negro's unique experience in the world," and this is because it is a project in keeping with the conventions of the intellectual community at large. Given that Frazier recognizes that black philosophers ought to grapple with the traditional "fundamental problems" of philosophy that emanate from the intellectual community at large, it follows that the philosophical perspective emerging out of the black experience has boundaries that are forged out of the fundamental questions. Maintaining the uniqueness of the black experience is not a summons to step out of these boundaries or to call for their destruction or nihilism. We are not to act as if we are engaged in the "hermeneutics of suspicion," instead these boundaries are the very background conditions from which black particularity (uniqueness) is anchored.[9]

Frazier's suggestion does not imply that Hegel's or Kant's or James's philosophies are not in any way relevant to the black experience; rather he argues that it is not enough to cite and memorize them and consequently believe with such an exercise the task of philosophizing has successfully been undertaken. In effect Frazier offers a critique of pursuing a mimetic approach to philosophy. The uniqueness affixed to the black experience is not reducible to some form of black exceptionalism, and subsequently this freedom from exceptionalism opens up the possibility for the quest for particularity without subjectivism and the negation of objectivity.

Why is this the case? It is because of the same reasons why Frazier does not fall into the trap of nihilism. Frazier's acknowledgment that the fundamental philosophical problems adjoined to the intellectual community at large amounts to the recognition that the scope of black philosophical inquiry is not narrowly restricted to a domain that excludes European thought as relevant to black philosophers. Frazier claims that the conventional designation of 'philosopher' remains an empty signifier, for African Americans, when the interests and experiences of the black community are omitted from investigation.

Two salient points from Frazier's ascriptions are relevance to our quest for establishing the locus of King as a black philosopher. First, the substance of black philosophy and the determination of what is a black philosopher derive from the African American experience. Second, the scope of black philosophy does not exclude the fundamental questions that have framed the course of philosophical discourse in the intellectual community at large. I contend that these two points shine a particular light on the present discourse about King as philosopher.

Over the past twenty-five years or so, there has been an intense debate in the secondary literature about the treatment and interpretation of King's philosophical and theological ideas. Some argue that the treatment of King the philosopher (as well as theologian) has been unduly and primarily circumscribed within the intellectual milieu of white intellectual culture. The studies of David Levering Lewis, John Ansbro, and Kenneth L. Smith and Ira G. Zepp, among others, given their emphasis respecting Western philosophical influences on King, are thus severely criticized for their alleged myopic vision.[10]

The charge is that the aforementioned scholars (Lewis, Ansbro, Kenneth L. Smith, and Ira G. Zepp) have a putatively limited and hence distorted perspective that places King within the orbit of white philosophy, which in turn grossly ignores his roots in the African American community. My concerted response to these claims will come shortly. What is of import to our mapping project is how Frazier's recognizes the fact that engagement in Western philosophy is not per se the abandonment of philosophical discourse on the black experience. In my view, Frazier's methodological treatment of black particularity, as mutually inclusive with fundamental philosophical questions at large, is a telling safeguard against our conflating the omission of the black experience with the activity of addressing the fundamental questions that are constituent with, but not exclusively contained within, Western philosophy.[11]

My immediate interest is the criteria for the justification and location of King. Frazier's grid provides allowances for King to undertake philosophical work focused on European/white thinkers in the expressed capacity as black philosopher—that is, if and when the issues at hand have relevance to the African American community. On Frazier's account, King's study of Henry David Thoreau, for instance, could very well be something that black philosophers can and perhaps ought to do. Particularly if Thoreau offers ideas, in their fundamental significance, provide an avenue for critical engagement of the black experience.

Lewis V. Baldwin brings to our attention, "Several well-known black professors greatly influenced King's intellectual and spiritual development at Morehouse. . . . Samuel Williams, a formally trained minister and professor of philosophy, introduced King to Plato, Socrates, Kant, Machiavelli, Henry David Thoreau, and other Western philosophers. . . . It was in Williams's class that King first read Thoreau's *Essay on Civil Disobedience*, a treatise that he said afforded 'my first intellectual contact with the theory of nonviolent resistance.'" [12]

From Frazier's standpoint, King's study of Thoreau would be an example of a black philosopher that learned valuable lessons from studying the fundamental questions of philosophical anthropology, which engages the intellectual community at large. Far from acting in a mimetic manner, we should acknowledge that King (as well as his mentor Williams) is a black philosopher. King's philosophically rooted social activism, on behalf of the black community, I submit, constitutes passing Frazier's litmus test for obtaining the status of black philosopher.

In view of Jones and Frazier's grid, I would argue that scholarly assessment of King's philosophical sojourn, especially works concerning white philosophers and their influences, would not of necessity constitute a breach or distortion of King's philosophical development as a black philosopher. To argue otherwise is to fall into the trap of the genetic fallacy. The source of King's ideas (Western philosophers or even for that matter Eastern thinkers such as Gandhi) does not in any way tell us about the validity and veracity of his claims. It surely does not address the fact that African American thinkers, long before King, found in Thoreau a basis for the philosophy of nonviolence.

King drew from many philosophical sources including the aforementioned African American tradition of the philosophy of nonviolence. Samuel W. Williams was one of several black philosophers that found in Thoreau's ideas a viable means that was relevant to black people via the philosophy of nonviolence. Hence, when King studied Thoreau and Gandhi's works, this process of inquiry did not exist in an intellectual vacuum, separated from the black intellectual experience. [13]

The fact that this black intellectual tradition of the philosophy of nonviolence in part owes some allegiance to non-black sources does not in any manner speak to the prospects of its viability for black people. The sources neither guarantee nor invalidate the truth about claims concerning nonviolence. We cannot construct a truth table on nonviolence where these sources are foundational. It could very well be determined that the philosophy of nonviolence is an approach that cannot effectively serve the interests of African American liberation. However, this conclusion cannot rest on an argument that supposes that if one begins with a non-black source then accordingly, due to these origins, it becomes inapplicable to the African American cause. Such is the nature of the genetic fallacy.[14]

Besides the genetic fallacy, I think there is an additional issue about the specificity of philosophical consciousness and how that significantly shapes our evaluation of King as black philosopher. The matter centers on the distinction between socialization as such and the specificity of the process and development of philosophical consciousness through intellectual inquiry. All of us as social beings are products of the process of socialization. We are all subjects to the influences of significant others, which have an immediate impact of our personal identity and psychological makeup. King expressed early on when at Crozer Seminary how his upbringing played a major role in his religious outlook. We should have no doubts about this fact.[15]

Yet, the recognition of the facts surrounding King's socialization within his family environ, the African American community and black church is not identical with the specificity of the formation of his philosophical consciousness. Philosophical consciousness is not merely holding beliefs that we gain through the course of our growing up to become adult. An ethical disposition to act and behave in a certain manner (Christian ethical orientation) is not the same as a philosophical inquiry into the nature of ethics or meta-ethics.[16]

Philosophical inquiry may or may not reinforce certain beliefs held prior to the study of philosophy. But it is the process of philosophical inquiry that supplies the ground for our philosophical beliefs by mandating that we justify our beliefs through rational assessment and logical argumentation and not merely holding to them due to the authority of community traditions, the impact of our cultural milieu, or parental influences.

The impact of various family relationships and community experiences indubitably had an impact on King's thinking and personal development. Yet they do not of necessity constitute *philosophical* influences. I think that King's early moral development and his subsequent Christian ethical outlook, for example, was a direct product of his upbringing. The key point rests in the fact that we must demarcate what are specifically and explicitly *philosophical* influences from other kinds of personal factors adjoined to the process of socialization. What we can gather from King's own reports is quite transparent; he encountered philosophical instruction for the first time during his Morehouse years.[17]

King stresses time and again that his Christian upbringing was personally stifling. What he describes as the Christian "fundamentalism" of his upbringing was a constraint that he sought to break and not embrace. King remarks, "my college training . . . brought many doubts into my mind. It was then that the shackles of fundamentalism where removed from my body. More and more I could see a gap between what I learned in Sunday school and what I was learning college. My studies made me skeptical, and I could not see how the many facts of science could be squared with religion."[18]

Hence, King's formal study of Western philosophers and theologians and his subsequent philosophical outlook was not something endemic to his early family and church life. The formal study of philosophy is the substantive matter, which is pivotal for the comprehension of his philosophical perspective. Those critics that seek to subordinate the impact of Western philosophical thought on King's thinking, to his childhood upbringing, ignore a crucial and salient factor in locating King as a philosopher.[19]

BROADUS N. BUTLER AND THE DEFENSE OF
THE BLACK PHILOSOPHER

Now we must return to addressing whether or not King fits Jones's and Frazier's grid for the black philosopher. We have a considerable body of scholarship, I think, that would support the idea that King was precisely what Jones describes and Frazier prescribes in terms of what is and should be the black philosopher. Of particular note is how philosopher Broadus N. Butler directly responds not only to Frazier's prescription as to what black philosophers should be, but also to Frazier's scathing assessment, namely there are no black philosophers of intellectual repute.[20]

As a philosopher himself, Broader Butler has an insider's view of what it means to be situated and identified as a black philosopher, especially living under the shadows of segregation and under the weight of academic racism. Additionally, Butler keenly comprehends how the white professional philosophical establishment functions vis-à-vis black philosophers' professional status and African American philosophical discourse.[21]

Butler's "In Defense of Negro Intellectuals " is actually a polemic with Frazier's "The Failure of the Negro Intellectual." Butler's article, as with Frazier's, appears precisely in 1962 and in the same publication, *Negro Digest*. Butler's essay appears one year before King's famous "I Have a Dream" speech at the March on Washington and six years following the bus boycott in Montgomery. When we inspect the corpus of Butler's works, many of his essays do not appear in professional (white) philosophy journals; instead they were published in African American journals, magazines, newspapers, and other periodicals and proceedings. As a black philosopher, Butler's own scholarly output was drastically different than the Frazier portrayal of mimetic pandering. [22]

Butler agrees with Frazier that there are some black thinkers who, in their rush to assimilate, would comfortably fit the mimetic description. However, Butler thinks the overall tenor of the African American philosophical tradition is far from reflecting black carbon copies of white philosophical discourse. Indeed, the roots of this tradition can be found in the works of Frederick Douglass, which unabashedly critique white racism and all forms of oppression. [23]

The general thrust of Butler's thesis is not on the failures of black philosophers, rather Butler has a critical assessment of the white philosophical establishment. This critique amounts to upbraiding certain white scholars, which in Frazier's terminology are constituents of "the intellectual community at large." Butler offers the following statement: "Almost all contemporary professional philosophers generally have abdicated their responsibility to profound moral and ethical issues in their theoretical pursuit of the image of the physical sciences and the image of the technological model of mathematics." [24]

In my estimation, Butler's vision and insights probe deeper, and his critique is more profoundly substantive than Frazier's—that is, to the extent that Butler's shifts the grounds of attack from solely focusing the failures of black philosophers, and forward to the criticism concerning the inherent contradictions of professional philosophy, which de facto amounts to white philosophers and their ancillary research program. I must add, however, that Frazier's charge of mimetic tendencies is not without measure and warrant. [25]

Granted the limited veracity of Frazier's charge, I think what Butler brings to the table are valuable insights for our efforts to structure criteria for the location and justification of King as a black philosopher. What is of prime importance is Butler's critique of the white philosophical establishment. The dominant white philosophical manner of philosophizing, Butler thinks, ultimately fosters benign neglect of pressing social concerns and a reactionary conformism that anchors and upholds what remains to be an unjust status quo. [26]

Here it is evident that Butler shares with King a critical stance toward white moderates that fail to take action to address ethical concerns of injustice and racism. King in his "Letter from Birmingham City Jail" declares,

> I have been greatly disappointed with the white moderate. I have almost reached the regrettable conclusion that the Negro's great stumbling block in the stride toward freedom is not the White Citizen's Counciler nor the Ku Klux Klanner, but the white moderate who is more devoted to "order" than to justice; who prefers a negative peace which is the absence of tension to a positive peace which is the pres-

ence of justice. . . . Shallow understanding from people of good will is more frustrating than absolute misunderstanding from people of ill will. Lukewarm acceptance is much more bewildering than outright rejection.[27]

Additionally, Butler recognizes that King was a philosopher that took what he formally studied and sought to construct a philosophy that would advance the African American struggle. From Butler's view, Frazier did not intend to include King among those that failed to assume the banner of black philosopher. Butler goes on to say, "Among academic scholars, Prof. Frazier did not intend to assert that men like Dr. Howard Thurman, Dr. Benjamin Mays, or Dr. Martin Luther King are not among the great philosophical minds of our nation."[28]

Butler conveys to us, "The Negro philosopher, by contrast, who begins as philosopher or theologian like Dr. Martin Luther King or Rev. Fred Shuttlesworth, find that they must release their creative genius as a Socratic gadfly to pepper the conscience of the nation with practical demonstrations of how this nation was grown in the difficult learning of abstract and absolute truth but in this role, he is neither conceived to be nor accorded the title of philosopher-even as Socrates was not acclaimed philosopher by his contemporaries."[29]

Butler holds to the idea that King belongs to the African American philosophical tradition, and this tradition, in its essential thrust, remains antithetical to the hegemonic thinking, which prevails within the ranks of professional philosophy. What follows is that, from the standpoint of the professional (White) philosophical establishment, the very notion of having the status of philosopher is denied to black thinkers.

For our purposes we must ask: does such denial mean that King's work remains outside of the vision of the (White) intellectual community at large? Is the lack of respect for King's philosophical work at base due to its mimetic character? Or is racism, in the ranks of professional philosophy, the source the lack of respect? Clearly Butler seeks to affirm that we are justified in the belief that Martin Luther King is a black philosopher. What is problematic is not King's de facto status as philosopher rather it is in seeking to anchor his philosophical placement by means of gaining approval from the white intellectual establishment. In Butler's estimation King is a black philosopher, and his philosophy is explicitly directed at social analysis and change. This view of philosophy is low on the professional philosopher's totem pole. In another essay Butler argues,

> Black American thinkers, with few exceptions, have not indulged themselves in the luxury either of pure speculative pursuit or of phenomenological analysis that disclaims consequences of analysis. This has been a matter of their historical attitude toward the relationship between knowledge and social responsibility. Their methodology and their goals of inquiry have been different from and often disquieting to

those who are accustomed to the accepted academic pursuit of philosophy. The most profound and penetrating philosophical contributions by black Americans have emerged in the context of social analysis, social decision and/or social action in pursuit of national social change. That role for philosophy generally has been either shunned or unheralded in the academic annals of the profession in America.[30]

Butler's description of the African American philosophical thought is also pivotal with our efforts to establish the precise specification of King's academic credentials. Butler offers us the factual (evidential) grounds for Jones's normative claims about the black philosopher. Butler is unequivocal in his judgment; King's academic locus is that of black philosopher, and this is because his works are exemplary achievements, which emanate from the African American philosophical tradition. Even if we take into account the differences in Jones, Frazier, and Butler's conceptions of philosophy vis-à-vis the black experience, it is transparent that King stands solidly as a black philosopher in all of the respective mappings. The weight of their combined arguments suggest that we are not justified in viewing King outside of his moorings within the African American intellectual culture.

However, if we grant King's place within African American intellectual culture, is that sufficient grounds for the justification that he is a black philosopher? Let's assume King is part and parcel of African American intellectual culture and instead of philosopher, we conclude he is a theologian. This assumption prima facie would not conflict with the prior claims about King's fit within this black experiential framework, but it would require greater specification about disciplinary differences between philosophy and theology.

Now we must shift our concerns about method and King's place as philosopher vis-à-vis other possible considerations within African American intellectual culture. For instance we can with substantial veracity and without much question offer up that he is a theologian. The philosophe-versus-theologian contrast is of particular importance from the standpoint of academic specialization. Not only is it a fact that Dr. King received his doctorate in systematic theology, there is also a considerable body of scholarship on his work as theologian. [31]

THE DIALECTIC OF PHILOSOPHY AND THEOLOGY: AFRICAN
AMERICAN INTELLECTUAL CULTURE REVISITED

I think a summary review of the literature would show that research on King the theologian far exceeds that of the scholarship on King the philosopher. I think that anyone with the cursory understanding of African American intellectual history would readily acknowledge that the function and role of theologian and philosopher, along with the relationship of theology and philosophy, particularly in African American intellectual culture, is far from being mutually exclusive. In fact a substantial number of African American thinkers have worn the hat of both theologian and philosopher. I submit that this is why Butler identifies not only King but also Mays and Thurman as philosophers despite the fact that their academic credentials were in religion and theology.[32]

Additionally among this group of African American intellectuals, we discover not only the presence of the philosopher/theologian but also the glaring fact that some of them were moreover ordained ministers. For example, the philosophers Thomas Nelson Baker, Marquis Lafayette Harris, Charles Leander Hill, Samuel W. Williams, Wayman B. McLaughlin, Carlton L. Lee, Richard McKinney, and George D. Kelsey were philosophers/theologians as well as "men of the cloth."[33]

Also we discover that Williams and Kelsey (both Morehouse alums) served as mentors to Martin Luther King Jr. during his Morehouse years. Additionally both men were Baptist ministers and in part through their scholarly work and academic approach to religion (along with the pivotal role of President Benjamin Mays of Morehouse) made such an impact on King that he ultimately decided, after considerable doubts, to become a Baptist minister.[34]

In Kelsey's course on Bible, King did very well and received his only "A" as an undergraduate student. Initially King decided to pursue the major in sociology at Morehouse. The young King had doubts about pursuing the ministry because he thought that black religious preaching and ritual was too emotionally driven and thus had little that was suitable for intellectual substance. Kelsey's academic approach to biblical studies via historical criticism fueled King's desire, on the one hand, to move away from biblical literalism, which fosters the emotionalism affixed to superstition and irrationalism, and on the other hand, King could remain within the province the Christian ministry with a higher level of intellectual respectability and sustenance.[35]

King stated in his autobiography, "I wondered if it [religion] could serve as a vehicle for modern thinking, whether religion could be intellectually respectable as well as emotionally satisfying. This conflict continued until I studied the course in the Bible in which I could see that behind the legends and myths of the Book were many profound truths which one could not escape. Two men-Dr. Mays, president of Morehouse college . . . and Dr. George Kelsey, a professor of philosophy and religion-made me stop and think."[36]

Although there has been considerable scholarly notice concerning Kelsey's influence on King, less has been said about Samuel W. Williams's influential role. Williams was for a number of years chair of the philosophy department at Morehouse. I must point out that King's formal introduction to philosophy was a year-long course that he took with Samuel Williams. Where King, during his junior year, had managed an "A" in

Kelsey's course on Bible, he only received a grade of "C" in Williams's introduction to philosophy course as a senior at Morehouse. Williams introduced King to philosophical ideas that had a lasting effect on his later activism. The King Collection at Morehouse in its "Background Information" on the collection reports, "Professor Samuel W. Williams exposed him [King] to Henry David Thoreau's 'Essay on Civil Disobedience.' King often stressed how reading Thoreau, along with Gandhi, was crucial in the formation of his ideas about the philosophy of nonviolence. Specifically King states that Thoreau was the motivation behind the tactics of the Montgomery bus boycott."[37]

Although King decided not to pursue an academic career in philosophy, he nevertheless taught philosophy for a short period during 1961 at Morehouse. This relatively unknown fact about King's stint at teaching, as a professor of philosophy, is undoubtedly an important additional factor we must take into account for any justification of King as black philosopher. The great majority of black philosophers, before the 1970s, were teachers at Historically Black Colleges and Universities. Most of the published works of black philosophers, as we observed earlier with Butler, appeared in African American scholarly journals. Many black philosophers, who in addition to facing academic racism were also saddled with heavy teaching loads and other administrative duties, were less inclined to publish their research and thus devoted an inordinate amount of energy to teaching and service.[38]

Given King's academic role at Morehouse, this is an important consideration about King the philosopher, and especially given the long and storied tradition of philosophers teaching at HBCUs. At least one of King's former students thought that King "knew a great deal" about philosophy. This particular student was none other than civil rights activist Julian Bond. Bond remarked, "I've talked to my classmates, the ones I can track down today, and almost none of us remember anything that was taught in the class. I do remember that he co-taught the class with the man [Samuel Williams] who had taught him philosophy when he had been at Morehouse. This man [Williams] probably knew much more about philosophy than Martin Luther King did, although King knew a great deal."[39]

Within the African American philosophical tradition at Historically Black Colleges and Universities, we note philosophers, Williams and many others, often taught courses in philosophy and religion. Many institutions had in fact combined religion and philosophy departments. However, we should not overlook the substantive academic differences between philosophy and theology. In opposition to such philosophical tasks, the apologetic function of theology overrides the need for a critique of the presupposition that God exists.[40]

For a comparative look at philosophy and theology let's visit the definition tendered by theologian J. Deotis Roberts. Roberts defines theology,

"Theology is *logos* of *theos*-reasoning about God. Thinking about God includes God's action in creation and history. 'God' implies creation, Providence, and redemption. . . . Theology may begin with the divine existence, or it may begin with human existence. Either way we have to do with God."[41]

What stands out with Roberts's definition is the notion that the concept of "God" is presumed without any critical inquiry into the existence or reality of God. Theology starts with the idea that God's existence is divine. God, for Roberts, stands axiomatically, a given entity without questions about providing ontological justification of the concept. Roberts further remarks,

> Theology is a discipline of interpretation. We are concerned with nature, man, and God-how God creates, sustains, and redeems in creation and history. Revelation is the process of unveiling. Revelation is the divine self-manifestation or self-disclosure. . . . Theology is reflection upon experience from revelation. Theology is concerned about God, man, world, and history. Revelation is both an objective and subjective experience. God speaks from beyond, but he also speaks with banner human experience, both personal and social. Revelation is universal and particular.[42]

In my estimation, although revelation is theologically considered as experiential, it nevertheless defies all social scientific description and rational reflection. This is because God is presumed to be supernatural and not subject to the social scientific empirical analysis and rational conception, which is the objective of philosophy. Thus God cannot be understood in the manner that objects of this world are so deemed. In speaking about the Montgomery Bus Boycott, Martin Luther King argues, "So every rational explanation breaks down at some point. There's something about the process that is suprarational; it cannot be explained without the divine dimension. . . . Whatever the name, some extra-human force labors to create a harmony out of the discords of the universe. There is a creative force that works to pull down mountains of evil and levels hilltops of injustice. God still works through history his wonders to perform."[43]

At the heart of the line of demarcation between theology and philosophy is the question of the relationship between faith and reason and how this relates to questions about God's existence and Christian doctrine. Those who place faith as the overriding principle fall into the camp of theology; this is because it is presumed that faith is not subject to rational critique and instead theologians hold that reason offers grounds for the interpretation and affirmation of faith. Theologian James Evans argues "Black theology is also a formal, self-conscious, systematic attempt to interpret the faith of the church."[44]

EARLY SCHOLARS THAT PRESUME KING WAS A PHILOSOPHER

A critical look at some of the earliest texts that presume King is a philosopher would no doubt provide evidence for a concrete demonstration as to how King is treated in the fashion of philosopher. However, given our distinction concerning philosophy and theology, I intend to point out to the reader that the act of merely referencing works that ostensibly identify King as philosopher does not offer a sufficient basis for reaching the conclusion he is in fact a philosopher. The presumption of King the philosopher must come under critical scrutiny. This is prime importance because of the possibility that the vital demarcation between philosophy and theology may be blurred and hence the presumption misplaced.

Some of those works that early on explicitly aim to view King as a philosopher, rather than theologian, are: Hanes Walton's book, *The Political Philosophy of Martin Luther King Jr.* (1971), Warren E. Steinkraus's article "Martin Luther King's Personalism and Non-Violence" (1973), and David Levering Lewis's *King: A Biography* (1978). All three publications are relatively early attempts to grapple with King as philosopher in some manner or fashion.[45]

Walton's text is completely devoted to the topic of King's political philosophy. Lewis presents in his biography of King what is a single chapter entitled "The Philosopher King." Steinkraus has a scholarly article that appears in *Journal of the History of Ideas* (1973). With respect to Walton's book, it is more a text driven by the nuances of a political scientist than a strictly considered philosophical examination. Therefore, I will not examine Walton's treatment of King in this paper. [46]

With Lewis's chapter, we uncover somewhat critical judgments with respect to the measure of King's philosophical acumen. Steinkraus also affirms King the philosopher and in contrast to Lewis presents a more favorable assessment of King's philosophical acuteness. I will aim to demonstrate that Steinkraus actually conflates the idea of King as a philosopher with what are manifestly theological considerations.

Lewis asserts that when King was a doctoral student studying philosophy at Boston University: "His exam books during this period reveal a vast program of reading whose dividends were reflected in the knowledge that range from superficial to highly derivative to not so superficial and bordering on original." Lewis goes on to point out that "He [King] have prepared for his qualifying examination in the history of philosophy by reviewing introductory works in philosophy. His treatment of the Milesian, Pythagorean, Eleatic, and Atomist philosophers of Greece is correct and competent though largely confined to the scrapings of key elements in summary generalizations from standard texts."[47]

Ultimately Lewis concludes that King "was not an original philosopher, although after Morehouse, it was perhaps the things he most desired to be. In an assessment of King's self-conscious effort to assume the mantle of philosopher Lewis adds, "But there was, undeniably, also an element of self-deception and self-mystification as to his philosophical acumen."[48]

Lewis's critical evaluation reminds us of Frazier's depiction of the black philosopher that at best cites and memorizes Western philosophers without having anything to say that would amount to creative contributions to the field of philosophy. Utilizing a similar method to Lewis, but with a drastically different judgment, Warren Steinkraus in his article "Martin Luther King's Personalism and Non-Violence" confirms that King is a philosopher. Steinkraus declares, "The late Dr. Martin Luther King, Jr. was a trained philosopher. He began studying philosophy as an undergraduate in Morehouse College, continued when at Crozer Seminary by enrolling for courses in the University of Pennsylvania, and took his doctor's degree in philosophical theology in 1955 at Boston University. But King is far better known as a civil rights leader, Nobel Prize winner, and martyr in the cause of racial justice. His popular writings are well known."[49]

Steinkraus's summation appears to fit within the conceptual framework, which Lewis offers to locate King's status as philosopher. As with Lewis, Steinkraus highlights King's formal study of Western philosophy as pivotal to establishing that King is undoubtedly a philosopher. From the standpoint of the above statement, however, we cannot determine if King, from Steinkraus's view, is specifically a black philosopher—that is, if we follow along the lines of Jones, Frazier, and Butler's grid. If we elect to assume the viewpoint of Cone and Garrow about the deficits of the method of citing King and the place he gives to white philosophers, then Steinkraus, as with Lewis, is on the wrong track for identifying King the philosopher.[50]

When we examine further commentary from Steinkraus, it is apparent that he is actually on board with Jones, Frazier, and especially Butler's grid about King as black philosopher. Steinkraus points out: "Is there any connection between King the famed apostle of nonviolence and King the contemplative philosopher? The answer must be in the affirmative. He is probably the only professionally trained philosopher of this century who has had a world-wide impact on large numbers of ordinary citizens and in the halls of government."[51]

Where Steinkraus slightly differs from Butler comes in the emphasis on King's place in professional philosophy. Steinkraus gives expression to how King standouts among professional philosophers. Although I think Butler would not disagree with Steinkraus that King stands apart, Butler is more of the inclination to demonstrate that King is an oppositional figure to professional philosophy and this would be the basis for why King stands out and apart from professional philosophers.

The statement directly relevant to the philosophy-versus-theology distinction comes when Steinkraus also adds, "On a superficial level, King's debts to philosophy are obvious because his six books are full of references to philosophers and philosophic concepts. He knew his way around in the history of philosophy far better than in theology."[52]

Steinkraus does not present any evidence to support his claim about King's knowledge of the history of philosophy versus that of theology. But he does show his hand when he says "a superficial level" of analysis would lead to his conclusion. I think Steinkraus's position follows less from grounding his views in evidential sources and is more due to his initial assertion that foremost King "was a trained philosopher" that later pursued philosophical theology. What Steinkraus's presumption—King is a trained philosopher—does in effect is to cloud the fact that King's encounter with academic philosophy was fundamentally instrumental to forging his theology.

It is clear that none of King's papers in philosophy were done outside of the objective of developing a foundation for his theological outlook, which is subsequently the basis to his practical activities in civil rights and social activism. Most debates about King's concept of God and the ethics surrounding his views on nonviolence are all situated in the framework of theology. Despite his accent on King the philosopher, I think Steinkraus affirms my point about theology when he argues, "King of course does not see his doctrine of non-violence as a short-term thing but as a fundamental law of the universe itself, rooted in the very nature of a good God. And to this is linked the perspective of immortality. In Personalism he found such a world-view."[53]

Rufus Burrow's *God and Human Dignity: The Personalism, Theology, and Ethics of Martin Luther King Jr.* is a scholarly advancement and improvement on Steinkraus's early efforts on King and personalism. As the title of his text indicates, Burrow explicitly situates King within theology. However, Burrow, who himself is an African American personalist, does refer to personalism as a philosophy.[54] Indeed King identifies personalism as his basic philosophical orientation.

> I studied personalistic philosophy—the theory that the clue to the meaning of ultimate reality is found in personality. This personal idealism remains to be my basic philosophical position. Personalism's insistence that only personality—finite and infinite—is ultimately real strengthened me in two convictions: it gave me metaphysical and philosophical grounding for the idea of a personal God, and he gave me a metaphysical basis for the dignity and worth of all human personality.[55]

I think the personalist worldview contains a particular metaphilosophy, where the definition of philosophy is dependent on religion and also on the presumption, rather than proof, of God's existence. Personalist Ralph

Flewelling argues that Bowne (one of the founders of personalism) held that "religion cannot be proved or explained in ordinary words. . . . Religion, therefore, would have to be proved through something of a still higher nature, and as we have access to nothing higher, it must remain unproved. Consequently, we must not try to prove it but to illustrate it; and this we made do by showing that every phenomenon depends closely upon it, and also, that an intelligent being is the established basis of every reality."[56]

Hence in the instance of personalist metaphilosophy the distinction between philosophy and theology is effectively extinguished. And what results is the blurring of the line of demarcation separating theology from philosophy, which is pivotal, at this juncture, to our discussion of King's location as a philosopher. This is true whether we take the position that King is a black philosopher or otherwise. The conflation of philosophy and theology is amplified in African American intellectual culture, particularly given the salient tradition of the philosopher/theologian and philosopher/preacher connection. This feature of co-mingling theologian (preacher) and philosopher obscures the real differences between theology and philosophy. We can safely say that Steinkraus's conflation does not take place in a vacuum.

All of the above notwithstanding, I think Burrow is closer to the mark than Steinkraus in locating King in theology. Furthermore, Burrow supplies viable arguments for King's personalism and he is especially astute in answering the charge of Garrow and Miller that personalism, as associated with Boston University had little or no significance on King, particularly given the black church/community influences. Just as with the philosophy of nonviolence, personalism has an African American tradition of formal academic standing. It begins with J. W. E. Bowen, and includes among others Gilbert Haven Jones, Willis J. King, and Martin Luther King Jr. as well as Burrow himself.[57]

Burrow's chapter on "King's Conception of God" is arguably one of the most detailed and thorough examinations regarding King on this topic. Throughout the chapter, we are informed about King's complex views on God. Burrow challenges other black theologians respecting King's commitment to personalism and its implications for his allegiance to the idea that God is omnipotent. The central point of contention is whether King held the more classical Christian theological perspective concerning the omnipotence of God. Burrow claims,

> If we trace King's view of divine power seminary to the mature period of his ministry, it will not be difficult to understand why I contend that he was, and was not, a proponent of divine omnipotence. That is, at times he talked, wrote, and acted as if he believed God possesses absolute power, while at other times he seems more comfortable proclaiming the "matchless power of God," which did not at all mean for him

that God possesses perfect, absolute power. Nor did it mean that God
was in any way a weak God. [58]

Burrow thinks King shifted his emphasis depending on the audience that
he addressed. When speaking to black audiences, King spoke in terms of
omnipotence, for he was well aware that most African Americans were
traditionally committed to divine omnipotence in their conception of
God. From Burrow's vantage, King did not want to alienate black people
from his central message that God was in concert with the African
American struggle to overcome racism.

However when speaking to white audiences, King was more inclined
to give full expression to his belief that an omnipotent God was not
necessarily foundational to Christian theology. An omnipotent God was
problematic in terms of theodicy and the issue of nonmoral evil. Nevertheless, where one might place King on the question of the nature of God,
what is most transparent in Burrow's analysis is that King was foremost a
theologian when he addressed whatever group he sought to gain for the
civil rights movement. Burrow's summarily states, "King's doctrine of
God grounds everything else that King took to be important in his work.
It provides the foundation for his doctrine of dignity, the beloved community, the objective moral order and moral laws, as well as the application of the latter." [59]

In conclusion, depending on our map of choice, King can be located as
a black philosopher—one who stands in opposition to conventional notions of philosophy, especially those attached to the professional (white)
philosophical establishment. For others, King is a black philosopher and
theologian, the substance of his philosophy/theology resides in his early
family and black church experiences. Lastly, when we review David Levering Lewis's notion that King was not an original philosopher, we see
that this view is predicated on King as philosopher qua philosopher, and
this conclusion stands in accord with E Franklin Frazier's mimetic philosopher. Lewis does not consider the theological dimension or the practical
application of philosophy in his assessment.

I think when we consider the matter of the relationship between theology and philosophy, we have the basis to understand why most scholars
on Martin Luther King Jr. place him within theology. This is because the
extent to which King embraced philosophy it was instrumental to the
task of constructing a theological framework for his social activism. I
would add to Burrow's conclusion that King's personalist doctrine of
God also shaped his metaphilosophy. The instrumental function of philosophy derives from King's overriding principle, which was his faith in
God. King explicitly states how his idea of God extended beyond philosophical reasoning and even systematic theological considerations of a
metaphysical sort.

The agonizing moments to which I have passed during the last few years have also draw me closer to God. More than ever before I am convinced of the reality of a personal God. True, I have always believed in the personality of God. But in the past the idea of a personal God was little more than a metaphysical category that I found theologically and philosophically satisfying. Now it is a reality that has been validated in the experiences of everyday life. God has been profoundly real to me in recent years. In the midst of outward dangers I have felt an inner calm. In the midst of lonely days and dreary nights I have heard an inner voice saying, "Lo I will be with you." When the chains of fear and the manacles of frustration have all but stymied my efforts, I felt power of God transforming the fatigue of despair into the buoyancy of hope.[60]

NOTES

1. Ernest Shaw Lyght, *The Religious and Philosophical Foundations in the Thought of Martin Luther King Jr.* (New York: Vantage Press, 1972). Warren E. Steinkraus, "Martin Luther King's Personalism and Non-Violence," *Journal of the History of Ideas* 34, no. 1 (January–March 1973). John Ansbro, "Martin Luther King's Debt to Hegel," *The Owl of Minerva* 26, no. 1 (1994). Adam Faircloth, "Was Martin Luther King a Marxist?," *History Workshop: A Journal of Socialist and Feminist Historians* 15 (Spring 1983): 117–23. William P. DeVeaux, "Immanuel Kant, Social Justice, and Martin Luther King, Jr.," *Journal of Religious Thought* 37, no. 2 (Fall–Winter 1981). Blake D. Morant, "The Teachings of Dr. Martin Luther King Jr. and Contract Theory: An Intriguing Comparison," *Alabama Law Review* 50, no. 1 (1998): 63–113. Miller argues that King was a black preacher seeking to gain a white audience via philosophical rhetoric; see Keith Miller, *Voice of Deliverance: The Language of Martin Luther King Jr. and Its Sources* (New York: Free Press, 1992).

2. James H Cone, "Martin Luther King Jr., Black Theology-Black Church," *Theology Today*, no. 41 (1984): 409–20; and David J. Garrow, "The Intellectual Development of Martin Luther King Jr: Influences and Commentaries," in David J. Garrow, ed., *Martin Luther King, Jr. and The Civil Rights Movement* (New York: Carlson Publishers, 1989). James Evans, "Keepers of the Dream: The Black Church and Martin Luther King Jr.," *American Baptist Quarterly* 5 (March 1986).

3. For representative essays on the philosophical examination of blackness consult Thomas F. Slaughter Jr., "Epidermalizing the World: A Basic Mode of Being Black," in Leonard Harris, ed., *Philosophy Born of Struggle* (Dubuque: Kendall/Hunt Publishing Company, 1983). Jesse N. McDade, "Towards an Ontology of Negritude," *The Philosophical Forum* IX, nos. 2–3 (Winter–Spring 1977–1978). Robert Birt, "Blackness and the Quest for Authenticity," in George Yancy, ed., *White on White/Black on Black* (Lanham, MD: Rowman & Littlefield, 2005). John H. McClendon III, "Blackness as Material Conditions, Presumptive Context, and Social Category," in George Yancy, ed., *White on White/Black on Black* (Lanham, MD: Rowman & Littlefield, 2005).

4. William R Jones, "The Legitimacy and Necessity of Black Philosophy: Some Preliminary Considerations," *The Philosophical Forum* IX, nos. 2–3 (Winter–Spring 1977–1978): 152–53.

5. William R Jones, "The Legitimacy and Necessity of Black Philosophy," 152.

6. For a critique of ontological blackness see Victor Anderson, *Beyond Ontological Blackness: An Essay on African American Religious and Cultural Criticism* (New York, Continuum, 1995).

7. E. Franklin Frazier, "The Failure of the Negro Intellectual," *Negro Digest* 11, no. 4 (February 1962): 32. Also consult Kevin Gaines, "E. Franklin Frazier's Revenge: Anticolonialism, Nonalignment, and Black Intellectuals' Critiques of Western Culture," *American Literary History* 17, no. 3 (Fall 2005): 506–29.

8. For representative texts from late nineteenth century and early twentieth century, which give expression to philosophical works that follows along Frazier's recommendation for grounding philosophy in the black experience see W. D. Johnson, "Philosophy," in James T. Haley, ed., *Afro-American Encyclopedia* (Nashville: Haley and Florida, 1895); and C. V. Roman, "Philosophical Musings in the By-Paths of Ethnology," *The AME Church Review* 28, no. 1 (July 1911). For a historical treatment on African American philosophical works of the black experience see John H. McClendon III, "The African American Philosopher and Academic Philosophy: On the Problem of Historical Interpretation," *American Philosophical Association Newsletter on Philosophy and the Black Experience* (Fall 2004); and John H. McClendon III, "Philosophers and the African American Experience in the United States," in Carol Boyce Davies, general ed., *Encyclopedia of the African Diaspora Volume 3* (Santa Barbara: ABC-CLIO Publisher, 2008).

9. For a treatment of African American philosophical tradition from the standpoint of the "hermeneutics of suspicion" consult Cornel West, "Philosophy, Politics, and Power: An Afro-American American Perspective," in Leonard Harris, ed., *Philosophy Born of Struggle* (Dubuque: Kendall/Hunt Publishing Company, 1983), 55.

10. David L. Lewis, *King: A Biography* (New York: Praeger Publishers, 1978). John J Ansbro, *Martin Luther King Jr.: The Making of a Mind* (Maryknoll, NY: Orbis Books, 1982). Kenneth L. Smith and Ira G. Zepp, *Search for the Beloved Community* (Valley Forge, PA: Judson Press, 1974). For critical treatments of the above authors see Keith Miller, *Voice of Deliverance: The Language of Martin Luther King Jr. and Its Sources* (New York: Free Press, 1992). David J. Garrow, "The Intellectual Development of Martin Luther King Jr: Influences and Commentaries," in David J Garrow, ed., *Martin Luther King, Jr. and The Civil Rights Movement* (New York: Carlson Publishers, 1989). James H Cone, "Martin Luther King Jr., Black Theology-Black Church," *Theology Today*, no. 41 (1984): 409–20. James Evans, "Keepers of the Dream: The Black Church and Martin Luther King Jr.," *American Baptist Quarterly* 5 (March 1986).

11. For a treatment of philosophy, beyond the limits of Western philosophy, which explicitly demonstrates that many of the philosophical questions that are conventionally rendered as "fundamental" are in fact global, see Randall Collins, *The Sociology of Philosophies: A Global Theory Intellectual Change* (Cambridge: The Belknap Press and Harvard University Press, 1998).

12. Lewis V. Baldwin, *There Is a Balm in Gilead: The Cultural Roots of Martin Luther King Jr.* (Minneapolis: Fortress Press, 1991), 26. Clayborne Carson, "Martin Luther King Jr.: The Morehouse Years," *The Journal of Blacks in Higher Education*, no. 15 (Spring 1997).

13. Dennis Dickerson, "Teaching Nonviolence: William Stuart Nelson and His Role in the Civil Rights Movement," *The A.M.E. Church Review* (July–September 2009). On Nelson's role in founding *The Journal of Religious Thought* and his leadership in the philosophy of nonviolent movement, see the special issue of *The Journal of Religious Thought* 35, no. 2 (Fall–Winter 1978–1979.). On Nelson and the Gandhi Memorial Lectures read Rayford W. Logan, *Howard University: The First Hundred Years, 1867–1967* (New York: New York University Press, 1968), 543-44.

14. For critical views regarding the viability of King's philosophy of nonviolence read William R Jones, "Liberation Strategies in Black Theology: Mao, Martin, or Malcolm?," in Leonard Harris, ed., *Philosophy Born of Struggle* (Dubuque: Kendall/Hunt Publishing Company, 1983); and Charles P. Henry, "Delivering Daniel: The Dialectic of Ideology and Theology in the Thought of Martin Luther King Jr.," *Journal of Black Studies* 17, no. 3 (March 1987).

15. Martin Luther King, Jr., "An Autobiography of Religious Development," paper written at Crozer Theological Seminary for the course Religious Development of Per-

sonality taught by George Washington Davis, (September 12–November 22, 1950], folder 22, box 106, Martin Luther King Jr., Papers (Mugar Memorial Library, Boston University).

16. Rufus Burrow Jr., *God and Human Dignity: The Personalism, Theology, and Ethics of Martin Luther King, Jr.* (Notre Dame: University of Notre Dame Press, 2006). Willis J. King, "Personalism and Race," in Edgar S. Brightman, ed., *Personalism in Theology* (Boston: Boston University Press, 1943), 204–24. Roy D. Morrison, "Black Philosophy: An Instrument for Cultural and Religious Liberation," *The Journal of Religious Thought* 33, no. 1 (Spring–Summer, 1976): 11–24. Walter Kaufmann, *Critique of Religion and Philosophy* (Princeton, NJ: Princeton University Press, 1958). Anthony Flew, *God and Philosophy* (Amherst: Prometheus Books, 2005).

17. Martin Luther King Jr., *The Autobiography of Martin Luther King Jr.*, Clayborne Carson, ed. (New York: Warner Books, 2004), 19. Also read Martin Luther King Jr., "Pilgrimage to Nonviolence," in James M. Washington, ed., *The Essential Writings and Speeches of Martin Luther King Jr.* (New York: HarperCollins, 1991).

18. Martin Luther King Jr., *The Autobiography of Martin Luther King Jr.*, Clayborne Carson, ed. (New York: Warner Books, 2004), 19.

19. Clayborne Carson, "Martin Luther King Jr.: The Crozer Seminary Years," *The Journal of Blacks in Higher Education*, no. 16 (Summer 1997).

20. Broadus N. Butler, "In Defense of Negro Intellectuals," *Negro Digest*" 11, no. 10 (August 1962).

21. Broadus Butler was president at Dillard University, Texas Southern, as well as vice president of the University of the District of Columbia, among other administrative posts at HBCUs. See Wolfgang Saxon, "Broadus Butler, 75, ex-Tuskegee Airmen and College Leader," *New York Times* (January 13, 1996). Also consult "UDC Official Broadus N. Butler, 75, Dies." *Washington Post* (January 15, 1996) p. B. 04; and "In Memoriam: Broadus N. Butler," *Water Highlights: DC Water Resource Center Washington, College of Life Sciences,* University of District of Columbia 16, no. 1 (Winter 1996).

22. A sampling of Butler's publications in black periodicals and other African American sources include: Broadus N. Butler, "The Negro Self-Image," *Negro Digest* 11 (March 1962). "Economic Emancipation Greatest Imperative for Negroes Today," *Crisis Magazine* (May 1962). "The Time Is Now," *Negro Digest* 12 (May 1963). "Booker T. Washington, W. E. B. Du Bois, Black Americans and the NAACP-Another Perspective," *Crisis* 37 (1960). "Black Arts in Higher Education: A Situation Report," *Proceedings of the Second Annual Invitational Workshop on Afro-American Studies,* Bennett college, Greensboro, North Carolina (May 1971).

23. Broadus N. Butler, "Frederick Douglass: The Black Philosopher in the United States: A Commentary," in Leonard Harris, ed., *Philosophy Born of Struggle* (Dubuque: Kendall/Hunt Publishing Company, 1983).

24. Broadus N. Butler, "In Defense of Negro Intellectuals," *Negro Digest* 11, no. 10 (August 1962): 43.

25. I do attend to the problem of the mimetic characteristics of African American philosophical tradition in another essay; see John H. McClendon III, "On the Politics of Professional Philosophy: The Plight of the African American Philosopher," in George Yancy, ed., *Re-framing the Practice Philosophy: Bodies of Color, Bodies of Knowledge* (Albany: SUNY Press).

26. Butler's critique is more exhaustive in his "Frederick Douglass: The Black Philosopher in the United States: A Commentary," in Leonard Harris, ed., *Philosophy Born of Struggle* (Dubuque: Kendall/Hunt Publishing Company, 1983).

27. Martin Luther King Jr., "Letter from Birmingham City Jail," in James M. Washington, ed., *The Essential Writings and Speeches of Martin Luther King Jr.* (New York: HarperCollins, 1991), 295.

28. Broadus N. Butler, "In Defense of Negro Intellectuals," 43.

29. Broadus N. Butler, "In Defense of Negro Intellectuals," 43. William R. Jones, "The Legitimacy and Necessity of Black Philosophy."

30.   Broadus N. Butler, "Frederick Douglass: The Black Philosopher in the United States: A Commentary," in Leonard Harris, ed., *Philosophy Born of Struggle* (Dubuque: Kendall/Hunt Publishing Company, 1983), 1.

31.   For a comparative treatment of King's theology consult Roger D. Hatch, "Racism and Religion: The Contrasting Views of Benjamin Mays, Malcolm X, and Martin Luther King, Jr.," *Journal of Religious Thought* 36, no. 2 (Fall–Winter 1979–1980): 26–36. William R Jones, "Liberation Strategies in Black Theology: Mao, Martin, or Malcolm?," in Leonard Harris, ed., *Philosophy Born of Struggle* (Dubuque: Kendall/Hunt Publishing Company, 1983); and Noel Leo Erskine, King *Among the Theologians* (Cleveland: The Pilgrim's Press, 1994). Also consult the following on King's theology, Rufus Burrow, *God and Human Dignity: The Personalism, Theology, and Ethics of Martin Luther King Jr.* (Notre Dame: University of Notre Dame Press, 2006). Paul R Garber, "King Was a Black Theologian," *Journal of Religious Thought* 31 (Fall–Winter 1974–1975): 16–32. Frederick L Downing, "Martin Luther King Jr. as Public Theologian," *Theology Today* 44 (April 1987): 15–31. Harold L. DeWolf, "Martin Luther King Jr. as Theologian," *The Journal of Interdenominational Theological Center* 4, no. 11 (Spring 1977): 1–11. Lonme Edmonson and Archie Logan, "Martin Luther King, Jr Theology in Context," *Duke Divinity Review* 40 (Spring 1975). Clayborne Carson with Peter Holloran, Ralph E. Luker, and Penny Russell, "Martin Luther King, Jr., as Scholar: A Reexamination of His Theological Writings," *The Journal of American History* 78, no. (June 1991): 93–105. For a relatively recent doctoral dissertation on King as theologian review George Russell Seay Jr., *Theologian of Synthesis: The Dialectical Method of Martin Luther King Jr., As Revealed in His Critical Thinking on Theology, History, and Ethics*, Dissertation Submitted to the Faculty of the Graduate School at Vanderbilt University (December 2008)

32.   See Carlton L. Lee, *Patterns of Leadership in Race Relations: A Study in Leadership among American Negroes* (Doctoral Dissertation, University of Chicago, 1951); Carlton L. Lee, "Black American Studies." *Negro History Bulletin* 34 (1971); and Carlton L. Lee, "Toward a Christian Critique of British Socialism," *Journal of Religious Thought* 6, no. 1 (Autumn–Winter 1949): 18–32. Richard Ishmael McKinney, *Religion in Higher Education among Negroes* (Doctoral Dissertation, Yale University, 1942). Richard I. McKinney. "Religion in Negro Colleges," *Journal of Negro Education* 13, no. 4. (Autumn 1944); and Richard I. McKinney, "Existentialist Ethics and Protest Movement," *Journal of Religious Thought* 22, no. 2. (1965–1966).

33.   For case study on the combined role of philosopher and theologian by an African American scholar consult John H. McClendon III, "Charles Leander Hill: Philosopher and Theologian," *AME Church Review* CXIX, no. 390 (April–June 2003): 81–105. For scholarship on King as minister and preacher, see Michael Franklin, "Martin Luther King Jr., as Pastor," *The Iliff Review* (Spring 1985): 4–20; and Mervyn Warrens *King Came Preaching* (Downers Grove, IL: InterVarsity Press, 2001). For Nelson see George Yancy, "Thomas Nelson Baker: Toward an Understanding of a Pioneer Black Philosopher," *The APA Newsletter on Philosophy and the Black Experience* 95, no. 2 (Spring 1996). Marquis Lafayette Harris was the first African American to receive a PhD in philosophy from The Ohio State University. Marquis Lafayette Harris, *Some Conceptions of God in the Gifford Lectures during the Period 1927–1929* (Doctoral dissertation, Ohio State University, 1933). Harris served as president of Philander Smith College. See M. Lafayette Harris, *The Voice in the Wilderness* (Boston: The Christopher Publishing House, 1941).

34.   Clayborne Carson, "Martin Luther King Jr.: The Morehouse Years," *The Journal of Blacks in Higher Education* 15 (Spring 1997). Lawrence Edward Carter Jr., ed., *Walking Integrity: Benjamin Elijah Mays, Mentor to Martin Luther King, Jr.* (Macon: Mercer University Press, 1998). Also read George D. Kelsey, *Racism and the Christian Understanding of Man* (New York: Scribner's Sons, 1965); and "Religion: Samuel W. Williams: Religion Is Justice." *Time Magazine* (April 6, 1970), http://www.time.com/time/magazine/article/0,9171,943986-1,00.html.

35.   Clayborne Carson, "Martin Luther King Jr.: The Morehouse Years." *The Journal of Blacks in Higher Education* 15 (Spring 1997). Christian Hartlich, "Historical-Critical

Method: In Its Application to Statements Concerning Events in the Holy Scriptures." *Journal of Historical Criticism* 2, no. 2 (Fall 1995): 122–39.

36. Martin Luther King Jr., *The Autobiography of Martin Luther King Jr.*, Clayborne Carson, ed. (New York: Warner Books, 2004), 18–19.

37. Martin Luther King Jr., *The Autobiography of Martin Luther King Jr.*, Clayborne Carson, ed. (New York: Warner Books, 2004), 45.

38. On King as philosophy teacher, see John W Whitehead, "A Powerful Figure: An Interview with Civil Rights Activist Julian Bond," *Old Speak: An Online Journal Devoted to Intellectual Freedom*, http://www.rutherford.org/oldspeak/Articles/Interviews/bond.html; and David J Garrow, *Bearing the Cross* (New York: HarperCollins Publishers, 1986), 164. For an assessment of the contribution of black philosophers in the role of teacher at an HBCU, see John H. McClendon III, "My Tribute to a Teacher, Mentor, Philosopher and Friend: Dr. Francis A. Thomas (March 16, 1913 to September 17, 2001)," *APA Newsletter on Philosophy and the Black Experience* 3, no. 1 (Fall 2000). John H. McClendon III, "Dr. Richard Ishmael McKinney: Historical Summation on the Life of a Pioneering African American Philosopher," *APA Newsletter on Philosophy and the Black Experience*, no. 2 (Spring 2006); and Joan Morgan, "Teaching the Young Keeps Him Young: 90 Year Old Dr. Richard McKinney of Morgan State Still Going Strong," *Black Issues in Higher Education* (August 22, 1996).

39. John W Whitehead, "A Powerful Figure: An Interview with Civil Rights Activist Julian Bond." *Old Speak: An Online Journal Devoted to Intellectual Freedom*, http://www.rutherford.org/oldspeak/Articles/Interviews/bond.html.

40. Louise Emma Anthony, *Philosophers without God* (Oxford: Oxford University Press, 2007). Michael Lackey, *African American Atheists and Political Liberation: A Study of the Sociocultural Dynamics of Faith* (Gainesville: University Press of Florida, 2007).

41. J. Deotis Roberts, "Black Theology in the Making," in James H. Cone and Gayraud Wilmore, eds., *Black Theology, a Documentary History: Volume One: 1966–1979* (Maryknoll: Orbis Books, 1993), 114.

42. J. Deotis Roberts, "Black Theology in the Making," 114–15.

43. Martin Luther King Jr., *Stride toward Freedom* (San Francisco: Harper & Row, 1986), 69–70.

44. James Evans, *We Have Been Believers: An African American Systematic Theology* (Minneapolis: Fortress Press, 1992), 13.

45. Hanes Walton, *The Political Philosophy of Martin Luther King Jr.* (Westport: Greenwood Press, 1971). Warren E. Steinkraus, "Martin Luther King's Personalism and Non-Violence," *Journal of the History of Ideas* 34, no. 1 (January–March 1973). David Levering Lewis, *King: A Biography* (Urbana/Champaign: University of Illinois Press, 1978).

46. In addition to Hanes Walton, *The Political Philosophy of Martin Luther King Jr.*,other works of political scientists on King include: Charles P. Henry, "Delivering Daniel: the Dialectic of Ideology and Theology in the Thought of Martin Luther King Jr.," *Journal of Black Studies* 17, no. 3 (March 1987).

47. David Levering Lewis, *King: A Biography* (Urbana/Champaign: University of Illinois Press, 1978), 39.

48. David Levering Lewis, *King: A Biography*, 44–45.

49. Warren E. Steinkraus, "Martin Luther King's Personalism and Non-Violence," *Journal of the History of Ideas* 34, no. 1 (January–March 1973): 97.

50. Steinkraus's article is one of the first scholarly papers to address the question of King the philosopher. Of significant note Steinkraus consulted with Samuel W. Williams, among others, in the preparation of his paper, Warren E. Steinkraus, "Martin Luther King's Personalism and Non-Violence," 97.

51. Warren E. Steinkraus, "Martin Luther King's Personalism and Non-Violence," 97.

52. Warren E. Steinkraus, "Martin Luther King's Personalism and Non-Violence," 97.

53. Warren E. Steinkraus, "Martin Luther King's Personalism and Non-Violence," 110.

54. Rufus Burrow, *God and Human Dignity: The Personalism, Theology, and Ethics of Martin Luther King Jr.* (Notre Dame: University of Notre Dame press, 2006), 69–73.

55. Martin Luther King Jr., *The Autobiography of Martin Luther King Jr.*, Clayborne Carson, ed. (New York: Warner Books, 2004), 30.

56. Ralph Flewelling, *Personalism and the Problems of Philosophy* (New York: The Methodist Book Concern, 1915), 12–13. Also consult Borden Bowne, *Philosophy of Theism* (New York: Harper and Brothers, 1887).

57. Rufus Burrow, *God and Human Dignity*, 73–77. Rufus Burrow, "The Personalism of John Wesley Edward Bowen," *Journal of Negro History* 82, no. 2 (Spring 1997): 224–56. Gilbert Haven Jones, *Lotze und Bowne Eine Vergleichung ihren Philosophschen Arbeit* (Doctor dissertation, University of Jena, 1909). George Yancy, "Gilbert Haven Jones as an Early Black Philosopher and Educator." *APA Newsletter on Philosophy and the Black Experience* 2, no. 2 (Spring 2003). Willis J. King, "Personalism and Race," in Edgar S. Brightman, ed., *Personalism in Theology* (Boston: Boston University Press, 1943), 204–24.

58. Rufus Burrow, *God and Human Dignity*, 95.

59. Rufus Burrow, *God and Human Dignity*, 123.

60. Martin Luther King Jr., *Strength to Love* (Cleveland: Collins Publishers, 1963), 154.

TWO

Dr. King's Philosophy of Religion

Theology of Somebodiness

George Yancy

All prejudice is evil, but the prejudice that rejects a man because of the color of his skin is the most despicable expression of man's inhumanity to man.

—Martin Luther King Jr.

In our sometimes difficult and often lonesome walk up freedom's road, we do not walk alone. God walks with us.

—Martin Luther King Jr.

[The Negro] has come to feel that he *is* somebody. And with this new sense of "somebodiness" and self-respect, a new Negro has emerged with a new determination to achieve freedom and human dignity whatever the cost may be.

—Martin Luther King Jr.

CONTEXT: LIVING WITHIN THE DENSITY OF WHITE RACISM

King's understanding of white racism—and the existential, religious, and political importance of militating against it through theological, ethical, and political reflection *and* praxis—grows out of his own personal experiential context vis-à-vis white racism. As an embodied black male born in 1929 to a middle-class family in Atlanta, Georgia, King was marked with the "stain" of so-called racial inferiority, and racial degeneracy. King's life is rooted within the funk of the everydayness of white racism, its insults, its hegemony, and power. My point here is that prior to King's

43

explicitly philosophical and theological espousal of a *doctrine* of personalism, a doctrine that is indispensable to understanding his conceptualization of human dignity, and prior to a *conceptually* rich understanding of the nature of white racism as a site of marking and dehumanizing the so-called other, King was a victim of white racism. Like so many black people, he felt the sting of white racism at the site of the black body, a site of marked "difference" and "degradation." Hence, to understand King, it is important to get a sense of his specific *lived* situation, a sense of his embodied encounters with white racism and how such encounters functioned as sites of interpellation, hailing him as a "nobody," an ontological cipher.

So, what is the context of King's *Erlebnis* vis-à-vis white racism? During one encounter, when King was a young child, he was slapped in the face by a white woman for accidentally stepping on her foot. He writes, "When I was about eight years old, I was in one of the downtown stores of Atlanta and all of a sudden someone slapped me, and the only thing I heard was somebody saying, 'You are that nigger that stepped on my foot.' And it turned out to be a white lady."[1] Of course, King may not have been the person who stepped on her foot. King talks about how he would not even dare to retaliate against a white person. He told his mother what happened. She was angry, and the two of them immediately left the store. White America had already granted the white woman permission to slap a black child or adult. Moreover, White America had effectively silenced many black people. King was aware of the rules of race relations in Atlanta, Georgia. The white woman not only physically assaulted and dehumanized King, but she truncated his being through the appellation "nigger." In short, King's young body was returned to him as a fixed entity, a "nigger" whose epidermal logic, so to speak, had already identified him as guilty, as violable with impunity. On the one hand, King was the "dark other," the nigger who was born to be disrespected and hurt. On the other hand, the white woman was the site of *white* law and order; King was the problem—ontologically so. Her slap was a violent act that reinforced the color line. King had literally stepped into her white embodied space, a "sacred" space. As a result, she needed to reinforce the ironclad rules of segregation.

King also recalls the time when he had an inseparable friendship with two white boys who lived close to him. King began to notice that when he went to play with them their parents said that they could not play. He notes that the parents were *not* hostile, but that they "just made excuses."[2] The white parents of those two white boys were no doubt loving and perhaps even Christian. Yet the damage had already been done; the color line had been enforced. As Lillian Smith writes, "The mother who taught me what I know of tenderness and love and compassion taught me also the bleak rituals of keeping Negroes in their 'place.'"[3]

King was also well-aware of how segregation was often brutally maintained. He writes, "I remember seeing the Klan actually beat a Negro. I had passed spots where Negroes had been savagely lynched."[4] It is no wonder that the young King was shocked by white racism and that around this time "was . . . determined to hate every white person."[5] The irony is that this is the same King who would later preach a gospel of love that entailed loving precisely those whites who would not think twice to disrespect, dehumanize, brutalize or lynch a black person.

King also knew firsthand what it was like to live within segregated spaces in Atlanta, Georgia. He knew that he could not eat at certain restaurants, swim in certain pools, and attend certain theaters. In short, within the context of the larger white world, King knew that he was "undesirable," "unwanted," and "untouchable" because his blackness had been historically marked as a curse.

Given the historical and daily bombardment of such negative racist assumptions, King knew the difficulty of undoing such assumptions. He writes, "The job of arousing manhood [or personhood] within a people that have been taught for so many centuries that they are nobody is not easy."[6] Returning from Simsbury, Connecticut, where he had worked on a tobacco farm to earn additional money, King recalls the journey home to the South. He writes about having "to change to a Jim Crow car at the nation's capital in order to continue the trip to Atlanta. The first time that I was seated behind a curtain in a dining car, I felt as if the curtain had been dropped on my selfhood."[7] In short, King felt that his very sense of himself as a person was negated. The curtain was like a veil, a cloak that rendered him invisible. Undergoing such blatant acts of racism, one can understand King's later doubts about liberal theology with its doctrine of the goodness of human nature. It was such early experiences that challenged, though they did not deplete, King's moral fortitude and religious outlook: "How could I love a race of people who hated me?"[8]

Yet, despite such experiences, King's sense of dignity and his sense of self-respect were nurtured by his family and religious community. King's mother, Alberta Williams King, taught him that he "should feel a sense of 'somebodiness.'"[9] King understood that he "had to go out and face a system that stared me in the face every day saying you are 'less than,' you are 'not equal to.'"[10] King's mother did not withhold from him her opposition to and hatred of racial segregation. She did not want him to feel inferior based upon a system of white supremacy. Indeed, he writes, "Then she said the words that almost every Negro hears before he [she] can yet understand the injustice that makes them necessary: 'You are as good as anyone.'"[11] At this early stage in King's life, his mother had already begun to instill in him a sense of "somebodiness." She had already begun to counter the ideology of white supremacy, its racist epistemic orders, and its axiological frames of reference.

King was also able to bear witness to his father's open protestation against white supremacist disrespect. Martin Luther King Sr. (known as "Daddy King"), who was steeped in political organizing to encourage black people to vote, who was also chairman of the Committee on the Equalization of Teachers' Salaries, and who insisted that the Christian church ought to play a vital role in civil rights activities,[12] enacted a form of antiracist praxis that helped to shape King's sense of existential fortitude in a white world that was openly hostile to his very being. To get a sense of his father's resistance (etymologically, "taking a stand") to white supremacy, King relates the story of shopping for some shoes with his father. He and his father decided to sit in the empty seats at the front of the store. A white clerk refused to serve them, and would do so only if they moved to the seats in the back of the store. King's father retorted, "We'll either buy shoes sitting here or we won't buy shoes at all."[13] With son in hand, King Sr. immediately left the store.

King also relates a story about his father being pulled over by a white police officer as a result of accidentally failing to stop at a stop sign. The white police officer pulled up and demanded that King's father, referring to him as "Boy," show him his driver's license. Infuriated and indignant, King's father said, "Let me make it clear to you that you aren't talking to a boy."[14] King's father went on to tell the white police officer that he would not listen to him if he persisted in referring to him as a "Boy." King says that the white police officer nervously and hurriedly wrote the ticket. In both situations, King's father was being reminded of his status as a "nigger." In the latter case, the white police officer attempted to degrade King's father through a process of infantilization—challenging King's father in terms of his sense of adult authority and autonomy.

James Cone notes that "thinking like a free person was not easy for a black child growing up in the South during the 1930s and 1940s."[15] Yet, King witnessed his father return the power of the black gaze. He witnessed his father fight back against a racial Manichean system that privileged white people and dehumanized black people, one that was designed to deny black people their sense of self-worth. These were crucial learning experiences for King, experiences that demonstrated the importance of theory in action. As Rufus Burrow writes, "Young Martin didn't know it at the time, but he was witnessing personalism in action. One who recognizes that as a person he is an end unto himself and is sacred by virtue of being imbued with God's image is morally obligated to defend and enhance his dignity. King witnessed this attitude in his father, who refused to passively receive words and treatment that were intended to undermine his humanity and dignity."[16]

King was also protected from the virulence and dehumanizing impact of the white gaze at Atlanta's Ebenezer Baptist Church. King's maternal grandfather, A. D. Williams, who had also been active in civil rights protestation through the lens of the social gospel, became pastor there in

1894. It was after his death in 1931 that King's father became pastor, expanding "the scope of his predecessor's politically engaged ministry."[17] James Cone asks, "If blacks were going to believe that they were somebody in spite of what whites did to them, from what sources could they derive that belief?"[18] Ebenezer Baptist Church, as many black churches did, functioned as a space within which black people could enact anti-white racist semiotics, a place where black people could explore a range of bodily expansion and articulation through collective worship, and a place where they could narrate their own stories about being *somebody*, especially somebody in the sight of God. Hence, for King, the home and the church were continuous. Both functioned as places where dignity and self-respect were installed. King notes, "The church has always been a second home for me."[19]

Through collective praise and mutual respect black people could find reprieve from being identified as "inferior niggers" and "second class citizens." They were able to use this "segregated space" as a space for freedom of expression, a space for the development of political consciousness, and as a space for the construction of an ontology of somebodiness that was fundamentally linked to a theological perspective that spoke to them about the metaphysical and historical reality of a God that underwrites their somebodiness. The site of the family and the church provided the young and adult King with the existential fortitude to keep on keeping on and to make a way out of no way, especially when the barriers of injustice seemed insurmountable and impenetrable. King's autobiographical reflections provide profound metaphilosophical insights into his philosophical and theological formation. Indeed, in stream with a (broadly construed) pragmatist position regarding the importance of metaphilosophical influences that impact our philosophical *Weltanschauungen*, King was aware of how philosophy and theology are shaped by place and time and how they may reflect, as Alain Locke says, "a personality, its temperament and dispositional attitude."[20] In a non-reductionist fashion, King observes:

> It is quite easy for me to think of a God of love mainly because I grew up in a family where love was central and where [loving] relationships were ever present. It is quite easy for me to think of the universe as basically friendly mainly because of my uplifting hereditary and environmental circumstances. It is quite easy for me to lean more toward optimism than pessimism about human nature mainly because of my childhood experiences.[21]

Yet, whites had created a larger systemically racist society that inevitably relegated King and other black people to their "nigger-status," their thing-like existence, a form of social and psychological attrition that challenged (and at times vitiated) black ego-stability. King writes:

The experience of having to enter a rear door and sit in a filthy peanut gallery was so obnoxious that I could not enjoy the picture. I could never adjust to the separate waiting rooms, separate eating places, separate rest rooms, partly because the separate was always unequal, and partly because the very idea of separation did something to my sense of dignity and self-respect.[22]

Not only did King's experiences speak to the lie upheld by the Supreme Court in *Plessy v. Ferguson* (the so-called separate but equal doctrine), but King felt that the color line impacted his sense of dignity and self-respect. The color line was predicated upon a deeper lie, a myth created by white people to keep blacks, in this case, oppressed. Whiteness was constructed as the transcendental norm, as that which marks nonwhites as "different," "deviant," and "raced." By implication, of course, whiteness is that which remains unmarked/the same through a field of "difference."

Whiteness creates the myth of a "metaphysical" division where what is white is deemed pure, good, and scared, whereas that which is black is deemed impure, bad, and evil. King insightfully indicts semantics in the perpetuation of such a vicious color line or racial Manicheanism. He writes:

In Roget's Thesaurus there are some 120 synonyms for "blackness" and at least sixty of them are offensive—such words as "blot," "soot," "grime," "devil," and "foul." There are some 134 synonyms for "whiteness," and all are favorable, expressed in such words as "purity," "cleanliness," "chastity," and "innocence." A white lie is better than a black lie. The most degenerate member of a family is the "black sheep," not the "white sheep." Ossie Davis has suggested that maybe the English language should be "reconstructed" so that teachers will not be forced to teach the Negro child sixty ways to despise himself and thereby perpetuate his false sense of inferiority and the white child 134 ways to adore himself and thereby perpetuate his false sense of superiority.[23]

King is aware of the fact that "epidermal differences" are normatively neutral. The problem has to do with a superimposed racial and racist ideology that marks epidermal differences as morally significant. Hence, blackness qua inferior is a function of whiteness qua superior. "Black alterity," then, is intelligible within the context of an anterior (perhaps even simultaneous) stipulation of whiteness as normative/the same. As Simone de Beauvoir argues, "Thus it is that no group ever sets itself up as the One without at once setting up the Other over against itself."[24] King's theorization of white racism captures the logic of whiteness, a logic that requires whiteness's alterity to be defined as inferior according to a hierarchical scale of "racial" value.

REFLECTION: KING ON WHITE RACISM

King's understanding of white racism effectively shifts a critical gaze toward the actions of white people. He writes, "To find the origins of the Negro problem we must turn to the white man's problem."[25] King also writes, "The dilemma of white America is the source and cause of the dilemma of Negro America."[26] King's observations point to the profound ways in which white racism obfuscates its role in inventing black people as *the* problem, while simultaneously denying its role in the process. King, though, does not obfuscate the historical role of white racism, declaring that black people "are the heirs of a past of rope, fire, and murder."[27] Indeed, he is unequivocal in marking whiteness as the source of the problem. This marking is reminiscent of Richard Wright's contention when asked by a French reporter about his opinion regarding the so-called Negro problem in the United States. Wright, cognizant of the tendency to stigmatize black people as the "problem people," stated: "There isn't any Negro problem; there is only a white problem."[28] Frantz Fanon was also aware of how racism presupposes a larger space of sociality, a space where white people continue to denigrate black people and yet distance themselves as the perpetrators of such acts of denigration. Fanon writes, "It will be seen that the black man's alienation is not an individual question."[29] In other words, the question of black peoples' profound sense of alienation is a question of sociogeny; it is not a question that speaks to the human species qua human species, and it is not what happens to individuals qua individuals. Rather, black existence must be understood within the context of a unique socially and historically constituted reality, within the context of racist discourses and structures of oppression within which black people attempt to make sense of themselves. Black experiences of alienation and existential malaise, then, presuppose a larger context of anti-black racism, a context of whiteness against which blackness is deemed undesirable, inferior, and wretched. Concerning this history of anti-black racism, King writes:

> For years the Negro has been taught that he is nobody, that his color is a sign of his biological depravity, that his being has been stamped with an indelible imprint of inferiority, that his whole history has been soiled with the filth of worthlessness. All too few people realize how slavery and racial segregation have scarred the soul and wounded the spirit of the black man. The whole dirty business of slavery was based on the premise that the negro was a thing to be used, not a person to be respected.[30]

King was also aware of and saw through the empty rhetoric of our so-called forefathers. Concerning Thomas Jefferson, he writes, "Jefferson's majestic words 'all men are created equal' meant for him, as for many others, that all *white* men are created equal."[31] Within this context, King is critical of the hypocrisy of a form of "humanism" that has built into it a racist philosophical anthropology that valorizes whiteness. It was this same valorization of whiteness that functioned to privilege those immigrants who came to North America and "became white." King is critical of the conflation of histories and forms of historical amnesia that discard the brutal trajectory of black peoples' arrival to North America. He writes:

> Negroes were brought here in chains long before the Irish decided voluntarily to leave Ireland or the Italians thought of leaving Italy. Some Jews may have left their homes in Europe involuntarily, but they were not in chains when they arrived on these shores. Other immigrant groups came to America with language and economic hardships, but not with the stigma of color.[32]

The point here is that the "stigma of color" presupposes the existence of whites who have created and superimposed a racist epidermal color-schema. For example, experiencing his body as an object among other objects, as a thing to be manipulated by the white gaze, Fanon realizes that he does not constitute a site of self-imposed racial pathology. Rather than seeking to discover human psychology through instinctual, genetic or intrapsychic reductionism . . . Fanon's project in psychology was to outline how inseparably enmeshed the individual was in their sociohistorical and cultural context. [33] Making explicit reference to the sociogenic, Fanon marks the source of the problems from which he suffers as that which comes from "the other, the white man, who had woven me out of a thousand details, anecdotes, stories."[34] My argument is that King is aware of how the source of black pain and suffering is centrifugal; pointing beyond a "congenital" racial sickness or a soul diseased by a self-imposed nihilism. Describing enduring pain experienced by black people within a world of anti-black racism, King writes, "The central quality in the Negro's life is pain—pain so old and so deep that it shows in almost every moment of his existence."[35] It is a pain that is inextricably linked to white hatred, power, and privilege. It is white America that King indicts: "White America must assume the guilt for the black man's inferior status."[36] And yet, King is also aware of the liberating praxis required of black people. He writes:

> And, with a spirit straining toward true self-esteem, the Negro must boldly throw off the manacles of self-abnegation and say to himself and to the world, "I am somebody, I am a person. I am a man [woman] with dignity and honor. I have a rich and noble history. How painful and exploited that history has been. Yes, I was a slave through my foreparents and I am not ashamed of that. I'm ashamed of the people who were so sinful to make me a slave." Yes, we must stand up and say, "I'm beautiful," and this self-affirmation is the black man's [women's] need, made compelling by the white man's crimes against him.[37]

In formulating his conceptual understanding of white racism as a problem coming from whites, King draws from the work of George Kelsey who was an African American philosopher and theologian who received his PhD in philosophy from Yale University in 1946 and whom King studied with at Morehouse. Kelsey theorized racism as a form of idolatry. The racist makes whiteness into his/her god, one that is worshiped in daily life. Indeed, Kelsey saw white racism as a form of polytheism,[38] a polytheism filled with contradiction and a framework that is fundamentally misanthropic. King also pulled from the work of anthropologist Ruth Benedict and concluded that racism's "ultimate logic is genocide."[39] Given the reality of segregation, King was aware that the issue faced by black people was not simply about civil rights, but about being. Segregation sends the message that black people do not deserve to be, because their "existence is corrupt and defective."[40] To the extent that whiteness negates the existence of the so-called black other, for King, "racism is a philosophy based on a contempt for life. It is the arrogant assertion that one race is the center of value and object of devotion before which other races must kneel in submission."[41] As such, for King, "racism is a total estrangement. It separates not only bodies, but minds and spirits."[42] And even for those whites who deemed themselves liberals, King detected the limits of their integrationist sensibilities, sensibilities that had become calcified by the longstanding myth that black people are impure and inferior. He writes:

> Often white liberals are unaware of their latent prejudices. A while ago I ran into a white woman who was anxious to discuss the race problem with me. She said: "I am very liberal. I have no prejudices toward Negroes. I believe Negroes should have the right to vote, the right to a good job, the right to a decent home and the right to have access to public accommodations. Of course, I must confess that I would not want my daughter to marry a Negro."[43]

What I find intriguing are the existentialist sensibilities that inform King's understanding and description of white racism and its impact on black bodies. In other words, King is able to give voice to the deep alienation, enduring pain, and depth of suffering experienced by finite and embodied black people within the context of their historical facticity. Rather than describing universal experiences that all persons undergo, King is able to telescope specific existential and contextual trauma resulting from ways in which black bodies are reduced to things and denied transcendence. Of course, even here, one must be cognizant of the ways in which black male and black female bodies experience racist trauma differently, a point that King, from what I can tell, did not examine in any detail.[44] Drawing from the language King uses to describe existentialism, one might say that throughout history in the United States black people have been faced with "a series of unreconciled conflicts" and that their "existence is filled with anxiety and threatened with meaningless"[45] caused by the unabashed assertion of white racial domination. King did not turn his back on the nightmare of history as experienced in the *individual* lives of black people. Perhaps this is partly why he objected to Hegelian absolute idealism, "because it tended to swallow up the many in the one."[46] It should be noted, though, that King was influenced by Hegel's emphasis upon rational coherence, that "Truth is the whole," and Hegel's (as well as Heraclitus's) insights into the importance of opposition or struggle as a prerequisite for growth/progress.[47]

My point here is that while King did not accept the atheistic strain in the existentialist movement, for he was committed to Christian theism, and while he came to reject Kierkegaard's understanding of faith as an irrational leap in the dark, though King did agree with Kierkegaard's stress on the significance of the individual to have a direct relationship with God, a relationship in which one does not fall victim to a superficial religious herd mentality,[48] his existentialist sensibilities were evident. In a powerful illustration of the importance of a Kierkegaardian religious nonconformism, King writes:

> When people think about race problems they are too often more concerned with men than with God. The question usually asked is: "What will my friends think if I am too friendly with Negroes or too liberal on the race question?" Men forget to ask: "What will God think?" And so they live in fear because they tend to seek approval on the horizontal plane rather than spiritual devotion on the vertical plane.[49]

King was particularly attentive to the existentially *concrete* sociopsychological pain and suffering endured by the majority of black people due to the "crushing weight of poor education, squalid housing and economic strangulation."[50] Reminiscent of Ralph Ellison's *Invisible Man* and Richard Wright's *12 Million Black Voices*, King writes, "Being a Negro in America means being herded in ghettoes, or reservations, being constantly ignored and made to feel invisible."[51] The black problem, as King makes clear, is not only about being rendered invisible, but also about having the power to enforce that invisibility through the material and structural arrangement of how bodies occupy lived space.

Addressing the issue of how one's sense of dignity is linked to issues of material existence, King writes, "But dignity is also corroded by poverty. . . . No worker can maintain his [her] morale or sustain his [her] spirit if in the market place his [her] capacities are declared to be worthless to society." Reflecting on the phenomenology of being embodied-as-black, King writes, "Because the society, with unmitigated cruelty, has made the Negro's color anathema, every Negro child suffers a traumatic emotional burden when he [she] encounters his [her] black skin."[52] King raises the problem of embodied black self-hatred or what Fanon calls "the burden of that corporal malediction."[53] Within this context, King is being critical of the ways in which blackness signifies an "it" and whiteness signifies a "thou." Pulling from the work of Martin Buber, which Kelsey had already done, King writes that "segregation substitutes an 'I-it' relationship for the 'I-thou' relationship, and ends up relegating persons to the status of things."[54] It is through the white imaginary that blacks are "seen" as "things," because, "the white racist chooses to deal with his own images of the Negro."[55] In this way, whiteness is narcissistic, which is another form of idolatry. The white racist, then, fails to acquire genuine self-knowledge because he/she experiences blacks "as antithetical to himself [herself] in the order of humanity, and thereby excludes the communion that is the condition for this self-knowledge."[56] On this score, whiteness is a form of inner brokenness predicated upon a larger social brokenness. Whiteness, as the site of the *Ubermenschen*, is homicidal; it inflicts social, psychological, and physical genocide on black bodies, those deemed *Untermenschen*. Given the history of black pain and suffering, enslavement and segregation, bodies mutilated and raped, existentially degraded and disciplined through acts of violence, psyches constantly bombarded by a racist ideology of nobodiness, it is no surprise when King writes, "The marvel is, as Frederic Douglass once said, that 'Negroes are still alive.'"[57]

PRAXIS: A THEOLOGY OF SOMEBODINESS

Whiteness/white racism/white supremacy is the denial of black dignity, *somebodiness*, and personhood, an ideology that is diametrically opposed to King's conceptualization of each person being made in the image of God—the *Imago Dei*. In short, then, King understood that whiteness/ White racism was antithetical to a theology based upon the belief that all persons are created in the image of God, and that God endowed each human person with dignity. In fact, King writes, "The greatest blasphemy of the whole ugly process was that the white man ended up making God his partner in the exploitation of the Negro."[58] This ugliness creates the problem that God actually works on the side of whites to oppress black people. This would make God an accomplice in the oppression of black people, suggesting the possibility of "Divine racism." If true, this would be theologically profane. In contrast, King embraced a species of liberation theology, one that emphasized the everyday sufferings of black people and the belief that God works on behalf of those who constitute the least of these. His father and mother, through their love, moral instruction, and Christian faith, had already provided King the self-understanding that he possessed intrinsic dignity through having been made in the image of God. Moreover, King witnessed his father, a social gospel pastor, protest the evils of white supremacy. Hence, prior to reading the work of Boston Personalists Borden Parker Bowne, Edgar S. Brightman, and L. Harold DeWolf, King was already being taught about a *personal*

God that works through human history and is eternally concerned with the existential and spiritual welfare of human *persons*. James Cone writes, "Belief in a personal God and in the dignity and worth of the human person has always been a deeply held conviction in the African-American Christian community. Therefore, it was easy, also most natural, for King to embrace the philosophy of personalism."[59] Also, before reading Walter Rauschenbusch's *Christianity and the Social Crisis* in the early 1950s, King had already personally borne witness to the doctrine that it was the *whole man* that constituted the hub of concern to which Christianity ought to attend.

King was critical of Rauschenbusch's identification of "the Kingdom of God with a particular social and economic system"[60]; however, it was after formally reading Rauschenbusch that King's conviction regarding the importance of social gospel activism became even stronger. Indeed, after reading Rauschenbusch, King thought that any religion that concerned itself with the souls of people, but is not just as concerned "about the slums that damn them, the economic conditions that strangle them, and the social conditions that cripple them is a spiritually moribund religion only waiting for the day to be buried."[61] King was not simply concerned with a theology of the spirit, but a theology of the body, the material well-being of human beings. Indeed, King's theology vertically points toward the transcendent and horizontally points toward embodied humanity. It is the overlapping of these two axes that gives weight to King's theology as a *liberation* theology, as one that does not turn a blind eye to the suffering of human beings and one that does not bracket out a God that is engaged in human history, a God on the side of those who suffer. This is not a God of sheer abstract metaphysics, but a suffering God, a God concerned with the existential facticity of the human predicament. As Noel Erskine writes, "It is an attempt to do theology in this context, to allow the divine law to call into question the injustice in the society, that points to the praxeological cutting edge of King's theology."[62]

King's understanding of humanity and his politico-theological mission are inextricably linked to his personalist conception of God. While critical of Brightman's theistic finitism, King, from a formal academic perspective, was apparently most influenced by Borden Parker Bowne's claim that "no term is as applicable to God as personality."[63] King writes, "Personalism's insistence that only personality—finite and infinite—is ultimately real strengthened me in two convictions: it gave me a metaphysical and philosophical grounding for the idea of a personal God, and it gave me a metaphysical basis for the dignity and worth of all human personality."[64] For King, however, God qua personal is not limited. He writes:

To say that God is personal is not to make him an object among other objects or attribute to him the finiteness and limitations of human personality; it is to take what is finest and noblest in our consciousness and affirm its perfect existence in him. It is certainly true that human personality is limited, but personality as such involves no necessary limitations. It simply means self-consciousness and self-direction.[65]

King's understanding of humanity presupposes the existence of a *personal* God that is the guarantor of each person's self-worth and somebodiness. Hence, for King, the value of each person is *not* something that is determined based upon the way in which *we* have historically constructed a moral vocabulary to talk about human beings. For King, the source of human dignity is grounded in that which is transhistorical; the source is beyond a moral/ethical community of intelligibility. Yet, for King, through political praxis, the deployment of moral suasion, and the power of love, we are able, along with an *immanent* and *loving* God, the metaphysical source of the human *person*, to transform the social order.

King's personalist conception of God is consistent with, and indeed supports, his conception of human persons as *free*. Freedom and somebodiness are mutually implicative. King says that "the essence of man is found in freedom."[66] Hence, having been created in the image of God, the somebodiness of human persons and their freedom are underwritten by God. For King, freedom is the capacity to deliberate, to make decisions, and to be responsible.[67] Hence, to be free, for King, is what it means to be a human *person*.[68] White supremacy is precisely predicated upon the denial of freedom and the denial of the personhood of black people. Indeed, on this score, white supremacy is a denial of the universal love of God and the Christian theological assumption that God endowed each person with freedom and that they were made in the image of the Divine. King used the metaphysics of personalism to indict the bitter reality of white supremacy and as a tool to fight on behalf of those denied dignity. In short, King's personalism was operationalized on the existential ground, as it were, through a form of social praxis, not simply eloquent locution. "King's most original and creative contribution to the personalist tradition," according to Rufus Burrow, "was his persistence in translating it into social action by applying it to the trilogy of social problems—racism, poverty/economic exploitation, and militarism—that he believed plagued this country and the world."[69] Moreover, it is also important to note that white supremacy truncates the freedom of whites as well by superimposing a restrictive and poisonous racist metanarrative that damages their sense of personhood. Indeed, white supremacy is fundamentally antithetical to a form of *Mitsein* that inclusively respects the dignity and personhood of all human beings. King writes, "All segregation statutes are unjust because segregation distorts the soul and damages the personality. It gives the segregator a false sense of superiority, and the segregated a false sense of inferiority."[70] Hence, segregation, by implication, is a form of sin. It is a denial of the humanity and personhood of black people. White supremacy, then, is anti-Christian; it is a site of idol worship—the privileging and valorizing of whiteness.

A theology that places a premium on freedom and dignity cannot be content with the status quo, but must actively and urgently seek a disruption of historical complacency and racist ideologies that sustain and prolong the suffering and pain of black people. King's famous "Letter from Birmingham City Jail" was addressed to white clergy who felt that King should not be in Birmingham, Alabama. In response, King was quite clear about why he was there. He writes, "I am in Birmingham because injustice is here."[71] King felt compelled; he felt that it was his *prophetic* duty, like the Apostle Paul, "to carry the gospel of freedom beyond [his] particular hometown."[72] For King, it was a question of Kairos time or the opportune moment. He writes, "For years now I have heard the words 'Wait!' It rings in the ear of every Negro with a piercing familiarity. This 'Wait' has almost always meant 'Never.'"[73] When it comes to suffering and angst under conditions of white oppression and dehumanization, and "when your first name becomes 'nigger' and your middle name becomes 'boy,'" and "when you are forever fighting a degenerating sense of 'nobodiness,'"[74] why should black people wait for whites to "set the timetable for"[75] their freedom? The time to usher in freedom and a sense of somebodiness is always Kairos time. The suffering endured by the oppressed might be great and the oppressive structures seemingly immovable, but as King states, "Only God is able."[76] In short, God will prevail.

Burrow delineates four indispensable motifs that constitute King's personalism and that capture what I have argued thus far. They are:

- For King, God is personal and loving
- Emphasis on the inherent dignity of persons
- The importance of a personal-communal spirit
- Protesting injustice and social evil and the establishment of a community consistent with the ideals of the Kingdom of God or what King referred to as the beloved community[77]

While the African American Civil Rights Movement and the Poor People's Campaign functioned as clear manifestations of the efforts of King and others to achieve justice and equality before the law, King's theological perspective was grounded upon a deeper soteriology that envisioned a spiritually redemptive/salvific outcome. As liberation theologian Gustavo Gutierrez writes: "Society will be just, and in a certain sense new, to the degree that it places the dignity of the human person at its center—a dignity that for a Christian has its ultimate foundation in the condition of being the 'image of God' which Christ saves by reestablishing the friendship between human beings and God."[78] King saw his struggle, and the larger struggle of the civil rights movement, through the theological *Welt-bild* of a living and personal God, a God that listens in the hour of need, a God that is like an unfailing friend. This is partly why King found the conceptions of God of both Paul Tillich and Henry Nelson Wieman so problematic. For King, Tillich's conception of God as "being-itself" and Wieman's conception of God as the "source of human good"[79] were too theologically deflationary. As King wrote, "The God whom we worship is . . . able to beat back gigantic waves of opposition and to bring low prodigious mountains of evil."[80]

Hence, King's concern for humanity, and black people in particular, is inextricably linked to his theology, a theology that takes seriously a form of political praxis that speaks to oppressors with parrhesia (or fearless speech). In a world that would rather remain ethically asleep, fearless speech is disturbing; it is jarring; it is unsafe. King was a philosophical gadfly, the sort that is needed "to create the kind of tension in society that will help men to rise from the dark depths of prejudice and racism to the majestic heights of understanding and brotherhood."[81] Through his brilliant, moving, and gripping oratory, clearly shaped by the tradition of African American homiletics, King practiced philosophical elenchus, publicly challenging white American power at home and abroad. He knew that "injustice anywhere is a threat to justice everywhere."[82] His aim was to create an aporetic United States and world citizenry in the face of moral apathy, and to fight to unhinge the United States from its white racism, its imperial tendencies, and its disregard for the poor. Yet even as King sought the best in humanity, he was, like all of us, a broken vessel. He knew that "following every affirmation of greatness is the conjunction 'but.'"[83] He knew the personal pains of Good Friday. Yet, in his indefatigability, his eyes no doubt remained focused on Easter Sunday, an event, for King, signifying restorative transcendence. God-talk, for King, was about reconciliation, human fellowship, consolation, *agape*, and liberation. It was a mode of fearless discourse and a mode of fearless listening that was always ready to "respond to the Macedonian call for aid,"[84] to come to the aid of those in need, in pain, in poverty—for those who needed reminding that they are *somebody*.

NOTES

1. Martin Luther King Jr., *The Autobiography of Martin Luther King, Jr.*, edited by Clayborne Carson (New York: Warner Books, 1998), 8–9.

2. James M. Washington, ed., *A Testament of Hope: The Essential Writings and Speeches of Martin Luther King, Jr.* (New York: HarperSanFrancisco, 1986), 420.

3. Lillian Smith, *Killers of the Dream* (New York: W. W. Norton, 1949), 27.

4. King, *The Autobiography of Martin Luther King, Jr.*, 10

5. James H. Cone, *Martin & Malcolm & America: A Dream or a Nightmare* (Maryknoll, NY: Orbis Books, 1991), 23.

6. Washington, *A Testament of Hope*, 580.

7. King, *The Autobiography of Martin Luther King, Jr.*, 11–12.

8. King, *The Autobiography of Martin Luther King, Jr.*, 7.

9. King, *The Autobiography of Martin Luther King, Jr.*, 3.

10. King, *The Autobiography of Martin Luther King, Jr.*, 3.

11. King, *The Autobiography of Martin Luther King, Jr.*, 3–4.

12. Clayborne Carson, "Martin Luther King, Jr., and the African-American Social Gospel," in *African-American Christianity: Essays in History* (Berkeley: University of California Press, 1994), 162.

13. King, *The Autobiography of Martin Luther King, Jr.*, 8–9.

14. King, *The Autobiography of Martin Luther King, Jr.*, 8.

15. Cone, *Martin & Malcolm & America*, 24.

16. Rufus Burrow Jr., *God and Human Dignity: Personalism, Theology, and Ethics of Martin Luther King, Jr.*, foreword by Lewis V. Baldwin and Walter G. Muelder (Notre Dame: University of Notre Dame Press, 2006), 81.

17. Carson, "Martin Luther King, Jr., and the African-American Social Gospel," 162.

18. Cone, *Martin & Malcolm & America*, 25.

19. King, *The Autobiography of Martin Luther King, Jr.*, 6.

20. Leonard Harris, ed., *The Philosophy of Alain Locke: Harlem Renaissance and Beyond* (Philadelphia: Temple University Press, 1989), 34.

21. King, *The Autobiography of Martin Luther King, Jr.*, 2–3.

22. Washington, *A Testament of Hope*, 421.

23. Washington, *A Testament of Hope*, 580–81.

24. Simone De Beauvoir, *The Second Sex*, translated by H. M. Parshley (New York: Vintage Books, 1989), xxiii.

25. Martin Luther King Jr., *Where Do We Go from Here: Chaos or Community?*, foreword by Coretta Scott King and introduction by Vincent Harding (Boston: Beacon Press), 66.

26. King, *Where Do We Go from Here*, 92.

27. Washington, *A Testament of Hope*, 588.

28. George Lipsitz, "The Possessive Investment in Whiteness: Racialized Social Democracy and the 'White' Problem in American Studies," *American Quarterly* 47, no. 3 (September 1995). http://jdmil4.people.wm.edu/LipsitzEssay.pdf (accessed June 28, 2011).

29. Frantz Fanon, *Black Skin, White Masks*, translated by Charles Lam Markmann (New York: Grove Press, Inc., 1967), 11.

30. King, *Where Do We Go from Here*, 45.

31. King, *Where Do We Go from Here*, 71.

32. King, *Where Do We Go from Here*, 92.

33. Derek Hook, "Frantz Fanon, Steve Biko, 'Psychopolitics and Critical Psychology'" (2004). http://eprints.lse.ac.uk/961/1/PsychopolitcsMasterPDF.pdf (accessed June 28, 2011).

34. Fanon, *Black Skin, White Masks*, 111.

35. King, *Where Do We Go from Here*, 92.

36. King, *Where Do We Go from Here*, 66.

37. Washington, *A Testament of Hope*, 246.

38. Burrow, *God and Human Dignity*, 107.

39. Burrow, *God and Human Dignity*, 67.

40. King, *Where Do We Go from Here*, 67.

41. King, *Where Do We Go from Here*, 67.

42. King, *Where Do We Go from Here*, 67.

43. King, *Where Do We Go from Here*, 82.

44. For more on King's myopia regarding the political needs of women and his alleged sexism, see Rufus Burrow Jr., *God and Human Dignity: Personalism, Theology, and Ethics of Martin Luther King, Jr.*, especially chapter 5.

45. Washington, *A Testament of Hope*, 37.
46. King, *The Autobiography of Martin Luther King, Jr.*, 32.
47. John J. Ansbro, *Martin Luther King, Jr.: Nonviolent Strategies and Tactics for Social Change* (New York: Madison Books, 2000), 119–23.
48. Ansbro, *Martin Luther King, Jr.*, 92–105.
49. Washington, *A Testament of Hope*, 479.
50. King, *Where Do We Go from Here*, 62.
51. King, *Where Do We Go from Here*, 97.
52. King, *Where Do We Go from Here*, 95.
53. Fanon, *Black Skin, White Masks*, 111.
54. Washington, *A Testament of Hope*, 293.
55. Ansbro, *Martin Luther King, Jr.*, 108.
56. Ansbro, *Martin Luther King, Jr.*, 108–9.
57. King, *Where Do We Go from Here*, 75.
58. King, *Where Do We Go from Here*, 71.
59. Cone, *Martin & Malcolm & America*, 29.
60. Washington, *A Testament of Hope*, 37.
61. Ansbro, *Martin Luther King, Jr.*, 18.
62. Noel Leo Erskine, *King among the Theologians*, foreword by Bernice A. King (Cleveland: The Pilgrim Press, 1994), 133.
63. Burrow, *God and Human Dignity*, 94.
64. Carson, "Martin Luther King, Jr., and the African-American Social Gospel," 168.
65. Washington, *A Testament of Hope*, 40.
66. Washington, *A Testament of Hope*, 120.
67. Washington, *A Testament of Hope*, 120.
68. Burrow, *God and Human Dignity*, 173.
69. Burrow, *God and Human Dignity*, 86.
70. Washington, *A Testament of Hope*, 293.
71. Washington, *A Testament of Hope*, 290.
72. Washington, *A Testament of Hope*, 290.
73. Washington, *A Testament of Hope*, 292.
74. Washington, *A Testament of Hope*, 293.
75. Washington, *A Testament of Hope*, 295.
76. Washington, *A Testament of Hope*, 508.
77. Burrow, *God and Human Dignity*, 80.
78. Gustavo Gutierrez, *The Density of the Present: Selected Writings* (Maryknoll, NY: Orbis Books, 1999), 180.
79. Carson, "Martin Luther King, Jr., and the African-American Social Gospel," 170.
80. Washington, *A Testament of Hope*, 504.
81. Washington, *A Testament of Hope*, 291.
82. Washington, *A Testament of Hope*, 290.
83. King, *Where Do We Go from Here*, 71.
84. Washington, *A Testament of Hope*, 290.

THREE

Dr. King as Liberation Theologian and Existential Philosopher

James B. Haile III

Living is a cross
That any one of the rock-faces
Comprehends...
Living is a fire
That any one of the wave-lashes
Comprehends.

—Ben Okri, *An African Elegy*

Black theology claims that in the life, death, and resurrection of Jesus of Nazareth there is an unprecedented *disclosure* of who we are as a people and who we are called to *become*.

—Noel Leo Erskine, *King among the Theologians* (emphasis mine)

It goes without saying that Martin Luther King Jr. was black. What is not so well agreed upon is what exactly constitutes this blackness and what exactly this blackness constitutes.[1] There is, perhaps, no more contested ground than the being, existence, and meaning of blackness, so that when the term is applied one must proceed with extreme care, and, with what many hope is caution, to not essentialize and simplify history, human freedom (autonomy), human existential expression, and the social as well as the economic and political life-world. So what is it that I mean when I say that King was undoubtedly "black"? What I mean to suggest by the usage of the term "black" is not a fundamental and unchangeable *a priori*: some quality of mind, body, or soul; nor do I mean to suggest simply the recall of historical experiences and images pronounced in the hanging of black bodies from poplar trees. Rather, blackness suggests an episteme brought about by the very facts of an existence and illuminates the particular position(s) one comes to inhabit therein. Blackness, thus, is not simply an examination of history or the reaction of persons to history—there is no pure moment of agency accounted for; rather, it is a mixture, an exchange between the human person and the world, what has been called a productive or fruitful contamination,[2] of being and meaning.

What, then, is said to be enduring of/in/about the human person that allows for introspection about justice, freedom, and reconciliation? What (theological) message(s) does God provide for us in human existence and through the historical existence of Jesus of Nazareth? What phenomenological and existential insights can be gleaned from black theology in addition to or perhaps beyond "general" theological concerns? Or, as James Cone asks, "What can black theology say about man?"[3] What does thinking of Martin Luther King Jr. as a black theologian tell us/add to our in depth knowledge of his message? Does a "racialized" perspectival negate, and necessarily so, the existence and our understanding of a beloved community, or is it the condition (in the sense of a prolegomena) for any understanding of a beloved community whatsoever?

This chapter seeks to locate Martin Luther King Jr. within the black church and liberatory theological traditions and, at the same time, to make a case for his thought to be considered existential as well.

BLACK THEOLOGY, LIBERATION

My Presence in my black body is Divined,
How can it be?
Why *must* it be?
The world is a difficult place.

—Anonymous

Theologian James H. Cone opens his text *A Black Theology of Liberation* with the following claim: "Christian theology is a theology of liberation."[4] The importance of this claim is that it is works to both thematize and galvanize his larger project of black theology, and, at the same time, to theoretically ground his work as epistemological *and* historical. This claim rests on four fundamental principles of black theology, principles that will shape the entirety of this chapter. Firstly, God's presence in human history with those oppressed persons who strive toward freedom and justice; secondly, God as a personal God; thirdly, the significance of community for knowledge of and truth in justice and freedom; and, lastly, the significance of the life, death, and Resurrection[5] of Christ. All four of these claims/modes, for Cone, rest on blackness and the historical being and becoming of black folk in America.

Cone's opening claim is a general one that is meant to apply to all those practicing the Christian faith, and not just black Christians alone. This definition of Christian theology as liberatory, "as that discipline which seeks to analyze the nature of the Christian faith in light of the oppressed arises chiefly from the Biblical tradition itself," namely, "the gospel, which is Jesus Christ."[6] Cone finds Biblical proof in both the Old and the New Testament, in the presence of God in the event of Exodus, and in the presence of God in the life, death, and Resurrection Jesus of Nazareth. What connects the former to the latter (and vice versa) is the transmission of God's will in and through human history; the former substantiates the necessity and importance of the religious community in the understanding and revelation of God's Word and God's work; the latter, both the unique and ubiquitous nature of revelation itself.[7] The Christian community, as "the community of the oppressed which joins Christ in his fight for liberation of men," then, becomes the foundation for understanding the revelation of the Word.[8] The community illuminates and helps to articulate the idea that God's presence is with oppressed persons. This means materially and historically, that, "one can never engage in conversation about the nature of God without confronting those elements of human existence which threaten man's existence as a person."[9]

For Cone, the "righteousness of God is not an abstract quality in the being of God, as with Greek philosophy. It is rather God's active involvement in history, making right what man made wrong."[10] Here Cone is expressing some fundamental principles of black theology: one, God is present in human history, not as an abstract quality or personae, but as an active element in human freedom and liberation. And, secondly, God is with the oppressed, helping to alleviate oppression, making right what has gone socially eschew. Both principles point to a larger principle: God is a personal God. God is *in* human history, uniting himself with man in the singular event of Jesus of Nazareth.

Black theology not only points out the material social reality of man on earth and in oppressive states, but that God's righteousness is not an abstract quality of *existenz*—that is, a philosophical discourse of the nature of God—or theoria alone, but is a revolutionary praxis expressed through the community. This, for Cone, is what separates theology from philosophy: philosophy is an individualized enterprise coming to terms with God and revelation through reason alone; theology, though, is an understanding of God's nature and God's will as *experienced* by a community of persons in human history: that is, the events that take place within historical time. Theology, thus, points to the importance of community for religious faith, particularly Christian faith. This, for Cone, is especially true for black people who, in their traditional "Southern, slave" worshipping roots, phenomenologically understand and express their rootedness in God through the spirit of fellowship and worship. Cone writes that in the black church

> [t]he word is more than *words* about God. God's Word is a poetic happening, an evocation of an indescribable reality in the lives of the people. This is the meaning behind the occasion when a black preacher "who after reading a rather cryptic passage took off his spectacles, closed the Bible with a bang and by way of preface said, 'Brothers and sisters, this morning—I intend to explain the unexplainable—and unscrew the inscrutable.'"[11]

Such is an interesting and revelatory occurrence of the preacher's sermon in the prologue of Ralph Ellison's *Invisible Man*[12] including both blackness and God, in a sermon *about* blackness.

> *Brothers and sisters, my text this morning is the "Blackness of Blackness."*
> *And the congregation of voices answered: "That blackness is most black, brother, most black . . ."*
> *"Halleluiah"*
> *". . . It'll put you, glory, glory, Oh my lord, in the WHALE'S BELLY."*
> *"Preach it, dear brother . . ."*[13]

"Here," Cone writes, "the preacher is not only affirming his freedom in relation to the text; he is also making a sharp distinction between the *words* of text and the *Word* disclosed in the text."[14] Black preaching and black worshipping, that is, the phenomenal intertwining of both (the audience echoing/reflecting the preacher and the preacher echoing the audience) in the experience of God in flesh as community, which, for Cone, is explicitly racialized—it is black, not because it relates to some genetic disposition to *be*, but because it reflects the historical situatedness and existential expressiveness of historical people, *black* people. "When the Word is spoken as truth and the people feel the presence of truth in the midst of their troublesome situation, they respond to the preached word by ratifying it with resounding 'Amens.'"[15]

Again, Ralph Ellison's speakerly preacher resounds,

> *"In the beginning . . ."*
> *"At the very start," they cried*
> *". . . there was blackness . . ."*
> *"Preach it . . ."*[16]

"Can I get a witness," "these are appeals to the people to let him or her know whether divine truth is being mediated through the proclamation-event."[17] Cone gives a phenomenological description of the importance and significance of the community to understanding and disclosing the being of God in human history and in one's personal life. For Black theology, the black community is important as foci of black thinking and black religious expression, but also as the galvanizing point of God's presence in human history as the redeemer and liberator of the oppressed. What, though, makes worship black; that is to ask, Why *black* theology? Cone writes,

> If the history of Israel and the New Testament description of the historical Jesus reveal that God is a God who is identified with Israel because she is an oppressed community, the resurrection of Christ means that all oppressed peoples become his people. [18]

The historical account of Jesus of Nazareth comes to play a significant dual role for black theology. Jesus of Nazareth is both a terrestrial figure and a transcendent figure, representing the ontological as well as the metaphysical reality of what it means to *be* a human being. His death and his Resurrection come to signify a specific exchange between man and God: man's law sentenced Jesus of Nazareth to death only to be overcome by God's will upending the metaphysical reality of beginning and end, life and death, with an intervening justice in the Resurrection event. Moreover, the Resurrection signifies both the *theoria* and *praxis* of black theology as both *eidos* and *material reality*. For Cone, "the resurrection conveys hope in God" [19] not just an eternal or ethereal reality, but also the material reality on earth. The interrelation of immanence and transcendence echoes the claim of fruitful contamination gestured toward earlier and helps to ground a further and central claim of black liberation theology: Jesus, in his Resurrection, *becomes* black—that is, after having suffered on earth as man, Jesus returns to earth as the redeemer with an historical memory of oppression tying him to, not men generally, but to a specific community of oppressed persons. It is from this particular historical encounter (of suffering, death, *and* redemption) with oppression that is the *blackness* of Christ.

Revisiting one of the initial concerns of the chapter, the expression and understanding of blackness and what it means to be black (and, what it means that Martin Luther King Jr. was black), the claim of the blackness of Christ requires further explanation. The blackness of Christ is for Cone both a theological and experiential/historical/existential claim. Firstly, Jesus becoming black takes place within a broader discourse of religious knowledge, which, like any other kind of knowledge—that is, historical and social—is contextualized with a people. As such, the blackness of Christ is to be understood as an epistemological, hermeneutic position, an articulation of Being through the doing-*in*-the-being, thought, and discourse of black people. [20] "The task of Black Theology," Cone writes, "is to take the Christian tradition that is so white and make it black, by showing that the white man does not know really what he is saying when he affirms Jesus as the Christ." [21] Black people, as those who suffer and have an existential account of their suffering in community building and creative exchange, understand "the meaning of his spirituality from his own *vantage point*." [22] Which means, Jesus emerges as Christ through the historical community of oppressed persons, in this case black persons.

Secondly, the incarnation of Jesus in the flesh as man—to live and die with man, *as* a man; to experience the joys, the sorrows, the pains, and the pleasures of existence—solidified the link between man and God as well as man *with* God; unified the damned with God, the spirit with the dust of dust, the clay of earth, the being of the world. Jesus' incarnation like the "rainbow sign" offered divine reconciliation in addition to terrestrial liberation. For black people the incarnation meant that God was one *with* the poor, the oppressed, one *in* the struggle for reconciliation: God loved us so much that He sent His only son to dwell with and die with the oppressed. Within the community of the oppressed and through the re-valuation of the Word made flesh, Jesus *became black*.

Thirdly, the life, death, and Resurrection of Christ works as a principle of/for life for black folk. James Cone writes, "[B]lack people expressed the contradictions of existence while affirming the need to live in history without being conquered by it."[23] Here one can witness the productivity that emerges from the *chiasmus* of God and Jesus as Christ: the funda-mental tension between the transcendence of a God outside of time, and the immanence of a God constricted by time reflected in the being and becoming of a people consigned to the building of a nation based on a principle for living—thought to be inherent to the human condition, his-torical, yet universal and *trans*historical—that was nevertheless offered to them conversely, as a principle of death. The creative tension between immanence and transcendence bridged within concrete human history is more than a simple contradiction or an existential paradox reconciled by thought, or even by God himself, but a fundamental structure of Being expressed in multiple forms. This means in concrete terms that the gospel carries within it a certain *praxis*, a determined (and determinate) action to bring about in the human world what Christ brought about in his death: reconciliation. This reconciliation, though, does not solve the problem of the tension; rather it utilizes the tension to create a dynamic interaction out of which *truth* emerges.

Black theology as a theology of liberation, a theology concerned with the praxis of human freedom following the metaphysical model of Jesus as Christ, thus, interprets reconciliation as the *cause* of justice,[24] which is liberating the oppressed not only from their specific oppressive condi-tions, but from the conditions that make oppression itself possible—that is, the structural elements of a society that create differences and hier-archies, the means of oppression: sexism, racism, classism, to name a few. In focusing on these structures, black theology is concerning itself with human freedom, mirroring metaphysically the condition of Jesus Christ the risen Messiah. Jesus's metaphysical liberation is what made the meta-physical reconciliation between man and God, and thus truth and justice possible. In the same way, human liberation from oppression is what makes reconciliation possible. For black theology you cannot have one without the other. That would be Absurd, but not in a creative way, but in a destructive way. For black theology, the problem of white theology and the white church is that they attempt to *solve* the tension; they want to have reconciliation without liberation; their theological system is not in line with the gospel of Jesus Christ. (More will be said of this later.)

Man's relation to one another in society is the immanence of God in human history expressed in the gospel of Jesus of Nazareth. This history mirrors the divine relation of God to man in God's history as the transcendence of the Resurrection of Christ. The importance of Jesus is that he is both immanent and transcendent, belonging to both man and God, he unites God to man (and vice versa) and is the linchpin of Christian fellowship and the beloved community. As such, the focus of black theology on the gospel of Christ articulates the commitment to human freedom/liberation and reconciliation. Black theology embraces both the immanent and transcendent qualities of man's condition in the world.

The question of the blackness of Christ can be simplified with the question, "How does one experience God?" Is there something within the historical experience of being black that reveals the Word of God in ordinary experience? That is, what does it mean to *experience* God, or for God to be revealed through concrete everydayness? If the phenomenological encounter of God, or the experience of God, is articulated through the concrete everyday, within human history, is ordinary experience, then, a fundamental manner or way of the spirit coming to *know* itself as itself and, thus, also coming to *know* God? What is the ontological range of the everyday, and what has it to do with blackness? If it is true that blackness is, as Cone writes, both particular and universal—meaning, both historically grounded as well as a site for understanding history—then, blackness is necessarily phenomenological as well as epistemological: there is a black way of *knowing* and phenomenally *experiencing* God to reveal Christ *as* black.

The blackness of Christ, though, is not to be understood as a limit case in which blackness is the simple negation of whiteness, or even the boundedness of blackness itself as in the claim, the blackness of Christ necessarily entails that Christ cannot *not be white*; rather, the blackness of Christ affirms both the historical groundedness of being as well as the transhistoricalness of blackness as a principle of life as the *chiasmus* out of which man continually strives towards justice in freedom: blackness in this sense is an epistemological frontier that expresses the revelation of God's intention in human history.[25] Cone writes,

> To focus on blackness doesn't mean that *only* blacks suffer as victims in a racist society . . . but that blackness is an ontological symbol and a visible reality which best describes what oppression means in America.[26]

Black theology, unlike its white counterpart theology does not begin with an ahistorical position of abstract universalism or humanism—that is, the generic human person as embodied spirit before God—nor is this sort of abstraction its goal; rather, black theology begins with the particular form of human as manifestly present within space and time, and generates out of this experience a truth grounded in concrete reality: Word is revealed in the concrete as the historical Jesus reveals that God is the God of the oppressed. Cone writes,

> As with the sermon and prayer, the spirituals and gospel songs reveal the truth of black religion is not limited to the literal meaning of the words. Truth is also disclosed in the movement of the language and the passion created when a song is sung in the right pitch and tonal quality. Truth is found in the shout, hum, and moan as these expressions move the people closer to the source of their being.[27]

Blackness, thus, becomes, for Cone, a site of truth and knowledge and religious experience. Reason, truth, even revelation, is and must be, contextualized within a specific history, a specific narrative, and from a particular perspective. The reason this is so is because "Truth," for Cone, "cannot be separated from the people's struggle and the hopes and dreams that arise from that struggle. Truth is that transcendent reality, disclosed in the people's historical struggle for liberation, which enables them to know that their fight for freedom is not futile. The affirmation of truth means that the freedom hoped for will be realized."[28]

God is with black people as those oppressed persons struggling for liberation from white racism in America. Black theology not only defines what a liberatory Christianity is, but what *blackness* itself is in light of the gospel of Christ and the history of those folk in the Western world that are labeled and label themselves "black." Black liberation theology, thus, is a defining moment as well as an intellectual movement. It also serves to explain the relation between blackness and those darker hued persons.[29]

The task of black theology, thus, is to combine the practices of human freedom with the voice of God. Faith must meet social theory to eradicate the ills of the human world.

> The presence of the crucified Christ and risen savior in the community of the oppressed empowers this community to say yes to all that affirms its right to liberation and no to all that encroaches on and frustrates its being.[30]

On a basic level or in a basic way black theology of liberation argues that the black church as a space emerges, like any other church, to meet the specific needs of the community (of knowers, of believers, of worshippers) and reflects the specific modes and moods of the being or existence *of* the community. In short, black theology and the black church brings together *theoria* and *praxis*, social transformation and eschatology. To be a black church means to meet the needs of the community, both terrestrial and beloved, to address the needs of the people, both ontological and metaphysical recognizing each as mutually necessary. As such, the gospel of Christ as its doctrine is understood and mediated through the epistemological positioning of the community. In this basic interpretation, the gospel of Christ as both Crucified Christ and Risen Messiah means that Jesus *as* Christ (as revealed in the gospel) is concerned with the oppression of persons on earth and their liberation *both* terrestrially and metaphysically. With this message, then, the black church, like all churches, have the expressed call to also be one with the oppressed and to organize and act out for the sake of human liberation.

The point being made here is that black theology is not solely concerned with the ontology of oppression, nor with metaphysical reconciliation, but the confluence of immanent reality of sojourn and suffering, and the transcendence of freedom as justice (and vice versa). It is from this basic confluence—the *chiasmus*—that Martin Luther King Jr. emerged and can be located with the black liberation theological tradition.

KING BLACK THEOLOGY, LIBERATION

> It is impossible to get at the roots of one's religious attitudes without taking into account the psychological and historical factors that play upon the individual.
>
> —Martin Luther King Jr. "Autobiography of
> Religious Development," 1949

Martin Luther King Jr. was born January 15, 1929, in Atlanta, Georgia, to Martin Luther King Sr. and Alberta Williams King on a street (in a neighborhood) ironically named Sweet Auburn Avenue: "Sweet" because the concentration of black ownership and wealth overcame the original intent of whites to disenfranchise blacks at the turn of the century. Auburn Avenue, previously named Wheat Street, served as an important influence for King's life and for his personal development. Mostly a middle-class neighborhood of small businesses, Auburn Avenue also housed Atlanta University, Ebenezer Baptist Church, where three generations of King's family had preached, offices for the Urban League, the NAACP and the Masons, and, the *Atlanta Daily*, the nation's first successful black owned newspaper.[31] In short, Atlanta's Auburn Avenue was "Sweet" because it represented a life-world previously thought denied by the whites that had segregated black bodies for them to die. This was the birthplace of Martin Luther King Jr.

Martin Luther King Jr. also was born into and grew up during/in the era of Jim Crow segregation. His birthplace was Southern, his upbringing was Jim Crow, his being, though, was Sweet Auburn. The King family's religious fervor emerged out of the social context of American history and the concrete conditions of chattel slavery and the present Jim Crow segregation, and engaged the need for and the importance of freedom in justice. The church and the ministry became places and spaces for confronting injustices, organizing principles and persons, and coming to terms with the feelings of anger, vengeance, and, ultimately, love.

King's great grandfather, grandfather, and father "were not only Baptist ministers but also pioneering exponents of a distinctively African-American version of social gospel Christianity."[32] King's great grandfather, Willis Williams "was a slave and fire-and-brimstone preacher in the Shiloh Baptist Church in Greene County, Georgia, about seventy miles east of Atlanta."[33] King's grandfather, A. D. Williams, arrived in Atlanta, Georgia, in 1893 to preach Ebenezer Baptist Church in 1894. In addition to preaching, Williams founded and organized many community and political activities ranging from the National Baptist Convention (1895), the largest black organization in the United States; to the Georgia Equal Rights League (1906), formed with five hundred other black Georgians; to the Atlanta branch of the NAACP (1917). King's grandfather expounded what James Cone would call pre-Civil War black church ideas that would come to summate the principles of black liberation theology set forth two decades later at the National Council of Black Clergymen (NCBC).[34] Not solely concerned with self-reliance, the pre-Civil War black church offered an interpretation of the Word that allowed for the idea of a personal God in human history unfolding, that is, delivering, justice and human freedom. King's grandfather concerned himself with making the Word flesh (*enfleshing* the Word) with the concrete of political action, insisting that, "whosoever carries the word must make the word flesh."[35] The church, thus, is the space wherein the flesh is made divine, and the divine is made flesh—a confluence of immanence and transcendence at the heart of black theology—and manifests as the place for liberation of the individual human person and the community at large.

King's father took over Ebenezer after Williams's death in 1931, following his father-in-law's commitment to service and justice. In 1935 King Sr. organized meetings to encourage blacks to vote, and organized a march for equal pay at City Hall.

King's family, in addition to being preachers were also proud people, people who often fought segregation and the attempts of white people to "put" them in their places and to dehumanize them.[36] King Jr., too, was expected to carry out both of these "traditions." It seemed as if King Jr. was destined to take on or go down the same path as the men in his family. King biographer Roger Bruns went as far as to write, "In Martin Luther King Jr.'s veins flowed the blood of generations of fiery black preachers, figures around whom congregations turned for word of redemption, the affirmation that the crosses of injustice and prejudices that plagued their days would be made right by God's power."[37] Once again we have to be careful with blackness and the semblance of what can be called essentialism, especially of the biological sort. What is to be understood with Bruns is a phenomenological description of the *process* of coming to be, that is, the development and unfolding of consciousness, and relation of the physical world on this development. In other words, the confluence of concrete history and the metaphysical principles of transcendence once again emerge, wherein *metaphysically* speaking, the phenomena of spirit—or the presencing of an impulse grown out of the historical—transposes truth *through* the concrete.

King's father certainly expected that his son would follow in the family "tradition" and take over Ebenezer Baptist Church upon his retirement. He wrote of his son: "M. L. was still a son of the Baptist South, there'd never be any doubt about that."[38] But King Jr. had to find his way. He had to locate his own historical roots—Southernness and the black Baptist preacher and church traditions—within himself. Early in his life King would characterize the black Baptist traditions as emotional rather than intellectual, which would often embarrass him. In the Biblical tradition, King had to lose himself in the Northern landscape of intellectualism and liberalism to find himself at home as a Southern Black Baptist minister, discovering that in the emotionalism of the Baptist tradition that had embarrassed him in the past was not only a sophisticated form of worship and knowledge, but was also his foundation. In this finding, King moved from his initial position of embarrassment, "religion was intellectually respectable. I revolted against the emotionalism of Negro religion, the shouting and the stamping. I didn't understand it and it embarrassed me"[39] to a deep appreciation for the place of "emotions" in the religious experience of God. Clayborne Carson writes,

> King's theological education distinguished him from all but a few African American preachers and temporarily separated him from his childhood environment, but theological studies ultimately led King to a deeper appreciation of traditional African-American conceptions of God as a source of support, especially in times of personal crisis.[40]

King would later speak of himself in the following way acknowledging, embracing, and mining his own Southern Baptist roots,

> I am many things to many people, but in the quiet recesses of my heart, I am fundamentally a clergyman, a Baptist preacher. This is my being and my heritage for I am also the son of a Baptist preacher, the grandson of a Baptist preacher and the great-grandson of a Baptist preacher.[41]

It seemed as if King had come full circle. After finishing Boston University King turned down preaching and teaching positions in the North to take over Dexter Avenue Baptist Church in Montgomery, Alabama—even against the protest of his then new wife, Coretta. King grew up in the church, and despite his desire to go against the "simple emotive nature" of the black church tradition, he always found himself drawn back to the *blackness* of it; he discovered that it was part of who he was. Both King's family history and his place of birth signified blackness, that is, a black community of persons understood in the concrete and expressed in the sublime experience of God.

King's blackness, too, could be attributed to both conscious and unconscious motivations. King's conscious influences were his family and his family history; in addition to his immediate family King was also consciously influenced by Reverend William Holmes Borders, family friend and classmate of King Sr. at Morehouse College; Howard Thurman, Professor George D. Kelsey, and, most importantly, Dr. Benjamin Elijah Mays, his mentor at Morehouse College.[42]

King's unconscious influences were more mystical, simpler, more basic. More than the words of his grandfather, the voice of his father, or the rituals of the church, King imbibed from his community a sense of belonging, a sense of what it meant to be a Southern, Baptist, black. What is more, he imbibed from this community the manner, the way in which this place, this space emerged, and the meaning of its emergence. Phenomenally, King wrote that his own religious development was more of an organic intaking, an urge to serve, than a deliberate *choice*:

> Conversion for me was never an abrupt something. I have never experienced the so called "crisis moment." Religion has just been something that I grew up in. Conversion for me has been the gradual intaking of the noble ideals set forth in my family and my environment, and I must admit that this intaking has been largely unconscious.[43]

More than an "inherited faith," King's religiosity emerged both alongside *and* in spite of his many influences growing up.

King's own blackness, though, did not negate other influences in his intellectual and religious development. Rather, his blackness was an epistemic position, a way in, a site of synthesis, and synoptically dynamic syncreticism—a *chiasmus*. It was King's ability to bring together disparate traditions while maintaining his established black Baptist identity that made him an eclectic thinker. Yet, this eclecticism did not negate or supersede his blackness, rather it reflected the eclectic nature *of* blackness.[44] For example King adopted Reinhold Niebuhr's assessment that one must make realistic moral choices,[45] putting it to work with his own experiences with racism and his own striving for freedom in justice. What is more, King used Niebuhr's assessment as a criticism of American liberalism and of the liberalism of his fellow white clergymen. In graduate school, King wrote that liberalism "confuses the ideal itself with the realistic means which must be employed to coerce society into an approximation of that ideal."[46] It should be noted that within black liberation theology the concrete human being is of principal concern and not the universal person of liberalism.

King's American dream, that of a reconciled beloved community, was born, not of liberal conceptions of equality or the importance of the human person qua *human person*, but of a black community of persons whose experiences and concomitant ideas date back to their slave ancestors. James Cone writes of King,

> With so many references to Martin King's dream, it is not only easy to distort what he meant but also to trivialize it. . . . [T]he meaning of King's dream has deep historical roots in the African-American struggle for justice in the United States. Equally important was the influence of his social development in Atlanta, Georgia.[47]

There is no contradiction to think that King developed his vision of one America, of the beloved community from his own historical roots in the black church, sentiments that were further bolstered in his graduate school days at Crozer and Boston University. In fact, the cornerstone of the black church is the gospel of Christ in whose body and historical life the idea of redemption, reconciliation, and the beloved community were expressed both materially and metaphysically. To speak of King in transracial terms, that is, in terms sans his blackness, is to discount his own personal history and its influences on his moral and intellectual development. What is more, it is to discount the Americanness and moral scope of black Americans generally. It is to posit white intellectualism as the center of the moral universe and to further bolster that "old tried and true" belief that black slaves and their ancestors were/are so bereft of intellectual and moral capacities that they failed to ever fully grasp the extent to which the institution of slavery and racism violated/s their freedom. The ideals of black liberation theology are reflected in his writings and in his sermons, which themselves reflect his own upbringing in the black church: redemption, reconciliation, and the beloved community.

Though King has often been considered a political integrationist—to the detriment of his blackness—and there is much in his work that can be taken this way, this particular reading does not separate him from nor negate his blackness, or the blackness of his intellectual and spiritual roots in the black church and the black community of Sweet Auburn Avenue. King was linked to blackness and the South both temporally and existentially as the space and place of the unfolding of the righteous gospel of Christ in justice and in love. King was not simply historically or abstractly indebted to his roots for the "now" moment of his existential reality, rather his roots were an expression of space made place—the "fiber and liquids" of his personality and the marrow of his *eidos* of redemption, reconciliation, justice in love.

A hermeneutics of black liberation theology reveals that God's existence/presence does not necessarily impose *teleogy* or a *telos*—that is, a determinative or *a priori* logos. What this means for black theology is that there is not an imposition, on the metaphysical level, of an essential nature or quality of kinds or beings mapped onto either history or bodies, wherein blackness would come to constitute something solely transcendent and ephemeral rather than contaminated *chiasmus* (of immanence and transcendence) represented in the thought of King. What God provides is not only an historical backdrop, but an existential one as well against which and in the name of which the revolt for freedom is issued. Rather than a stolid debate over the ontology of God or proofs for God's existence, what black liberation theology offers is a metaphysically driven assessment of concrete history *in the service of* human freedom from oppression.

BLACK THEOLOGY LIBERATION, EXISTENTIALISM

Who do men say that I am?

—Matthew 16:13

But who do *you* say that I am?

—Matthew 16:15 (emphasis mine)

God was in Christ reconciling the world to himself.

—St. Paul (II Corinthians 5:19)

Walter Kaufmann, the architect of the secular turn in existential philosophy in his seminal collection *Existentialism from Dostoevsky to Sartre*[48] writes that existentialism itself cannot be defined using traditional philosophical ways and means; existentialism is its own animal. "Existentialism is not a philosophy," Kaufmann notes, "but a label for several widely different revolts against traditional philosophy."[49] Moreover, "existentialism is not a school of thought nor reducible to any set of tenets."[50] Rather, existentialism is constituted by "[T]he refusal to belong to any school of thought, the repudiation of the adequacy of any body of beliefs whatever, and especially of systems, and a marked dissatisfaction with traditional philosophy as superficial, academic, and remote from life— that is the heart of existentialism."[51] What existentialism is, according to Kaufmann, is simply "a timeless sensibility."[52] The "philosophy" of existentialism is not simply a doctrine or a system of knowledge or a series of beliefs, but a *way of life* or a *way of doing things, handling things* that is presupposed by a particular view of man (humanity) articulated through a single point, "the individual."

Existential philosophy became, largely through Kaufmann, a philosophy of the individual. That is, human existence became articulated and articulable through a moment, the individual. Moreover, in the American academy of philosophy, European existential philosophy not only took a subjectivist turn as well as secular turn, but also, and problematically, a universalist turn. What is German philosophy or Danish philosophy or French philosophy came to stand in for human philosophy. Along with the subjectivist turn in existential philosophy, the idea of universal humanism was given new strength. Heidegger, for example, became existentialism per se, not German existentialism, European, or Continental but *existential* philosophy.

Given that we have such a thing as European Continental philosophy *as* existential philosophy, the "insights" of black folk have become relegated to "black" existential philosophy, a particularized philosophy wherein *the* individual becomes a *black* individual taking away the universality of individualism, leaving only the "blackness of individuation." Blackness is not and cannot be universal, nor can it speak to or for the universal. And, yet it is still somehow existential.

Yet, what is termed "black philosophy" — the *black* here serving a dual role of both accenting philosophy with concrete history, but also adding a metaphysics of blackness *to* the discipline of philosophy where what is being expressed *is* history and yet the surpassing of *mere* history — and its antecedent existential contour, black philosophy displays much of the "true" aspects of Continental philosophy: the collapse of the individual, autonomous purely rational and ahistoric subject for ambiguity, *chiasmus* giving birth to an anxiety, angst, forlornness, and despair necessary for self-conscious humanity. What the black of black philosophy offers is a perspective of the historic, but not solely perspective alone, but the confluence of the concrete with the transcendence of consciousness; what the black offers philosophy, especially existentialism, is a critical insight into *how to live chiasmus*: transience and the unfolding of history mirrored in faith, the revelation of the historical and historicized Word, enfleshed spirit made Holy Spirit through God-Man Christ.

In this *chiasmic* figure we witness his being as the slain Christ and the Resurrected Messiah, in whom the historical and metaphysical, individual and universal are brought together in fruitful contamination. For black liberation theology, as existential philosophy — positing not only what the historical facts of black life, but also an interpretation of these facts — the revelation of the Word in the body of Jesus as Christ means that human reality is freely chosen and that those who suffer and are oppressed in this world stand arm in arm with Jesus as Christ in their liberation. As such, black liberation theology as existential philosophy does not posit the existentially individuated subject through whom human reality is understood as both particular and universal, rather it posits a community that is not a hindrance to this individual, but a precondition for individual freedom as liberation.

In much the same way Continental existential philosophy constitutes an anti-tradition tradition, which expresses an *attitude* more than produces a doctrine, black liberation theology is an anti-tradition tradition. 'Making a way out of no way,' going against the theological and cultural grain of the Academy and the cultural milieu at large, black liberation theology, with its focus on the concrete as well as the metaphysical, constitutes its own "tradition," "is immanent in its own eyes. . . . [I]t is its own following,"[53] out of which a *disposition* of/for freedom and human liberation emerges.

The existential elements of black theology are organized around the following claims: one, God overturned, that is, overcame our terrestrial understanding of Being in the Resurrection of Christ, *the* moment where God's face in human history is most illuminated; and, two, man is Reconciled with man, and with God through the death and Resurrection of Jesus. Jesus is the *chiasmatic* figure in whom life and the negation of life exists—both the presence of death and the presence of life—simultaneously; his death and his Resurrection are two figurative moments, phenomenologically and metaphysically—the twin pillars of existential philosophy—where he both adheres to and yet rejects being, at the same time, in the same respect.[54] These claims are but the existentially turned furtherance of the already named claims of black liberation theology—one, God's presence in human history; two, God as a personal God; three, the importance and necessity of fellowship and community; and four, the life, death, and Resurrection of Christ. These claims are organized around and philosophically grounded by the existential claims of the metaphysical implications of the Resurrection and the concomitant metaphysical paradigm of reconciliation and the beloved community that follow the Resurrection. And, what is more, the existential claims help to further link Martin Luther King Jr. philosophically and spiritually to black liberation theology. The concept of reconciliation lies at the heart of the metaphysics of Jesus as Christ, and, thus, is at the heart of black liberation theology. Philosophically, the concept of reconciliation is what makes black liberation theology not a traditional metaphysical "system." The concept of reconciliation is what makes black liberation theology philosophically significant; it is also what makes it existential, but not in the sense of the noted distinction between *essence* and *existence*, but in the sense of the relation of being *to* ontology, being *with* ontology. The fundamental question of existence, and the nature of Being, is given through the life, death, and Resurrection of Christ in whose material being God's immaterial Being is shone through. Tying being to Being, articulating Being through being (*and* vice versa), Jesus is the *best* example of what Heidegger called das Dasein *and* a fundamental ontology. Black liberation theology's starting point for understanding being and Being is Jesus as Christ, the reconciler, and God's ability to overcome traditional metaphysics—life and death; being and Being; temporality and infinity; transcendence and immanence; essence and existence; chaos and order—

is *accomplished* in the life, death, and Resurrection of Christ. Christ was Resurrected so that God could *reconcile* the world to himself.

Black theology's Jesus is similar to, yet different from the Greek figure Dionysus, a figure that signified a challenge to traditional metaphysics, brought to life by Friedrich Nietzsche and further reified in the non-traditional postmetaphysical stance of contemporary existentialists. While similar to Dionysus in the transfiguration of traditional metaphysics—rebirth, the eternal return of the same—the figure of Jesus is markedly different in that Dionysus is not a reconciler; rather Dionysus is simply a celebrator. Jesus is both reconciler and celebrator. Perhaps, if Nietzsche were a black American, he would celebrate Jesus *as* Christ instead of Dionysus.[55] It is Jesus' reconciliation of the world that differs him from philosophical muses of the Greeks and Romans, and from the philosophical thoughts of those of pre-Socratic antiquity—with exception to Heraclitus of Ephesus.[56] Jesus becomes, for black liberation theology, a figure, metaphor, hero, and folk narrative of divine materiality for black culture.[57] Jesus restores order; he is at once a creator of disorder and the restorer of divine order. One can see the inspiration in black ministers and black folk culture.

King's idea of nonviolent resistance, too, sought to disrupt the white racist structural order, creating disorder, yet, at the same time restoring a *new order* of justice. King writes,

> Long ago the Greek philosopher Heraclitus argued that justice emerges from the strife of opposites, and Hegel, in modern philosophy, preached a doctrine of growth through struggle. It is both historically and biologically true that there cannot be birth and growth without birth and growth pains. Whenever there is the emergence of something new, we confront the recalcitrance of the old. So the tensions which we witness in the world today are indicative of the fact that a new world order is being born and an old order is passing away.[58]

This principle—the necessity of strife for growth—is why King argued that black Americans could not wait for change, but had to be the agents of change. King found inspiration not only in Heraclitus and Hegel, but in the figure of black theology and the black church: the figure of Jesus served as inspiration as that being who overcame material *death* to bring eternal *life*; who overcame discord and disunity to bring about metaphysical *unity*.

Black theology presses us to answer who and what we are and what we must do and become in presence of God as Jesus: Who does Jesus compel us to *be*? What does Jesus compel us to *do*? Immanuel Kant's speculative questions—what can I know, what ought I to do, and what may I hope[59]—become transposed into: who are we to become, what ought we to do given who we are to become? The *who*, which is the thinking being for Kant, becomes temporalized as an existential being grounded within human history, yet more than mere history, within black liberation theology.

The problem inherent with white theology and the white church—a problem to which black liberation theology indirectly responds—is its failure to engage the troubles of human existence—oppression, disappointment, fear, uncertainty, doubt—concretely and critically; rather, the white church favors a more abstract, intellectual, one might say, philosophically formalistic manner in their understanding of human existence and the nature of God. In the white church the Jesus of scripture becomes a transcendental figure more than a transcendent figure, a canonical archetype, but certainly not a figure of terrestrial importance: "Jesus is the one who heard my cries," or "I told Jesus, it would be alright if He changed my name." The historical experiences of black Americans necessitate a personal God who not only walks with them but is one with them in oppression. This is the element of black liberation theology that spiritually binds man to man and man to God *in* forgiveness articulated in the being of Christ's re-animated body. Black liberation theology, thus, does not ignore or lack the scholarship of Academic theology; rather, it forces us to make the Word *stir to life* in the living moments of its worshippers.

The white church, then, in its intellectual formalism, does not link itself to Being phenomenologically, that is, through concrete historical experience; rather it is linked to Being formally, through argumentation, in a sort of "brute" intellectual formalism. The white church articulates and illuminates Being—the Being discovered in experience itself— through an abstract quality—through rules, regulations, and norms, that work to illuminate life and living purely on rationalistic grounds.[60] While there may be discourse on phenomena as such—gender, sexuality, even class—it is done in terms of an intellectual formalism wherein multiples and differences are subsumed under the sameness of some principle *for difference itself*—for the sake of an intellectual reason, system, or rule. What this formalism 'forsakes' in the interconnection of Being to being through pure reason is an existential truth. King, in his famous essay, "Letter from a Birmingham Jail," writes,

> So, afterall, maybe the South, the nation and the world are in dire need of creative extremists. I had hoped that the white moderate would see this. Maybe I was too optimistic. Maybe I had expected too much. I guess I should have realized that few members of a race that has oppressed another race can understand or appreciate the deep groans and passionate yearnings of those that have been oppressed and still fewer have the vision to see that injustice must be rooted out by strong, persistent and determined action.[61]

And, encountering the white church and white church leadership, he writes,

Let me rush on to mention my other disappointment. I have been so greatly disappointed with the white church and its leadership. . . . I had a strange feeling when I was suddenly catapulted into the leadership of the bus protest in Montgomery several years ago that we would have the support of the white church. I felt that the white ministers, priests, and rabbis of the South would be some of our strongest allies. Instead, some have been outright opponents, refusing to understand the freedom movement and misrepresenting its leaders; all too many others have been more cautious than courageous and have remained silent behind the anesthetizing security of the stained-glass windows.[62]

Here, King is critical of the formalism and status quo of the white church when he writes,

But again I have been disappointed. I have heard numerous religious leaders of the South call upon their worshippers to comply with a desegregation decision because it is the *law*, but I have longed to hear white ministers say, "Follow this decree because integration is morally *right* and the Negro is your brother." In the midst of blatant injustices inflicted upon the Negro, I have watched white churches stand on the sideline and merely mouth pious irrelevancies and sanctimonious trivialities.[63]

Once more, King makes note of the disinterestedness of the white church to the existential condition of man in the world:

In the midst of a mighty struggle to rid our nation of racial and economic injustice, I have heard so many ministers say, "Those are social issues with which the gospel has no real concern," and I have watched so many churches commit themselves to a completely otherworldly religion which made a strange distinction between body and soul, the sacred and the secular. . . . I have looked at her beautiful churches with their lofty spires pointed heavenward. I have beheld the impressive outlay of her massive religious education buildings. Over and over again I have found myself asking: "What kind of people worship here? Who is their God?"[64]

"I told Jesus, it would be alright, if He changed my name." Black liberation theology, unlike white theology, doesn't suffer from "brute formalism" because it is productive. Rather than merely reproducing ideology without activity in the social, political, and aesthetic worlds, black liberation theology creatively interprets the Word wherein the fire in the eyes of Jesus shines bright through the darkness of oppressive moments. At its core, because of what James Cone calls the context of black liberation theology—that is, historic experience of black Americans and the metaphysical expression of Being in Christ—black liberation theology *has* to be syncretic, *chiasmatic*, and, thus, creative and productive.

Black theology and black existentialism demonstrates, or perhaps better, illustrates not only the epistemological problems inherent in white theology, but an ontological, dare we say it, *philosophical* problem in white theorizing of the divine or of Being. Black theology and black existentialism illustrate the relativity of white theology as not universal, a historically grounded theological perspective.

And, yet we have to ask ourselves the question that frames the existential quality of black theology—Jesus's question: who do you say that I am?—to fully embrace the irony of oppression in its fundamental epistemic construction. Black theology is necessarily a theology of liberation and existential in tone; it is a Christ-centered theology that emerges out of the specific and unique experiences of black Americans. Christ's significance for black theology is not simply philosophical, or even theological, but personal: "Jesus is the one who heard my cries."

CONCLUSION

Before I awoke, I was already reconciled.
The sea was already red; the waters already parted.
And I stood there before it all.
And, opened my eyes, and it, too, was already there.

—Anonymous

Black liberation theology is an existential philosophy of rebellion, the striving of human beings toward freedom. At its heart, black theology expresses the basic fact that human being is freedom, and that this is so due to man's existential reality of being-in-the-world-with-others. Black liberation theology acts as a reminder not only of human suffering and oppression, but of the possibilities of human creation in the midst of chaos and disorder, and the redemption that follows existential revolt— and the redemptive possibilities of existential revolt.

And, a racialized worldview is what is up for debate philosophically, what is called to concern. It seems, what is disturbing about a black liberation theology and its black existential strains, is that 'black' is not somehow additive, but necessary for analysis and understanding. Philosophically, the cause to concern deals with what is thought to be its metaphysical implications and, thus, exclusionary possibilities. Yet, for both Cone and King, the human and the epistemic contours of conscious existence always take place within an already coded, embedded concrete history; yet man is more than a simple collection of events. Cone writes, "Because black theology begins with the black condition as a fundamental datum of human experience, we cannot gloss over the importance of man."[65] Martin Heidegger writes in his lectures on religion, *Phenomenology of Religious Life*, that "life experience is more than mere experience which takes cognizance of. It designates the whole active and passive pose of the human being toward the world."[66] This is precisely the historical and existential contour of black American experience and of blackness: they are but inflections, tones of the writing of Cone, in the speeches of King; they are also the elements that excite the call for abstract humanism, and the critique of a reductionary or exclusionary essentialism. This departure from the universal to the particular is structurally echoed theologically in the New Testament in the being and body of Christ. But, this is not solely what makes black liberation theology philosophically important—in addition to this ontology, there is also the reversal of it; the departure from the particular back to the universal *through* the concrete and historical, a *chiasmic dialectic*, man to God, man to man, is the major contribution of black liberation theology. Jesus *as* Christ announces the presence of God in concrete human history, and yet gestures toward the metaphysical in the Resurrection of Christ—man is brought to God *and* God is brought to man, in justice, in love. This ontological reversal, as truth seeking, as immanent and transcendent, as justice for the oppressed, is an epistemic horizon for the disclosure of ourselves to ourselves, and truth through Christ.

The presence of God in human history takes God and God's will out of the mystical and places it in the concrete living situation of man. Within the context of human suffering a different understanding of God's will toward human liberation is given, calling forth man authentically in revolt, in rebellion, love, and in freedom.

NOTES

1. This is both an intriguing philosophical question, but also an historical question concerning roots and influences that shape an individual consciousness, in this case Martin Luther King Jr. Many words have been written, text filled with the idea that King's work signified a post-black moment of transraciality, a moment in which we could, as a nation, "get past this race thing" altogether through a man who would claim, "We are all one in Christ Jesus." In addition these words and texts suppose, and dangerously so, that King's work was the result of a liberal education at Crozer Seminary and Boston University, only mentioning his Morehouse days, and rarely his own family background. See John Ansbro's *The Mind of Martin Luther King, Jr.* (Maryknoll, NY: Oribis, 1982) for a good example of how King's work has been interpreted in terms of white theology and white philosophy. Throughout this essay I will reference Ansbro's arguments about King's influences, especially his philosophical influences.

2. While much of contemporary philosophy, especially French philosophy, in the last thirty years, and to some extent the history of American philosophy, has sought to distance itself and rewrite the metaphysical assumptions and principles that emerged from Aristotlean logic—principally the logic of noncontradiction that is predicated on a sort of onto-metaphysical stasis, if not purity, not of thought alone, but of the living world—black experience in the West has been a living unity of the disunity of this principle. The idea of impurity, then, as experienced and theorized with the black lifeworld—often characterized as the contradiction of "American values" and "American practice"—should be more aptly understood in terms of what it reveals theoretically (and practically): a fundamental *chiasmus* philosophical position of impurity and structural and cyclical instability within being itself. A now novel (rediscovered) concept, the truth or the reality of the world is impure and contaminated with essences that, according to traditional metaphysics, were thought to be separate, has long been part

of the black intellectual worldview. A simple example of this worldview could be found in W. E. B. Du Bois' notion of double-consciousness in *Souls of Black Folk*, or in Nella Larsen's contamination of conceptual being in the phenomena of "passing" as described in her novel *Passing*. For our usage, the idea of contamination is twofold: one, the idea that truth is not *a priori*, but is adjudicated in the historical becoming and happening of a community of persons, and, thus, is a mixture of materiality and human imagination; and, two, that the theological assumptions of Christian faith centered on the life, death, and Resurrection of Christ challenges traditional metaphysical assumptions about life and death, *and*, materiality and immateriality. For us, black theology is making a philosophical claim—one that is both epistemological, the community's adjudication of the truth of Christ, *and* metaphysical, God as personal through the life, death, and Resurrection of Christ—*from* the experiences and life-world of black people.

3. James Cone, *A Black Theology of Liberation* (New York: J. B. Lippincott Company, 1970), 159.

4. James Cone, *A Black Theology of Liberation*, 17.

5. I capitalize "Resurrection" because it represents a singular event in God's overcoming of the death principle in the rebirth of Christ after his domestic, or terrestrial crucifixion.

6. James Cone, *A Black Theology of Liberation*, 17–18.

7. What is important to note here for black liberation theology is the epistemological and metaphysical claim that God's presence in human history is both universal, *and*, simultaneously particular. God acts as both transcendent force outside of human history *and* principal actor *within* human history; God both activates those metaphysical realities of space and time (life and death) *and*, at the same time, is constricted by them (in the suffering and death of Christ), yet overcomes them as well (in the Resurrection). These both/and's exemplify the sort of contaminated ontological reality spoken of previously.

8. James Cone, *A Black Theology of Liberation*, 20.

9. James Cone, *A Black Theology of Liberation*, 22.

10. James Cone, *A Black Theology of Liberation*, 19.

11. James Cone, *God of the Oppressed* (Maryknoll, NY: Orbis Books, 1975), 17.

12. Ralph Ellison, *Invisible Man* (New York: Vintage Books, 1952).

13. Ralph Ellison, *Invisible Man* (New York: Vintage Books, 1952), 9.

14. James Cone, *God of the Oppressed*, 17–18.

15. James Cone, *God of the Oppressed*, 18.

16. Ralph Ellison, *Invisible Man*, 9.

17. James Cone, *God of the Oppressed*, 18.

18. James Cone, *A Black Theology of Liberation*, 21.

19. James Cone, *A Black Theology of Liberation*, 21.

20. The fellowship—the phenomenological relation between the preacher and the audience, and the audience with one another—through which truth is expressed and Word revealed is an example of the doing-in-being as thought and practice within a religious community.

21. James Cone, *A Black Theology of Liberation*, 29.

22. James Cone, *A Black Theology of Liberation*, 29; emphasis added.

23. James Cone, *God of the Oppressed*, 28

24. By proxy, philosophically, the tension between immanence and transcendence, wherein *chiasmus* is its structure is also the foundation for justice as well as truth.

25. Wherein "race" is generally understood to be a concept separating out human beings into kinds, demarcating one from the other—in a sense, its boundaries are constructed by as much what one *is not* as much as what one *is*—blackness in black theology is understood as historically grounded—whereas race is simply historically emergent, in the same way that concepts can have a history without having a constructive historical consciousness.

26. James Cone, *A Black Theology of Liberation* (New York: J. B. Lippincott Company, 1970), 27.

27. James Cone, *A Black Theology of Liberation* (New York: J. B. Lippincott Company, 1970), 21.

28. James Cone, *A Black Theology of Liberation* (New York: J. B. Lippincott Company, 1970), 16.

29. For a detailed account of the cultural and historical context of black theology, that is, the black experience see James Cone, *God of the Oppressed* (Maryknoll, NY: Orbis Books, 1975), especially chapters 1 and 2; James Cone, *A Black Theology of Liberation* (New York: J. B. Lippincott Company, 1970). For an interesting counterview to Cone's see Victor Anderson, *Beyond Ontological Blackness: An Essay on African American Religious and Cultural Criticism* (New York: Continuum International Publishing Group, 1999).

30. Noel Leo Erskine, *King amongst Theologians* (Cleveland: The Pilgrim Press, 1994), 109–10.

31. For a good book on the history of Auburn Avenue, see Clifford M. Kuhn, Harlon E. Joye, and E. Bernard West, *Living Atlanta: An Oral History of the City, 1914–1948* (Athens: University of Georgia Press, 1990).

32. Clayborne Carson, "Martin Luther King, Jr. and the African-American Social Gospel." In *African-American Christianity: Essays in History*, Paul E. Johnson, ed. (Berkeley: University of California Press, 1994), 161.

33. Roger Bruns, *Martin Luther King, Jr.: A Biography* (Westport, CT: Greenwood Press, 2006), 1–2.

34. For a brief history of the term "black theology," see James Cone's *For My People: Black Theology and the Black Church* (Maryknoll, NY: Orbis Books, 1984).

35. Clayborne Carson, Ralph E. Luker, and Penny A. Russell, eds., *Papers of Martin Luther King, Jr.*, vol. 1, *Called to Serve, January 1929–1951* (Berkeley and Los Angeles: University of California Press, 1992), 89; cited in *African-American Christianity: Essays in History*, Paul E. Johnson, ed. (Berkeley: University of California Press, 1994), 162.

36. James Cone writes of Martin Luther King's father, lovingly called "Daddy King," that "Martin observed that his father did not 'turn the other cheek' to the brutalities of the white man but 'had begun to strike back.' Daddy King did not 'bow and smile' when he was insulted, but was always 'straightening out the white folks.' 'When I stand up,' he often proclaimed, 'I want everyone to know that a *man* is standing there.'" (23) (Martin Luther King, Jr. *Strive toward Freedom* (New York: Harper and Brothers, 1958; cited in James Cone, *Martin & Malcolm & America: A Dream or a Nightmare*).

37. Roger Bruns, *Martin Luther King, Jr.: A Biography* (Westport, CT: Greenwood Press, 2006), 1.

38. Martin Luther King Sr., with Clayton Riley, *Daddy King: An Autobiography* (New York: William Morrow, 1980), 127; cited in *African-American Christianity: Essays in History*, Paul E. Johnson, ed. (Berkeley: University of California Press, 1994), 171.

39. James Cone, *Martin & Malcolm & America: A Dream or a Nightmare* (Maryknoll, NY: Orbis Books, 1998), 27.

40. Clayborne Carson, "Martin Luther King, Jr. and the African-American Social Gospel." In *African-American Christianity: Essays in History*, Paul E. Johnson, ed. (Berkeley: University of California Press, 1994), 173.

41. Martin Luther King Jr., "The Un-Christian Christian," *Ebony* 20 (August 1965): 76; cited in *African-American Christianity: Essays in History*, Paul E. Johnson, ed. (Berkeley: University of California Press, 1994), 173.

42. For more on these influences see, Clayborne Carson, "Martin Luther King, Jr. and the African-American Social Gospel," in *African-American Christianity: Essays in History*, Paul E. Johnson, ed.

43. Martin Luther King Jr., "Autobiography of Religious Development," *Papers of Martin Luther King, Jr.*, vol. 1, 361; cited in *African-American Christianity: Essays in History*, Paul E. Johnson, ed. (Berkeley: University of California Press, 1994), 164.

44. Carson wrote of King's synoptic method: "He skillfully incorporated into his sermons those aspects of his theological training that affirmed his ties to the religion of his parents and grandparents" (171).

45. Martin Luther King Jr., "Autobiography of Religious Development," *Papers of Martin Luther King, Jr.* 1: 361; cited in *African-American Christianity: Essays in History*. Paul E. Johnson, ed. (Berkeley: University of California Press, 1994), 168.

46. Martin Luther King Jr., "Niehbur's Ethical Dualism," *Papers 2, Rediscovering Precious Values 1951–1955* (Berkeley and Los Angeles: University of California Press, 1994); cited in *African-American Christianity: Essays in History*, Paul E. Johnson, ed. (Berkeley: University of California Press, 1994), 168.

47. James Cone, *Martin & Malcolm & America: A Dream or a Nightmare* (Maryknoll, NY: Orbis Books, 1998), 20.

48. Walter Kaufmann, *Existentialism from Dostoevsky to Sartre* (New York: Meridian Press, 1975).

49. Walter Kaufmann, *Existentialism from Dostoevsky to Sartre* (New York: Meridian Press, 1975), 11.

50. Walter Kaufmann, *Existentialism from Dostoevsky to Sartre* (New York: Meridian Press, 1975), 11.

51. Walter Kaufmann, *Existentialism from Dostoevsky to Sartre* (New York: Meridian Press, 1975), 12.

52. Walter Kaufmann, *Existentialism from Dostoevsky to Sartre* (New York: Meridian Press, 1975), 12.

53. This is a metaphysical and ontological argument presented in Franz Fanon's famous text, *Black Skin, White Masks* (New York: Grove Press, 1967), 135. This particular fragment is part of a larger claim of the being or ontological status of black folk. And though Fanon's argument is within the space and place of the Antilles rather than America, the site for black liberation theology, what is to be taken from this, for our use, is that (1) the Fanonian loop, is the loop of humanity, and (2) not all circles, especially those that are "raced," are vicious.

54. One needs to only look at Paul's experience on the road to Damascus, where Christ, already known to have been slain, appears, a voice without body, presence and being, without figuration. In this experience Christ is most present, though already dead, and yet there is no indication that Paul had experienced a ghost, but something alive, transfigured (1 Corinthians 15:3–8; Acts 9:3–9).

55. On the intersection of African American culture and continental philosophy, in particular Nietzsche see Jacqueline Scott and Todd Franklin's *Critical Affinities* (New York: State University of New York Press, 2006).

56. Interestingly, Heraclitus's philosophy of the chiasmus and cross-wise logic comes closest to the figure of Jesus as Christ within black liberation theology, and the presence of fluidity within black American culture at large. For more of Heraclitus's philosophy of chiasmus see Patrick Miller's *Becoming God: Pure Reason in Early Greek Philosophy* (New York: Continuum, 2011).

57. James Cone argues that the cultural context of black theology is the black community and the black historical experience, which means that alongside Jesus are other more traditional folk heroes such as High John the Conqueror out of Africa. While Jesus was central to black theology and the black church, other important figures stood next to him in the folklore of black persons, and especially in the older black church. See James Cone, *God of the Oppressed* (Maryknoll, NY: Orbis Books, 1975), 15–25.

58. Martin Luther King Jr., "Facing the Challenges of a New Age," p. 25; cited in Ansbro, p. 120.

59. Immanuel Kant, *Critique of Pure Reason* (New York: Cambridge University Press, 1998).

60. For example, theologian Paul Tillich, whose "presence" in King's work, and "presence" in black theology generally, has to be problematized given Tillich's own silence to the suffering of oppressed persons in America. As Erskine writes,

Tillch's theology is colored by his theological perspective, and in essence he deals with questions that emerge from the general situation and seeks to shape his answers according to that situation. This in part may account for Tillich's silence on the struggle of the civil rights movement for justice and freedom in America. This may seem surprising since the economic, political, and theological foundation of America was shaken by the civil rights movement. Tillich lectured in the midst of the revolution without speaking a word in reference to that revolution. (*King among the Theologians*, 134)

61. Martin Luther King Jr., "Letter from Birmingham Jail," in *The Essential Writings and Speeches of Martin Luther King, Jr.*, James M. Washington, ed. (New York: Harper Collins, 1991), 298. The usage of the word "infamous" is to signify the idea that King's essay is often used in philosophy courses or political science courses on the question of just and unjust laws. Also, the essay is often used in combination with other texts on political activity—for example, Plato's *Euthyphro*, where the lead character Socrates has an imagined conversation with the law of the land, which tells him he has to obey even if he does not agree because he is a citizen, is often contrasted with King's idea that an unjust law need not be followed. Yet, rarely is King's critique of whiteness and white theology critically analyzed for its political or philosophic insight.

62. *The Essential Writings and Speeches of Martin Luther King, Jr.*, James M. Washington, ed. (New York: Harper Collins, 1991), 299.

63. *The Essential Writings and Speeches of Martin Luther King, Jr.*, James M. Washington, ed. (New York: Harper Collins, 1991), 299; emphasis in original.

64. *The Essential Writings and Speeches of Martin Luther King, Jr.*, James M. Washington, ed. (New York: Harper Collins, 1991), 299.

65. James Cone, *Black Theology of Liberation* (New York: J. B. Lippincott Company, 1970), 154.

66. Martin Heidegger, *The Phenomenology of Religious Life*, Matthais Fritsch and Jennifer Anna Gosetti-Ferencei, trans. (Bloomington: Indiana University Press, 2004), 8.

FOUR

The Philosopher King

An Examination of the Influence of Dialectics on King's Political Thought and Practice

Stephen C. Ferguson II

Hegel once wrote, a great man condemns posterity to the necessity of explicating him.[1] The truth of these words is clear when we examine the proliferation of literature, both scholarly and popular, on Dr. Martin Luther King Jr. While few would deny King's historical significance as an intellectual and activist in the African American liberation movement, there is no agreement on the meaning and substance of his political thought and practice.

What constitutes the *essence* of King's social and political thought? Examining the social and political thought of Martin Luther King Jr. presents one with a riddle of sorts. Is the King of "I Have a Dream" fame the same King who spoke out against the Vietnam War? Did King's thought remain the same over the course of his life? Or did King's thought change? What was the relationship between philosophical thought and political practice for King?

When we critically scrutinize the corpus of writings on King's thought, one thing becomes apparent. There are few works from a philosophical perspective and even fewer that undertake the study of King's philosophical outlook and influences. In some instances, we find prominent African American intellectuals such as Cornel West distorting King's philosophical vision. While West does not formally bring King into the pantheon of prophetic pragmatism, he does argue that King's "all-embracing moral vision" is an exemplar of the possibilities of pro-phetic pragmatism.[2]

In fact, many scholars pay little attention to King as a philosopher vis-à-vis theologian. Rare exceptions are articles by the African American philosopher William R. Jones entitled, "Liberation Strategies in Black Theology: Mao, Martin or Malcolm?"; Robert Michael Franklin entitled, "In Pursuit of a Just Society: Martin Luther King, Jr. and John Rawls"; and Dwayne A. Tunstall's recent book *Yes, But Not Quite: Encountering Josiah Royce's Ethico-Religious Insight*, which philosophically engages King's concept of the Beloved Community. Perhaps, John J. Ansbro's *Martin Luther King, Jr.: The Making of a Mind* remains the most compre-hensive philosophical examination of King to date.[3]

In far too many examinations of King, his work as a social and politi-cal activist is separated from his philosophical (as opposed to theological) thought. When we examine King's political and ideological development dialectically, we see that there are stages in the development of his thought. From the standpoint of methodology, my analysis assumes that the material context of the African American liberation struggle, as a process of objective development, shaped and directed his thinking as a dialectician. Consequently, the material context of the African American liberation movement served as a dynamic process that greatly affected King's cognitive grasp of dialectics as a tool of analysis.

I should note at the outset that my intention is not to discount the importance of Personalism or African American religious thought on King's political thought and practice. The central focus of this chapter is the neglected topic of King's comprehension and employment of dialec-tics. Or more formally, what is the role of dialectics in the philosophy and political practice of King? In the first section of the chapter, I outline three different conceptions of dialectics as presented by Mortimer Adler that will serve as a heuristic device to situate King's theory of dialectics. In the next section, I examine King's introduction to and critical study of Heg-el's philosophical architectonic, specifically Hegel's dialectic, during his graduate studies at Boston University's School of Theology. Here we will determine to what extent King viewed his theory of dialectics as Hege-lian. In the third section, we will turn to King's subjective idealist critique of Hegel's objective idealism. In the last section, we will be concerned with situating King's theory of dialectics according to Adler's typology in light of his critique of Hegel's absolute idealism. Ultimately, I conclude that King's *early* conception of dialectics is not Hegelian, but rather reflex-ive in character, and hence truth finds its ground in consensus, concilia-tion, and compromise. However, after 1965, King as dialectician becomes more Hegelian, approximating what Mortimer Adler characterizes as a regulative dialectic.

ON THE MEANING OF DIALECTICS

What is dialectics? It has been assumed up to this point that the notion of dialectics is an understood concept. Aristotle credited Zeno of Elea with the invention of dialectic (derived from the Greek dialectikê) in his famous paradoxes, which were designed to vindicate the Eleatic cosmology by drawing intellectually unacceptable conclusions from its rejection. But the term was first generally applied in a recognizably philosophical context with Socrates's mode of argument, or elenchus, which was differentiated from the Sophistic rhetorical method. Plato himself regarded dialectic as the supreme philosophical method of scientific knowledge. Of course, Aristotle's opinion of dialectic was considerably less exalted, regarding it as a mere propaedeutic to the syllogistic reasoning expounded in his *Analytics*. The sense of dialectic as conversational interplay and exchange, involving the assertion, contradiction, distinction, and qualification of theses, was retained in the practice of medieval disputation. Later, Kant regarded dialectic as that part of transcendental logic that showed the mutually contradictory or antinomies into which the intellect fell when not harnessed to the data of experience. Finally, dialectics reached its highest expression in the work of Hegel, Marx, and Engels. Recently, Roy Bhaskar has attempted to revive dialectics once again in his monumental (yet cryptic) work *Dialectic: The Pulse of Freedom.*[4]

Before we can take a critical look at King as a dialectician and at the dialectical unfolding of his thought and practice, we must be clear on the meaning of this crucial concept. Despite the lack of agreement concerning what dialectics is and the long history in which the dialectical method has been put to many uses, I think the philosopher Mortimer Adler offers a valuable typology in his article, "The Idea of Dialectic."[5] Adler begins with the following point:

> A theory of dialectic is, like a theory of science or of art, a philosophical theory. If the dialectician has a conception of dialectic itself, in addition to having and using a certain method, he does so in virtue of being a philosopher, not a dialectician. On the other hand, his conception of dialectic must square with the principles and objectives of his method. We have already seen that his method commits him to certain philosophical positions—about truth, human reason, the laws of thought, language and meaning. It also commits him to a certain theory of dialectic.[6]

So, one's conception of dialectics commits one to a particular philosophical methodology and philosophical assumptions as it relates to such issues as truth, reason, laws of thought, language, and meaning. On this basis, Adler suggests that there are three theories of dialectics: (1) noetic dialectic, (2) regulative dialectic, and (3) reflexive dialectic. Adler comments that these theories of dialectics "only appear to be in conflict but are actually in nonagreement rather than disagreement."[7]

The first, noetic dialectic, involves a method of philosophical inquiry of which knowledge of reality is the outcome of this inquiry. Plato's dialectic as contained, for example, in the *Republic* is representative of this theory, where dialectics is identified with "philosophy as knowledge of the ultimate reality."[8] Plato sets dialectic in opposition to the unfair questioning of disputation (characteristic of the Sophists) in which the purpose is simply to make a point. Plato's dialectical method, which has some analogies to the sophistic method, frees the mind of error, contradiction, and the effects of verbal ingenuity and quibbling. Dialectic avoids the confusion and verbalisms of disputation by its attention to the essential nature of things: it consists of the processes of dividing and collecting, cutting things into classes where the natural joints are.[9] Dialectic yields the truest kind of knowledge, which has to do with being, reality, and eternal immutability.[10]

Second, regulative dialectic consists of those thinkers who maintain that there are fundamental dialectical laws that govern the development of thought, nature, and society. Here Hegel and Marx would be leading proponents.[11] This can be seen, for example, in Hegel's systematic elaboration of a dialectical method and its application to epistemology, logic, metaphysics, and history. Within the Hegelian architectonic, the identity of thinking and being is not only a metaphilosophical foundation, but also a metaphysical axiom—the real is rational, and the rational is real. The connecting thread that links the metaphysical to the metaphilosophical for Hegel is objective (or absolute) idealism. Hegel's Absolute idealism posits the existence of a transhistorical mind or consciousness (the Absolute) of which nature and history are mere semblances of its development toward self-realization. On the metaphilosophical plane, the subordinate relationship of history to reason (consciousness) serves as the basis for Hegel's idealism. Hegel thought that Absolute Spirit itself (which is to say, the sum total of reality) develops in a dialectical fashion toward an ultimate end or goal. As the Absolute undergoes this development, it manifests itself both in nature and in human history. Nature is Absolute Spirit objectifying itself in material form. Finite minds and human history are also the process of the Absolute manifesting itself. Hegel's dialectical perspective furnishes the basis for the presupposition that reason as transcendent mind governs all motion and activity in the material realm, that is, nature and human history.

Third, reflexive dialectic is not concerned with knowing reality directly nor regulating reality. Rather, it is "a method auxiliary to philosophy by which men think about things, not as they are in themselves, but as they are reflected in human thought."[12] Here Aristotle and Kant give us a representative statement. According to Aristotle, dialectic is not the unique method of philosophy as posited by Plato. Far from being the science of sciences, it treats of probability and opinions rather than of certainty and the nature of things. It is not identical with scientific demonstration, although it may serve to clarify issues and define terms in the absence of scientific proof. To use Hegelian language, it is a subjective dialectic.

Adler's typology will serve as a heuristic device to situate King's theory of dialectics. This is of prime importance since King is often located by most commentators on his dialectic, specifically Ansbro within the orbit of a regulative dialectic via Hegel. The following questions are before us. First, did King view his theory of dialectic as Hegelian? And, second, to what extent is King's conception of dialectics Hegelian? I will show that it is, in reality, the conflating of these two questions that invariably pushes one to the conclusion that King's conception of dialectics was Hegelian.

KING CONFRONTS HEGEL: FROM MOREHOUSE TO BOSTON UNIVERSITY

During the Montgomery Bus Boycott, King declared (in an interview with the *Montgomery Advertiser*) that the German philosopher G. W. F. Hegel was his favorite philosopher.[13] Throughout his life, King appealed to Hegel for insights not only into the African American liberation movement, but also in shaping his political philosophy. As King notes, in his classic work *Stride toward Freedom*, his study of Hegel's dialectic "helped me to see that growth comes through struggle."[14]

King was first introduced to Hegel during his undergraduate studies at Morehouse. In a two-semester required course in philosophy under Professor Samuel Williams, the young fifteen-year-old learned of the German philosopher among others.[15] According to King biographer David Levering Lewis, "he succumbed to an almost uncritical fascination with the Hegelian dialectic." Unfortunately, he did not do very well in the class and only managed to get a "C" in the course.[16]

King's early "uncritical fascination" with Hegel's dialectic developed into a critical study when he arrived at Boston University for his doctoral work. As a graduate student, he read Hegel's *Phenomenology of Spirit*, *Philosophy of History*, and *Philosophy of Right* and the so-called smaller *Logic* published as *Part One of the Encyclopedia of the Philosophical Sciences*. There is no evidence that King read the *Science of Logic*. King was spellbound by Hegel's dialectical idealist philosophy.

During a two-semester seminar at Boston University with Edgar S. Brightman and Peter A. Bortocci, King undertook a study of Hegel's dialectical logic. In this seminar King's study was concentrated on the so-called smaller *Logic*. King wrote an essay for this seminar on the Doctrine of Being examining the categories of being, nonbeing, and becoming.[17] The fact that King read the *Encyclopedia* is significant because this is a mature work of Hegel and represents a systematic construction of the dialectic as a logical method. What becomes apparent from King's exposition of Hegel's dialectic, however, is more a generic (almost superficial) grasp of the Hegelian dialectic. (This is a point, in my estimation, missed by Ansbro in his discussion of Hegel's influence on King.[18]) We should mention that King relied heavily on W. T. Stace's *The Philosophy of Hegel*.

Of particular note during his tenure at Boston University, King, Wayman B. McLaughlin, an African American doctorate student in philosophy, in conjunction with other African American graduate students organized a philosophical club called the Dialectical Society, "a group that was mainly interested in certain philosophical and theological ideas and applied them to the black situation in the country." Between ten and thirteen graduate students would gather once a week at King's apartment to discuss the existence of God, Hegel, Kierrkegaard, and a variety of other philosophical and theological topics. While the Dialectical Society was primarily composed of African American male graduate students, it occasionally involved participation from non-Blacks such as Dr. Harold DeWolf and women such as Coretta Scott and female friends of other members. Some of the members of the Dialectical Society were Cornish Rogers who served as vice-president, Percy A. Carter Jr. who served as secretary, Major J. Jones, David W. Bridell, Jack Clark, among others. According to Taylor Branch,

> Graduate students interested in philosophy or religion gathered one evening a week to share a potluck supper and a rarefied discussion about God or knowledge. One student read a formal paper, and the others then jumped in to criticize or support it. The club lasted throughout King's student life in Boston, becoming so popular that white students dropped in occasionally and Professor DeWolf once delivered the paper for discussion. A rather stiff decorum prevailed early in the evening, as pipe smoke and abstract jargon mingled in the air, but the hard core of participants usually settled into a bull session late at night.[19]

According to Branch, there was relatively little discussion about racism and other political matters. "At the Dialectical Society," Branch claims, "discussions of politics were largely confined to the issue of whether it was wise for them to choose 'race-related' topics for papers, theses, and doctoral dissertations. King concurred with the general consensus that to do so might cheapen their work in the eyes of influential Negroes as well as whites." At one of the meetings, King presented a paper on the theology of Reinhold Niebuhr.[20] During May of 1954, L. Harold De Wolf attended the Dialectical Society's meeting and lectured on "How the Kingdom Will Come." According to notes from the meeting, DeWolf presented two views of how Jesus expected the Kingdom to come: the apocalyptic view as opposed to the view that the Kingdom is already present.

According to the meeting notes, DeWolf attempted to reconcile these two views, arguing that a solution "may lie in a synthesis of both views."[21]

Of all Hegel's works, the *Phenomenology of Spirit* (1807), particularly Hegel's discussion of the master-slave dialectic, proved to be the most attractive to King during his philosophical and theological studies at Boston University. According to Dr. Peter Bertocci, King "almost took over the class" in the graduate seminar on Hegel in his enthusiasm for Hegel's insight on the master-slave dialectic.[22] In one of the most famous sections of the *Phenomenology*, Hegel claims that the slavemaster/slave relationship is not limited to the slave's dependency on the slavemaster. Rather, the slavemaster's consciousness qua slavemaster is only possible through his relationship to the slave, consequently the consciousness of the slavemaster as slavemaster is a dependent one.

Hegel first takes up the task of presenting his philosophical system in the *Phenomenology*, which he refers to as the propaedeutic to his philosophical architectonic.[23] The *Phenomenology* describes, in prose both tortuous and elegant, the development of consciousness from its most primitive or naïve form—which Hegel names sensuous certainty—to its most mature form—self-knowing spirit or "absolute knowing" or dialectical reason. Unlike Hegel's *Philosophy of History*, the *Phenomenology* does not unveil the historical development of consciousness.[24]

Hegel's aim is to set forth a philosophical system so comprehensive that it would encompass the ideas of his predecessors and create a conceptual framework in terms of which both the past and future could be philosophically understood. Such an aim would require nothing short of a full account of the historical development of and self-realization of the Absolute. "It is this coming-to-be of *Science as such* or of *knowledge*," Hegel explains, "that is described in this *Phenomenology* of Spirit."[25]

We can see the influence that Hegel's *Phenomenology* had on King's political philosophy in his biographical work *Stride toward Freedom*. When discussing the philosophy of nonviolence King makes the following reference:

> Like the synthesis in Hegelian philosophy, the principle of nonviolent resistance seeks to reconcile the truths of two opposites—acquiescence and violence—while avoiding the extremes and immoralities of both.[26]

Here we can see that the philosophy of nonviolence as a species of moral suasion has as a key feature an appeal to the conscience of the oppressor. This idea that the oppressor's identity and consciousness is dependent on the oppressed was appealing, to King, because it projects a sense of interdependency and hence an intrinsic equality. For if the slave and slavemaster, as oppressed and oppressor, are interdependent, it then follows they share a common destiny. Consequently, an interdependent relation and common destiny create a space for political compromise and consensus (as exemplified, for instance, in Booker T. Washington's famous speech at the opening of the Cotton States and International Exposition in Atlanta on September 18, 1895).[27] We will come back to this point in our discussion of King's application of dialectics to the political direction of the civil rights movement.

KING'S SUBJECTIVE IDEALIST CRITIQUE OF HEGEL'S OBJECTIVE IDEALISM

Clearly there is good *prima facie* evidence that King was familiar enough with Hegel to claim him as his favorite philosopher. This should not be taken, however, to mean that King was a Hegelian. Indeed, he thought, "[t]here were points in Hegel's philosophy that I strongly disagreed with. For instance, his absolute idealism was rationally unsound to me because it tended to swallow up the many in the one."[28]

What does King mean when he criticizes Hegel's absolute idealism because it "tended to swallow up the many in the one"? At the heart of this criticism is King's identification of Hegel's absolute idealism with a monistic pantheism. For King, a monistic pantheism necessarily devalued the individual worth of each and every person. And it simultaneously meant relegating God to being one with the universe rather than conceptualizing God as a distinct personality.

King's adoption of personalism as the basis of his philosophical outlook left no room for a monistic pantheism. His embrace of personalism began during his doctoral study at Boston University under the mentorship of Edgar Brightman and L. Harold De Wolf. He comments in *Stride toward Freedom*:

> Both men greatly stimulated my thinking. It was mainly under these teachers that I studied personalistic philosophy—the theory that the clue to the meaning of ultimate reality is found in personality. This personal idealism remains today my basic philosophical position. Personalism's insistence that only personality—finite and infinite—is ultimately real strengthened me in two convictions: it gave me metaphysical and philosophical grounding for the idea of a personal God, and it gave me a metaphysical basis for the dignity and worth of all human personality.[29]

King's interpretation of Hegel as a monistic pantheist is directly due to the influence of the Boston Personalists and their acceptance of Soren Kierkegaard's critique of Hegel.[30]

Kierkegaard's critique of Hegel was in its social implications a reaction to what he thought to be Hegel's denial of individual freedom and hence a dehumanization of intellectual life. The merging of all opposition, for Kierkegaard, negates the element of the "either/or" so critical to decision making. This results in the denial of freedom and thus nullifying what Kierkegaard believes is central to human existence. Furthermore, Kierkegaard rejects Hegel's identification of epistemology and ontology—that is, thinking and being. He, in turn, asserts that existence cannot be reduced to thought, for the concreteness of existence can never be fully captured in thought. Kierkegaard argued that thought necessarily abstracts from existence, it collapses the differences encountered in concrete existence. Hence one can neither think nor talk about concrete existence. One does not think existence but rather lives it.[31]

It is probably most obvious now that Kierkegaard's critique of Hegel is an existentialist response to Hegel's absolute idealism. Both existentialism and personalism are species of subjective idealism, hence their common response to Hegel's objective idealism. As a Christian, King does not fully embrace existentialism but he does claim, "there is much here by which the theologian may describe the true state of man's existence."[32] King further expresses his appreciation for existentialism in "Pilgrimage to Nonviolence." He noted,

> Its understanding of the "finite freedom" of man is one of existentialism's most lasting contributions, and its perception of the anxiety and conflict produced in man's personal and social life as a result of the perilous and ambiguous structure of existence is especially meaningful for our time. The common point in all existentialism, whether it is atheistic or theistic, is man's existential situation is a state of estrangement from his essential nature. In their revolt against Hegel's essentialism, all existentialists contend that the world is fragmented. History is a series of unreconciled conflicts and man's existence is filled with anxiety and threatened with meaninglessness.[33]

Is it possible for King to accept the Kierkegaardian critique of Hegel, yet remain a proponent of Hegelian dialectics?

King's existentialist critique of "Hegelian essentialism," while concurrently propagating a Hegelian dialectic, is, at the very least, problematic. And here I differ with Ansbro's analysis of King. Ansbro asserts,

> King tried to adopt a Hegelian approach even in his interpretation of Hegel. While deeply impressed with those truths found in Hegel's system, he was not reluctant to reject as false those portions of that system which he thought either ignored or neglected the freedom and dignity of the individual.[34]

Ansbro's above statement contradicts a point he brings to the reader's attention in a footnote regarding Kierkegaard's critique of Hegel. I want to quote more substantially Ansbro's claim. He states,

> It would seem, however, that Kierkegaard was not accurate in some of his criticisms of Hegel. Kierkegaard's criticism that Hegel's system was pantheistic ignored Hegel's emphasis on the eternal Trinity, distinct from and prior to creation, which is its manifestation. . . . His further criticism that Hegel emphasized the importance only of the movements

of the World-Spirit or Absolute in the development of "objective truth" and deprived the individual of his self-identity, self-determination, and dignity neglected Hegel's emphasis on the value of the individual's achievement of "subjective freedom" by consciously interiorizing and contributing to the rational element in the objective political, artistic, religious, and philosophical orders. . . . The criticism that Hegel destroyed the meaning of Christianity failed to appreciate the role of belief in the unique person of Christ as the source of the insight in the Hegelian system that the divine and the human have already been implicitly reconciled in the Incarnation.[35]

In contrast to King, McLaughlin argues, in his dissertation, "Both Kierkegaard and Hegel were aware of the significance and value of the individual. Although Hegel did not place sufficient stress upon the individual, Kierkegaard's accusation against Hegel that he did not treat the individual is untrue. Kierkegaard's over-emphasis upon the individual leads to a false individualism which Hegel's doctrine overcomes."[36] At several points in his dissertation, McLaughlin astutely notes that Kierkegaard was not completely accurate in some of his criticisms of Hegel. For example, McLaughlin notes,

Did not Kierkegaard misinterpret Hegel's meaning at this point? For example, when Hegel identified thought with being, he did not intend by the use of a magic wand to close the door to all existential reality. The contrary seems to be true that Hegel sought to reveal the multidimensional passions of the human soul, not "a ballet of bloodless categories." In speaking of the unity of thought and being, Hegel insisted upon an identity in difference.[37]

At another point, McLaughlin argues,

Kierkegaard's objection to Hegel's identification of logic and metaphysics as an abstract identity misses the empirical side of Hegel's thought. Hegel's view of essence is formulated to give existence its due respect, since the point of departure for thought and philosophy is from experience.[38]

What Ansbro and McLaughlin have so astutely brought to our attention, concerning the pitfalls of the Kierkegaardian critique, is lost on King. Two points should be clear. One, there are limitations to the Kierkegaardian critique of Hegel. Two, King's criticism of Hegel are precisely Kierkegaardian in substance. Ultimately, can King accept the Kierkegaardian critique of Hegel and yet remain a proponent of Hegelian dialectics?

If one is to answer in the affirmative, as in the case of Ansbro, then what transpires is the conflation of the question "To what extent or not is King's theory of dialectics Hegelian?" with the question "Did King view his theory of dialectics as Hegelian?" The former question is one that can be objectively treated in view of Adler's typology. The latter question pertains to King's subjective understanding—that is, his belief that he was following a Hegelian dialectic.

ASSESSING KING'S CONCEPTION OF DIALECTICS

Where does King's theory of dialectics find its locus in Adler's typology? Is it a noetic, regulative, or reflexive theory of dialectics? A cursory observation of King's writings and public statements indicates he did view his theory of dialectic as Hegelian. He, for example, begins his book, *Strength to Love*, by counterpoising the opposites, "A Tough Mind and a Tender Heart," and he makes reference to Hegel saying, "The philosopher Hegel said that truth is found neither in thesis nor the antithesis, but in an emergent synthesis which reconciles the two."[39] In his *Stride toward Freedom* when discussing the philosophy of nonviolence, he makes the following reference:

> Like the synthesis in Hegelian philosophy, the principle of nonviolent resistance seeks to reconcile the truths of two opposites—acquiescence and violence—while avoiding the extremes and immoralities of both.[40]

King makes a concerted and conscious effort to employ what he thinks is the Hegelian dialectic. And this becomes pervasive, throughout his philosophical perspective, encompassing his philosophical anthropology, philosophy of history, his conception of life, and his analysis of the nature of political struggle. In explaining the role of Rosa Parks in lighting a spark that ignited the Civil Rights movement, King employed Hegel's dialectical analysis.

King saw in the Montgomery bus boycott the workings of what Hegel describes as the "cunning of reason."[41] King viewed "world-historical individuals" like Rosa Parks as catalysts who galvanized the passions of the masses at a crucial period in history. Parks was a lightning rod for what everyone was thinking without realizing it. To use Hegelian language, she brought unconscious Spirit to mass consciousness, and consequently her actions raised the universal out of the stormy mass of the particular. In *Stride toward Freedom*, King states, Parks was:

> anchored to that seat by the accumulated indignities of days gone by and the boundless aspirations of generations yet unborn. She was a victim of both the forces of history and the forces of destiny. She had been tracked down by the *Zeitgeist*—the spirit of the time.[42]

King's description of Rosa Parks mirrors Hegel's discussion of historically significant individuals. For Hegel, the "cunning of reason" speaks to the manner in which reason (or Absolute Consciousness) was at the root of historical development and the impulse for change. Reason in its pursuit of self-consciousness and freedom uses the passions of individuals to achieve its goals even though these individuals do not have full consciousness of the consequences of their actions. In this respect, Hegel noted:

> Such individuals had no consciousness of the general Idea they were unfolding, while prosecuting those aims of theirs; on the contrary, they were practical, political men. But at the same time they were thinking men, who had an insight into the requirements of the time—*what was ripe for development*.[43]

In his 1956 address to the First Annual Institute on Nonviolence and Social Change, King appealed to the thought of Heraclitus and Hegel to explain the significance of the Civil Rights movement. He observes,

> Now I am aware of the fact that there are those who would contend that we live in the most ghastly period of human history. They would argue that the rhythmic beat of the deep rumblings of discontent from Asia, the uprisings in Africa, the nationalistic longings of Egypt, the roaring cannons from Hungary, and the racial tensions of America are all indicative of the deep and tragic midnight which encompasses our civilization. They would argue that we are retrogressing instead of progressing. But far from representing retrogression and tragic meaninglessness, the present tensions represent the necessary pains that accompany the birth of anything new. *Long ago the Greek philosopher Heraclitus argued that justice emerges from the strife of opposites, and Hegel, in modern philosophy, preached a doctrine of growth through struggle.* It is both historically and biologically true that there can be no birth and growth without birth and growing pains. Whenever there is the emergence of the new we confront the recalcitrance of the old. So the tensions which we witness in the world today are indicative of the fact that a new world order is being born and an old order is passing away. (Italics added)

King makes the following point in the same speech,

> We must continue to struggle through legalism and legislation. There are those who contend that integration can come only through education, for no other reason than that morals cannot be legislated. *I choose, however, to be dialectical at this point.* It isn't either education or legislation; it is both legislation and education. I quite agree that it is impossible to change a man's internal feelings merely through law. But this really isn't the intention of the law. The law does not seek to change ones internal feelings; it seeks rather to control the external effects of those internal feelings. For instance, the law cannot make a man love me—religion and education must do that—but it can control his desire to lynch me. So in order to control the external effects of prejudiced internal feelings, we must continue to struggle through legislation.[44]

The salient feature of King's conception of the dialectic is the notion of the reconciliation of opposites via synthesis.[45] I think there is enough *prima facie* evidence—throughout King's speeches, interviews, and writings—to comfortably say that King did, in fact, view his theory of dialectics as Hegelian. Hegel's chief merit, King assumes, is a syncretic approach that allows for the possibility of resolving differences by finding a common denominator among opposing views.

The question remains, however, is this syncretic approach, the synthesis of thesis and antithesis, the fundamental core of the Hegelian dialectic? In the conventional introductory texts of philosophy, it is often the case that Hegel's dialectical logic is reduced to the simplistic formula of thesis, antithesis, and synthesis. But, for Hegel, dialectic does not follow the formalism of "thesis, antithesis, and synthesis." To attribute this conventional slogan to Hegel is a poor attempt to understand what is really going on in Hegel's dialectical logic. As Gustav Mueller comments, this myth about Hegel's dialectic is "a convenient method of embalming Hegel and keeping the mummy on display for curious visitors of antiquities."[46] The truth is that it was not Hegel but Fichte who introduces these categories.

Fichte, in response to the Kantian thing-in-itself (noumena) as the cause of consciousness (phenomena), argues that, in thought, the ego (not to be confused with the solitary individual) posits its object or the non-ego (Kant's noumena). This positing of the non-ego, by the ego, overcomes Kantian dualism and establishes a more consistent (monistic) idealism. The non-ego, as an alienation of the ego, acts upon the ego and, in turn, the ego acts upon it. The reconciliation of ego and non-ego is a synthesis of ego (thesis) and non-ego (antithesis) where alienation is overcome in the harmony of scientific knowledge (synthesis).[47]

While there is a line of continuity from Fichte to Hegel, nonetheless, Hegel's dialectic cannot be simply reduced to Fichte's as King does. The emergence of post-Kantian German idealism starts with Fichte and reaches its culmination with Hegel. Hegel's dialectic builds on Fichte, yet it is not identical to it. Although it is true that Hegel's dialectical logic is sometimes expressed in the form of a triadic process, he is nevertheless critical of the Fichtean dialectic. Prima facie, Fichte's dialectic appears as an evolving progression where the contradiction between thesis and antithesis finds resolution in a synthesis making the opposition and contradiction merely apparent, and in turn the new synthesis consequently becomes a thesis with its antithesis ad infinitum. However, Fichte's dialectic is not a progressive determination of meaning because he did not make the movement from the initial thesis to the antithesis as a strictly theoretical deduction from the initial proposition. The crux of Hegel's critique of Fichte is focused on this point. For Hegel, the categories must express logical necessity, that is, there must be a rational deduction wherein the initial category implicitly contains within itself its opposite. For the Fichtean triadic dialectic—similar to Kantian metaphysics—the overriding principle governing the historical process and hence human practice (freedom) was a regulative principle.

In contradistinction, the dialectical process, for Hegel, is a logical necessity. Yet it is not based on the laws of Aristotle's formal logic. Hegel's dialectical logic views Aristotle's formal logic as restrictive primarily because identity excludes difference. Hegel critically takes Aristotelian logic to be a limited form of reasoning centered on a formal identity. The principle of identity (A=A) is necessarily a tautology. We cannot, with formal logic, discover the dynamic content behind the apparent stable form(s). Aristotelian logic is a formal abstraction that leaves untouched the very nature of reality's essential contradictory and changing character. Hegel's dialectical logic—as presented, for example, in the *Science of Logic*—takes into account that identity contains difference and difference identity.

In contrast, Fichte's dialectic is void of the principle of contradiction as an internal relation. Fichte's failure to comprehend the dialectic, as an internal relation, has as its foundation a logical grounding, viz. the principle of identity. In Fichte's view, philosophy becomes a science (more accurately metascience) not due to objective necessity but as a construct emanating from the ego's will. He thought all necessity (determinism) ultimately pointed to materialism. Hegel's dialectic returns determinism and necessity into the idealist fold. Ergo, Hegel conceptualizes the historical process and human freedom in terms of necessity and attainability. "The truth of necessity," Hegel posits, "therefore, is freedom."[48]

What is important for us, at this point, is precisely Hegel's dialectical logic that Kierkegaard found to be at the foundation of Hegel's monistic dehumanization. Kierkegaard argues that Hegel's logic collapses all difference into identity and as such relegates individual differences to the scrap heap. Without the possibility for individual difference, as found in concrete human existence, there can be no freedom. What this amounts to is situating the notion of freedom within the classic debate of pluralism versus monism. Kierkegaard upholds pluralism, atomism, and individuality as the essence of freedom. Hegel, on the other hand, embraces the individual and the many as aspects (or moments) of a greater whole or movement. In Hegel's monism, the individual is part of the absolute, a moment in the dialectical movement of history, which at its various stages, brings us to greater freedom. King's dialectic cannot be properly placed in the camp of Hegel, for as long as his dialectic remains fundamentally Fichtean in character, and compatible with the Kierkegaardian critique of Hegel, it must stand in contradistinction to Hegel's dialectic. [49]

Now if we apply Adler's typology as a grid, it can reasonably be demonstrated that King's dialectic is not Hegelian. Is King's theory noetic or reflexive? A noetic dialectic identifies philosophy as knowledge of ultimate reality. In the noetic dialectic of Plato, knowledge is not obtained by merging partial truths because "partial truths" are untruths. Knowledge of reality is immutable, changeless, and complete within itself. The dialectic of thesis, antithesis, and synthesis is a dialectic of becoming. A noetic dialectic is a dialectic where there is a line of demarcation between being (ultimate reality) and becoming (the visible world). This demarcation, for Plato, while not absolute (as in the case of Parmenides) is, nevertheless, an objective relationship and condition. Thus truth is not reached by consensus or synthesis. Truth—knowledge of reality—is objective and no amount of agreement or reconciliation of opinion can get one to this realm. Obviously, since reconciliation and synthesis of differences are cardinal principles in King's conception of dialectics, it cannot be noetic.

A reflexive dialectic, on the other hand, is a dialectic that is auxiliary to philosophy. Its method is the approach one uses in philosophical discussion and debate. The accent is not on things-in-themselves as an objective reality (as in the Platonic architectonic) standing over and apart from social consciousness. Rather, the very core of the reflexive dialectic has as its aim a certain neutrality (though not necessarily jettisoned from partisanship) so as to remain open to finding agreement and consensus. I think King's initial conception of dialectic, is more appropriately, a reflexive dialectic where thesis, antithesis, and synthesis are not ontological categories but dialogical ones. King's theory of dialectic is reflexive, and hence truth finds its ground in consensus, conciliation, and compromise.

THE PILGRIMAGE TO SOCIAL DEMOCRACY: THE SOCIAL IMPORT OF DIALECTICS FOR UNDERSTANDING KING'S POLITICAL THOUGHT AND PRACTICE

What is the social import of dialectics for understanding King's political thought and practice? Why is it important to highlight King's application of dialectics to politics? The social import of King's dialectic, as a syncretic notion, is entailed in the fact that during his *early* foray into the African American liberation movement, he thought that reaching reconciliation, finding a middle ground, was indicative of how dialectics should be applied to the tactics and strategy of the movement as indicated earlier. A dialectic of synthesis translates into a politics of compromise. The benchmark of King's liberalism is the politics of consensus with an anchor in constitutionalism. This became most obvious during the 1963 March on Washington where the civil rights leaders including King compromised with the Kennedy administration. King's politics of compromise led Malcolm X to call the March on Washington, the "Farce in Washington." And again, during 1964, in the intense battle over the seating of the Mississippi Freedom Democratic Party (MFDP) at the Democratic National Convention, King relinquishes his support of the MFDP and joins forces with Lyndon Johnson and the Dixiecrat segregationists such as Senator James Eastland. Given King's political orientation during this period, Jack Minnis, a supporter of the MFDP and Director of the Research of the Student Non-Violent Coordinating Committee (SNCC) remarked, "Martin Luther

King, Jr., said, 'I am enough of a dialectician to believe that out of thesis and antithesis comes synthesis'—the philosopher of compromise."[50] It was King's politics of compromise that led people like Malcolm X to view him as an accomplice of the bourgeois (white) power structure.

Although King's early conception of dialectics was reflexive, it can be shown that his conception of dialectics was, in fact, qualitatively transformed from 1965 to 1968 and subsequently reflected in his sociopolitical practice and adoption of a social democratic framework. To see this point, one would have to reject the view that King's political outlook remained—throughout his life—liberal democratic in character. In fact, King's political philosophy and practice was far too dialectical to be encased in a simple, didactic legend designed to offend no one. King's political thought changed in conjunction with the concrete context, that is, the sociopolitical relations and material conditions that grounded his ideological and political formation. This popular misreading of King is precisely due to the failure to understand him at two levels, on the one hand, as a product of a changing movement and, on the other, as a dialectician attempting to comprehend the nature of these changes.[51]

Toward the end of 1965, King began to jettison his politics of compromise, viewed by Malcolm X and the Black Power advocates as selling out to the white bourgeois Establishment. In terms of political philosophy, King's evolution can best be described as a movement from liberal to social democracy. To be sure, King's social democratic stance was not Marxist in the classical or orthodox sense. However, his social democracy derived from the social gospel of Walter Rauschenbusch, modified by the Christian realism of Reinhold Niebuhr, and governed by personalism. His social democratic propensities left no room for compromise.[52]

After the Selma campaign in 1964 King's political thought and practice reaches a critical nodal point. Now, we can see that the imperatives of the movement required more than desegregation and the formal right to vote, it required a socioeconomic platform that would speak to poverty under capitalism. King's social democratic thought reaches its highest stage of development in his landmark speech, "Beyond Vietnam: A Time to Break the Silence." His anti-imperialist stance in support of the Vietnam War protest brought King against the mainstream civil rights leadership and the Johnson administration.[53] At this point, King fully and deeply comprehended the nature of the crisis sweeping the United States. Indeed, he had found this crisis was not only moral in character but also, in its very essence, to be profoundly social and political economic. Consequently, King joined the anti-imperialist forces in the campaign against the Vietnam War and denounced the liberal Lyndon B. Johnson as well as the conservative Nixon administrations.

Former liberal supports of Dr. King, both black and white, denounced him. They charged King was only a leader of the "civil rights" movement and therefore not qualified to speak on issues outside of its boundaries.

Moreover, they thought, King's proposed "Poor Peoples' March" went too far beyond civil rights and hinted at a kind of "Un-Americanism," fostering class struggle and socialism. They anxiously inquired, what happen to the King of "I Have a Dream"? King's historic and memorable elocution, wherein his rhythmic cadence about the "American Dream" brought hope of a liberal America, an America bereft of racism. Now, they declared, King had betrayed the liberal dream. In fact, his critics shouted King had fallen into the hands of the "Un-Americans," that motley and unsavory crew of antiwar activists, socialists, and Communists.

His support of the sanitation workers in Memphis and plans to create a coalition of the poor and to March on Washington are a further indication of his transition from a liberal to a social democratic worldview.[54] King's dialectics has increasingly become a dialectic of negation rather than synthesis. During this period, King rejected the idea of piecemeal reform within the existing socioeconomic structure. His final address to the Southern Christian Leadership Council best indicates how the dialectics of compromise would no longer be satisfactory. He states,

> For years . . . I have labored with the idea of reforming the existing institutions of the society. A little change here, a little change there. Now I feel quite differently. I think you've got to have a reconstruction of the entire society, a revolution of values.[55]

While I do not want to suggest that King ceased to be an advocate of nonviolence, it is, however, clear that he saw reformism as limited and increasingly became critical of the very socioeconomic foundations of capitalism. By 1966, King viewed himself as an enemy of capitalism and argued that America "must move toward a Democratic socialism."[56] King was convinced that capitalism was the common determinant linking racism, materialism, and militarism.

Unfortunately, King did not have the time to reformulate his theory of dialectic, in a systematic manner, as he had moved from a dialectic of synthesis, which more properly approximates Adler's reflective dialectic, to a dialectic of negation. King as a dialectician was more Hegelian, approximating Adler's regulative dialectic, in the post-1965 period. In Hegelian terms, he had made the transition from understanding to reason.

ACKNOWLEDGMENTS

I would like to thank John H. McClendon for his many insights into the influence of dialectics on Africana intellectual culture, particularly Kwame Nkrumah, C. L. R. James, and Martin Luther King Jr. Thanks, as well, to Robert E. Birt, Lani Roberts, and Andrew Fiala in addition to the two blind reviewers of *Philosophy in the Contemporary World* for their editorial assistance.

NOTES

1. Cited in Robert Stern, *Hegel and the* Phenomenology of Spirit (New York: Routledge, 2002), vii.

2. Cornel West, *The American Evasion of Philosophy: A Genealogy of Pragmatism* (Madison: University of Wisconsin Press, 1989), 234–35. For an excellent critique of West's Prophetic Pragmatism, see Robert Gooding-Williams, "Evading Narrative Myth, Evading Prophetic Pragmatism: Cornel West's *The American Evasion of Philosophy*," *The Massachusetts Review* (Winter 1991–1992).

3. William R. Jones, "Liberation Struggles in Black Theology: Mao, Martin or Malcolm?," in Leonard Harris (ed.) *Philosophy Born of Struggle* (Duboque, IA: Kendall/ Hunt Publishing Co., 1983), 229–41; Robert M. Franklin, "In Pursuit of a Just Society: Martin Luther King, Jr. and John Rawls," *Journal of Religious Ethics*; Dwayne A. Tunstall, *Yes, But Not Quite: Encountering Josiah Royce's Ethico-Religious Insight* (New York: Fordham University Press, 2009); John J. Ansbro, *Martin Luther King, Jr.: The Making of a Mind* (Maryknoll, NY: Orbis Press, 1982). See also Ira G. Zepp Jr., *The Social Vision of Martin Luther King, Jr.* (New York: Carlson Publishing Inc., 1989); Michael Eric Dyson, *I May Not Get There with You* (New York: The Free Press, 2000); Greg Moses, *Revolution of Conscience: Martin Luther King, Jr. and the Philosophy of Nonviolence* (New York: Guilford Press, 1997).

4. Roy Bhaskar, *Freedom: The Pulse of Freedom* (London: Verso, 1996). For an excellent critique of Bhaskar's dialectic, see Sean Creaven, "The Pulse of Freedom? Bhaskar's Dialectic and Marxism," *Historical Materialism* 10, no. 2 (2002): 77–141; and Alex Callinicos, "Marxism and Critical Realism: A Debate," *Journal of Critical Realism* 1, no. 2 (2003): 89–114.

5. Mortimer J. Adler, "The Idea of Dialectic," in Mortimer Adler (ed.), *The Great Ideas Today* (Chicago: Encyclopedia Britannica, Inc., 1986), 154–77; see also Richard McKeon, "Dialectic and Political Thought and Action," *Ethics* 65, no. 1 (October 1954): 1–33.

6. Adler, "The Idea of Dialectic," 166.

7. Adler, "The Idea of Dialectic," 166.

8. Adler, "The Idea of Dialectic," 167.

9. Plato, *Phaedrus*, 265E–266C.

10. Plato, *Philebus*, 57E–58A.

11. Adler, "The Idea of Dialectic," 167. See also Frederick Engels, *Dialectics of Nature* (Moscow: Progress Publishers, 1972); and V. I. Lenin, *Philosophical Notebooks*, in *Collected Works*, vol. 38 (Moscow: Progress Publishers, 1961).

12. Ibid., 167; see also Engel's *Dialectic of Nature* and Lenin's *Philosophical Notebooks*.

13. The interview conducted by Tom Johnson, *The Montgomery Advertiser*, January 19, 1956. Also see Lerone Bennett, *What Manner of Man* (Chicago: Johnson Publishing Co., 1976), 72. See also King, *Stride toward Freedom* (New York: Harper & Row Publishers, 1958), 100; Ansbro, *Martin Luther King, Jr.*, 298n63.

14. King, *Stride toward Freedom*, 101.

15. Clayborne Carson, "Martin Luther King, Jr.: The Morehouse Years," *The Journal of Blacks in Higher Education* 15 (Spring 1997): 121–25. George Kelsey (1946 Yale doctorate) also mentored King at Morehouse. Kelsey taught philosophy and theology at Morehouse from 1938 to 1945. Kelsey gave King his only "A" at Morehouse in theology. Both Williams and Kelsey were mentors to King and helped to cultivate an understanding of the civil rights movement and, more importantly, the philosophy of nonviolence.

16. David L. Lewis, *King: A Critical Biography* (Urbana: University of Illinois, 1978), 20.

17. Martin Luther King, Jr., "An Exposition of the First Triad of Categories of the Hegelian Logic—Being, Non-Being, Becoming," in *The Papers of Martin Luther King, Jr.: Rediscovering Precious Values, 1951–1955*, vol. 2, edited by Clayborne Carson (Los Angeles: University of California Press, 1994), 196–201. King's exposition relies heavily

on W. T. Stace's exposition of Hegel's dialectic. See W. T. Stace, *The Philosophy of Hegel* (New York: Dover, 1955).

18. For Ansbro's discussion on Hegel's influence on King see ibid., 119–20, 123–26, 162, 190–91, 217–18, 298n63; both *Logics* by Hegel are published after the *Phenomenology*. The *Phenomenology* is more properly viewed by Hegel as an introduction to his system.

19. Branch, *Parting the Waters: America during the King Years, 1954–1963*, 93.

20. *King Papers*, vol. 2: 269.

21. *King Papers*, vol. 2: 265.

22. Ansbro, *Martin Luther King, Jr.: The Making of a Mind* (Maryknoll, NY: Orbis Press, 1982): 298.

23. Hegel, *Science of Logic*, 28–29.

24. For a discussion of Hegel's historical importance and a critique of Hegel's dialectical idealism from the standpoint of dialectical materialism, see Frederick Engels, "Ludwig Feuerbach and the End of Classical German Philosophy," in *Selected Works of Karl Marx and Frederick Engels*, vol. 3 (Moscow: Progress Publishers, 1970), 341.

25. G. W. F. Hegel, *Phenomenology of Spirit*. Translated by A. V. Miller (New York: Oxford University Press, 1977), 15, § 27.

26. King, *Stride*, 132.

27. Booker T. Washington best expressed this point in his famous "Atlanta Compromise" speech, "The laws of changeless justice bind oppressor with oppressed and as close as sin and suffering joined we march to fate abreast. . . . In all things that are purely social we can be as separate as the fingers, yet one as the hand in all things essential to mutual progress." See Louis R. Harlan (ed.), *The Booker T. Washington Papers*, vol. 3 (Urbana: University of Illinois Press, 1974), 585. Cynthia Willet makes an insightful critique of the intersubjective relationship between slavemaster and slave. She states, "Hegel's incomplete familiarity with historical accounts of slavery also binds to a fundamental error in dialectical logic. While the slave may serve as mirror for the master, it is not all clear that the master serves as mirror for the slave." See Cynthia Willet, *Maternal Ethics and Other Slave Moralities* (New York: Routledge, 1995), 123; Cynthia Willet, "The Master-Slave Dialectic: Hegel vs. Douglass," in *Subjugation and Bondage: Critical Essays on Slavery and Social Philosophy*, edited by Tommy L. Lott (New York: Rowman & Littlefield, 1998), 151–70.

28. King, *Stride*, 100–101.

29. Ibid., 100.

30. On the influence of Kierkegaard's critique of Hegel on the Boston personalist consult Edgar S. Brightman, *The Problem of God* (New York: Abingdon Press, 1930). Ansbro offers a rebuttal to the Kierkegaardian critique of Hegel—see Ansbro, 299n83.

31. For Kierkegaard's monumental critique of Hegel, see *Either/Or*, vol. 1, trans. David R. and Lillian Marvin Swenson (Garden City, NY: Anchor Books, Doubleday and Co., 1959) and vol. II, trans. Walter Lowrie, 1959.

32. King, *The Strength to Love*, 252.

33. Ibid., 252.

34. Ansbro, *Martin Luther King, Jr.*, 128.

35. Ibid., 299n83.

36. Wayman B. McLaughlin, *The Relation between Hegel and Kierkegaard* (PhD diss., Boston University, 1958), 316.

37. Wayman B. McLaughlin, *The Relation between Hegel and Kierkegaard* (PhD diss., Boston University, 1958), 110–11.

38. Wayman B. McLaughlin, *The Relation between Hegel and Kierkegaard* (PhD diss., Boston University, 1958), 315.

39. King, *Strength*, 147.

40. King, *Stride*, 132.

41. G. W. F. Hegel, *The Philosophy of History*, translated by J. Sibree (New York: Dover Publications, 1956), 33.

42. King, *Stride*, 44.

43. Hegel, *The Philosophy of History*, 30.

44. King, "Facing the Challenge of a New Age," speech delivered to Institute for Nonviolence and Social Change, December 3, 1956.

45. See Ansbro, *Martin Luther King, Jr.*, 119–28.

46. Gustav E. Mueller, "The Hegel Legend of 'Thesis-Antithesis-Synthesis,'" *Journal of the History of Ideas* 19, no. 3 (June 1958): 414.

47. On the Fichtean origins of thesis, antithesis, synthesis, see Richard T. DeGeorge, *Patterns of Soviet Thought* (Ann Arbor: University of Michigan Press, 1966), 15; on the locus of Fichte in German Idealism from a Marxist-Leninist perspective see Evald Ilyenkov, *Dialectical Logic: Essays on Its History and Theory* (Moscow: Progress Publishers, 1977); especially chapter 4, "The Structural Principle of Logic: Dualism or Monism."

48. *Hegel's Logic*, edited by William Wallace, 220. See also Hegel, *Science of Logic*, 577–78.

49. By asserting that King's dialectic is Fichtean in character, I am not asserting that King embraces a Fichtean metaphysics. Fichte's ego is transcendental and consequently is "an absolute, trans-historical and trans-individual consciousness of which empirical egos are the finite instantiations." For Fichte, the individual ego, what King terms "finite personality," is relegated to secondary status vis-à-vis the transcendental ego. Such a reduction of the individual ego, from King's personalist perspective, would be tantamount to a family resemblance with Hegel's absolute idealism as monistic pantheism. The crucial link connecting King to Fichte is the dialectic of thesis, antithesis, and synthesis. It is not the metaphysical presupposition undergirding German idealism as a philosophy of consciousness. See Kate Soper, *Humanism and Anti-Humanism* (Lasalle, IL: Open Court Press, 1986), 27.

50. Jack Minnis, "The Mississippi Freedom Democratic Party A New Declaration of Independence," *Freedomways* 5, no. 2 (Spring 1965): 271. For a more extensive account of the 1964 Democratic Convention and King's role, see James Forman, *The Making of Black Revolutionaries* (Seattle: Open Hand Publishing Co., 1985), 292–93; Chana Kai Lee, *For Freedom's Sake: The Life of Fannie Lou Hamer* (Chicago: University of Illinois Press, 1999), especially chapter 5, "The National Stage."

51. There are a host of articles documenting King's move from a liberal to a social democratic posture, see David Garrow, "From Reformer to Revolutionary," 427–36; Vincent Harding, "Recalling the Inconvenient Hero: Reflections on the Last Years of Martin Luther King, Jr.," 525–40; Adam Fairclough, "Was Martin Luther King a Marxist?," 301–10; Robert M. Franklin, Jr., "An Ethic of Hope: The Moral Thought of Martin Luther King, Jr.," 349–60. All of the above appear in David Garrow (ed.), *Martin Luther King, Jr.: Civil Rights Leader, Theologian, Orator*, vol. II (New York: Carlson Publishing Inc., 1989). For a more recent treatment, see Thomas F. Jackson, *From Civil Rights to Human Rights: Martin Luther King, Jr. and the Struggle for Economic Justice* (Philadelphia: University of Pennsylvania Press, 2007).

52. See Adam Fairclough, "Was Martin Luther King a Marxist?," *History Workshop* 15 (Spring 1983): 117–25; and Thomas F. Jackson, *From Civil Rights to Human Rights: Martin Luther King, Jr. and the Struggle for Economic Justice* (Philadelphia: University of Pennsylvania Press, 2007).

53. See, for example, Adam Fairclough, "Martin Luther King, Jr. and the War in Vietnam," *Phylon* 45, no. 1 (1984): 19–39.

54. See, for example, William M. King, "The Reemerging Revolutionary Consciousness of the Reverend Dr. Martin Luther King, Jr., 1965–1968," *The Journal of Negro History* 71, no. 1 (Winter/Autumn 1986): 1–22; Douglas Sturm, "Martin Luther King, Jr., As Democratic Socialist," *The Journal of Religious Ethics* 18, no. 2: 79–105. For a more in-depth study of King's ideological and political evolution, see Thomas F. Jackson, *From Civil Rights to Human Rights: Martin Luther King, Jr. and the Struggle for Economic Justice* (Philadelphia: University of Pennsylvania Press, 2007). For a in-depth study of King and the Memphis Sanitation Strike, see Joan T. Beifuss, "At the River I Stand: Memphis, the 1968 Strike, and Martin Luther King,"*Martin Luther King, Jr. and the Civil*

Rights Movement, vol. 12 (Carlson Publishers, 1989); and Michael K. Honey, *Going Down, Jericho Road: The Memphis Strike, Martin Luther King's Last Campaign* (New York: W. W. Norton, 2008).

55. Quoted in Adam Fairclough, "Was Martin Luther King a Marxist?," 122.
56. Quoted in Adam Fairclough, "Was Martin Luther King a Marxist?," 120.

FIVE

Martin Luther King Jr. as Social Movement Intellectual

Trailblazer or Torchbearer?

Maurice St. Pierre

INTRODUCTION

This chapter provides an analysis of Martin Luther King Jr. as a social movement intellectual. It is contended that while much has been written about King's life and his participation in the civil rights movement,[1] his questionable academic qualifications,[2] and sexual peccadilloes,[3] hardly anything has been written about his role as a social movement intellectual, especially within a specific theoretical framework. This effort endeavors to fill that lacuna, but in so doing takes the position that while King and a number of black pastors gave the civil rights a "public face," the foundation of nonviolent resistance was laid by a number of mostly black women, who endured rapes that went unpunished and unprosecuted, lynching, beatings, and public humiliation by white males in general, and especially white male train conductors and bus drivers. The essay is guided by a theoretical perspective that combines social movement theory, especially cognitive praxis; and intellectualism, particularly in terms of antihegemonic activity that led to the civil rights movement as a producer of "new knowledge" and King as a social movement intellectual.

THEORETICAL GROUNDINGS

Earlier approaches to the study of collective action viewed such action as "nonrational," if not outright "irrational,"[4] and action participants as "misfits" and "sinners,"[5] or the alienated, or the anomic, in other words those who were marginalized in the society. However, with the realization that some social movements are led by well-educated individuals (like Martin Luther King Jr.), the theoretical focus shifted to resource mobilization theory, which speaks to resources used by leaders to educate and mobilize prospective collection behavior participants. These resources do not arise out of thin air, and indeed, are part of the sociohistorical experiences of the aggrieved, and may be part of a hierarchy of resource possibilities that reflect the scale of preferences of participants. Resources, furthermore, may be nonmaterial,such as time, energy, friendship, specialized knowledge (like philosophy and theology or history), and values; or they can be material, such as money or previously organized entities (like political parties or trade unions).[6]

Second the cognitive praxis approach maintains that social movements can be viewed as producers of new knowledge, to the extent that as leaders, social movement intellectuals interact with the challenged, mobilize their followers, and in the process educate them and raise their consciousness, often providing their own novel analysis, interpretations of, and solutions to, the grievance at hand.[7] However, in order to achieve the status of a movement intellectual, leaders have to create space for their beliefs, ideas and ideologies, strategies, and tactics (new knowledge) in the political landscape.[8] Beyond that, cognitive praxis provides a better understanding of the role of social movements in transforming scientific ideas into social and political beliefs. It is in this manner, that the historical function of social movements as social laboratories for testing social theories, and in providing critiques for existing paradigms and structures,[9] in other words as generators of knowledge, also becomes apparent. Finally, this approach helps us understand how social movement intellectuals create and exploit opportunities, thereby making space, for their views regarding systemic change.

Third, the intellectual perspective speaks to the extent to which events like social movements open up opportunities for intellectual activity on the part of movement intellectuals like Martin Luther King. Apart from the argument that intellectuals,[10] as Lewis Coser maintains, "never seem satisfied with things as they are,"[11] intellectuals may be viewed as "critics of existing regimes [and] creators of social or cultural orientations and activities opposed to tradition" and also as "guardians or would-be guardians of society's conscience–but only when that conscience was thought to be opposed to the established order";[12] or as individuals "whose ideas are such that they challenge conventional wisdom or, at least, invite us to see the obvious in a new light." [13]

Again, Antonio Gramsci identifies what he refers to as *organic* intellectuals, who under certain conditions emerge and seek to embody the aspirations of a social class of which the intellectual is a part, while others such as Lipset and Basu, Lipset and Dobson, and Flacks point to the efforts of intellectuals to make their knowledge socially relevant as well as transmissible. Also railing against the system enables the intellectual to move issues of concern from the periphery to the center for more serious consideration and ventilation, [14] thereby creating space for "new knowledge" in the sociopolitical fabric. This is done usually by efforts "to make 'scientific' sense of the world" and by generating various theories of society that in turn make history. Social theories, therefore, "are levers intellectuals used to influence power structures, to facilitate political outcomes, to enable groups interested in exercising control to improve their [chances of doing so], to justify their ascendancy, to achieve their goals, or to advance their interests" (Flacks: 3). Finally, intellectuals need a stage and a setting upon, and against, which to launch their ideas and theories, which may be the academy, a political party, or a social movement.

THE SOCIAL CONSTRUCTION OF A DISCREDITED STATUS

As sociologist Erving Goffman notes the term *stigma* referred to "bodily signs designed to expose something unusual and bad about the moral status of the signifier." Later in Christian times, the term referred to bodily signs of either grace or, as in the case of "Negroes," of a physical disorder. [15] However, while a stigma, like a missing limb, is not always apparent to the stigmatizer, what Goffman calls a tribal stigma, like race, is not only observable to stigmatizer and stigmatized alike, but is transmitted through lineages and thus equally contaminates members of a family. Lastly, stigmatization becomes systemic in that it is nourished by rewards provided for conformity and negative sanctions for deviation from its norms.

With respect to the condition of blacks in Montgomery, Alabama, in particular in the early 1950s, King notes in his book *Stride toward Freedom*, that the existing political subjugation, economic exploitation, and cultural underbelly of officially sanctioned violence and humiliation experienced by blacks conduced to fear among the lower class and indifference on the part of the black middle class. While this amounted to "a sort of tacit acceptance of things as they were" on the part of the black citizenry, he noted that there were always some educated people who stood in the forefront of the struggle for racial justice. These, however, were the exceptions. Beyond that, the lack of concern, King opined, had its basis in fear as many of the educated group felt that their job security would be jeopardized if they challenged the system.[16] King also wrote of crippling factionalism among the organized political forces before the emergence of the Montgomery Improvement Association, which was exemplified by several civic groups, each at loggerheads with the other.[17]

BLACK WOMANHOOD AS A SOCIALLY DISHONORED STATUS

A black woman's body was never hers alone.

—Fannie Lou Hamer

Black women are engaged in a painful, patient, and silent toil . . . to gain title to the bodies of their daughters.

—Anna Julia Cooper

Rape[18]

Driven by an intense and manifestly irrational fear occasioned by the end of enslavement and later the 1954 Supreme Court decision that proscribed the separate but equal doctrine in public places, many white citizens and public officials decided on an institutionalized campaign of sexualized violence aimed at black females involving unpunished rape and humiliating treatment on the buses, both by white males. On September 3, 1944, for instance, Recy Taylor, a twenty-four-year-old sharecropper and black mother and wife from Abbeville, Alabama, was abducted at gunpoint and raped by six white males who drove her to a secluded place. Upon hearing the news, Montgomery NAACP chairman E. D. Nixon promised to send his best investigator to Abbeville, a rural county ninety miles southeast of Montgomery. That investigator would launch a movement that would ultimately change the world. Her name was Rosa Parks. Although a grand jury failed to indict Taylor's assailants thereby effectively removing any prospect of a trial, the case mobilized and outraged the black community and a few outspoken whites in defense of Recy Taylor. In 1946 Viola White, a black female, was beaten by police after she refused to move out of her seat on a bus. She was later found guilty of "disobeying a bus driver." She appealed the case, and in apparent retaliation, her sixteen-year-old daughter was seized by a police officer and taken to a cemetery, where she was raped. A grand jury found no evidence of rape and refused to identify anyone.

On March 27, 1949, Gertrude Perkins, a twenty-seven-year-old black female was raped by two uniformed Montgomery police officers who pushed her into a patrol car, took her to a railroad embankment, and dragged her behind a building, where they raped her repeatedly and forced her to have "all types of sexual relations." They then shoved her into the car, dumped her in the middle of town, and sped away. Perkins reported the matter to the Reverend Solomon Seay, a black minister.

Among other things a committee was drafted to represent Perkins, and the Women's Political Council (WPC), which was formed in 1946 to protect and represent the interests of women, became involved.

In February 1951, Sam E. Green, a white grocery owner, raped a black teenager who did babysitting for him. After the all-white jury returned a verdict of not guilty after deliberating for five minutes, Rufus Lewis, a black American veteran, member of Dexter Avenue Baptist Church, and owner of Montgomery's largest black funeral home, organized a "Citizens Committee" to lead a boycott against Green's store. The boycott was successful, and he was driven out of business.[19] In all of these cases the assailants were either not brought to trial or, if so, found not guilty.

Public Humiliation

Alabama State College professor Mary Fair Burks recalls that she was first introduced to racism when her mother explained to her what she described as the "facts of life," after her brother was addressed with appellation "nigger." And although she embarked on her own "private guerila warfare" by entering restrooms for WHITE LADIES ONLY, she came to the realization that only organized efforts could remedy the intolerable racism in Montgomery. Thus after in 1946 she was arrested, stopped by a policeman's billy club for trying to explain that she had done nothing wrong during a traffic incident involving a white woman who cursed her, and thrown into a cell[20] (Burks, 1993: 78). She, Jo Ann Robinson, and Johnnie Carr, an old friend of Rosa Parks from Miss White's school in Montgomery,[21] formed the WPC.

Jo Ann Robinson, a college-educated, Alabama State College English professor, recalled that in December 1949, while traveling on a bus in Montgomery she was ordered to vacate her seat by the driver, who after she failed to do so, slammed on the brakes, raised his hand as if to strike her, and screamed at her, "Get up from there." Robinson also recalled that she walked back to the College "tears blinding her vision" and inundated by waves of humiliation. "I felt like a dog," she would later state, "I have never forgotten the shame, the hurt of that experience. The memory will not go away."[22] Robinson also recalls that it was only after she had called a meeting of the WPC, whose leadership she assumed in 1950, to tell them what had happened that she did learn that her experience was far from unique and that dozens of other mostly black women had experienced similar abuse from Montgomery bus drivers.[23] However, this form of racially stigmatized public humiliation was nothing new as far as black women were concerned. Indeed, as Paula Giddings observes, as far back as September 15, 1883, Ida Wells Barnett, the pistol-packing, anti-lynching crusader who had purchased a first-class ticket, was physically removed from the ladies car that was reserved for whites with first-class tickets after refusing to relocate to the colored car, where there was coarse behavior on the part of white males, in particular. As Giddings contends, "While conductors strictly enforced the rules against swearing, drinking, and smoking, in the ladies' car, they often failed to do so in the colored car, making it indistinguishable from the smokers' car, where second class passengers of both races rode together and behavior was unpoliced."[24]

On March 2, 1955, Claudette Colvin, a fifteen-year-old studious tenth grader at Booker T. Washington High School boarded a bus at a stop near the Dexter Avenue Baptist Church, and, after taking her seat, was instructed to give up her seat for a pregnant white woman. After refusing to do so, the bus driver stopped the bus and called the police, who demanded to know why Colvin ignored the driver's direct order. She would later state that "I couldn't. I had it in my mind that it was wrong." Amid shouts of "you black whore" by the police officer, a terrified Colvin was yanked from her seat and kicked "down the aisle toward the front of the bus," dragged down the steps of the bus and later pushed into a patrol car.[25] Colvin who was charged with violating *state* segregation laws and who was represented by Fred Gray, a bespectacled twenty-five-year-old black attorney just one year out of Cleveland's Case Western Reserve Law School, was found guilty of assault and battery, and sentenced to indefinite probation. Following Colvin's case Robinson, Burks and two carloads of women, and E. D. Nixon, started to draw up plans for a boycott of the buses, especially after as Robinson recalled, "large numbers [of women] refused to use the buses . . . for a few days."[26] However, since, allegedly, Colvin was pregnant out of wedlock, and both Nixon and Parks felt that her morals would be called into question by whites, plans were aborted for a boycott based on Colvin's case. Also, on October 21, 1955, Mary Louise Smith an eighteen-year-old black maid was arrested by police and fined for refusing to give up her seat and stand in the colored section of a bus so that a white woman could sit down. However, according to Nixon, since Smith lived in a "tar paper shack on the edge of town" and moreover "her father was a drunk,"[27] her case was also deemed to be unsuitable to test the law regarding segregated seating on the buses.[28]

On December 1, 1955, Rosa Parks, a black seamstress refused to relinquish her seat for a white male when ordered to do so by the bus driver, in defiance of the law. Mrs. Parks was duly arrested and charged with violating the law following a complaint by the white bus driver. Mrs. Parks explained it thus:

> People always say that I didn't give up my seat because I was tired, but that isn't true. I was not tired physically, or no more tired than I usually was at the end of a working day. I was not old, although some people have an image of me being old then. I was forty-two. No the only tired I was, was tired of giving in to white people. . . . There had to be a stopping place, and this seemed to have been the place for me to stop

being pushed around. . . . I had decided that I would have to know once and for all what rights I had as a human being and a citizen, even in Montgomery, Alabama.[29]

Parks also recalled that she always thought that the "laws and customs in the South that kept African Americans segregated from Caucasians and allowed white people to treat black people without any respect was not fair and it was very hard to do anything about segregation and racism when white people had the power of the law behind them."[30] She herself was often mistreated by bus drivers, and on one occasion, after she attempted to walk down the aisle after having paid her fare through the front door, "The driver ran after her, snatched hold of her, and pulled her to the door. Then he pushed her out and drove away."[31]

Additionally, Parks had attended a workshop during the summer of 1955 at the Highlander Folk School, an interracial meeting place and training ground for labor union and civil rights activists in Tennessee. This had occurred at a time when Parks had just about given up on white people, and which would change her life forever. The attendance at the workshop was at the suggestion of Virginia Durr, a white female described as a "reformed racist who as a freshman at Wellesley College had thrown a fit because she had to sit next to black in the dining hall,"[32] and whose husband, an attorney, was victimized by the society because he represented clients regardless of race. During the workshop Parks was encouraged to jettison her shyness and to tell her story about her life in Montgomery. And although Rev. Ralph Abernathy would later state that the Montgomery NAACP was thought to be "moribund,"[33] Rosa Parks together with Nixon were the mainstay of the organization during the 1940s and 1950s. Indeed, she not only worked in Nixon's office on her lunch hours, in the evenings after work, and on weekends, answering phones, handling correspondence, sending out press releases to newspapers, keeping track of the complaints that flooded in concerning racial violence and discrimination, but in the "the early 1940s, she helped organize the local NAACP Youth Council and became its adviser, encouraging its teenage members to try to integrate the local white library. Childless herself, she loved working with youngsters, who, in turn, responded to her warmth and enthusiasm."[34]

Finally, Parks had intimate knowledge of Montgomery's secret injustices—the mysterious killings of black men, the unpublicized rapes of black women by white men, the beatings and burnings that went unnoticed because the victims were black. "Everything possible that was done by way of brutality and oppression was kept well under cover," she recalled. Her friend Johnnie Carr recalled several instances of young black girls being raped. Nixon and the NAACP would push for prosecution but nothing would happen, but it always turned out that the assailant's granddaddy was the judge or his uncle was the sheriff, but if a black man was accused of raping a white woman, it was the electric chair.[35] This in a real sense explains Nixon's gleeful comment to Jo Ann Robinson upon hearing the news of Parks's arrest, that they had "arrested the wrong woman."[36]

The bus drivers all of whom were white were in the words of a white city commissioner, "mean as rattlesnakes." It was not unusual for them to drive past a stop where blacks were waiting or to drive off just as a black passenger who had paid his/her fare at the front door, was about to re-enter the bus through the back door. Some especially perverse drivers would accelerate or slam on the brakes so as to knock standing black passengers off balance, or to open the windows during winter days if a black person requested more heat. Additionally, drivers heaped obscenities on blacks, as was noted, the recipient of which risked being thrown off the bus, assaulted, or arrested. And, although there were empty seats in the unoccupied white section of the buses by the time the buses reached the black area of the city, exhausted maids, cooks, and other workers had to stand, clutching overhead bars, to prevent from falling as the bus jolted down the street. Since bus transportation was not optional, observed attorney Fred Gray, "Every day the bus situation put the issue of what it meant to be black squarely before you," as the buses were not merely means of transportation but spaces of abuse and contentious political activity. It was therefore not too difficult to understand why black women in particular were very partial to collective action in the form of a bus boycott.

DECONSTRUCTING THE SOCIALLY BLEMISHED STATUS

The Montgomery Bus Boycott

Having regard for her irreproachable background and her quiet demeanor, Nixon would later tell reporters, Parks could stand on her feet, was honest, was clean, and had integrity. Thus, Jo Ann Robinson, upon hearing the news, declared that the Women's Political Council (WPC) would not wait for either Nixon's approval or for Parks's permission and declared that the WPC will call for a boycott of the buses for December 5. A more detailed draft announcement was drawn up and with the help of a colleague and students at Alabama State College, 52,500 flyers were mimeographed referring to the Colvin case and the Parks arrest and ending with the exhortation "We are therefore asking every Negro to stay off the buses Monday in protest of the arrest and trial. Don't ride the buses to work, to town, to school, or anywhere on Monday. . . . Please stay off the buses Monday."[37] Contextually, among other things, drawing up the wording for, and typing of, the flyers, mimeographing the flyers, and most important delivering the notices on Monday, December 2, to schools and storefronts, beauty parlors and beer halls, barbershops and businesses, arguably, opened up opportunities for intellectual activity on the part of Robinson, Alabama State College students, and WPC personnel.

Again, despite the fact that he was deemed to be relatively uneducated with an unacceptable grasp of the English language by Abernathy and other black Ministers, E. D. Nixon was an organization man, fearless, and a pragmatist. Thus, he recalled that on hearing about Mrs. Parks's arrest and after securing her consent to use her case to challenge Jim Crow laws:

> I went home that night and took out a slide rule and a sheet of paper and I put Montgomery at the center of that sheet and I discovered that there wasn't a single spot in Montgomery a man couldn't walk to if he really wanted to. I said it ain't no reason in the world why we should lose the boycott because people couldn't get to work.[38]

On December 5, 1955, a meeting was convened at the Holt Street Baptist Church in Montgomery, Alabama, where the twenty-six-year-old Martin Luther King Jr. had recently been appointed Minister. King recalled that when he arrived at the Church, so large was the crowd that it took him fifteen minutes to get to the pastor's study. During the meeting, King was elected President of the recently formed Montgomery Improvement Association (MIA), and addressed a very excited audience. During his address Abernathy recalls that King skillfully invoked the ideas of Henry Thoreau and Mohandas Gandhi and America's democratic ideals when he repeatedly informed his audience of the injustice suffered by Mrs. Parks and stressed the democratic rightness of the decision to protest her arrest by invoking the Constitution of the United States and even Jesus Christ. Ironically, while Rev. Abernathy recalls that the pulpit and the platform were jammed with ministers and others who were anxious to speak "because the thing was hot," in response to Mrs. Parks's inquiry as to whether she should speak, one of the leaders responded "Why? You've said enough." "So she sat there mute, as King introduced and praised her, and the audience gave her a standing ovation."[39] Parks would later state, however, that she "did not feel any particular need to speak. I enjoyed listening to others and seeing the enthusiasm."[40]

Finally, as Gandhi might have done, King advocated nonviolence as he wanted "it to be known throughout Montgomery and throughout the nation that we are a Christian people." This would be a recurring theme as King would argue that violence, among other things, leads to a multiplicity of violence and is therefore counterproductive. The event, it may be said was akin to a spiritual rejuvenation and apart from the hymn singing between speeches, the meeting, as the city editor of the white daily newspaper who covered the event recalls, "was much like an old-fashioned revival with loud applause added."[41] In the end for 381 days, 17,000 black people in Montgomery walked to work or obtained lifts to work from the small car-owning black population. The ensuing loss of revenue and a Supreme Court decision forced the capitulation of the Montgomery Bus Company and acceptance of the three major demands of the MIA—courteous treatment for black passengers, the employment of black drivers for predominantly black routes, and seating on a first come first basis with blacks seating starting from the back and whites seating starting from the front of the bus—ending the boycott on December 20, 1956. Interestingly enough, Abernathy points out that the Company was most resistant to the idea of black drivers because that would mean blacks having power over whites.

However, while it was the males, especially the Ministers, who were the public face, this did not mean that females were either absent or not meaningfully involved in the boycott. Indeed, the public face of the boycott belied the crucial role played by Robinson in making it a success. It was she not King who served as the chief strategist for the MIA. She negotiated with city leaders and bus company officials, edited the MIA newsletter, and ferried blacks to and from work for nearly 381 days, all the while holding down a full-time teaching job at Alabama State College. "Few realize how much Jo Ann did," Fred Gray recalled, as "much of the activity . . . occurred at Jo Ann Robinson's house." [42] Her role and those of other women were kept secret because they were employees of the State and liable to lose their jobs if word leaked out of their involvement in the boycott. As Donald T. Ferron, an oral historian from Fisk University, put it, "The public recognizes Reverend King as *the* leader . . . but I wonder if Mrs. Robinson may be of equal importance. The organizational process is being kept secret, as well as the organizers." [43]

Beyond that, in addition to Ella Baker who left New York to return to the South, a number of females were instrumental in helping to raise money in order to sustain the boycott. For example, the Federated Women's Clubs threw parties to raise needed cash, and women went from door to door, canvassing neighborhoods for donations, so much so that within the first few months of the boycott when donations from outside organizations like the NAACP were rare, the MIA raised a quarter of a million dollars, primarily from local blacks. The most consistent fundraiser was Mrs. Georgia Gilmore, a nurse, midwife, and defiant mother of six, who had a long history of standing up for herself and fighting for justice. She refused to follow bus drivers' demands and insisted on being treated with dignity. Since she felt that what women could do best was to cook, she and other women called themselves the Club from Nowhere, and made sandwiches, and later full dinners and pies and cakes to sell to attendees at the mass meetings at the Holt Street Baptist Church. [44]

The Movement Intellectual and the Ideology of Nonviolence

Mass civil disobedience is a strategy for social change which is at least as forceful as an ambulance with its siren on full.[45]

While the term ideology has been associated with serving the interests of a particular social group, for social movement theorists the concept has shed its seemingly negative connotations and has come to be portrayed in less negative ways. For example, Anthony Oberschall suggests that ideology involves (a) an interpretation of the situation, in terms of what is desirable and who is to blame, (b) a blueprint for change, which may require overcoming the resistance of certain groups, (c) the introduction of a moral component that concerns the illegitimacy of the current situation and the legitimacy of the movement, and (d) the furnishing of a novel interpretation of history that provides a new sense of identity, pride, and values for the challengers.[46]

Again, Daniel Bell notes that while the analysis of ideology properly belongs to the intelligentsia, and that what the priest was to religion, the intellectual was to ideology, ideologies are ideas that are transmuted in such a manner as to rise to the level of "truth." Thus, they not only serve the interests of a particular group, but are converted into "social levers." Conceivably, also from the perspective of intellectual activity, certain ideas are (a) "selected out" for espousal and emphasis with a degree of passion by the social movement and (b) in so far as they can be simplified, used to establish a claim to truth and a demand for social action of an ameliorative nature.[47] Thus, a social movement can rouse people when it can simplify ideas, establish a claim to truth, and following from these two points, demand a commitment to action.[48]

In the case of nonviolence, King notes that he had grown up abhorring segregation and its inseparable concomitant the barbarous and brutish treatment visited on African Americans, as a consequence of which he had come perilously close to resenting all white people. And, although he had come from a home of economic security and relative comfort, he had also learned that the inseparable twin of racial injustice was economic injustice. Making use of the Hegelian notion of thesis, antithesis, synthesis, regarding dialectical reasoning, King set about constructing an ideology of nonviolence that combined philosophy and Christian theology with praxis.[49] King's ideology, furthermore, embraced the concept of personalism that emphasized the humanity of the individual, and as David Garrow[50] (1986) maintains in general was *rooted* in the story of Jesus Christ and the black Southern Baptist church into which he was born, and that, Cornel West contends, was the major institution created and sustained by blacks and functioned as a bridge between God and the forsaken.[51]

King states, for example, that during his student days at Morehouse he read and became fascinated with Thoreau's concept of the refusal to cooperate with a perceived "evil system." Since some of King's thought on justice and unjust laws became the cornerstone of the ideology, an iteration of some of Thoreau's ideas is contextually appropriate. Thoreau, for example, had indicated that to do what is right is more important than what is lawful, by which he meant action in accordance with a law, which may or may not be just. Finally, Thoreau notes that there are four alternatives when faced with an unjust law, namely, to obey, seek to amend, obey until the law is overturned, and, lastly, if the law "is of such a nature that it requires you to be the agent of injustice to another," transgression of the law.[52]

King also indicates that although he found much of value in Walter Rauschenbusch's *Christianity and the Social Crisis*, he was troubled by the latter's overoptimistic view of the "cult of inevitable progress." Moreover, King felt that "any religion which professes to be concerned about the souls of men and is not concerned about the social and economic conditions that scar the soul is a spiritually moribund religion, only waiting for the day to be buried."[53] It was from this posture that King's later emphasis on dealing with the *whole* person would flow. King also scrutinized Karl Marx's *Das Kapital* and Marx and Engels's *The Communist Manifesto*, from which he accepted communism's concern with the exploitation of the working class, but he rejected the eschewal of religion and the predilection toward totalitarianism that characterized communist states. Moreover, he noted that as far as Marxism pointed to the contradictions of traditional capitalism and challenged the social conscience of religion, he responded with a definite "yes."[54] As Cornel West[55] explains, King would have had to have taken a hard look at Marx's views regarding religion being the opiate of the masses or the sigh of an oppressed creature as well as an ideology emanating from the ruling class that was designed to perpetuate the immiserization of the masses, in view of the condition of the Negro in Jim Crow America. This would have been the case despite King's observations that the noble affirmations of Christianity notwithstanding, the church had often been derelict in its concern for social justice and had not always been faithful to its social mission regarding the issue of racial justice.[56] In addition, King familiarized himself with Utilitarianism from which he no doubt came to grips with the ideal of justice and ethical conduct especially in terms of the surfeit of pleasure over pain, the question of happiness, and Hobbes's view regarding the nature of man. King revealed also that he studied the works of Reinhold Niebuhr. And although he was initially perplexed by Niebuhr's critique of pacifism, especially his emphasis on "the irresponsibility of relying on nonviolent resistance when there was no ground for believing that it would be efficacious in preventing totalitarian tyranny," he concluded that Niebuhr seemed to have interpreted pacifism as a sort of passive nonresistance to evil, which was expressive of a naïve trust in the power of love.

King also revealed that he was deeply fascinated by Mohandas Gandhi's campaigns of nonviolent resistance, which helped to diminish his skepticism concerning the power of love in the context of social reform, and came to accept Gandhi's position that involved the resistance of evil with as much power and vigor as the violent resister, but within the context of love rather than hate. As King pithily observed, from the perspective of a social epistemology and with reference to the Gandhian concept of *Satyagraha* that is truth-force or love-force:

> The principle of nonviolent resistance seeks to reconcile the truths of two opposites—acquiescence and violence—while avoiding the extremes and immoralities of both. The nonviolent resister agrees with the person who acquiesces that one should not be physically aggressive toward his opponent; but he balances the equation by agreeing with the person of violence that evil must be resisted. He avoids the nonresistance of the former and the violent resistance of the latter. With nonviolent resistance, no individual or group need submit to any wrong, nor need anyone resort to violence in order to right a wrong.[57]

Beyond that, King contended that the method of nonviolent resistance "is effective in that it has a way of disarming opponents. It exposes their moral defenses, weakens their morale and at the same time works on their conscience. It makes it possible for the individual to struggle for moral ends through moral means."[58]

For King, therefore, nonviolence combined the best of both worlds in the sense that it was proactive rather than passive, and when it came to the resistance of injustice, it did so from a nonviolent rather than a violent perspective. Furthermore, and as is the wont of the intellectual who uses theory as a lever for social action, especially of an ameliorative nature, King observed that nonviolence "became more than a method to which I gave intellectual assent: it became a commitment to a way of life." Furthermore, as Richard H. King points out, nonviolence was not only political in that it underscored the individual's right qua freedom to choose a particular course of action that would ultimately transform his structural condition, for Martin Luther King it involved a transformation of the self, with deep historical implications. As Robert Birt put it, freedom is something that inheres in the being of the human being with community— read contextually collective action—being the "expression of freedom in a social mode."[59]

King, however, made it clear that nonviolence was not for everyone and therefore not for cowards; required involvement in a process of spiritual purification; does not seek to defeat or humiliate the opponent but to win his friendship and understanding; is not aimed at persons but the forces of evil—this explains his contention that the boycott was not directed at the bus company but at the injustice, hence the MIA's concern not "to put the bus company out of business, but to put justice in business";[60] and finally, involved a willingness to "accept suffering without retaliation, to accept blows from the opponent without striking back." Suffering, therefore, was self-redemptive, all of which placed the exponent of nonviolence at a higher level of morality within the realm of hate.

THOUGHT AND PRAXIS: THE MOVEMENT INTELLECTUAL AND THE SOCIAL MOVEMENT ORGANIZATION

The Southern Christian Leadership Conference

Reference has been made to the undergirding importance of ideology to King's activities as a social movement intellectual that enabled nonviolence as an ideology to secure space in the political terrain. However, crucial to the protractedness of a social movement is the existence of a social movement organization. This came into existence with the formation of the Southern Christian Leadership Conference (SCLC) in January 1957 by King, the Rev. Ralph Abernathy, and activist Bayard Rustin. Theoretically, it may be said that social movement organizations encapsulate the aims and aspirations of the movement, and provide an element of continuity essential to the life of a protracted movement.[61] Beyond that, since in a charismatic movement, authority is based on the personal qualities of the leader, when these begin to fail due to infirmity or age or both, the charismatic authority figure finds it convenient to routinize the charisma by, among other things, transferring it to an organization, in this case like the SCLC. The authority of the leader may then be based both on allegiance to the charismatic figure as well as the technical competence of his organizational abilities. Beyond the above the name of a social movement organization is important, because the naming of the organization opens up opportunities for intellectual activity. Thus, the Rev. T. J. Jemison, a foundation member of the SCLC, recalls that the name was chosen because of the feeling that "Since the NAACP was like waving a red flag in front of some Southern whites, we decided that we needed an organization that would do the same thing and yet be called a Christian organization."[62]

The Black Church

It should also be noted that social movement theorists have also viewed social movement organizations capitalizing on the prior existence of an enabling infrastructure.[63] As the decentralized arm of the black church the SCLC did not arise out of a vacuum, but was very much part of an evolving infrastructure, which involved the WPC, the NAACP, black colleges, barbershops, beauty parlors, and especially the black church.[64] With the rapid urbanization of blacks seeking a better life, black churches transitioned from being rural entities where a minister had to work elsewhere in order to make ends meet to organizations led by full-time ministers who concentrated on organization and maintaining the spiritual and economic viability of the flock. This development was much more important than a casual appraisal would indicate because, unlike the women who participated in the movement who worked as maids, domestics, sharecroppers, school teachers, and college professors, the shift on the part of the black church gave the pastors a sense of financial independence from the very people who might have been their employers. This explains why black pastors have always been in the forefront of the black struggle in America. Second, the black church functioned as a space for the acting out of specific behaviors related to a sense of community reinforced by a certain rhetoric, rhythmic freedom, and antiphonal forms of reaction involving call-and-response forms, all of which were part of the preacher-congregation relationship. In other words, blacks were able to manifest the *self* and act out frustrated emotions in a manner not permitted in the wider society. Again, as part of the infrastructure of which the SCLC was the beneficiary, the black church allowed the manifestation of passionate physical activity not otherwise available and for the development of a specific relationship between preacher and the flock that transformed the sermon into a performance.[65] This stood in stark contrast to the cultural perceptions and social roles imposed upon blacks in the wider society.[66]

In addition, since money has always been part of the lifeblood of a social movement, the sponsorship of revival meetings, whose purpose in addition to the conversion of new souls, was to increase membership and raise money, became an important part of the activities of black churches and helped to maintain the financial viability of the movement. Indeed, most of the community meetings and rallies sponsored by the church and its affiliates resembled the revival, and when an SCLC church affiliate was in need of money, a revival was arranged. As a result a renowned and often charismatic minister from the outside was often invited to preach a series of sermons.[67] Moreover, according to the Rev. Walker who became executive director of the SCLC in 1960, whenever local groups needed to raise money, because of his notoriety King in particular was invited. This helped to forge a collective identity among African Americans. As Walker put it:

> They wanted Martin and Ralph [Abernathy] to come. 'Cause they knew they could get the folk; you can't do anything without folk. And Martin and Ralph could get up the folk. . . . Charisma plays a great role. Martin Luther King's great leadership came from the fact that he was able to get more warm bodies in the street at one time than anybody else we've ever seen in American history. That's what gave him his tremendous influence and power.[68]

In other words because of the relevance of his thought—always a key factor in the production of knowledge by intellectuals—as a social movement intellectual, King was able to create not only space for his ideas but an audience for his thought. Finally, it was generally agreed that within the SCLC, King had the ultimate power, as Robnett contends in her discussion of the difficulty the bridge leader Ella Baker had in being recognized in the SCLC,[69] although strong personalities were also involved and suggestions from staff and specialized committees were accepted. The foregoing then speaks to King's role as a social movement intellectual in raising money, decision making, and in mobilizing, and raising the consciousness of his followers, as well as in converting the Church from an organization dealing with spiritual matters merely, to one that was invested with special meanings consistent with his vision of freedom.

The Movement Intellectual and the Fear Question

In addition to the formation of the SCLC, King found it necessary to address other manifestations of the oppression of African Americans. Therefore, as he did from his jail cell and in his "Letter from Birmingham Jail," written April 16, 1963, responding to a statement from a group of white clergymen describing his presence during demonstrations in Birmingham as "unwise and unhealthy" and him as an outsider, King not only distinguished between a just law and an unjust law, but explained why because of its moral deficiency, he was obliged to disobey an unjust law, and to encourage others to do so. As he put it on another occasion, "We cannot in good conscience obey your unjust laws and abide by the unjust system, because non-cooperation with evil is as much a moral obligation as is cooperation with good, and so throw us in jail and we will still love you."[70] Again, consistent with his contention that liberation theology should address the whole person and in an effort to galvanize his followers for collective action and especially as a reflection of the influence of personalism, King also found it necessary, in addition to commenting on democracy with its unfettered right to register and to vote, and freedom to be a human being, to focus on the underbelly of fear.

Thus, in a sermon titled "Antidotes for Fear,"[71] King told his listeners that although "normal fear protects us; abnormal fear paralyzes us," and that fear could have debilitating physical as well as psychological consequences. The problem, therefore, was not to rid oneself of fear, but rather to harness it. In order to do so, King counseled that one should unflinchingly face fear and be honest about asking ourselves why we are afraid. Second, fear can be mastered through one of the supreme virtues known to man, that is courage, which he defined as "the power of the mind to overcome fear." Third, King suggested that fear is mastered by way of love, the kind of love that keeps one unembittered, like Christ demonstrated on the cross, and that enables one to overcome the rough-hewn adversities of life. Contextually, he noted that many white men themselves fear retaliation in the face of the Negro's growth politically, culturally, and economically and that *The Negro must convince the white man that he seeks justice for both himself and the white man.*[72] Fourth, King noted that fear is also mastered through faith. The question of faith has deep and often unrecognized implications for efforts to forge a collective identity by social movement intellectuals. As others such as Ella Baker and Jo Ann Robinson have noted, the movement intellectual, particularly in oppressive situations, faces the daunting task of enjoining a group of similarly situated individuals, who have been beaten down by oppression related to systemic inequality based on ascriptive criteria such as race and color, and who have experienced humiliation, lack of hope for salvation, and the possible lack of faith, that a change for the better will come about. It is no simple matter then, "to convince timid people that the indignities of everyday life are not written in the stars and can be attributed to some agent, and that they can change their condition by taking action collectively."[73] To face this dilemma not only must the social movement and the social movement intellectual produce observable results that justify that faith, eventually, but as some social movements analysts have maintained, for collective action to take place leaders must also construct meaning and relevance to the task of collectively confronting an oppressive system. This King, in particular, did by contributing mightily to the denudation of the socially dishonored status of black Americans and by his exhortation that suffering could be redemptive, as well as productive.

SOME CONCLUDING REMARKS

In seeking to address the question, how do social movements like the civil rights struggle generate "new" knowledge, and inexorably social movement intellectuals like Martin Luther King Jr., it was seen that King and a number of biographical others railed against the oppression of African Americans with its economic exploitation, political exclusion, and culture of humiliation, brutality and fear. In doing so, King used various settings and both the written and especially the spoken word to educate, raise the consciousness of, and mobilize African Americans and others against the unacceptability of Jim Crowism, while making use of resources such as his knowledge of philosophy, history, and theology and perhaps more importantly, time, energy, and his charisma, and oratorical skills honed in the tradition of preaching in the church and the black Southern Baptist Church heritage. His overall strategy in this connection was to craft an ideology of nonviolence, which was rooted in a deeply held conviction of self-abnegation, and theology that in itself emanated from his readings of philosophy, in order to transform his ideology into a social movement organization that provided continuity to the struggle, and especially pivotal financial support.

Tactically, nonviolence manifested itself in the form of boycotts, mass demonstrations, sit-ins at lunch counters, where King and his associates as social movement intellectuals tested various theories of collective action and actions emanating from various unjust statutes. These tactics no doubt enabled him and the movement to create space in the political spectrum. In addition, King transformed many sites into locales of contestation and invested them with new meanings consistent with his views on freedom. The sites of contestation included churches, universities, buses, business places that discriminated against African Americans, the streets, his prison cell in Birmingham, and even the National Monument. In addition, King very skillfully used the mass media to obtain much needed publicity for his efforts and those of others, to trumpet the contradictions in American society that preached democracy and chided other imperialist nations to grant independence to their possessions while denying the same rights to African Americans as U.S. citizens. Thus, as a diasporan organic intellectual, King not only exemplified the best of life of the mind involved in public affairs,[74] but, as Manning Marable argued, raised such questions as: What is racism? How does racism manifest itself institutionally? Is there a connection between racism in the United States and the struggles for political independence in the colonies of various European countries?[75] Finally, by promulgating an epistemology of collective resistance to Jim Crowism, as a standpoint theorist, and in the role of movement intellectual as articulator, King *participated* in enjoining us to see the world through the shared experiences and the fractured identities of black Americans—both the "PhDs and the no Ds."

However, King's thinking does not adequately encompass a critical factor of oppression that concerns the existential nature of the experiences of women at the hands of white males. As Olson points out, not only was there systematic sexualized racial violence and humiliation directed against black women by white males, but white women were placed on a pedestal, and their chasteness was expected to be protected at all costs from so-called sexually predatory black males. Thus, it was that white women were expected to suffer in silence while their husbands and sons violated black females with impunity. It is in this context that John Stuart Mill's notion—King admitted that he had read Mill's work—that oppression is rooted in the unequal distribution of legal rights that involves the denial of freedom and liberty as well as the ability to realize one's intellectual capabilities, must be viewed. Like other tyrannies, therefore, the tyranny of the silent white majority was held in dread, and operated chiefly through the acts of public authorities, like the police and the legal system. In addition, Mill contended that the "social tyranny" is even more formidable than the political oppression because it "leaves fewer means of escape, penetrating much more deeply in the details of life, and enslaving the soul in the process." Thus, protection against the tyranny of the legal system is not enough. There needs to be protection against the tyranny "of the prevailing opinion and feeling against the tendency of society to impose, by *means other than civil* penalties its own ideas and practices as rules of conduct on those who dissent from them."[76] Moreover, this "despotism of custom" is everywhere the standing hindrance to human advancement and remains in unceasing antagonism with "the spirit of liberty, or that of progress or improvement."[77]

It is in this context that the experiences and *testimonies* of various females[78] as well as of subalterns like the black women who were sharecroppers, domestics, cooks, and maids who were raped and/or humiliated and the beating of Fannie Lou Hamer on June 10, 1963, by two black prison inmates who were forced to beat her at gunpoint by white guards must be seen. Hamer, who subsequently lost her left eye and suffered irreparable damage to her kidneys, opined that it is because freedom is of "divine origin. . . . [W]e can speculate as to where Christ is in the freedom struggle." Moreover, the Church "is that community that participates in Christ's liberating work in history, meaning that it can never endorse law and order while people are suffering . . . especially since itself causes much of the suffering."[79] Hamer also likened the current pain and suffering of blacks and other third world peoples to the cross experience, not unlike the crucifixion experience of Jesus and the persecution of the early church.[80]

Similarly, Ella Baker's comments about gender inequality in the movement on the part of black males—ministers and others—her extensive experience as a grassroots organizer, in the SCLC and the Student Nonviolent Coordinating Committee, and her pedagogical style that permitted her charges to discuss, and argue over strategies, as well as to think for themselves, constitute another epistemology emanating from the civil rights movement. Baker's experiences and her early involvement in the black women's missionary movement were reflected in her emphasis on the principles of Christian charity and service in the real world,[81] and were therefore instrumental in shaping her views regarding participatory democracy, which stressed grassroots empowerment of the people, group-centered leadership, and direct action involving opposition to violence and intransigent bureaucratic and legalistic obstacles that thwart the will of the people.[82] As Ransby put it,[83] Baker's intellectualism parallels Gramsci's contention that "the mode of being the new intellectual can no longer consist in eloquence, which is an exterior and momentary mover of feelings and passions, but in active participation in practical life, as constructor, organizer, 'permanent persuader' not just a simple orator."[84]

Again, adverting to a social epistemology that privileges the experiences of women precludes the likelihood of Rosa Parks slipping through the shadows of civil rights history, and belies the image of her, merely as a "tired seamstress," created by King and other male leaders. Indeed, in commenting on a documentary about the Montgomery bus boycott in which Parks was hardly mentioned, Septima Clark was driven to remark that Parks "gave Dr. King the right to practice his nonviolence" and it was she "who started the whole thing." Clark was a grassroots organizer with whom Parks discussed her work with the NAACP as an advisor to the youth, when they both attended the Highlander Workshop in the summer of 1955. Clark, who was also a teacher, worked with Thurgood Marshall and the NAACP to get equal salary scales for black and white teachers.[85] Similarly, E. D. Nixon recalls that in response to a woman who remarked that she did not know what would have happened to black people if King had not been there to lead the boycott, he replied, "If Mrs. Parks had got up and given that white man her seat you'd never aheard (sic) of Reverend King."[86] Finally, this social epistemology also privileges the activities of students at Morgan State College and others whose non-violent sit-in demonstrations in June 1955 led to the desegregation of various eating places in Baltimore, Maryland, and the nonviolent resis-tance of Mrs. Parks, who opined that the laws and customs that allowed blacks to be disrespected "were not fair," and Claudette Colvin whose comment that "I had it in my mind that it (the bus situation) was wrong" are reflective of the Kantian categorical imperative that views some ac-tions as immanently right in and of themselves. Thus, it is apparent that intellectualism is a socially constructed phenomenon, involving in King's case the contributions of previously organized entities, the efforts of fe-males in different social strata, church members, other ministers, individ-uals who raised funds, and typed, proofread, produced, and distributed the printed word in the form of his sermons, articles, leaflets, and books, and who organized various nonviolent, antihegemonic activities, to name some. It would not be an exaggeration to conclude, as Mary Burks does,[87] that the females in particular, were trailblazers in that they were pioneers with respect to nonviolent resistance, and that King as one who followed the trailblazer was in reality a torchbearer.

NOTES

1. See, for example, Branch, *Parting the Waters*; Garrow, *Bearing the Cross*; Morris, *The Origins of the Civil Rights Movement*; and Washington, *A Testament of Hope*.

2. Lewis, *King: A Critical Biography*.

3. Garrow, *Bearing the Cross*; O'Brien, "Old Myths/New Insights"; and Dyson, *I May Not Get There with You*.

4. See, for example, the earlier work of LeBon, *The Crowd*, Smelser, *Collective Behavior*, and Smelser, "Theoretical Issues of Scope and Problems," who viewed beliefs systems that power, arguably the most important component of, collective action as being "akin to magical beliefs." For a suggestive statement that speaks to the need to emphasize the social context and the structure of collective action as opposed to per-sonal qualities see Couch, "Collective Behavior," and for a similar argument that

privileges the ideas, the articulators, and the social environment see Nettl, Ideas, "Intellectuals and Structures of Dissent."

5. Hoffer, *The True Believer.*

6. For a critique of resource mobilization theory that speaks to the need to take into account the social history and the whole human actor see Ferree, "The Political Context of Rationality"; Morris, "Reflections on Social Movement Theory"; and especially McAdam, *Political Process and the Development of Black Insurgency.* For a helpful statement of various theoretical approaches to the study of social movements see Morris, *The Origins of the Civil Rights Movement,* chapter 11.

7. The major proponents of this perspective are Eyerman and Jamison, *Social Movements,* and Eyerman, *Between Culture and Politics.*

8. For a very helpful application of this approach to the U.S. Civil Rights movement that entails a fourfold phase, that includes a discussion of nonviolence as the main strategy, and protest demonstrations, sit-ins as legality tactics, and religiosity and spirituality of the cosmological, as main tactics, see Eyerman and Jamison, *Social Movements,* especially chapter 5.

9. Eyerman and Jamison, *Social Movements,* pp. 92–94; and Bottomore, *Critics of Society,* especially chapter 5.

10. The literature on intellectuals is voluminous. For our purposes, helpful statements include Lasch, *The New Radicalism in America 1889–1963*; Shils, "The Intellectuals and the Powers"; Feuer, "What Is an Intellectual?"; Gella, *The Intelligentsia and the Intellectuals*; Mannheim, *Ideology and Utopia*; Goldfarb, *Civility and Subversion*; and Gouldner, *The Future of Intellectuals and the Rise of a New Class.*

11. Coser, *Men of Ideas,* p. viii.

12. Eisenstadt, "Intellectuals and Tradition," p. 1.

13. Goulbourne, "The Institutional Contribution of the University of the West Indies to the Intellectual Life of the Anglophone Caribbean," p. 21.

14. Habermas, *The Structural Transformation of the Public Sphere.* For a similar approach but with respect to the role of ideologies in this manner, about which more will be said, see Daniel Bell, *The End of Ideology,* An Epilogue.

15. Goffman, *Stigma,* p. 1

16. King, *Stride toward Freedom,* p. 35.

17. Ibid., p. 34.

18. For more on this point see McGuire, *At the Dark End of the Street.*

19. Ibid., p. 39.

20. Burks, "Trailblazers," p. 78.

21. Officially known as the Montgomery Industrial School for Girls, Miss White's school was founded by white teachers from New England to teach black girls domestic skills as well as academic subjects. The teachers were shunned by the white community, and on two occasions the school was set on fire. See Olson, *Freedom's Daughters,* p. 96.

22. Robinson, *The Montgomery Bus Boycott and the Women Who Started It,* p. 16; and Olson, *Freedom's Daughters,* p. 90.

23. Garrow, *Bearing the Cross,* p. 22.

24. Giddings, *Ida: A Sword among Lions,* p. 61.

25. McGuire, *At the Dark End of the Street,* p. 70.

26. Ibid., p. 74.

27. However, many years later both Colvin and Smith would challenge Nixon's version as to why they were found to be unsuitable. Colvin claimed that while she subsequently became pregnant, she was not pregnant or even "visibly pregnant" as Giddings states, (*Where and When I Enter,* p. 263) at the time of Colvin's arrest. "We weren't in the inner circle," she opined, "The middle-class Blacks didn't want us as a role model," *Freedom's Daughters,* p. 95; while Smith said that she grew up in a "two story, three-bedroom frame home" and a former neighbor of Smith claimed that "Mary Louise's father was sober and 'rock solid.'" Ibid.

28. Olson, *Freedom's Daughters,* p. 94.

29. Olson, *Freedom's Daughters*, p. 108; and Parks, *Tired of Giving In*, p. 61.

30. Parks, *Rosa Parks: My Story*, p. 2.

31. Greenfield, *Rosa Parks*, p. 19.

32. Olson, *Freedom's Daughters*, p. 99.

33. Abernathy, *And the Walls Came Tumbling Down*, p. 143.

34. Olson, *Freedom's Daughters*, p. 99.

35. Ibid., p. 98.

36. McGuire, *At the Dark End of the Street*, p. 80.

37. Robinson, *The Montgomery Bus Boycott and the Women Who Started It*, pp. 45-46.

38. Quoted in Morris, *The Origins of the Civil Rights Movement*, p. 52.

39. Olson, *Freedom's Daughters*, p. 110.

40. Parks, *Tired of Giving In*, p. 70.

41. Azbell, "At Holt Street Baptist Church," p. 53.

42. McGuire, *At the Dark End of the Street*, p. 89.

43. Ibid.

44. Ibid., p. 99.

45. Martin Luther King Jr., "The Trumpet of Conscience," in *A Testament of Hope*, p. 647.

46. Oberschall, *Social Conflict*, chapter 4, note 1.

47. Daniel Bell, *The End of Ideology*, pp. 394 ff.

48. Ibid., p. 401.

49. For a revealing statement of the process by which he came to nonviolence as an ideology and eventually a way of life see his "Pilgrimage to Nonviolence," in King, *Stride toward Freedom*. For a truncated version of this statement by the same title see King, *Strength to Love*. This book contains a classic collection of his sermons.

50. Garrow, *The Intellectual Development of Martin Luther King, Jr.*

51. West, *The Cornel West Reader*.

52. Thoreau, *Civil Disobedience and Other Essays*, p. 8.

53. King, *Stride toward Freedom*, p. 91.

54. Ibid., p. 95.

55. West, *The Religious Foundation of the Thought of Martin Luther King, Jr.*

56. King, *Strength to Love*, p. 102.

57. King, *The Words of Martin Luther King, Jr.*, p. 65.

58. *The Case against Tokenism*, in *A Testament of Hope*, p. 109.

59. Birt, *Of the Quest for Freedom as Community*, p. 89.

60. King, *Stride toward Freedom*, p. 51. King would also note that he "conceived of our movement as an act of massive noncooperation. From then I rarely used the word 'boycott,'" ibid., p. 52.

61. Oberschall, "Protracted Conflict."

62. Morris, *The Origins of the Civil Rights Movement*, p. 86.

63. Morris, *The Origins of the Civil Rights Movement*.

64. McAdam, *Political Process and the Development of Black Insurgency, 1930–1970*, p. 141.

65. West, *The Religious Foundation of the Thought of Martin Luther King, Jr.*

66. West, *The Cornel West Reader*.

67. Morris, *The Origins of the Civil Rights Movement*, p. 92.

68. Ibid.

69. Robnett, *How Long? How Long?: African-American Women in the Struggle for Civil Rights*.

70. *The Words of Martin Luther King, Jr.*, p. 72.

71. See King, *Strength to Love*, chapter 2.

72. Ibid., p. 121. Italics supplied by King.

73. Tarrow, *Power in Movement*, pp. 122–23.

74. West, *The Cornel West Reader*.

75. Marable, *Black Leadership*.

76. Mill, *On Liberty and Other Writings*, p. 8.

77. Ibid., p. 70.
78. For a very informative statement of the stories and narratives of these mostly movement participants—black, white, and Latina; young and old; southern and northern—who were associated with the Student Nonviolent Coordinating Committee and the Civil Rights Movement, and who experienced fear, sexual harassment, and imprisonment, see Faith Holsaert et al., *Hands on the Freedom Plow*.
79. Grant, "Civil Rights Women," p. 46.
80. Ibid., p. 47.
81. Ransby, *Ella Baker and the Black Freedom Movement*, p. 45.
82. Mueller, "Ella Baker and the Origins of Participatory Democracy."
83. *Ella Baker and the Black Freedom Movement*, p. 361.
84. Gramsci, *Selections from the Prison Notebooks*, p. 10.
85. Rouse, "We Seek to Know...in Order to Speak the Truth," p. 102.
86. Olson, *Freedom's Daughters*, p. 130.
87. *Trailblazers*, p. 71.

2

King as Engaged Social and Political Philosopher

SIX

Martin Luther King Jr.'s *Agape* and World House

Richard A. Jones

Today our very survival depends on our ability to stay awake, to adjust to new ideas, to remain vigilant and to face the challenge of change. The large house in which we live demands we transform this world-wide neighborhood into a world-wide brotherhood. Together we must learn to live as brothers or together we will perish as fools.
— Martin Luther King Jr.

Painted on a wall in an elementary school in La Güinera, a community of twenty-six thousand on the southern edge of Havana, Cuba, is the following quote:

All can be great . . . because all can serve. One need not have a university degree to serve. One need not use subject-verb agreement to serve. All one need is a HEART filled with grace. A soul borne of LOVE.

MARTIN LUTHER KING[1]

In 1986 poor women started building in the La Güinera community. These women, who had no previous practical knowledge of construction, built apartments, dining rooms for the elderly, a primary school, and a community center. To accomplish this task, these women engaged in a battle of ideas to make changes in the community in a collective way. Social development, building housing, healthy families, and self-motivation required a vision. Teresa Rimada Reyes, one of the La Güinera organizers, commented on the quote painted on the wall, "Martin Luther King inspires us to keep on working."[2]

In this chapter I argue that Martin Luther King Jr.'s utopian ideal for "Beloved Community" through *agape* in the "World House" is a highly philosophical trope that serves to remind us that "Where there is no vision, the people perish."[3] Moreover, I will argue that King is also a "philosopher"—a *Philosopher King*—transcending the narrow disciplinary boundaries of what it means to be a "philosopher." In the current post-modern era where dystopian futures or "No Future"[4] and "the end of history"[5] reinforce Marxian alienation, Neitzschean nihilism, and terror-ist wars against terrorism, King's positive vision for *a* future is as impor-tant as Plato's *Republic*, Kant's *Perpetual Peace*, or Rousseau's *Social Contract*. "Professional," Western, analytic philosophers need to reevalu-ate King, as he was and is an important social philosopher. King's social, political, and axiological philosophies should assume as important a place in graduate seminars as they have, more importantly, in the praxes by which they inform a world—a world like La Güinera.

The Struggle for Loving Communities

As the twenty-first century begins, "community" has become the reg-nant ideal for constructing a "new world order." As philosopher Robert Birt acutely observes:

> Our quest for freedom requires a rethinking of freedom. It requires a shift of focus from individualist notions of liberty so deeply rooted in American culture to an emphasis on the communality of freedom— indeed, to a vision of a cooperative community of freedom. A revision-ing of freedom is crucial because a really human experience of freedom is hardly possible without community, and also because one of the most salient features of contemporary social unfreedom is precisely the negation of community and the atomizing of human bonds.[6]

Thus King's struggle for "Beloved Community" represents more than African American longings for freedom beyond enslavement and Jim Crow racism. It represents the ongoing longings for, as Birt correctly locates, human freedom in community. Sociologist Zygmunt Bauman also believes that longings for community mark the so-called postmodern era. He writes, "Thus postmodernity, the age of contingency *für sich*, of self-conscious contingency, is for the thinking person also the age of com-munity: of the lust for community, search for community, invention of community, imagining community."[7] In traditional models for commu-nity, philosophical Marxism continues to animate the moral imagination. In Martin Luther King Jr.'s "Beloved Community" are elements of Marx's vision.[8]

King's conceptions of communal political life continue to coincide with Marx's ongoing critique of capitalism. For if this *is not* "the end of history," then, as Sean Sayers argues, "forces of opposition to capitalism will surely emerge. This is the faith of socialism."[9] The *faith* of socialism, as an immanent critique of capitalism, is what links King to Marxian thought, despite his protestations. King's revolution of conscience, like the Cuban women at La Güinera and analytical historical Marxism, is a moral revolution. It is the transvaluation of morals that unite them, for without a change in the human spirit there is no possibility for normative moral community. For King, the key to the moral revolution was a transformation of values. Marxist Marshall Berman writes:

> It was vital for the community of revolutionaries to avoid degenerating into just another "illusory community" themselves; and Marx felt that personal independence could be protected only in a *moral* community, in which individuals act not primarily for their own benefit, or for that of the group as such, but for the sake of all mankind. Only a "world-historical class," one whose interests and ideals are fused, is capable of decisively enlarging the scope of freedom for all.[10]

King's "Injustice anywhere is a threat to justice everywhere"[11] couples the "world-historical class" in the individual agencies required for collective freedom. In a review of *To the Finland Station*, a 1940 novel by Edmund Wilson recounting Lenin's triumphal entry onto the world stage, Berman writes:

> It is a dream [romantic dream of revolution] of people taking their lives into their own hands, coming together to forge a common destiny, to create a wholly new kind of society: a community based on liberty and equality, in which men and women can express themselves as individuals more freely, and love one another more intensely and deeply, than human beings have ever done before.[12]

King's prophetic visions of community exist in a continuous nexus of social thought. King, like Marx, understood that the perfectibility of human beings was "humanity creating itself."[13]

Where King's written works provide little justification for, and if anything indicates an antipathy to, Marxism, the kernel of his social philosophy was decidedly socialistic. In realizing the relationship between possibilities for individual freedom and the requirement for moral social transvaluations, King arrived at a formula Marx had exacted from history a century earlier. "For 'only in community with others has each individual the means of cultivating his gifts in all directions, only in the community, therefore, is personal freedom possible.'"[14] King's indebtedness to Hegelian and Marxian dialectical historical processes, which stressed Hegel's *Geist* as the evolution of human freedom at the expense of Marx's evolution of material modes of production, has been exhaustively researched. The point is to locate King in a continuum of philosophical thought concerning the nature of human freedom and political community. At a historical moment wherein history has not ended, and individuals on many parts of the globe have their species being increasingly denied by capitalist excesses, issues of visions for global community emerge as fundamental. Martin Luther King's mid-twentieth-century philosophical ideals for a worldwide community averse to poverty, war, and racism—by-products of capitalism—remain architectonics for hope.

Beloved Community and Agape

When Nietzsche fell stricken in the street after seeing a man beat a horse, he had already predicted that human beings would endure one hundred years of nihilism, and that it would require yet another century before the rancorous pall dissipated. This prophecy, made real in the nerve gas trenches of the First World War, atomic explosions at Hiroshima and Nagasaki, Kamir Rouge killing fields, and machete-mangled corpses of Rwandan genocide, has entered its second century in the postmodern ironies of an American unipolar military world. Yet the consolidation of U.S. military power did not create a new world social community. The excesses of capitalism, and its new forms of transnational corporatism, exacerbated the hopes and holdings of the global haves and global have-nots. Pragmatic political philosophies for alleviating the conditions contributing to these realities have been wanting, especially given the assumptions that history has ended in a stalemated American exceptionalism. Martin Luther King's "Beloved Community," based on agape—or other-regarding love—remains the social ideal for ending the Nietzschean nihilistic epoch. King said:

> This call for a worldwide fellowship that lifts neighborly concern beyond one's tribe, race, class, and nation is in reality a call for an all-embracing and unconditional love for all mankind. This oft mis-understood, this oft misinterpreted concept, so readily dismissed by the Nietzsches of the world as a weak and cowardly force, has now become an absolute necessity for the survival of man.[15]

"Without a vision, the people perish!" King's vision of Beloved Community is the palliative that offers social hope. In the postmodern condition, political quietism, the retreat to ludic irony, orgies of consumption driven by false consciousness and false needs, prevent willful moral action. It is as if individual moral agency and collective economic exploitative action are disconnected by a litany of excuses, rationalizations, and philosophical accounts of *human nature.* As Marshall Berman reminds us, "We need to strive for the precarious, dynamic balance that Antonio Gramsci, one of the great communist writers and leaders of our century, described as 'pessimism of the intellect, optimism of the will.'"[16] King's Beloved Community represents an optimism of the will in the face of an unavoidable intellectual pessimism. All the violent struggles of King's Birmingham, Cicero, and Selma campaigns were *means* to an *end.* King himself describes this end: "The end is reconciliation, the end is redemption, the end is the creation of beloved community."[17]

Where other factions in the African American struggle for equality and equity clamored for "Black Power," in terms of the political and economic, King's vision of Beloved Community was driven by "Love Power." "When I talk about power and the need for power, I'm talking in terms of the need for power to bring about . . . the creation of the Beloved Community."[18] The upward path of the inner strength, necessary to overcome negative racial stereotypes in loving oneself in "somebodiness," translated into a loving community that prepared the way for a loving worldwide community. Facing the massive hatreds personified by Birmingham, Alabama's savage dogs, police billy clubs, and skin-stripping water cannons, King's response to these forces was the counterforce good Christians had always meted out to tyrants: a meek and mild turned cheek. This instantiates King's genius and lends credence to his status as an important but often unacknowledged philosopher worthy of continuing relevance.

King said, "We will meet the forces of hate with the power of love. . . . We must say to our white brothers all over the South, we will match your capacity to inflict suffering with our capacity to endure suffering. . . . Bomb our homes and we will still love you. . . . We will so appeal to your heart and conscience that we will win you in the process."[19] In Nietzsche's condemnation of Christianity as a "herd mentality" and the "religion of the weak," King reconceptualizes love for one's enemies as love for oneself. King's sublime insights into the graces of self-conceptions, self-love, and other-directed love are political and social philosophical praxes toward the requisite holism denied in commodified and monological notions of self. For it is King's ideal of social love—*agape*—that rekindles Rousseau's conception of the *General Will* trumping the individual's individual will. King's politicized *agape* is the social instantiation of Hegel's *Giest* as the evolution of human freedom, which is only possible in community.

King counters the racist syllogism of "God made man in his image, God is not a Negro, therefore the Negro is not a man," with "God loves all creation, Those who hate you are God's creations, therefore you must love your enemy because God loves him." In direct quotes from Birmingham, Marshall Frady quoting King says,

> "Now, we say in this nonviolent movement that you've got to love this white man. And God knows he *needs* our love," going on to expound again for these congregations the concept of agape: "And when you rise to love on *this* level . . . you love those that you don't like, you love those whose ways are distasteful to you. You love *every* man—because *God* loves him!"[20]

This appropriated passion play of the Jesus-like persecuted servant personified in the oppressed southern black is "applicable to any black theologian who adopts the theodicy of vicarious suffering, including Martin Luther King, for example."[21] If community, by definition, is the manifestation of people overcoming their separateness to live together in harmony, then it is their love for one another—rather than the power they can manifest in collective conquest by domination—that creates the possibility of this miracle of human closeness. Thus the parable of Schopenhauer's "Porcupines" and the answer to the question of "What is the good we can know together that we cannot know alone?" are answered by King's invocation of the most apparently misunderstood and misrepresented of human emotions. Reimagining love as more than mutual sexual exploitations, the marginal production of excess value, or human nature, King identified it in the universal, cosmic, natural essence of the divine. This property of the universe is so essential that human beings cannot escape its ineluctable grasp. "As King observes, the love advocated by Jesus was expressed by the Greek word agape, defined as unconditional, disinterested goodwill toward all men. Agape aims 'to preserve and create community.'"[22]

This community-building love as a cosmic manifestation of the "summum bonum" is not to be confused with other definitions of love. According to King, this agapistic "outpouring" is uniquely defined:

> In the Greek New testament are three words for love. The word *eros* is a sort of aesthetic or romantic love. In the Platonic dialogues *eros* is a yearning of the soul for the realm of the divine. The second word is *philia*, a reciprocal love and the intimate affection and friendship between friends. We love those whom we like, and we love because we are loved. The third word is *agape*, understanding and creative, redemptive goodwill for all men.[23]

Students of philosophy cannot help but be impressed by this paralleling of Aristotle's arguments in the *Nicomachean Ethics* concerning friendship and community.[24] Aristotle holds that there are three kinds of friendships: self-interested (using others as means to ends), reciprocally exploitative (mutual means/ends reasoning), and disinterested (where equals recognize one another and cannot employ them as means to any end). Further, Aristotle employs these categories to discuss types of communities where these friendships evoke political community. King's reasoning on the role of love, in its various forms from erotic, through filial, to personally disinterested, is Plato's upward path from the *Symposium* and Aristotle's evolution of the *Polis*. The point is not the derivative aspects of King's *agape* from canonical philosophy, but the nuanced appreciation of a philosophical tradition of which he is rightly an integral and necessary part. King's agapistic love is not only universalizable in its Western Kantian disinterestedness in its historical, cultural, political, or racial located-ness, as it is also universalizable from non-Western perspectives.

Eliding "Otherness" (big "O" otherness) is an accomplishment that few Western thinkers have achieved. King's loving struggle for community transcends black/white binaries, as increasingly his vision became focused on Beloved Community for the world. King was informed by Mahatma K. Gandhi's nonviolent manifestation of Hindu philosophy's *Satyagraha*, which

> is pure soul-force. Truth is the very substance of the soul. That is why this force is called *satyagraha*. The soul is informed with knowledge. In it burns the flame of love. If someone gives us pain through ignorance, we shall win him through love. "Non-violence is the supreme *dharma*." [25]

Forging the relationships among self, love, nonviolence, and community, King writes, "The whole Gandhian concept of *satyagraha* (*satya* is truth which equals love and *graha* is force; *satyagraha* thus means truth-force or love-force) was profoundly significant to me." [26] In his book, *Stride toward Freedom: The Montgomery Story*,[27] King describes *agape* as

> a willingness to go to any length to restore community. It doesn't stop at the first mile, but it goes the second mile to restore community. It is a willingness to forgive, not seven times, but seventy times seven to restore community[28]

King's theological, political, and philosophical praxes are all committed to achieving livable, sustainable, nurturing human communities. En-meshed as we all are in the deteriorating structural fragmentations of postmodern nationalisms and cultures in the "clash of civilizations," the momentum of the destructive trajectories of war, racism, and poverty can only be countered by a powerful secular humanism. King's nonvindictive God of the New Testament is sufficiently ecumenical to transcend relig-ious sectarian interests, in the name of cooperative human love, to moti-vate a unifying global politic. "Love" as a political instrument is more efficacious than the economics of production or the coercions of militar-ism. King believed that "a genuine revolution of values means in the final analysis that our loyalties must become ecumenical rather than sectional. Every nation must now develop an overriding loyalty to mankind as a whole in order to preserve the best in their individual societies." [29] The interconnected poverties of the mind, the soul, and larder can only be assuaged by Kingian *agape*. Revealing the knowledge of the *Philosopher King*:

> "Love is the most durable power in the world." This has been the chief quest of ethical philosophy. This was one of the big questions of Greek philosophy. The Epicureans and the Stoics sought to answer it; Plato and Aristotle sought to answer it. What is the *summum bonum* of life? I

think I have found the answer, America. I have discovered that the highest good is love. This principle is at the center of the cosmos. It is the great unifying force of life. God is love. [30]

The "personalism" of a conscious God who loves the individual is different from a God who is in essence love itself. A God who *is* literally love and pervades the universe *is* a unifying substrate, a Leibnizian *monadology*, a Spinozian *hylozoism*, and an ahistorical Hegelian *Giest*. King's God is understandable by Hindus, Baptists, and Marxian atheists. A unifying rather than divisive God is a requirement for human beings with different religious beliefs to live in a World House.

World House

King became aware of the rapidly shrinking global differences and distances affected by early satellites, intercontinental ballistic missiles, and the interconnectedness of global markets. The erosion of these transnational and geographical boundaries was exacerbated by the concomitant crises of absolute authority in the philosophical sphere. Cornel West writes:

> Demythologizing of the institution of science . . . demystifying the role of authority makes the function of philosophy suspect. . . . This demystifying is not simply a revolt against intellectual, social, and political authority, it calls into question the very notion of and need for authority. . . . [T]he disclosure of a deep sense of impotence tends to support the view that philosophy is superfluous. [31]

King understood that while the world was shrinking, the bases for unity were dissolving. Cornel West's "anti-realism in ontology, anti-foundationalism in epistemology, and detranscendentalism of the Kantian subject" [32] represent the reinvigorated Nietzschean nihilism, existential angst, and hopelessness of the final decades of the twentieth century. Thus philosophy itself answers Kant's famous questions: "What can I know? What ought I to do? And for what can I hope?" with anti-realism (it's all a human construct), anti-foundationalism (there is no truth), and detranscendentalism (there is no spiritual reality). King's *agape* attempts to answer Kant's questions, against all arguments to the contrary, affirmatively with the reality of love, the truth of love, and the reality of the human soul.

Hence, King's philosophy represents what has come to be called "social hope" where there was, and is, no other vision. Philosopher Maurizio Valsania's characterization of social hope as a basis for a "New Socialism" is particularly effective:

> Hope is a choice whose content is substantially amenable to a form of assertive awareness of the inventive power of individuals and human groups, to a desire to participate and cooperate, to freedom from war,

injustice and subjugation, to a refusal of passivity, pessimism, and every postmodern fascism. Individuals, groups, institutions which are committed to hope enhance the human power to invent solutions to problems.[33]

Without vision, the people perish. And without hope, there is no vision. Jesse Jackson's closing refrain during his 1988 Democratic National Convention address, "Keep hope alive!" was an invocation reaching back to Martin Luther King's vision for the social hope of *agape* working for beloved communities to create the World House.

"Martin didn't make the movement, the movement made Martin."[34] As he gained the confidences of the successful Birmingham bus boycott, the 1963 March on Washington and "I Have a Dream" speech, and the 1964 Nobel Peace Prize, King began to believe he could use his philosophy of nonviolence worldwide. Beloved Community within national boundaries could be linked to produce a World House. For if "in my father's house there are many dwellings,"[35] and these rooms are indeed mansions, then as denizens of the World House all humanity shares responsibilities for any "room" where poverty, war, or racism dwells. King believed to the core of his inner experience that "there is something in the very structure of the cosmos that will ultimately bring about fulfillment and the triumph of what is right."[36]

The reticulated cosmic holism King recognized in *agape* within World House presages the growing consensus in Western thought that human beings are inextricably united in an ontological oneness. King writes, "We are caught in an inescapable network of mutuality, tied in a single garment of destiny. Whatever affects one directly affects all indirectly."[37] Thus, at a time when the lay public continued to grapple with the ramifications of Einstein's equivalence of matter and energy, unity of space—time, and the emergence of Wittgensteinian holistic thought, King was extrapolating these unifying principles to "cosmic citizenship."[38]

King scholar Lewis V. Baldwin's *To Make the Wounded Whole*[39] offers a compelling examination of King's conception of World House. In chapter 4, "Caught in an Inescapable Network: A Vision of World Community," he writes:

> King used the metaphor of the "Great World House" to explain his world perspective in intellectual and theoretical terms. This metaphor captured for him the ideal of a totally integrated world based on love, justice, and equality of opportunity—a world in which loyalties to race, class, sex, tribe, religion, philosophical orientations, political differences, ethnicity, and nationality would be transcended in the interest of total human community.[40]

Then, as we do now, King realized that the potential was great for human beings to destroy the world with the ever-growing arsenal of thermonuclear weapons. The never-ending Hobbesian "war of all against all," driven by geopolitical struggles for territory, goods, markets, and pride in national sovereignties, not only resulted in poverty and war. It also legitimized racism as a means of justifying the hatreds necessary to pursue war and produce poverty within the United States and abroad. When King deciphered the intertwined relationships between poor people in the rice paddies of Vietnam and the poor people in the ghettoes of Chicago, he found the key to unlock the many disparate and desperate rooms in his "Father's House." King, again:

> Our only hope today lies in our ability to recapture the revolutionary spirit and go out into a sometimes hostile world declaring eternal hostility to poverty, racism, and militarism. With this powerful commitment we shall boldly challenge the status quo and unjust mores, and thereby speed the day when "every valley shall be exalted, and every mountain and hill shall be made low, and the crooked shall be made straight, and the rough places plain."[41]

It is time once again to "Break the Silence." As the war on terrorism propels the world toward Armageddon, King's solution reemerges as superior to strategies of mere "If we withdraw our troops we will fight the terrorists on our own soil," or escalating "troop surges." The silence denies the obvious reality that late market capitalism's need to expand markets, and the gross asymmetries of wealth between the global East and West (as well as South and North), structurally perpetuate poverty, racism, and war. The political quietism—the sense of impotence that the forces of historical necessity lie beyond the control of individuals—allows us to drift in postmodern uncertainty, where "the center cannot hold."[42] The centers of Western authority, including unilateral militaristic American exceptionalism driven by the white arrogance of global white supremacy, produce the poverty of three billion human beings. This is what King intended by his famous remark that "today we have a choice: Chaos or Community." "King said in 1967 that 'a final problem that mankind must solve in order to survive in the world house that we have inherited is finding an alternative to war and human destruction.'"[43]

Carol Bragg, analyzing King's "World House" essay, writes:

> In "The World House," Dr. King calls us to: 1) transcend tribe, race, class, nation, and religion to embrace the vision of a World House; 2) eradicate at home and globally the Triple Evils of racism, poverty, and militarism; 3) curb excessive materialism and shift from a "thing"-oriented society to a "people" oriented society; and 4) resist social injustice and resolve conflicts in the spirit of love embodied in the philosophy and methods of nonviolence.[44]

King continued:

> All over the world like a fever, freedom is spreading in the wildest liberation the great masses of people are determined to end the exploitation of their races and lands. They are awake and moving toward

their goal like a tidal wave. You can hear them rumbling in every
village street, on the docks, in the houses, among the students, in the
churches and at political meetings.[45]

Freedom in the house! As King postulated "World House" as a normative utopian vision, the Vietnamese were successfully resisting American
military power, African nations were claiming their independence from
their colonial masters, U.S. students were demanding more freedoms at
universities, French workers and students were producing anarchy in
protesting restrictions on their perceived rights, and young people all
over the globe were "on the road" in search of human liberation. Thus
more than mere rhetoric, King's prophetic and inspirational words were
translated into praxes.[46]

Beyond the postmodern deconstructive philosophies that analyze
without providing reconstructive strategies, King's transvaluation of the
moral bases for human communities represents a path toward the fulfillment of the promises of modernity. The High Renaissance in Europe
promised the enlightenment of scientific progress and human equality.
Rather than prosperity and equity, modernity produced poverty and
war. Rather than human equality, modernity produced enslavement and
human immiseration. In his "World House" speech, King said, "The rich-
er we have become materially, the poorer we have become morally and
spiritually. . . . Enlarged material powers spell enlarged peril if there is
not proportionate growth of the soul."[47] This sounds much like Marx:
"The *devaluation* of the human world grows in direct proportion to the
increase in the value of the world of things."[48] Whereas, "King's world
perspective included the concepts of *civil egalitarianism, economic egalitarianism, international egalitarianism,* and *spiritual egalitarianism,*"[49] "World
House" begins to resemble a Marxian "Kingdom of Freedom."

Martin Luther King Jr. and Communism

It would be incorrect to suggest that Martin Luther King Jr. was a
communist sympathizer. It would also be an error to read socialism back
into King's activism. But it would not be an overdrawn conclusion to
argue, despite the words "communism" and "socialism" attached to the
changing social and political arrangements described and prescribed by
these terms, that King was a "fellow traveler." Where his own words
indicate his criticism of Marxism, he is also equally critical of capitalism.
Given the historical and political realities of Cold War America in the
1960s, I maintain that King's understanding of the economic, spiritual,
and political forces shaping possibilities for World House was an implicit
recognition of historical materialism.

Thus King's practical politics were, like Wittgenstein's, "outwardly
dissimilar, yet inwardly similar" family resemblances. Outwardly, King's
political alliances were firmly within the liberal, democratic, capitalistic

sphere. Yet inwardly, given his understanding of the pivotal causal role capitalism played in the creation of poverty, racism, and militarism, King's espousal of *economic and international egalitarianism* was clearly socialistic. In fact, I would go so far as to suggest that "World House" is Marx's "Kingdom of Freedom," that final moment in the historical dialectical process where technology frees mankind from the necessities of scarcity. From the safe standpoint of a half-century, it is easy to advocate socialism, but for King and other Western academic and activist Cold War ideologues, it was a matter of life or death.[50] In what follows I will motivate an argument that King was a socialist—if not in name, in spirit—and that it is this spirit that is, and will in the future be, his contribution to political philosophy. In his 1964 Nobel Prize lecture, King said,

> All over the globe men are revolting against old systems of exploitation and oppression, and out of the wombs of a frail world new systems of justice and equality are being born. . . . We in the West must support these revolutions. It is a sad fact that, because of comfort, complacency, a morbid fear of Communism and our proneness to adjust to injustice, the Western nations that initiated so much of the revolutionary spirit of the modern world have now become the arch anti-revolutionaries. . . . Communism is a judgment on our failure to make democracy real and to follow through on the revolutions that we initiated.[51]

Here, King reveals a subtle recognition that the opposition between communism and democracy is a marked binary, a false dichotomy. Further, he posits the central premise in contemporary efforts to resurrect socialism after the collapse of the Soviet Union: "socialism is a critique of capitalism." Most political observers, then and now, are wont to point out that Marxist/Leninist Soviet "communism" was not "pure" communism, just as U.S. "democracy" is not "pure" democracy. Both systems have flaws. King continued:

> Truth is found neither in traditional capitalism nor in classical Communism. Each represents a partial truth. Capitalism fails to see the truth in collectivism. Communism fails to see the truth in individualism. Capitalism fails to realize that life is social. Communism fails to realize that life is personal. The good and just society is neither the thesis of capitalism nor the antithesis of Communism, but a socially conscious democracy which reconciles the truths of individualism and collectivism.[52]

In this speech, King has posited a synthesis. His approach rejects the naïve Maxism characterized by simple economic class conflict. By this reading, "World House" is a final historical moment where agape in the individual is the unifying force for the collective. Being a Christian, King could not have accepted the Marxian rejection of religion as the "opiate of the masses," but even with Marx's antipathy toward religion, Marx recognized its value. Opiates not only induce the false-consciousness of sleep and quietism, but they also alleviate the pains of alienation and death. Philosopher Alasdair MacIntyre writes, "There has also persisted within Marxism a quite different emphasis upon religion as not merely 'the opiate of the people' and 'the sigh of the oppressed creature,' but also 'the heart of a heartless world.'"[53] MacIntyre continues his analyses of the millennial secularization of the European working classes by saying, "Both Marxism and Christianity rescue individual lives from the insignificance of finitude (to use the Hegelian expression) by showing the individual that he has or can have some role in a world-historical drama."[54]

Attempting to straddle the universal and particular, the chaos of the contingently historical, and the community of universal love (*Chaos or Community?*) in his *Stride toward Freedom*, King is at once down on all fours with practical Marxian economic realities and "in his father's house." Michael Eric Dyson argues, "In truth, King had a rather flat and unreflexive reading of Marx's views of religion and ethics, a trait he shared with many on the right. At the same time, King's reading of Marx made him miss just how faithfully he embodied progressive Marxist principles in his own fight for the poor against capitalism."[55] Where Dyson locates King's politics on the "right," presumably because of King's belief in liberalism's systems of laws, Manning Marable is more willing to emphasize King's critique of liberalism. Marable writes,

> Martin now understood the structural limits of liberal reform, even in the context of political democracy. What was necessary was to connect the struggle for civil rights with the democratic restructuring of America's economic system. "The dispossessed of this nation—the poor, both white and Negro—live in a cruelly unjust society," Martin insisted.[56]

Whereas we will never know exactly how Martin Luther King Jr. reconciled his spiritual and political beliefs, evidence for his growing awareness by the time of his death of the internal contradictions between democracy and capitalism abound.

Taylor Branch, one King's foremost biographers, offers an informative perspective on King's insights into his own internal conflicts concerning Marxism and Christianity. Branch, recounting a conversation between King and Hosea Williams, writes:

> Just as they must "not be intimidated" to speak out against the war in Vietnam, he said, they could not let charges of communism silence misgivings about capitalist distribution of wealth. "Maybe America must move toward a democratic socialism," King bluntly suggested, and the movement must consider economic critiques by taboo thinkers such as Karl Marx. "If you read him, you can see that this man had a great passion for social justice," he said. You know Karl Marx was born a Jew, had a rabbinic background. . . . "The great weakness is...he did not recognize that the means and ends must cohere."[57]

The "bloody revolution" between the bourgeois and proletariat—class struggle—was natural anathema to King's Christian nonviolent *agape* and even more to his ecumenical *satyagraha*. Yet his willingness to "consider" a scientific Marxian historical analysis, and his suggestion that perhaps capitalism ought be mediated by socialism, is evidence that he was at least sympathetic to ideological or philosophical Marxism—if not its means, at least its ends. These ends were the social, economic, political, international, and moral egalitarian requisites for denizens of World House.

There could be no poor, disenfranchised, exploited people in the World House. "The social crisis in America, he [King] declared, was, 'inseparable from an international emergency which involves the poor, the dispossessed, the exploited of the whole world.'"[58] King's epiphany was Marxian. When he spoke of the "thingification" of people, King was alluding to Marxian alienation and commodification. On King's view of the objectification of people, Marshal Frady writes, "The primal Cain act of racism—its denial of a natural connection to other human beings, reducing them to objects, which then allows any manner of violence against them—inexorably evolved into an evangelism against what he saw as the moral coma of the country's whole corporate, technological order."[59]

Thus, if King publicly decried communism for political reasons, I argue he privately embraced many of its analytical methodologies. "In all, King was to arrive in the end at a kind of Christian socialism of conscience."[60] King's secular humanism was more Christian than Marx's, but their visions for social justice remain compellingly harmonious.

King's Holistic Legacy

King's insistence that "racism, poverty, and war [are] the greatest impediments to the actualization of world community"[61] remains the focus of all postmodern political analyses. Yet in celebrating King, "we have sought to remember him by forgetting him."[62] Extricating King the philosopher—the *Philosopher King*—from the canonized historical figure, the preacher, the civil rights leader, the prophet, the orator is controversial. Whether his celebrated status represents contrition and racial redemption or white guilt is debatable. For the purposes of this paper, his public legendary status is not the issue. What is more important is King's status as a *philosopher*. Answering this question has many ramifications.

First, if King *is* a philosopher, then his thought should be part of Western academic philosophical training. Second, if King's thought is marginalized, and he *is* a philosopher, then metaphilosophical concerns are raised concerning the nature of philosophy itself. Third, if King is a philosopher, what are the contours of his thought that normatively ought to continue to inspire? King's philosophical legacies—the ideals and concepts that make him a *Philosopher King*—are metaphilosophical, transvaluative, and philosophically holistic. Moreover, his ideals remain important because "World House" remains as necessarily difficult to achieve today as when King had this "dream."

In *Disciplinary Decadence*,[63] Lewis Gordon argues that academic policing of disciplinary boundaries contributes to their lifelessness. As twenty-first-century philosophy struggles to redefine itself, Gordon points out that priests (Augustine and Aquinas), mathematicians (Descartes), physicians (Locke), librarians (Leibniz), historians (Hume), Anglican bishops (Berkeley), theologians (Hegel), and philologists (Nietzsche) were not philosophers by training, but were added to the canon by subsequent judgments. Gordon writes:

> If racial prejudice were suspended, to this pantheon we could easily add, for example, a lawyer and anthropologist (Anténor Firmin), a historian and sociologist (W. E. B. Du Bois), a literary scholar (Anna Julia Cooper), and a psychiatrist (Frantz Fannon).[64]

Unfortunately, racial prejudice has not been suspended. Hence Martin Luther King Jr., for whatever he was and is now, has not been included in the philosophical canon. At best, in academic philosophy, he is relegated to introductory philosophy courses and a brief discussion of his "Letter from Birmingham Jail." Beyond that, serious King scholarship is found in African American divinity schools. But this, as Gordon powerfully understands, should come as no surprise, as black philosophers and philosophy have been systematically marginalized to the basement of the World House. Rather than representing the brotherhood, agape, and solidarity King advocated, academic philosophy has become a nihilistic instrument for maintaining bourgeois power. There are one thousand biographies in *Biographical Dictionary of Twentieth-Century Philosophers*,[65] but not one is African American.[66] Given this continuing racist aspect, philosophy itself must come under increasing scrutiny. If there are no African American philosophers, King cannot be considered a philosopher. In a period of intense self-scrutiny and the postmodern critique that there are no *grand narratives*, philosophy *qua* philosophy needs to become, as Gordon argues,

> an act of *teleological suspension* . . . when a discipline suspends its own centering because of a commitment to questions greater than the discipline itself. Ironically when philosophers do this—attempt to think beyond philosophy to greater commitments—they ironically breathe life into philosophy's gasping lungs.[67]

As Georg Lichtenberg held, "philosophy . . . must always speak the language of unphilosophy."[68] No philosopher should ignore King's contributions to ethical, political, and social philosophy. As philosophy attempts to resuscitate itself, it should peer beyond its self-imposed disciplinary borders to its original aims—the pursuits of Socrates—figuring out how to live well in the world with others. This is King's World House.

The present global anti-community remains mired in poverty, racism, and war. King's Poor Peoples Campaign of 1968 "reflected Dr. King's recognition of the centrality of the economy for social justice. That campaign was designed to lead the movements of the day in the direction of class struggle."[69] King's transvaluation of values was more than an ethical transformation from nihilism, alienation, and hopelessness. His transvaluation was also economic and political. "Most of the nations in the world still have not realized the truth implicit in King's contention that a solution to global poverty requires a fundamental shift in values, economic priorities, and a more democratic sharing of decision-making power."[70] "King ranks in history with other so-called extremists such as Socrates, Jesus, and Gandhi. Martyrs for their ideals, each challenged humanity to transcend itself."[71]

Beyond being a dreamer, King was also pragmatic, in the style of John Dewey and Alain L. Locke: "a great synthesizer—as one who borrowed from many schools of theological and philosophical thought 'without becoming a mere disciple of anyone.'"[72] In the axiology of action, King was a "process philosopher," who valued practice as much as theory. He was more philosopher than contemporary activists and more of an activist than contemporary philosophers. This philosophically informed activism marked King as a radical philosopher. Philosopher and King scholar Greg Moses writes:

> At heart, King was a process philosopher; he had no fondness for static categories. The concept of justice, in particular, was not to be subjected a paralysis of analysis. For King, the concept of justice necessarily compelled further action, because injustice was both pervasive and intolerable.[73]

In the contemporary world, where transnational corporations (TNCs) mock capitalism's new world order by masquerading as democratic agents, pervasive injustice remains intolerable. Because of increasing global population growth and the proliferation of thermonuclear weapons, knowledge of King's transvaluative philosophical revolution of the economic, ethical, and egalitarian is essential. Moses's evaluation of King's importance is essentially correct. King required a revolution, then and now—in a synchronic and diachronic historical global white supremacy—in white *conscience*. If whites could not achieve *The Strength to Love*, blacks would teach them by sacrifice, by *satyagraha*, to keep the hope alive that agape could create beloved communities within a World House.

Hans A. Baer, reviewing Moses's *Revolution of Conscience*, writes:

> Greg Moses argues that King also was a significant philosopher who has too often been ignored by Eurocentric philosophers. . . . [O]n read-

ing *Revolution of Conscience,* I strongly suspect that many philosophers will not be convinced of Moses's claim that Martin Luther King, Jr., was a noteworthy philosopher. If indeed this is the case, such a refusal is in keeping with the larger society's tendency to sanitize the radical King, who in his last years viewed the struggle for African American civil rights within a larger context, namely that of U.S. and international capitalism.[74]

The failure of Western "analytic" philosophers to recognize King as a philosopher is not King's failure, but their own.

Finally, within the framework of the World House elaborated above, I would argue that Martin Luther King Jr.'s vision of world brotherhood and sisterhood is presciently holistic. As satellites beamed back images of the earth during his lifetime, King increasingly became a proponent of what has come to be termed James Lovelock's *Gaia* hypothesis[75] —the earth is one living organism.[76] King's theological reading made him aware of Teilhard de Chardin's idea of the *noosphere.* Noosphere (nous, or mind + atmosphere), where "a new realization arose: 'Time and space are organically joined again so as to weave, together, the stuff of the universe.'"[77] The point is that King embraced an early philosophical sensitivity to the whole planetary perspective that has fueled environmentalism.

The "World House" was not a structure constructed in or on the world, it *was* the world. "[King's] metaphor of the 'World House' or the 'world-wide neighborhood,' and his assessment of the major obstacles to world community, have significant implications for the shaping of a new humanity and a new world."[78] Moreover, beyond social and political world holism, King's philosophy is also holistic.[79] For it is the holism King offered by social hope in agape that transvalues the nihilism and hopelessness that characterizes modernity. Mark Bevir offers the following account of philosophical holism:

> [It] has been integral to the changing concerns and arguments of philosophers over the last twenty or thirty years. . . . [I]t encourages . . . a contextualizing and synthetic approach. Indeed, because holism challenges the rigid distinction between synthetic and analytic propositions, it prompts us to put the prefix "post" in front of the whole "analytic philosophy."[80]

Therefore, because of his role in the ongoing redefinition of philosophy, his transvaluative philosophies, and his holistic normative dreams and visions for all human beings, I am eager to conclude that Martin Luther King Jr. was a philosopher. And until "either philosophers become kings in our states or those whom we now call our kings and rulers take to the pursuit of philosophy . . . there can be no cessation of troubles."[81] King was a philosopher: now we who are not Kings need to help educate our leaders to be philosophers.

NOTES

1. "Todos pueden ser grandes. . . . Porque todos pueden servir. Para servir no hace falta un título universitario. Para servir no hace falta concordar el sujeto y el verbo. Solo se necesita un CORAZÓN lleno de gracia. Un alma generada por el AMOR." Martín Luther King.

2. Teresa Rimada Reyes, June 18, 2007, at the Jo Jo White Center in the Arroyo Naranjo Municipality de Cuba. These people working together, mainly poor, black women, accomplished the nearly impossible task of constructing cinderblock buildings without any knowledge of the construction trades. The women of La Güinera were celebrated by Fidel Castro for their feats. Reyes also said, "In real life all of us are important; we must respect everyone's particulars. With physical change we needed to change minds as well."

3. Proverbs 29:18.

4. Nihilistic lyrics by Johnny Rotten of the punk-rock group Sex Pistols from the 1977 album *God Save the Queen*: "When theres no future how can there be sin/ Were the flowers in the dustbin/ Were the poison in your human machine/ Were the future in your future/ . . . No future for you no future for me."

5. Francis Fukuyama's memorable phrase connotes that because the West has won, for the foreseeable future, the future will resemble the present.

6. Robert E. Birt, "Of the Quest for Freedom as Community," in *The Quest for Community and Identity*, ed. Robert E. Birt (Lanham, MD: Rowman & Littlefield, 2002), 89.

7. Zygmunt Bauman, *Intimations of Postmodernity* (New York: Routledge, 1992), 134.

8. Johnny Washington, *Alain Locke and Philosophy: A Quest for Cultural Pluralism* (New York: Greenwood Press, 1986):

> King admired certain traditional philosophers, such as Socrates, Kant, Hegel, Bentham, Mill, and Marx who were concerned with political and moral issues. Because of Marx's concern with the oppressed class, King held that Marx's theory possessed merit, but King never accepted it in its entirety. (17)

9. Sean Sayers, *Marxism and Human Nature* (London: Routledge, 1998), 11.

10. Marshall Berman, *Adventures in Marxism* (New York: Verso, 1999), 54.

11. Martin Luther King Jr., "Letter from Birmingham Jail," in *Voices of Wisdom: A Multicultural Reader*, ed. Gary E. Kessler (Belmont, CA: Wadsworth, 2001), 197.

12. Berman, *Adventures in Marxism*, 59.

13. Ibid.

14. Ibid., 109. Here, Berman is quoting from Marx's *German Ideology (1845–1846)*.

15. Martin Luther King Jr., "Beyond Vietnam—A Time to Break Silence," delivered April 4, 1967, at a meeting of clergy and laity convened at Riverside Church in New York City, www.americanrhetoric.com/speeches/mlkatimetobreaksilence.htm (accessed January 26, 2011).

16. Berman, Ibid., 137.

17. Marshall Frady, *Martin Luther King, Jr.* (New York: Penguin, 2002), 5.

18. Ibid., 183.

19. Ibid., 5.

20. Ibid., 102.

21. William R. Jones, *Is God a White Racist?: A Preamble to Black Theology* (New York: Anchor Press, 1973), 80. Reflecting on this ubiquitous paralleling of black suffering with the servant (or the chosen people "wandering in the desert"), William R. Jones discusses the following argument from Joseph Washington's major work *The Politics of God* (Boston: Beacon Press, 1969), 155: "As a result of this suffering by a whole people for four centuries and placed in the perspective of the Bible, we contend . . . that the

Negro cannot be understood or understand himself except as another 'chosen people.'. . .

> If blacks are the suffering servant / chosen people,
> The charge of divine racism is disproved.
> *Blacks are the suffering servant / chosen people.*
> Therefore the charge of divine racism is disproved."

See also Lewis V. Baldwin, *There Is a Balm in Gilead: The Cultural Roots of Martin Luther King, Jr.* (Minneapolis: Fortress Press, 1991):

> King interpreted the suffering, humiliation, and death experienced by his people under oppression in light of some great divine purpose, an interpretation that led him to propound a concept of black messianism. Black Americans, he held, had a special redemptive role to play in American history and in world civilization. King espoused this concept so consistently that it should be accounted a fundamental component of his thought. (230)

22. James A. Colaiaco, *Martin Luther King, Jr.: Apostle of Militant Nonviolence* (New York: St. Martin's Press, 1993), 24. The quotation is from King's *Stride toward Freedom*, 105.

23. Martin Luther King Jr., *Strength to Love* (New York: Harper, 1963), 36.

24. See Aristotle's *Nicomachean Ethics*, trans. Terence Irwin (Indianapolis: Hackett, 1985), Book viii, chapters 29, 9.2–9.6, 209–24.

25. Mahatma K. Gandhi, "On Satyagraha," in *Social and Political Philosophy: Classical Western Texts in Feminist and Multicultural Perspectives*, ed. James P. Sterba (Belmont, CA: Wadsworth, 1998), 301.

26. Martin Luther King Jr., *Strength to Love*, 138.

27. Martin Luther King Jr., *Stride toward Freedom: The Montgomery Story* (New York: Harper, 1958).

28. Ibid., 105.

29. Martin Luther King Jr., "Beyond Vietnam—A Time to Break Silence," delivered April 4, 1967, at a meeting of clergy and laity convened at Riverside Church in New York City, www.americanrhetoric.com/speeches/mlkatimetobreaksilence.htm (accessed January 26, 2011).

30. Martin Luther King Jr., *Strength to Love*, 133.

31. Cornel West, "Philosophy, Politics, and Power: An Afro-American Perspective," in *Social and Political Philosophy: Classical Western Texts in Feminist and Multicultural Perspectives*, ed. James P. Sterba (Belmont, CA: Wadsworth, 1998), 497.

32. Ibid., 499.

33. Maurizio Valsania, "Social Hope and Prophetic Intellectuals in a 'Hopeless World,' " in *Toward a New Socialism,* eds. Anatole Anton and Richard Schmitt (Lanham, MD: Lexington Books, 2007), 200.

34. See http//www.amazon.com/Martin-Luther-Routledge-Historical-Biographies/dp /0415216648 for the source for this quotation (accessed January 26, 2011).

35. John 14:2. The various translations of "rooms" to dwellings and mansions are important. A Christian ontology, where the "upper rooms" represent heaven, leaves the basement rooms as the dwellings of servants. But in a universe of love, even the lower rooms are mansions, *In My Father's House* (to quote the title of Anthony Appiah's book).

36. Frady, *Martin Luther King, Jr.*, 119.

37. Martin Luther King Jr., *Why We Can't Wait* (New York: The New American Library, 1964), 77.

38. What I intend to suggest here is that King understood Carl Sagan's "We are citizens of the universe." In tracing King's indirect influence on the ascendancy of ontological, epistemological, and social holism, I am struck by the fact that 1967's

"Summer of Love" and the ethos of "Flower Power" coincided with King's resurrection of love.

39. Lewis V. Baldwin, *To Make the Wounded Whole: The Cultural Legacy of Martin Luther King, Jr.* (Minneapolis: Fortress Press, 1992).

40. Ibid., 251.

41. Martin Luther King Jr., "Beyond Vietnam—A Time to Break Silence."

42. The reference is to William Butler Yeats's "The Second Coming": Turning and turning in the widening gyre / The falcon cannot hear the falconer; / Things fall apart; the centre cannot hold; / Mere anarchy is loosed upon the world, / The blood-dimmed tide is loosed, and everywhere / The ceremony of innocence is drowned; / The best lack all conviction, while the worst / Are full of passionate intensity." This is also a more contemporary reference—for many of the same reasons—to Chinua Achebe's *Things Fall Apart*.

43. Baldwin, *To Make the Wounded Whole*, 269.

44. Carol Bragg, "Introduction: The World House Essay," http://www.theworldhouse.org/whessay.html (accessed January 26, 2011).

45. Martin Luther King Jr., "The World House," http://www.theworldhouse.org/whessay.html (accessed January 26, 2011).

46. Even beyond these "social movements" and "political revolutions," King influenced the creation of "Peace Studies" and peace institutes. Liberation theology, a nebulous concept during the 1950s, took more concrete forms because of King.

47. Martin Luther King Jr., "The World House."

48. Karl Marx, "Estranged Labor," *Economic and Philosophical Manuscripts*, 1844.

49. Baldwin, *To Make the Wounded Whole*, 254.

50. To recount the pressures on King to separate himself from Stanley Levison (an avowed communist), FBI wiretaps, and bomb threats and actual bombings would be to go too far afield. Suffice it to say that once King entered the antiwar movement, scrutiny of his national loyalty (and political allegiances) became more important than his civil rights campaigns. Hence, dissimulation concerning his actual beliefs was a protective measure.

51. Martin Luther King Jr., "The World House."

52. Ibid.

53. Alasdair MacIntyre, *Marxism and Christianity* (Notre Dame: University of Notre Dame Press, 1984), 109.

54. Ibid., 112.

55. Michael Eric Dyson, *I May Not Get There with You: The True Martin Luther King, Jr.,* (New York: The Free Press, 2000), 130.

56. Manning Marable, *Speaking Truth to Power: Essays on Race, Resistance, and Radicalism* (Boulder: Westview, 1996), 137.

57. Taylor Branch, *At Canaan's Edge: America in the King Years 1965-68* (New York: Simon and Schuster, 2006), 555–56.

58. Frady, *Martin Luther King, Jr.*, 199.

59. Ibid., 6.

60. Frady, 25.

61. Baldwin, *To Make the Wounded Whole*, 254.

62. Frady, *Martin Luther King, Jr.*, 7. Here Frady quotes King biographer David L. Lewis.

63. Lewis R. Gordon, *Disciplinary Decadence: Living Thought in Trying Times* (Boulder: Paradigm, 2006).

64. Ibid., 34.

65. Stuart Brown, et al., *Biographical Dictionary of Twentieth-Century Philosophers* (London: Routledge, 1995).

66. "No Black Americans Included in the Biographical Directory of 1,000 Twentieth-Century Philosophers," *The Journal of Blacks in Higher Education*, no. 14 (Winter 1996/1997): 144.

67. Gordon, *Disciplinary Decadence*, 34.

68. Alfred Nordmann, *Wittgenstein's Tractatus: An Introduction* (New York: Cambridge, 2005), 21.

69. Harry Targ, *Challenging Late Capitalism, Neo-Liberal Globalization, and Militarism: Building a Progressive Majority* (Chicago: ChangeMaker Publications, 2006), 90.

70. Baldwin, *To Make the Wounded Whole*, 310.

71. Colaiaco, *Martin Luther King, Jr.: Apostle of Militant Nonviolence*, 203.

72. Ibid., 125.

73. Greg Moses, *Revolution of Conscience: Martin Luther King, Jr., and the Philosophy of Non-Violence* (New York: Guilford, 1997), 8.

74. Hans A. Baer, "Revolution of Conscience: Martin Luther King, Jr., and the Philosophy of Nonviolence—Book Reviews," *African American Review* (Summer 1998), http://findarticles.com/p/articles/mi_m2838/is_n2_32/ai_21059973/ (accessed January 26, 2011).

75. The Gaia hypothesis—"Gaia was a Greek goddess in whose body all living things were organs" (Seieland, 1983: 135)—has influenced deep ecology, environmentalism, and I would also suggest feminist philosophy (e.g., "Gynecology" and "In a Different Voice"). Beyond these important movements, I would also suggest that quantum physicist David Bohm's "Implicate Order," which emphasized an emergent coherent ontology, was also instrumental in the changing holistic paradigms concerning the interrelatedness of persons, nature, and communal arrangements. In Africa, at the same historical moment, Kwame Nkrumah was delineating a non-European form of socialist communalism—consciencism—which, "taking its start from the present content of the African conscience, indicates the way in which progress is forged out of the conflict in that conscience" (Hord and Lee, 1995: 56). King's "World House" speech reveals a deep sensitivity to all these emerging holistic paradigms.

76. See Stephen Miller, "Gaia Hypothesis," http://erg.ucd.ie/arupa/references/gaia.html (accessed January 26, 2011).

77. Phillip. J. Cunningham, "Teilhard de Chardin and the Noosphere," http://www.december.com/cmc/mag/1997/mar/cunning.html (accessed January 26, 2011).

78. These "new" people we now strive to be, who would live in King's "World House," are what leftists in the 1970s called the "Tribe." In Gary Snyder's *Earth House Hold* (New York: New Directions, 1969), he describes these new people:

> The signal is the bright and tender look; calmness and gentleness, freshness and ease of manner. Men, women and children—all of whom together hope to follow the timeless path of love and wisdom, in affectionate company with the sky, winds, clouds, trees, waters, animals and grasses—this is the tribe. (116)

See also Baldwin, *To Make the Wounded Whole*, 316.

79. I also intend to suggest that King's philosophical holism is an early form of what Bruno Latour develops in *Politics of Nature: How to Bring Sciences into Democracy* (Cambridge: Harvard University Press, 2004):

> Whereas the moral question of the common good was separated from the physical and epistemological question of the common world, we maintain, on the contrary, that these questions must be brought together so that the question of the *good* common world, of the *best* of possible worlds, of the *cosmos*, can be raised again from scratch. (93)

80. Mark Bevir, "Taking Holism Seriously: A Reply to Critics, 2001," http://escholarship.org/uc/item/7z9394vw?query=taking%20holism%20seriously;hitRank=1#page-1 (accessed January 26, 2011).

81. Plato, *The Collected Dialogues of Plato*, eds. Edith Hamilton and Huntington Cairns (Princeton: Princeton University Press, 1989), 712–13.

SEVEN

King's Radical Vision of Community

Robert E. Birt

"I" cannot reach fulfillment without "thou." The self cannot be a self without other selves.... All men are *interdependent*.
— Martin Luther King Jr., *Where Do We Go from Here: Chaos or Community?*

[T]he inmost growth of the self is not accomplished, as people like to suppose today, in man's relation to himself, but in the relation between the one and the other, between men...
— Martin Buber, *The Knowledge of Man*

Only in community [with others has each] individual the means of cultivating his gifts in all directions; only in community, therefore, is personal freedom possible.
— Karl Marx, *The German Ideology*

An individual has not started living until he can rise above the narrow confines of his individualistic concerns to the broader concerns of all humanity.
— Martin Luther King Jr., *The Measure of a Man*

Can we truly understand Dr. Martin Luther King's vision of freedom and social justice without understanding his moral vision of community? King's vision of community is the philosophical locus of his social radicalism as well as the ultimate goal (and ethical realization) of the freedom movement that he led. At the center of his vision of community and social justice is the primacy of the human person—the unalienable dignity of *every* human being. Yet this person is not the disconnected atom of aggressive self-interest so esteemed in our tradition of "rugged individualism." The human person is always uniquely individual, but as an individual is always a person-in-community.[1]

Personhood and Community are inseparable in the thought of Dr. King. For human personality can only flourish in a community of freedom, and community can only flourish as a free and loving association of autonomous human individuals. Personhood and community are essential to the very metaphysics of Personalism, which Dr. King regards as his "basic philosophical position."[2] This philosophical position (which King calls "personal idealism") afforded him a "metaphysical basis for dignity and worth of all human personality."[3] It also offered him a metaphysical basis for community via its idea of the interrelated structure of reality, and of the interrelatedness of self and other. Personalist metaphysics, with its idea that reality itself is "*through and through social, relational and communal*," also holds that the individual never experiences self in total isolation.[4] "We are made to live together," King insists, "because of the *interrelated structure* of *reality*."[5] King's idea of the communal nature of reality and persons is grounded in metaphysical principle.

But whatever his philosophical grounding in metaphysics, King is not primarily a metaphysician. King is primarily a moral (and social) philosopher, and his notions of personhood and community are moral ideals. It was for the sake of these ideals that King engaged in civil disobedience and nonviolent resistance to racial segregation. It was for the sake of the dignity of the human personality and the ideal of community that he came to oppose militarism and economic exploitation as well as racial oppression of America's black people. Indeed for Dr. King the end sought by the black freedom movement was not merely liberation from repressive racial caste restrictions, and not only the improvement the social status of blacks in America. Ultimately, the "end is the creation of the beloved community."[6] Community is essentially an *ethical* relation between human beings—between *persons*—that enables the flowering of the human personality, and the affirmation of the inherent worth of every human being.

Dr. King's idea of community seems to be bound up with three basic principles: the *sacredness* (or dignity) of the human personality, the essential importance of *freedom* to the very *being* of the human, and recognition of the *solidarity* of the human family.[7] As a Christian thinker, King largely derives his belief in the sacredness of the human person from the "Hebraic-Christian tradition," which conceives the "inherent dignity of man" as being created in "the *image of God*."[8] This innate human dignity is universally shared in "equal portions" by all human beings. God has created "no graded scale of essential worth," and "no right of one race which differs from the divine right of another." For King "every human being has etched in his personality the indelible stamp of the Creator."[9]

Thus Dr. King reveals himself as heir to an ancient and renowned tradition of religious dissent and radicalism that has for centuries inspired millions of reformers and revolutionaries—a tradition that infers from a doctrine of human spiritual equality before God the moral duty of social equality in a human community. No social order may rightfully make unequal whom God has made equal. King argues that racial segregation is evil because it is "diametrically opposed to the principle of the sacredness of the human personality."[10] King also argues that while we have a moral duty to treat "all men as ends and never as mere means," racial caste necessarily treats human beings as means rather than ends in themselves. Racism thus reduces people to the status of "things rather than persons."[11] But the human being is not a thing, nor (as in Aristotle's description of the slave) an "animated tool," but "a person sacred in himself."[12]

Yet King does not base his belief in human dignity on religious conviction alone. For King human dignity is inconceivable without freedom. Like Immanuel Kant, he sees human dignity as bound up with moral freedom and autonomy, moral autonomy or self-determination being the essential condition of human dignity. But unlike Kant, King does not narrowly equate moral freedom with freedom or autonomy of will. For he holds that "the very phrase, freedom of will, abstracts freedom from the person to make it an object." But "an object almost by definition is not free." Thus freedom cannot be "abstracted from the person, who is always subject as well as object." Rather, when one speaks of freedom one is speaking of "the freedom of man, the *whole* man, and not one faculty called the will."[13] Freedom is no mere property that we *have* but rather the peculiar mode of being that we *are*. Dr. King's idea of freedom here resembles existentialist ideas of freedom. And John Ansbro may have a point in seeing the influence of Sartre in King's conception of freedom.[14] For King, freedom is constitutive of the being of the human, as is indicated by his inferring that "the essence of man is found in freedom." He notes with apparent approval the existentialist idea that "man *is* freedom," and specifically the claim by existentialist theologian Paul Tillich that "Man is man because he is free."[15]

Freedom is the capacity to deliberate and weigh alternatives, as when I ponder and decide between bachelorhood and marriage, or between an intellectual vocation and climbing the corporate ladder. A decision in one direction excludes alternatives in another. King notes that many "existentialists say we must choose . . . and that if we do not choose we sink into thinghood and the mass mind."[16] This is because freedom for King constitutes personhood. Freedom expresses itself as decision and responsibility. It involves a commitment to values for which I am accountable to others as well as myself. Hence the freedom that constitutes the human being also expresses itself as moral action. But moral action is expressed in interhuman relations, in community. Existential and moral freedom is thus bound up with social freedom. And Burrow correctly observes that King's emphasis "was on both metaphysical and social freedom."[17]

Recognition of human solidarity, the third principle underlying King's idea of community, implies the oneness of humankind and the essential importance of community for the realization of the freedom and dignity of the human personality. King thinks the oneness of humanity is made increasingly evident by the sciences, independently of religious teachings. Writing in 1963, he notes that anthropologists were already arguing that fundamental differences between major racial groups do not exist, and that most scientists "deny the actual existence of what we have known as race."[18] There are no superior or inferior races. Ultimately, there is only the *human* race, and the human race is one—however much our history has racially polarized the human family.[19]

But solidarity means not only that humankind is one, but that the human being is naturally a social creature. Freedom constitutes human personhood, but personhood is social as well as personal. King thinks that the human being "has been working from the beginning at the great adventure of community," which he describes as *mutually cooperative* and *voluntary* venture of man to assume a semblance of responsibility for his brother."[20] Dr. King seems to believe that the creation of a community of freedom is the ultimate meaning and purpose of human history. Thus he would probably agree with Martin Buber that "the primary aspiration of all history is a genuine community of human beings."[21] If for Hegel history "is the progress of the consciousness of freedom,"[22] for King the lived reality of freedom is realized through the historical creation of human community.

Thus, for King the quest for freedom is the quest for community, for a community of freedom that affirms the dignity of every human personality. Yet such a quest implies a *lack*. If King seeks a community of freedom, it is because he finds it absent. He experiences a world marked by a tragic *unfreedom*, a world sadly marked by an *estrangement* between self and other that corrodes the spirit of community. The communal nature of reality does not immediately ensure a flourishing human community. Where estrangement prevails, solidarity is diminished. Moreover, King lives in a land that proclaims freedom its national creed, and yet harbors a vicious system of racial caste that denies freedom to millions of America's black people. But if freedom truly constitutes human personhood, all oppression is a trampling upon the human personality. And where personhood is trampled, dignity is denied. For the sake of this trampled personhood, this dignity denied, this abrogated human freedom, King is morally committed to forming a new community of freedom that affirms the inherent worth of every human being on earth.

But what if the social order itself, by the very way it is structured, denies freedom, tramples dignity, and alienates "I" from "thou"? Then King's quest for community cannot be a seeking for what *is* but a striving for what is *not yet*—for what *can be*. It is a *transcendence* of the given toward the *possible*. King's movement becomes an effort at *creation*, the formation of a new social order. The struggle for freedom as community becomes a *transformative movement*, a *radically* transformative movement. The social transformation King seeks in quest of community is nothing short of revolutionary. And one may be astonished at the frequency with which the word "revolution" emanates from the mouth and pen of the allegedly "moderate" Martin Luther King Jr. It is no mere rhetorical flourish. King's quest for community is a *radical* quest to transform not only the situation of black America, but the entire social order. Not only racial caste, but the interrelated evils of economic exploitation, poverty, materialistic values that elevate things above persons (often relegating persons to the status of things), militarism and imperialism—all these mark the world that *is*, the world King seeks to *transcend* in thought and action toward a possible *new* world where freedom and dignity in a cooperative society of justice and love can be the birthright of every man, woman and child on earth.

Now to most Americans, it may seem odd to speak of King's social radicalism. It doesn't fit our sanitized image of the apostle of nonviolence committed to brotherhood and racial harmony. But commitment to brotherhood and racial harmony hardly precludes social radicalism, especially once one becomes convinced that a fundamental change in the social order and (in King's words) a "revolution of values" is needed to realize it. Such would be the fruits of the beloved community. Moreover, it is the commitment to transformation that makes one radical. Nonviolence hardly precludes radicalism. Even famous advocates of armed revolution like Frantz Fanon and Karl Marx acknowledge that in *some countries*, under *certain circumstances*, nonviolent radical change is possible. And C. L. R James, renowned black Trinidadian Marxist thinker, activist and man of letters who corresponded with King, seems quite confident of the radicalism of Dr. King and nonviolent resistance. Comparing King's methods of nonviolence in Montgomery with Kwame Nkrumah's "positive action" in Ghana, James expressly describes nonviolent resistance as "a technique of *revolutionary struggle* characteristic of our age."[23] Perhaps the recent "Arab Spring" evidences at least the *possibility* of revolutionary nonviolence in our era.

Yet King's social radicalism lies not only in technique, and nonviolence for him is not merely a technique. "The aftermath of nonviolence" he writes "is the creation of the beloved community."[24] King's social radicalism lies in a moral and social vision of which community is the heart and soul. We might say that community—especially the notion of "beloved community" bound by Agapic love—is the essential normative value in King's ethical thought, the moral impetus behind his activism, and the moral criteria by which he politically challenges and philosophically critiques the prevailing status quo. Naturally, this is first manifested in King's opposition to racism. As a black youth in the Deep South, his first encounter with violated personhood and radical estrangement of self from other was his experiences with segregation. When as an adolescent he was first compelled to ride in a segregated part of a train—curtain drawn as if to protect privileged whites from the pestiferous presence of an untouchable—King recalls that "I felt as if a curtain had been *dropped on my selfhood.*"[25] This curtain of segregation, like the "veil" of caste in W. E. B Du Bois' *The Souls of Black Folk*, symbolizes an imprisonment that denies our personhood by denying our freedom. It offends the young King not only because "separate but equal is inherently unequal," but also because "the very idea of separation did something to my *sense of dignity* and *self-respect.*"[26] Like Du Bois' veil, the curtain of segregation not only estranges one from others but also estranges one from self.

Thus we see the denial of *freedom,* the trampling of *dignity,* and by virtue of that radical separation or estrangement inherent to racial caste, a negation of *human solidarity* essential to all genuine communal life. In short, young King suffers as a *lived experience* the violations of three principles or values (freedom, dignity, and solidarity) that would underlie his adult philosophy of community and his primary ethical commitment. In his famous 1963 "Letter from Birmingham Jail," Dr. King argues:

> Any law that uplifts the human personality is just. Any law that de-grades the human personality is unjust. All segregation statutes are unjust because segregation *distorts the soul* and *damages the personality.* It gives the segregator a false sense of superiority, and the segregated a false sense of inferiority. To use the words of Martin Buber, the great Jewish philosopher, segregation substitutes an *"I-It"* relationship for an *"I-Thou"* relationship, and ends up relegating persons to the status of things.[27]

These five sentences contain the core principles of Dr. King's critique not only of racism but of every form of oppression and injustice. Racism violates the human personality of blacks by denying them freedom and thus relegating them to the status of things. By imbuing in many of them a false sense of inferiority it engenders "a degenerating sense of nobodi-ness."[28] And by reifying relations between self and other—substituting an "I-It" relation for an "I-Thou" relation—it estranges self from others thereby eroding possibilities of community. But if King is committed to community, to freedom, dignity of human personality, and a more af-firming relation between human beings, he is morally obligated (as is *everyone* on his view) to defy the existing order of things.

Of course, any number of moderates or liberals might well concur with King regarding the injustice of *De Jure* segregation without calling into question the entire social order. Certainly, the eradication of Jim Crow laws, while an historic achievement in the quest for freedom, hard-ly amounted to a revolutionary transformation of society. Nor has King any such illusions. Racism and oppression run much deeper, and its inju-ries are far more insidious, than the coercive restrictions of segregation laws. Moreover, desegregation is not the ultimate end but actually a vital step toward that end. According to King, "Desegregation is only a *partial*, though *necessary*, step toward the final goal which we seek to realize, *genuine intergroup* and *interpersonal living*."[29] It is the *transformation of life* that is sought. For King "desegregation is only a first step on the road to the good society."[30] The question remains "How fundamental a change in the present society is needed to achieve the good society?" The answer depends on whether one views racism and related injustices as *endemic* to the social order, or as a mere aberration or superficial blemish.

Now what if racism is more than a superficial blemish on the lovely countenance of the Republic? What if it is more than an aberration from the norm of an otherwise healthy American democracy? And what if it is inseparably bound up with other forms of injustice, especially economic injustice, in a total system of injustice and unfreedom? King comes to realize (especially after Selma, if not sooner) that racism is *endemic* to the American social order, that it involves more than overt discrimination and segregation laws. That is one reason why he sees desegregation as only one step toward the good society. Racism is not reducible to mere ignorance and prejudice. It is a way of life, a maleficent life-denying way of life. It is the antithesis of community, the negation of "genuine intergroup and interpersonal living." A genuine community would *affirm* life and the dignity of every human being. But according to King, "Racism is a philosophy based on a contempt for life." It is total negation. "Racism is *total estrangement*,"[31] King writes. Racism, especially in America, is a way of life that is contemptuous of life. But if we are to create a way of life that affirms life, then we cannot simply reform racial caste. We must do away with it. For King this is a moral imperative with revolutionary sociopolitical implications.

Why revolutionary? Because King finds racism to be too endemic, too insidious, too deeply rooted in the social order to be remedied by reforms achieved by civil rights victories in Birmingham and Selma. It is too deeply rooted in the social structure. But one of the reasons, perhaps the main reason, racism is so deeply rooted in the social structure is that it is inseparably bound up with (though not reducible to) economic exploitation. Without fundamentally transforming the socioeconomic structure you cannot abolish American racism with its myriad delusions, depersonalizations, and estrangements of self from other. Moreover, the economic system also inclines toward dehumanization, violations of personhood, and estrangement of I from Thou. The social order itself must be restructured if community is to be fully realized.

That King doesn't see racism as a separate problem all to itself is clear from his own words. In *Stride toward Freedom* (1958), King claims that as a *youth* he had already "learned that the inseparable twin of racial injustice was economic injustice."[32] Since poor whites were also subject to the latter injustice, he grew up "deeply conscious of the varieties of injustice in our society."[33] But the *relation* between these varieties of injustice he was also aware of. And in *Where Do We Go from Here* (1967), Dr. King—Christian theist and philosophical idealist—offers an analysis of the origins of racism rooted in a system of economic profiteering and exploitation that is strikingly similar to analyses offered by many Marxists. He argues that the "the basis for the birth, growth and development of slavery in America was primarily economic,"[34] that the slave trade was lucrative commerce, and slavery a profitable enterprise. Africans were legally reduced to the status of property, and blacks stripped of all human and civil rights. All this was done for the purpose of producing "commodities for sale at a profit, which in turn would be privately appropriated." And the effort to give "moral sanction" to this "profitable system gave birth to the doctrine of white supremacy."[35] This doctrine is sanctioned by law, philosophy, science, and religion until racism that begins as a central element of economic exploitation evolves into a culture, ethos, value system, and way of life.

Moreover, Dr. King rejects the idea of white supremacist ideology having its origins with the "unlettered, underprivileged, poorer-class whites." Au contraire, "the social obstetricians who presided over the birth of racist views in our country were the *aristocracy*: rich merchants, influential clergymen, men of medical science, historians and political scientists from some of the leading universities of the nation."[36] And with the *"elite* working so assiduously to disseminate racist views," King infers that there was little to "inspire poor, illiterate and unskilled" white laborers to think differently. Hence King, while acknowledging the racism of the white poor, places the largest burden and blame for the evils of racism at the doorstep of the exploitative white ruling class. It is they who invented it, and they who to this day profit most from it. Inscribed in law, "imbedded in every textbook, and preached in practically every pulpit," racism "became a *structural part of the culture.*"[37]

Thus, it would seem to follow from King's own perspective that if the realization of community requires the transcendence of racism, it must also entail the transcendence of the system of economic exploitation that gave birth to racism. In short, community requires the transcendence of capitalism and its alienations. King's critique of capitalism, which some writers think begins only post-Selma, actually precedes Montgomery, and proceeds from the same moral principles as does the critique of racism. This is evident from some of his writings from his student days, including at least one letter written in 1952 to Coretta Scott, his future wife.[38] While King was not a Marxist—being philosophically opposed to Marx's materialism, and morally opposed to the bureaucratic authoritarianism of the USSR—he was nonetheless deeply concerned "about the gulf between superfluous wealth and abject poverty."[39] And his reading of Marx only intensified that concern. Furthermore, King thinks that Marx exposed the "danger of the profit motive as the sole basis of an economic system: capitalism is always in danger of inspiring men to be more concerned about making a living than about making a life." In the relentless pursuit of profit, we are "prone to judge success by the index of our salaries or the size of our automobiles, rather than the quality of our service and relationship to humanity."[40]

In short, the same profiteering system that begat slavery and the total estrangement of racism also begets a great alienating divide between wealth and poverty. It creates the injustice of destitution amidst immense wealth. And the values of a system that sanctifies wealth and acquisitiveness over all human values and relationships, naturally engenders an estrangement that is the antithesis of a communal spirit. Our relations to things become for us more real (or at least more valued) than our relations to each other. The deepening cultural blight of consumerism in our time, the corrosive privatization of life which virtually blinds our social conscience, the ever-widening gap between haves and have-nots with its growing social miseries stoking the flames of racial antagonisms and xenophobia, and that "free market fundamentalism" that (in Cornel West's words) "makes an idol of money and a fetish of wealth"[41] — evils that in our time far exceed the scale they had attained in the time of Dr. King — clearly indicate the prescience and continued relevance of his critique.

But King deepens this critique in later years, especially after Selma in 1965. I do not quite agree with the claims of some, including Robert Mitchell Franklin, that it was only after Selma that Dr. King "began to articulate a more radical analysis of oppression." I don't quite agree that Dr. King only later "expanded from a mono-causal focus on racism to include the increasing significance of economic dimensions of oppression."[42] Given King's holistic philosophical outlook, which stressed the interrelated nature of reality, he would never have been inclined to a *mono-causal* focus on race. But his *primary emphasis* (not exclusive focus) would have been on the fight against racism until at least the *legal* shackles of racial caste were broken by the civil rights movement. The themes of economic justice versus exploitation, and indeed the need for a *global* struggle against poverty and imperialism, are to be found even in the pre-Movement expressions of his thinking.[43] But after Selma there does seem to be an increasing *emphasis* on themes of poverty and exploitation, on militarism and imperialism — and on the *interrelation* of these with each other and with racism. And in his critique of these social evils the concern is always for a community of freedom, and underlying values of dignity, freedom, and human solidarity.

The increasing emphasis on the interrelations of racism, economic injustice, and militarism are sometimes taken as indicative of a shift from civil rights to human rights in the thought and praxis of Dr. King. Civil rights are commonly seen as those rights and liberties that are *legally* conferred on citizens by the Constitution, rights largely denied to African

Americans before the Movement. But while many civil rights activists advocated a "dual agenda" of civil rights and economic rights—"Jobs and Freedom" as some of the placards stated at the March on Washington—economic rights are not guaranteed by the Constitution. Hence by 1966 we find King arguing that "We have left the realm of constitutional rights and we are entering the area of *human rights*."[44] There are some rights that people have, some things to which they are *morally entitled* whether these are acknowledged by the Constitution or not. "It is not a constitutional right that men have jobs, but it is a human right," he insists.[45] Dr. King's increased emphasis on economic justice and opposition to economic injustice and exploitation, proceeds from the same moral perspective as his general opposition to racial discrimination—and still with the aim of the creation of a beloved community of freedom.

King was aware that civil freedoms won by southern Movement victories would be compromised, or have little effect when confronted with concentrated urban poverty in the North and rural poverty in the South. He noted that after the Civil War the freedom gained by former slaves was an "abstract freedom" since "they found themselves with no bread to eat, no land to cultivate, no shelter to cover their heads."[46] They lived in an agrarian economy but were "given no land to make liberation *concrete*."[47] King is clearly concerned that the civil rights newly won by black Americans during the 1960s might be rendered—like the rights won by their ancestors during Reconstruction—largely abstract and ineffectual unless combined with economic rights needed to make true self-determination possible. The right to dine in a desegregated restaurant meant little if you couldn't afford the meal. The poor and those of modest means still find themselves ostracized—doubly ostracized if black and bearing also the stigma of race—but ostracized even when they are persons of European descent unable to procure a decent life in a society whose Protestant ethic tends to scorn the poor, viewing their deprivation of means as sign of a depravity of character. But for King, this contempt for the poor is contempt for human dignity, the *inherent dignity* of *every* human being. And the resulting ostracism is a denial of the reality of that "network of mutuality" that binds us as one human family, a disregarding of the interrelatedness of all life that can express itself in community. Even allowing poverty to exist in a nation with the means to end it is an injustice that shows contempt for the dignity of the human person.

But to demand economic rights not recognized by the Constitution is to press against the authority of the State. Community is hardly realizable without economic rights that the Constitution fails to recognize. Either community cannot exist at all or its freedom is compromised and communal life deformed by material servitude to the masters of wealth. Thus, King's commitment to the creation of community virtually puts him in radical opposition to the existing political order. But what choice has he? If he is *really* committed to the dignity of the human person—and if this dignity and commitment is to have for him a *concrete* meaning rather than a merely abstract and metaphysical one—then he must demand economic rights and well-being essential to a dignified life. He must demand *concrete* freedom. For it was not only *legalized* racial discrimination and denial of liberties that violated the dignity of the American black. King infers that in the African American's "search for human dignity he is handicapped by the stigma of poverty in a society whose measure of value revolves around money."[48] Of course the stigma of poverty, though compounded for blacks by the malicious stigma of race, is an affliction imposed upon *all* the poor in our society. At least the danger of such a stigma hangs over the heads even of the educated middle classes, like an omen of a coming evil should they lose their footing in society.

For Dr. King, the quest for community must liberate human beings from the stigma of poverty even as it must liberate them from the stigma of race. It must end the ravaging of human lives by material deprivation and the ravaging of their spirits by a system of values that elevates things and property above people, and judges the worth of human beings by the size of their wallets. Just as it is morally wrong, and a violation of human dignity, to judge someone worthless on account of his or her race or skin color, it is unjust to judge someone worthless on account of his or her lack of money and wealth. "The dignity of the individual will flourish when the decisions concerning his life are in his own hands," King writes, "when he has the assurance that his income is stable . . . and when he knows he has the means to seek self-improvement."[49] A new order of values that affirms the *intrinsic worth* of the human being rather than measuring human worth in dollars and cents can greatly humanize interpersonal relations. Even familiar relations could then become less stressed, and more mutually affirming. "Personal conflicts between husband, wife and children will diminish when the unjust measurement of human worth on a scale of dollars is eliminated."[50] Quite possibly such a change in values accompanied by greater economic rights and well-being for *everyone* would also greatly diminish racial antagonisms among the disinherited and dispossessed. And this in turn would increase the chances of realizing the beloved community.

Now from the perspective of Dr. King, the conception and realization of this community is radical in at least two respects. First of all, its realization would require a radical transformation of the entire social order—the entire socioeconomic structure. Secondly, beloved community requires a fundamental transformation of *persons* themselves, a radical *self-transformation* that involves radically different ways of living, and of relating to self and others. It would involve such a deep moral and spiritual self-transformation that it might even be seen as akin to Frantz Fanon's idea of setting "afoot a new man."[51] And it would involve such a qualitatively different order of values that its accomplishment would be, in King's words, a "revolution of values." In his 1966 "Gandhi Memorial

Lecture" at Howard University, King indicates that the deep structural change now required involves an emphasis on class as well as race. The achievements of the Civil Rights Movement from Montgomery through Selma were accomplishable without a fundamental change in the socioeconomic order. It cost the nation nothing economically to end segregation in public accommodations or to concede to blacks the right to vote. But as we shift from civil rights to human rights, fighting economic injustice that is the perpetual twin of racial injustice, "we are grappling with basic class issues between the privileged and underprivileged." Consequently, a "restructuring of the architecture of American society" will be necessary.[52] But this restructuring, and the addressing of issues between privileged and underprivileged, requires the dissolution of myths concerning capitalism, and a critique of the values of that system. In his 1967 address in Chicago at the "National Conference for a New Politics," Dr. King's anticapitalist critique becomes more explicit:

> [W]e have deluded ourselves into believing the myth that capitalism grew and prospered out of the Protestant ethic of hard work and sacrifices. The fact is that capitalism was built on the *exploitation* and suffering of black slaves and continues to thrive on the exploitation of the poor, both black and white, both *here* and *abroad*. . . . The way to end poverty is to end the exploitation of the poor. Insure them a fair share of the government's services and the nation's resources.
>
> We must recognize that the problems of neither racial nor economic injustice can be solved without a *radical redistribution* of political and economic power.[53]

King's repudiation of the delusions of the Protestant work ethic is, of course, a rejection of one of the ideological pillars of capitalism. This is a matter of no small importance for a man who is a Protestant minister. But his argument that the wealth of capitalism is based on exploitation, past and present, at home and abroad clearly resembles critiques by many Marxist and Marxist-leaning thinkers. And since he has already argued that the twin evils of economic injustice and racism have their origins or foundations in exploitation, which in turn cannot be ended without a radical redistribution of economic and political power, it stands to reason that King seeks a radical transcendence of capitalism itself. For no radical redistribution of power is possible *within* capitalism. Thus we see an attack on the *values* of capitalism through a rejection of the Protestant ethic, and an attack on the institutional *structure* of capitalism as exploitative.

That King does seek the radical transcendence of capitalism as a condition for the triumph of community is evident in his last presidential address to the SCLC (1967). He tells his coworkers that "the movement must address itself to the question of restructuring the whole of American society." It must ask why there are tens of millions of poor people in the world's richest nation. Why is there hunger amidst abundance? But when such questions are raised, "you are raising questions about the economic system, about the broader distribution of wealth. When you ask that question, you begin to question the capitalistic economy."[54] It is essential to call into question the *whole* society.

The call for radical transformation that transcends capitalism takes on global implications in his famous speech "A Time to Break Silence," where Dr. King publicly denounces the war in Vietnam. He doesn't think that Vietnam is simply a mistake made by well-meaning American leaders. After making his case against the war, he warns that the war is a symptom of a "far deeper malady within the American spirit" and a sign of some deep-seated flaws in the American social order. And he warns, with a prophetic prescience we can appreciate today given our current military entanglements in the Middle East, that if the deeper flaws in the American social order are not addressed, we would in the future (now our present) have to protest other expressions of American militarism and interventions in other countries. He questions why we have U.S. military "advisors" in Venezuela even while Vietnam is going on. And King infers that the "need to maintain the stability of our *investments* accounts for the counterrevolutionary action of American forces in Guatemala." This economic motive also explains why American helicopters are in action against guerillas in Columbia, and why "American napalm and green beret forces have already been active against rebels in Peru."[55]

Clearly, it will take more than piecemeal reforms to end this plague of militarism and aggression. This global expression of the "malady within the American spirit" is rooted in an economic system and structure of values that places property rights above human rights. The same system of profiteering exploitation that, according to King, gave rise to slavery and white supremacy, and that imposes poverty and the stigma of poverty on millions of Americans of all racial and ethnic backgrounds, is the motivating force behind military and other intrusive interventions by the United States in various countries around the world. King has always held that "injustice anywhere is a threat to justice everywhere." And here he recognizes that exploitation is global. Hence his solidarity will be global. As King's moral philosophy commits him to reverence the inherent dignity of *all* human personality, it is hardly surprising that his vision of beloved community reaches beyond the emancipatory strivings of black America and the borders of the United States to embrace the whole of humanity. He sees that the same system that oppresses us here creates oppression and war throughout the world.

To end this injustice both globally and domestically, King thinks that we need to challenge the values as well as the structure of capitalism, though not by insurrectionary violence as often proposed by Fanon and many Marxists. But to get on the "right side of the world revolution," America must undergo a "radical revolution of values." America must make a shift from a "thing-oriented society" to a "person-oriented society."[56] For when "machines and computers, profit motives and property rights are considered more important than people, the giant triplets of racism, materialism and militarism are incapable of being conquered." This revolution of values would be a kind of transvaluation of values. This "person-centered" revolution of values would commit to radically changing an unjust social structure. The new order of values would realize that "true compassion is more than flinging a coin to a beggar." Rather, it "comes to see that the *edifice* which *produces beggars* needs restructuring."[57] Revolutionary new values would never countenance the "glaring contrast of poverty and wealth." A true revolution of values, ever mindful of the oneness of humankind, would look abroad and see "capitalists of the West investing huge sums of money in Asia, Africa and South America, only to take profits out with no concern for the social betterment of those countries" and insist "This is not just."[58] It will find endless wars to be unjust as well. The new revolutionary values would be anti-militarist.

Finally, the revolution of values would embrace the whole of humanity in a kind of global beloved community. This means that "in the final analysis that our loyalties must become ecumenical rather than sectional." The new revolutionary values would involve every nation developing "an overriding loyalty to mankind as a whole in order to preserve the best in their individual societies." King envisions a "worldwide fellowship that lifts neighborly concern beyond one's tribe, race, class and nation," leading ultimately to an "all-embracing and unconditional love for all men."[59] This is the beloved community gone global. But a necessary condition of its realization both at home and abroad is a radical transcendence of the system of exploitation, a radical transformation of an entire social order that engenders war, poverty, and racial oppression. The achievement of such a community would be a revolutionary development, and only a revolutionary movement can bring it into being.

Now one may wonder what form this revolutionary community would take. As King's conception of it clearly involves the negation of capitalism as well as racism, the ending of class as well as caste oppression, what system might King be advocating? What new laws or institutions would he propose? And what new kind of property or economy would constitute the material grounding of this new community? What would be the content of the new values ushered in by the revolution of values?

King does not offer a detailed blueprint or an elaborate treatise. He is not a systematic philosopher, and one seeks in vain if one expects from him elaborate social and political theories such as one might derive from Locke, Rousseau, Marx, or Fanon. As steps on the way to a new community with revolutionary new values, King tried to popularize the idea of economic rights. And part of his plan for the Poor Peoples Campaign was to propose an Economic Bill of Rights that would guarantee a job to all able to work, and an income for those not able to work, as well as a number of other reforms akin to some of the provisions already common in other industrial nations. But he understood that these reforms, even if won, would be only more steps to the kind of society he envisioned.

Dr. King clearly favored a democratic *cooperative* society. And this would clearly be a radical shift from the current society marked by cut-throat competition, possessive individualism, and callous materialism. But unlike a collectivist society, which smothers individual freedom while forgetting that "life is individual," Kingian community is a *mutually cooperative* and *voluntary* endeavor. It cannot be forced or imposed from above. And for King a principle of free individuality is integral to his whole notion of the inviolability of the human person, the inherent dignity of the human personality. Yet community is not imbued with the rugged individualism (or possessive individualism) that is so much a part of the culture of capitalism. For the individualist tradition fails to see that life is social. It tends to see the individual as a presocial (or asocial) being, and community or society as artificial and often a threat to individual liberty. By contrast, King sees individuality and community as inseparable. "The self cannot be a self without other selves," according to King. "All life is interrelated. All men are caught in an inescapable network of mutuality."[60] Indeed, if there is no "I" without "Thou," the individualist tradition may be said (in Kingian terms) to be a negation of the individual. And like Marx (whose materialism he opposes) King believes that "The individual is the social being."[61] For it is only in community, in relation with others, that a flowering of individuality is possible. At this point King the revolutionary Christian coincides with the secular revolutionary, Marx.

Of course, I do not mean to imply that Dr. King was a Marxist. He clearly was not, and quite strongly opposed Marx's philosophical materialism. King is more akin to Christian left radicals like El Salvador's Bishop Oscar Romero or many of our own religiously inspired nineteenth-century Abolitionists. Yet the philosopher Richard A. Jones makes perhaps a cogent point in chapter 6 of this volume when he infers that there are elements of Marx's vision in Dr. King's idea of the beloved community. King certainly read Marx, and acknowledges that *The Communist Manifesto* was authored by "men aflame with a passion for social justice."[62] We have already seen that much of King's critique of racism and capitalism resembles many Marxian critiques even if King arrives at them from a different philosophical perspective. Furthermore, King does describe Marx's idea of a classless society as a "noble end," even if he doesn't find so noble Marx's recommendation of armed insurgency as the means to that end.[63] A society without class injustice, racism, or war would neatly coincide with King's own vision of a community of freedom that affirms the dignity of every human personality.

Moreover, we now know from recent research that Dr. King was sympathetic to the idea of a socialist society—a *democratic socialism*. Some of the Social Gospel theologians whom he studied leaned in a socialist direction. Also, we have it on record that at a 1966 SCLC staff meeting, he stated to the gathering that "something is wrong with capitalism . . . there must be a better distribution of wealth, and maybe America must move toward a Democratic Socialism."[64] And while in Scandinavia to receive the 1964 Nobel Prize, he evinced much interest in Scandinavia's democratic socialist tradition. But King was not a socialist theoretician or politician. He identified with no particular party or ideology. His commitment is more ethical than theoretical. He is morally committed to a society characterized by mutual cooperation, freedom, and brotherhood. And his solidarity knew no bounds.

In his vision of community, a cooperative spirit would supersede the acquisitive spirit of our exploitative society. Human beings would come to understand that true wealth "comes as a result of the *commonwealth*," and that there is no material treasure of equal or greater value than the human personality. Whether we are secular or religious, we would come to see that "life is sacred." We would cease to deify profits and property. We would see that "property is intended to serve life, and no matter how much we surround it with rights and respect, it has no personal being."[65] Of course, in such a community no one can be scorned on account of his or her race. There can be no illegal aliens, for no *fellow* human being can be *alien* to me. Humanity would be one, and with all its marvelous diversity. But to achieve this we would need to transform not only the institutional structures of society, we would have to transform ourselves. We must transform society in order to transform ourselves, and transform ourselves so as to transform society. We must bring about a moral and spiritual self-transformation whereby we "re-establish the spiritual ends of our lives in *personal character* and *social justice*."[66] In our own era—more polarized than in King's time between haves and have-nots, and with the racial divide far from healed—how well we rise to the challenge of personal and social transformation may soon determine whether our future will be one of loving communities or desolate chaos.

NOTES

1. It is to Dr. Rufus Burrows Jr. that I owe the expression "person-in-community" as a description of King's conception of human being and the relation of individual and community. For further reference see especially chapter 6 ("Personal Communitarianism and Beloved Community") in his book *God and Human Dignity: The Personalism, Theology and Ethics of Martin Luther King, Jr.* (Notre Dame: University of Notre Dame Press, 2006), 155–81.

2. Martin Luther King Jr., *Stride toward Freedom* (San Francisco: HarperCollins, 1986), 100.

3. Ibid., 100.

4. Burrows, 157.

5. Martin Luther King Jr., *The Trumpet of Conscience* (New York: Harper & Row Publishers, Inc., 1968), 69.

6. Martin Luther King Jr., "Facing the Challenge of a New Age," in *A Testament of Hope: The Essential Writings and Speeches of Martin Luther King, Jr.*, ed. James M. Washington (San Francisco: HarperCollins, 1986), 140.

7. *Testament of Hope*, 117–25. King describes these as "Ethical Demands of Integration."

8. Ibid., 118–19. Some scholars like Lewis Baldwin and Rufus Burrow also see this emphasis on the God-given dignity of man in the "homespun" social gospel or Personalistic philosophy that was deeply rooted in African American culture, and in the African cultural background of African American culture. This point is especially emphasized in Burrow's *God and Human Dignity*.

9. *A Testament of Hope*, 119.

10. *Testament of Hope*, 119.

11. *Testament of Hope*, 119.

12. Testament, 119.

13. *Testament*, 120.

14. John J. Ansbro, *Martin Luther King, Jr.: The Making of a Mind* (Maryknoll, NY: Orbis Books, 1992), 102–4. Ansbro reasons that Dr. King valued Sartre's doctrine of human freedom, even while rejecting Sartrean atheism. Ansbro also infers that King could subscribe to Sartre's notion that one must choose for all humanity, since this would coincide with King's own Personalist conviction about the interrelated structure of humanity.

15. *A Testament of Hope*, 120. It should be pointed out that Personalism, which King describes as his "basic philosophical position," also emphasizes the primacy of freedom. But unlike Sartrean existentialism, Personalism holds to the idea that there are objective "moral laws." One recalls appeals to eternal moral laws in King's famous "Letter from Birmingham Jail" where such laws form the criteria for justice in all human statutes. The importance for King of objective moral law and moral order of the universe is examined in some detail in chapter 7 of Burrow's *God and Human Dignity*.

16. *A Testament of Hope*, 120.

17. *God and Human Dignity*, 179.

18. *Testament of Hope*, 122.

19. However, King is not a proponent of that superficial liberal universalism (pilloried by Sartre) that "recognizes neither Jew, nor Arab, nor Negro, nor bourgeois, nor worker, but only man...." King is well aware of the historical-social reality of race and racial inequality. But while acknowledging its social reality, he denies it any metaphysical or "natural" status.

20. *Testament of Hope*, 122 (my italics).

21. Martin Buber, *Paths in Utopia* (Syracuse: Syracuse University Press, 1996), 133. While I am not certain of the degree to which King studied Buber, his frequent allusions to Buber's *I and Thou* indicates not only familiarity but a sense of affinity. Indeed, King's dialectical critique of the rapacious capitalism of the West and the coercive authoritarianism of the former Soviet East resembles (even in its manner of expression) Buber's critique of individualism and collectivism in *Between Man and Man*.

22. Georg Hegel, *Reason in History* (Upper Saddle River: NJ: Prentice-Hall, Inc., 1997), 24.

23. From *Martin Luther King, Jr. Papers Project*, vol. IV, *Symbol of the Movement* (San Francisco: University of California Press, 2000), 149–50 (my italics). I would like to thank Professor John McClendon III for bringing to my attention James's correspondence with Dr. King, and his evaluation of King's method and movement as revolutionary.

24. Martin Luther King Jr., *The Autobiography of Martin Luther King, Jr.*, edited by Clayborne Carson (New York: Warner Books, 1998), 125.

25. Ibid., 12.

26. Ibid.

27. *A Testament of Hope*, 293.

28. Ibid.

29. Martin Luther King Jr., *Strength to Love* (New York: Walker and Company, 1981), 48 (my italics).

30. *A Testament of Hope*, 119.

31. Martin Luther King Jr., *Where Do We Go from Here: Chaos or Community?* (Boston: Beacon Press, 1967), 70 (my italics).

32. *Stride toward Freedom*, 90.

33. Ibid., 90.

34. *Where Do We Go from Here*, 71.

35. Ibid., 71–73.

36. Ibid., 74–75.

37. Ibid., 75 (my italics).

38. See *The Autobiography of Martin Luther King, Jr.*, 36. In the letter to Coretta Scott he also mentions his own socialistic inclinations.

39. *Stride toward Freedom*, 94.

40. Ibid., 94.

41. Cornel West, *Democracy Matters: Winning the Fight against Imperialism* (New York: Penguin Press, 2004), 158.

42. Robert Franklin Mitchell Jr., "An Ethic of Hope: The Moral Thought of Martin Luther King, Jr.," *Seminary Quarterly Review* 40, no. 4 (January 1986): 41–43.

43. Historian Thomas F. Jackson argues that many activists (King included) believed even before the 1960s that "racial and economic justice were indissoluble." Since at least the 1930s, many civil rights organizations pursued a "dual agenda" of civil rights and economic justice. King would have inherited that legacy, of which his own father was an exemplar. Moreover, there was "tradition of often religiously inspired *democratic socialism*" within many black churches, progressive seminaries, on some campuses, and in some trade unions from the 1930s to the 1950s. King encountered this during this student days, and was deeply influenced by the ideas of the democratic left of the time. For further discussion see Thomas F. Jackson, *From Civil Rights to Human Rights: Martin Luther King, Jr. and the Struggle for Economic Justice* (Philadelphia: University of Pennsylvania Press, 2007).

44. *A Testament of Hope*, 58. Italics mine.

45. *From Civil Rights to Human Rights*, 5.

46. *Where Do We Go from Here?*, 79.

47. Ibid.

48. Ibid., 87.

49. Ibid., 164.

50. Ibid.

51. Frantz Fanon, *The Wretched of the Earth* (New York: Grove Press, 1968), 316.

52. Robert Franklin Mitchell Jr., "An Ethic of Hope," 45.

53. Ibid., 45.

54. *A Testament of Hope*, 250.

55. Ibid., 240.

56. Ibid.

57. Ibid, p. 241.

58. Ibid.

59. Ibid., 242.

60. Ibid., 122.

61. Karl Marx, *Writings of the Young Marx on Philosophy and Society*, ed. Loyd D. Easton and Kurt Guddat (Indianapolis: Hacket Publishing Company, 1997), 306.

62. *Strength to Love*, 172.

63. Ibid., 168.
64. "An Ethic of Hope," 46.
65. *The Trumpet of Conscience*, 56.
66. *Strength to Love*, 123.

EIGHT

Martin Luther King Jr.

Toward a Democratic Theory

Tim Lake

Democracy is an attractive political system because it is flexible and able to appropriate the changing and, often, conflicting needs, desires, and expectations of persons seeking to gain the maximum benefit from their lives. The grand idea of democratic rule—where ordinary individuals participate in the governance of the state—might be the greatest political idea that human beings have come up with for balancing individual liberty with a respect for the liberty of others. But there is no guarantee that a democratic state will be benign or materially beneficial for every person. In fact, there is no certain or truly democratic state.

Even America, the longest democratic experiment in the history of the world, has never been an absolute democracy; there have always been those who did not fully count. For all of its grandeur, democracy is, however, an approximate solution to the perpetual quest for a just society. It is difficult, to say the least, to establish political institutions and social networks that bring together liberal notions of (1) respect for the individual and the radical equality of persons with (2) the imperative of cooperative work and shared responsibility while (3) holding at bay the demons of warfare, intolerance, and, as Martin Luther King Jr. puts it, "man's inhumanity to man." "To complete a process of democratization which our nation has too long developed too slowly," writes King, "is our most powerful weapon for world respect and emulation." Therefore, for King at least, part of what it means to live a democratic life is to make a commitment to the work of making democracy a certainty—benevolent and gratifying—for all.

King understood the contradictions inherent in America's constitutional democracy in terms of its class, racial, and gender exclusivity. King was clear about the disjuncture between "thin paper" democracy and "thick action" democracy. "For a hundred years since emancipation, Negroes had searched for the elusive path to freedom," writes King. "The words of the Constitution had declared them free, but life had told them that they were a twice-burdened people—they lived in the lowest stratum of society, and within it they were additionally imprisoned by a caste of color."[1]

It is clear that neither the Declaration of Independence (1776) nor the Constitution of the United States of America (1787) has the power to make the benefits of democracy a reality for all persons. "As splendid as are the words," however, King laments over the shortcomings of the Declaration of Independence because "there are disquieting implications in the fact that the original phrasing was altered to delete a condemnation of the British monarch for his espousal of slavery."[2]

To make democracy true and certain for all requires more than words on paper, it requires individuals who are willing to commit their bodies and, in some cases, their lives to the work of freedom and human equality. The two ideas that dominate King's December 1955 address to the first mass meeting of the newly formed Montgomery Improvement Association (MIA) were love and democracy. He told the throng of people,

> We are here in a general sense because first and foremost we are American citizens and we are determined to apply our citizenship to the fullness of its meaning. We are here also because of our love for democracy, because of our deep-seated belief that democracy transformed from thin paper to thick action is the greatest form of government on earth.[3]

The Montgomery bus protest would be about, among other things, the work of democratic transformation and the application of a multiracial democracy. For King, the true value of democracy lies in a radical application of its tenets of human equality and liberty and, to a far lesser degree, in the written expression of those tenets.

King was, of course, cognizant of the democratizing potential of the U.S. Constitution with its Bill of Rights and subsequent amendments. In particular, the granting of the right of protest (i.e., the First Amendment) acts as a sort of counter-majoritarian protection for minority constituents. "The only weapon that we have in our hands," King told the Holts Street crowd, "is the weapon of protest. That's all."

But protest must be conducted with civility and within the spirit of democracy itself. Indeed, for King, the most constructive protest takes the form of nonviolent resistance and is directed by an ethic of love. "This is the glory of America, with all of its faults," continues King. "This is the glory of our democracy. . . . The great glory of American democracy is the right to protest for right."[4] Here the minority—the politically weak, economically poor, and otherwise disenfranchised—can mount an offensive against usurpations of their liberty or full recognition within the polity.

For King, the "promise of democracy" is liberty and equality. The choice is between "democracy's fulfillment or fascism's triumph; for social progress or retrogression. We can choose either to walk the high road of human brotherhood or to tread the low road of man's inhumanity to man."[5]

King's use of the phrase "human brotherhood" encapsulates his understanding of the social nature of human existence and the interrelatedness of all humanity. King's vision of the "beloved community," which also embodied the concepts of universal love and justice, represents the long quest of African Americans for an America where the principles of democracy would be afforded to all. "Ever since the signing of the Declaration of Independence, America has manifested a schizophrenic personality on the question of race. She has been torn between selves—a self in which she has sadly practiced the antithesis of democracy," exclaims King.

But freedom and equality cannot be distributed piecemeal as the "Founding Fathers" intended; the right to freedom is whole because it is constitutive of personhood.[6] Moreover, justice requires "that liberty not be divided into installments, doled out on a deferred-payment plan."[7] All oppressed people know that a partial liberty is no liberty and "a faltering democracy" can no longer be sanctioned.[8] "There comes a time," said King at the initial Holt Street mass meeting, "when people get tired of being trampled over by the iron feet of oppression."

King spoke to a Negro community, and for a generation, that possessed a keen sense of urgency for social equality and complete enfranchisement. Perhaps, King also perceived a similar sense of urgency—in the wake of anticolonial campaigns in India, Africa, and Latin America— among the world's oppressed people for their liberation. For King, however, it was a peculiar and "bitter irony" that "Negroes had seen their government go to the brink of nuclear conflict more than once" for the preservation of the freedom of those "in foreign lands." Meanwhile, America's "readiness for heroic measures in the defense of Negro liberty disappeared or became tragically weak."[9]

America can become a fully democratic society where individuals participate in decision-making processes at the highest levels and enjoy an equal share of the benefits of citizenship within the state, but this requires the collective involvement of all sectors of society. "There will be neither rest nor tranquility in America until the Negro is granted his citizenship rights," warns King. "The whirlwinds of revolt will continue to shake the foundation of our nation until the bright day of justice emerges."[10] It is not a matter of more or less democracy but full democracy. As King states, "We cannot be satisfied as long as a Negro in Mississippi cannot vote and a Negro in New York believes he has nothing for which to vote."[11]

For King, the work of democracy includes the formation and maintenance of a social personality that coheres with his philosophy of nonviolence and universal ethic of love. King's democratic vision rests upon a human psychology that posits a radical unity of all persons. This radical unity of humanity is captured in his oft-quoted catchphrase, "I cannot be what I ought to be unless you are able to be what you ought to be." This sense of human interconnectivity and interdependability leads King to view forced separation as sin and violence as self-defeating. Additionally, King argues that a universal ethic of love should beat within the chest of each democratic person. The desire for freedom, the desire for justice, and the desire for the affirmation of our personhood are natural yearnings of human beings. King's universal ethic of love requires that we pursue these natural desires in a manner that conjoins the possibility for others to also achieve their legitimate desires. For King, a democratic life means having a personality that is constituted by the philosophy of nonviolence and tempered by the spirit of love.

By the time that King completed his formal education, he had embraced nonviolent resistance against pacifism as a method for achieving social justice. King states, "At this time, however, I had merely an intellectual understanding and appreciation of the position, with no firm determination to organize it in a socially effective situation."[12] King did not initiate the Montgomery bus protest, he merely responded to the call to serve as its spokesperson.

King's philosophy of nonviolent direct action recognizes that individual persons can become caught in evil systems of their own making. However, it is the system that must be destroyed and not persons. Nonviolent direct action is the best moral response to oppression because it allows the oppressed to serve as agents of their liberation by transmuting hatred into constructive energy. The goal is freedom for both the oppressed and the oppressor. Here, the oppressed comes to see their oppressor as an individual person who is in need of transformation and not annihilation. Therefore, the oppressed should turn their energies toward defeating the evil system that enables the evil actions of individuals while seeking to save the individual.[13] It is the transformative aim of nonviolent direct action that makes it "a methodology and philosophy of revolution" as opposed to a mere call to revolt.

Nonviolent direct action seeks to create such a crisis and to foster such a tension that a reticent government is forced to confront, no matter the particular issue. The tension that nonviolence resistance seeks is a not "violent tension" but a "constructive tension." King explains,

Just as Socrates felt that it was necessary to create a tension in the mind so that individuals could rise from the bondage of myths and half-truths to the unfettered realm of creative analysis and objective apprai-sal, so must we see the need for nonviolent gadflies to create the kind of tension in society that will help men rise from the dark depths of prejudice and racism to majestic heights of understanding and brother-hood.[14]

An additional difference between these two types of tensions—violent and creative—rests in the ends for which they are employed. King con-cedes that the nonviolent position can be used as a political tactic to further both good and evil ends. For example, it is conceivable that a government can nonviolently impose sanctions upon those who, through nonviolent means, oppose laws that are themselves unjust. In such a situation, the tension created may be so latent that it does not register on the conscience or sufficiently disturb the "peace" of the polity. In such a case, the nonviolent protester may enjoy a "moral advantage" but not a "power advantage."

If we think of slavery as a morally indefensible system of exploitation and domination of relative powerless persons by powerful institutions under the control of a privileged group, then, it is possible to conclude that for 244 years the American government used its power advantage in the furtherance of unjust racial relationships despite the moral advantage of enslaved person over enslavers.[15] King answers this objection by pointing out that it is not enough to simply adopt a position of nonvio-lence; rather nonviolence must be connected to the moral bent of the universe—justice and human equality. "I have tried to make clear," argued King, "that it is wrong to use immoral means to attain moral ends. But now I must affirm that it is just as wrong, or perhaps even more so, to use moral means to preserve immoral ends."[16]

For King, justice requires action on the part of the just individual. This is the case because (1) "He who passively accepts evil is as much in-volved in it as he who helps to perpetrate it." King continues, (2) "He who accepts evil without protesting against it is really cooperating with it." We can see Reinhold Niebuhr's influence on King. For Niebuhr there is no way of distancing ourselves from the evil caused by the social systems that we create and, at least tacitly, endorse. What (3) justice re-quires is that we withhold our cooperation with social structures that oppress people. While this does not free us from responsibility for the evil generated from our social systems, it is the best option for those who seek to mitigate (it is not possible to eliminate completely) the effects of egoistic social systems. When (4) we refuse to participate in unjust sys-tems we make a positive gesture toward justice, which has the effect of highlighting the evil perpetrated by the unjust system and, thereby, un-masking the consequences of the actions of both the oppressed and op-pressor.

This unmasking is important because "often the oppressor goes along unaware of the evil involved in his oppression so long as the oppressed accept it." However, once forced to see the reality of the harmful effects of maintaining unjust social relations, both parties must consciously choose to either act in ways that will end the current oppressive arrangement or maintain it. For King, "a righteous man has no alternative but to refuse to cooperate with an evil system."[17]

King suggests that there is a psychological element in the philosophy of nonviolent direct action that works against attitudes of "complacency," "bitterness and hatred." "Nonviolence had tremendous psychological importance to the Negro," King wrote,

> He had to win and to vindicate his dignity in order to merit and enjoy his self-esteem. He had to let white men know that the picture of him as a clown—irresponsible, resigned and believing in his own inferiority— was a stereotype with no validity. This method was grasped by the Negro masses because it embodied the dignity of struggle, of moral conviction and self-sacrifice.[18]

For King, the philosophy of nonviolent resistance, however, must project an attitude of love. Oppressed people will not tolerate their oppression forever. The philosophy of nonviolence, however, offers a morality and political strategy that reflects the highest respect for the humanity of the oppressor while at the same time allowing for the legitimate right of the oppressed to resist. King surmises,

> Man was born into barbarism when killing his fellow man was a normal condition of existence. He became endowed with a conscience. And he has now reached the day when violence toward another human being must become as abhorrent as eating another's flesh. Nonviolence, the answer to the Negroes' need, may become the answer to the most desperate need of all humanity.[19]

Public demonstrations are ways to release pent-up anger without violent destruction. In short, they are acts of psychological therapy for a people who have a sense of legitimate discontent and rage. "So I have not said to my people: 'Get rid of your discontent.' Rather, I have tried to say that this normal healthy discontent can be channeled into the creative outlet of nonviolent direct action," explains King.[20] Complacency and bitterness are extreme attitudes toward the perpetrators of injustice, but the consequences of these two attitudes are objectionable to the cause of justice and love. "So, the question," wrote King, "is not whether we will be extremists, but what kind of extremist we will be." King argued that the healthy psychological attitude is to be an "extremist" for love and justice.[21]

King understood nonviolent resistance to be democratic in that it welcomes recruits on a nondiscriminatory basis.

To join an army that trains its adherents in the methods of violence, you must be of a certain age. But in Birmingham, some of the most valued foot soldiers were youngsters ranging from elementary pupils to teen-age high school and college students. For acceptance in the armies that maim and kill, one must be physically sound, possessed of straight limbs and accurate vision. But in Birmingham, the lame and the halt and the crippled could and did join up.[22]

In addition to these relaxed age and physical restrictions, the nonviolent army is classless. "In Birmingham, outside of the few generals and lieutenants who necessarily directed and coordinated operations, the regiments of the demonstrators marched in democratic phalanx. Doctors marched with window cleaners. Lawyers demonstrated with laundresses. PhDs and no-Ds were treated with perfect equality by the registrars of the nonviolent movement." King concludes, "In the nonviolent army, there is room for everyone who wants to join up."[23]

The army of nonviolence might accept all applicants; however, it imposes a special encumbrance upon those who suffer. Returning once again to Niebuhr, King writes:

Lamentably, it is an historical fact that privileged groups seldom give up their privileges voluntarily. Individuals may see the moral light and voluntarily give up their unjust posture; but, as Reinhold Niebuhr has reminded us, groups tend to be more immoral than individuals.[24]

It seems that the oppressed have to make a greater commitment to the transformation of oppressive systems. Here, liberation must be demanded by the oppressed because freedom does not come "by a passive acceptance of suffering. However freedom is won by a struggle *against* suffering. By this measure, Negroes have not yet paid the full price for freedom. And whites have not yet faced the full cost of justice."[25]

But it would not be easy to get Negroes to quit "sobbing" and pay the price of freedom—through the currency of nonviolence and love. The "work of democracy" would include a reconstruction of both black and white identities. To black Americans, King pleaded, "As long as the mind is enslaved the body can never be free." In order to begin the process of emancipation the internalization of their oppression must be challenged and surmounted. As King states, "Psychological freedom, a firm sense of self-esteem, is the most powerful weapon against the long night of physical slavery."[26]

For King, the oppressed come into a new self-awareness, a greater appreciation of their own value, when they resist their oppressor. King told his people that a "New Negro" was emerging on the American scene, and he attributes this rebirth to changes that were ushered in with the events that transpired at the turn of the century. In the wake of two World Wars, the stock market crash of 1929, the industrialization and urbanization of American cities, the great migration of blacks from south to north "all conjoined to cause the Negro to take a fresh look at himself."

Additionally, increased opportunities and mobility for the Negro citizen led to "a consciousness that he is an equal . . . and accordingly should be given rights and privileges commensurate with his new responsibilities." According to King, Negroes were in the process of constructing for themselves a new identity. "He has come to feel that he is somebody. His religion reveals to him that God loves all His children and that the important thing about a man is not "his specificity but his fundamentum"—his eternal worth to God.[27]

This "new consciousness" reflects a repudiation of the "tragic sense of inferiority" acquired during slavery and segregation. King used the mass meetings that started with the Montgomery bus protest as sites for black identity reformation through the philosophy of nonviolent direct action and universal ethic of love. King told the throng of black Montgomery citizens gathered at Holt Street Baptist Church in December of 1955 that there was "no alternative but to protest." The condition of their suffering had finally come to a head, and they would have to choose a different response other than "patience." He told them, "Tonight we have come here to be saved from that patience that makes us patient with anything less than freedom and justice."[28]

After redefining black patience, he launched into the work of shaping black America into a nonviolent army equipped with the sole weapons of love and peaceful protest. Over and over again he stressed the democratic character of their struggle; the third sentence he spoke that December night is particularly telling. King said, "We are here also because of our love for democracy, because of our deep-seated belief that democracy transformed from thin paper to thick action is the greatest form of government on earth." He said that they were "merely insisting on the dignity and worth of every human personality." And he went on to say that they had to be prepared to "sacrifice" and "maybe some of them will have to die" for justice. Shortly afterward King left the meeting.[29]

King would use his considerable media exposure as a public stage to reconstruct America's democratic identity by placing emphasis on the democratic content of his philosophy of nonviolence. He wrote,

> When a police dog buried his fangs in the ankle of a small child in Birmingham, he buried his fangs in the ankle of every American. The bell of man's inhumanity to man does not toll for any one man. It tolls for you, for me, for all of us.[30]

This was a different identity that King was asking both white Americans and black Americans to accept as their American identity. The struggle of reconstituting a new inclusive American identity went beyond matters of public policy. As the motto adopted by King's Southern Christian Leadership Conference (SCLC) proclaimed, this was a struggle "to save the soul of America."[31] King put it into his own words,

> Eventually the civil-rights movement will have contributed infinitely more to the nation than the eradication of racial injustice. It will have enlarged the concept of brotherhood to a vision of total interrelatedness.[32]

It is understandable that we should seek personal justice in our lives. Here, "personal justice" means the desire for internal harmony that Duane Cady argues for in his interpretation of justice in the *Republic*. "Justice," states Socrates, "isn't concerned with someone's doing his own externally, but with what is inside him" (*Republic* 443c7–9). The just individual, like the balanced state, is at peace within. Socrates makes the connection between justice and harmony clear when he states, "an action that destroys this harmony is unjust" (*Republic* 443e6–7).

In fact, there is no place in King's thinking for the very notion that humans possess the capacity to become beautiful, wise, or just absent the aid of divine power. Without getting into a protracted theological discussion on the nature of human sin and God's plan for human redemption, let me offer that King maintains a strong position regarding the need for Divine Grace (II Peter 1.3–4). The divine-human relationship is a Holy-sinner relationship, and therefore, Divine Grace involves forgiveness, love, and reconciliation.

Love respects the inherent goodness that's within "the best of us . . . and within the worst of us." This is an extension of the Christian idea that humanity was created in the image of God. Here, King interprets this as an "element of goodness that [we] can never slough off."[33] In a sense, King views good and evil as twin features of human psychology. He often exclaimed, "There is something within all of us that causes us to cry out with Plato that the human personality is like a charioteer with two headstrong horses, each wanting to go in different directions."[34] Additionally, these contrasting features of the human personality are also within the cosmology. King states, "There is a tension at the heart of the universe between good and evil." Again, he cites Plato for support, "Platonic philosophy used to refer to it as a tension between body and soul. . . . Whatever you call it, there is a struggle in the universe between good and evil."[35]

For King, to love someone is to respect the life-promoting creative goodwill for all that lies within each of us. When we operate out of this understanding of love, it becomes possible to love someone while seeking to defeat an evil system that they may be caught in. This is the sort of justice, in King's view, that we owe to our enemy.

Like Socrates, King acknowledges that the aim of injustice is to do harm, and he also assigns this attribute to hate.[36] However, he takes it a step further by asserting that hate harms both the hated and the hater. King put it this way:

> For the person who hates, you can stand up and see a person and that person can be beautiful, and you will call them ugly. . . . For the person who hates, the good becomes the bad and the bad becomes the good. For the person who hates, the true becomes false and the false becomes true. . . . Hate destroys the very structure of the personality of the hater.[37]

Love calls us to act toward others in beneficial ways because by doing so we benefit ourselves.[38] For King, justice and injustice are both linked to the collective state of the human personality. That is, individual dis/harmony is linked to the dis/harmony of others.[39] So, the rich individual is just when he/she uses his/her wealth as a resource to balance their individual harmony with that of others who are disharmonious.

It has already been pointed out that, for King, love is greater than justice. Moreover, love plays a determinative and evaluative role in human expressions of justice. It is the measure of one's love—respect for the dignity of the human person—that will determine whether or not our actions are genuinely just. It is not enough to be just because of some advantage or out of fear of penalty, but we must be just because we have love for others.

It is possible to perform good acts that result in positive consequences and to make right choices that correctly interpret reality. However, good acts and right choices are the measures of justice, but are not sufficient motives for justice. A crucial requirement of justice is to be motivated by love—a creative, redemptive, goodwill toward all persons. For King, to define justice in terms of our behaviors—that is, justice as an act or choice—makes us both the subject and object of justice. Defining justice as an act or choice is problematic because we are egoistic, finite, and, to King, sinners who lack the capacity to live consistent lives. King writes,

> A persistent schizophrenia leaves so many of us tragically divided against ourselves. On the one hand, we proudly profess certain sublime and noble principles, but on the other hand, we sadly practice the very antithesis of those principles. . . . This strange dichotomy, this agonizing gulf between the ought and the is, represents the tragic theme of man's earthly pilgrimage."[40]

In order to live a consistent life, where our deeds match our creeds, we need an inerrant guide and a source of empowerment. Philosophy cannot serve as our guide because it reflects our human limitations. Neither can human will power serve us because we experience a failure of will when it comes to matching our deeds with our creeds (see Romans 7.18–19). For King, the solution lies in the life and death of Jesus the Christ. King writes, "Never in history was there a more sublime example of the consistency of words and deed."[41] The life and death of Jesus represents the singular moment in history when someone lived a just life, possessed sufficient power to bring his actions in line with this noble desire, and was motivated by love. King confessed, "Every time I look at the cross I am reminded of the greatness of God and the redemptive power of Jesus Christ." He continues, "I am reminded of the beauty of sacrificial love and the majesty of unswerving devotion of truth."[42]

Jesus is the example of how loving others can lead to the just life. When our actions accord with God's agape power, we are freed from the faulty realms of human action and decision-making, and our actions acquire transhistorical and universal value. In the life and death of Jesus we learn how to live a consistent life with the love of God. Jesus's life and death was an act of loving-justice.

What we learn from the life and death of Jesus is that it is impossible to achieve justice without love. Following Niebuhr, King placed love, God, justice, reality, and humanity on a single continuum. Paraphrasing Niebuhr, King wrote in a student paper,

> Justice is never discontinuously related to love. Justice is a negative application of love. . . . Justice is a check (by force, if necessary) upon ambitions of individuals seeking to overcome their insecurity at that expense of others. Justice is love's message for the collective mind.[43]

King would later reduce this thought to the pithy phrase, "Justice is love in calculation."

For King, love is aligned with justice and, therefore, certain norms like giving each their due, paying debts, persuasion, and coercion without violence are "the tools of justice."[44] In this sense the philosophy of nonviolence is an educational tool for training persons in the tools of justice, but the Christian doctrine of love "is the regulating ideal." King writes, "Christ furnished the spirit and motivation, while Gandhi furnished the method."[45] In studying the life of Jesus we can see that justice—noble intentions accompanied with noble actions—is possible with "the love of God operating in the human heart."[46] Again, here, we are to understand the divine personality as participating in our private and public affairs and this enables us to perform justice.

Also, love provides an adequate assessment of human justice because love, as King understood it, has transformative powers. King said, "And I am foolish enough to believe that through the power of this love somewhere, men of the most recalcitrant bent will be transformed. And then we will be in God's kingdom."[47] We can satisfy the demands of justice only by mastering our will; however, the human tendency to sin is great, and our reason is insufficient for the task. What we need is an ethic of love to direct us toward the path of justice and the transformation of the human condition. That is, it directs justice toward the establishment of the "Beloved Community."

Love's transformative power is both personal and social. As a Christian minister, King understood his commitment to the love of others as the proper response to the creative love of God within everyone. As such, the love of God is demonstrated in the life and death of Jesus the Christ. King saw his Christian mission as twofold. He stated, "On the one hand I must attempt to change the soul of individuals so that their societies may be changed. On the other I must attempt to change the societies so that the individual soul will have a change."[48] The human condition can only be improved when our souls and social relationships are altered. Through our observations and reflections the soul can be conditioned and/or reconditioned toward true justice, but the highest direction is toward love. This is the basis of King's philosophical and theological orientation. He asserts, "Yes, it is love that will save our world and our civilization."[49] On a different occasion, King asserted that there is "something in human nature that can respond to goodness. So that man is neither innately good nor is he innately bad; he has the potentialities for both."[50]

If, as Socrates puts it, a just person seeks that which is good for others and not their own advantage, then, King would add that a just person loves everyone and seeks to transform the human soul and the social condition by serving humanity. Here, just persons are the "servants" of others—as opposed to "rulers" over others. On this point, King's own words best reveal his thinking. King said,

> If any of you are around when I have to meet my day, I don't want a long funeral. And if you get somebody to deliver the eulogy, tell them not to talk too long. And every now and then I wonder what I want them to say. Tell them not to mention that I have a Nobel Peace Prize— that isn't important. Tell them not to mention that I have three or four hundred other awards—that's not important. Tell them not to mention where I went to school.
>
> I'd like somebody to say that day that Martin Luther King, Jr., tried to give his life serving others.
>
> I'd like for somebody to say that day that Martin Luther King, Jr. tried to love Somebody . . .
>
> I want you to say that I tried to love and serve humanity.
>
> Yes, if you want to say that I was a drum major, say that I was a drum major for justice. Say that I was a drum major for peace. I was a drum major for righteousness.[51]

Love, service, justice, and peace are virtues to be used in the pursuit of a righteous and harmonious life within the will of God. Using the Judeo-Christian bible, King put the question of the virtue of justice within the context of African American history. He states,

> Centuries ago Jeremiah raised a question, "Is there no balm in Gilead? Is there no physician there?" He raised it because he saw the good

people suffering so often and the evil people prospering. Centuries later our slave foreparents came along. And they too saw the injustices of life, and had nothing to look forward to morning after morning but the rawhide whip of the overseer, long rows of cotton and the sizzling heat. But they did an amazing thing. They looked back across the centuries and they took Jeremiah's question mark and straightened it into an exclamation point. And they could sing, "There is a balm in Gilead to make the wounded whole. There is a balm in Gilead to heal the sin-sick soul."[52]

For King, justice is not merely a matter of dialectical reasoning, but a grave matter for those who suffer unjustly either by the direct hand of individuals or government policy. Justice must be concerned with the daily lives of those who are on the bottom as well as those at the top (and in the lagging middle) and is measured through our love for humanity. King insists that there is a mysterious force at work in the universe that grounds all reality—this force cannot be absolutely explained in material or metaphysical terms. Here, King's thinking displays the influence of antirationalist scholars who accepted the limitations of reason to make us better. He asserts, "History is ultimately guided by spirit, not matter."[53] Hence, spirit (read divine love) acts in human history by moving us along a preselected path toward the beloved community. While the destination is already determined, the contours of the journey will be fixed by our willingness to bend and turn as the spirit of love leads. And love allows us to see and correct our errors as we try to bring the just society into existence. King often exclaimed that the moral arc of the universe is long but it bends toward justice.

In concord with Socrates's reasoning regarding like things desiring to outdo their opposites, King declares that love responds to love and, hence, reveals our dependency on others.[54] As stated above, the idea that people possess the image of God (read Love of God) is central to King's philosophy and theology. It is this innate creative Love that ultimately gives humanity its inalienable dignity. So, when we love each other without conditions, we reflect the divine love ("creative goodwill for all") for each person, and this makes humanity a special part of the created order. That we are made in the image of God also means that we are all interconnected and interdependent. As King says, "We are tied together in life and in the world"—what affects one directly affects others indirectly."[55]

As to whether it is best to be just or unjust, King explicates the soul in somewhat different terms than Socrates. While he never offers a definition of the "soul" *per se*, it is clear that King takes it to be a constitutive element of human psychology. At certain points, however, King identifies the soul in terms of our heart's desire. But such desires are not measured by our success in achieving them. King warns, "As you set out to build the temple of peace you are left lonesome; you are left discouraged; you are left bewildered."[56] It is the intrinsic good (i.e., love) contained within our heart's desire itself that determines its value. King continues,

> Well, that is the story of life. And the thing that makes me happy is that I can hear a voice crying through the vista of time, saying: "It may not come today or it may not come tomorrow, but it is well that it is within thine heart. It's well that you are trying."[57]

In short, it is the trying and desire to be a just person and not the accomplishment of an actual just life that gives our lives value and indicates our love and respect for others.

> If any of you are around when I have to meet my day. . . . I'd like somebody to mention that day that Martin Luther King, Jr. tried to give his life serving others. . . . I want you to say that I tried to love and serve humanity.[58]

For King, the goal of living a just life should be our hearts desire, however, we may never obtain it. This is the case because the virtue of justice lies in the motivation to act out of love, which is the creative pursuit of corporate harmony, and not our potential for achieving internal harmony. Here, the function of justice is love conceived as understanding (empathy and compassion), creative (perpetual possibility) goodwill for all. And when justice aims at love, the transformation of the soul and society, it has virtue. In the final analysis, King reasoned that justice, at its best, is love correcting everything that stands against love.[59]

For King, the human family is an interdependent whole and the measure of a just world is displayed in the response shown to those who suffer and the respect shown to those with whom we disagree. King's approach to resolving conflict was to deploy the practice of nonviolent direct action. In his philosophy of nonviolent direct action, King was able to combine the love imperative of the Christian faith tradition with the demand of a long-aggrieved people for justice. But, as King said of the failure of the government to enforce the ruling of the Supreme Court in the 1954 case of *Brown v. Board of Education,* justice too long delayed is justice denied.

Enfranchisement is the linchpin of procedural democracy. The right to vote for our leaders also entails the right to reject certain leaders. The right to vote is the popular expression of the people's right to shape (and reshape) the body politic. King's criticism of the war threatened the passage of legislation aimed at securing the right of African Americans to have a voice in the selection of those who would govern.

Increasingly, King came to see that he could not remain silent about the war in Vietnam. Furthermore, he considered it his democratic duty to voice his objections to government policies and actions that he deemed wrong-headed and/or nonvirtuous. He told his staff, "We have moved from the era of civil rights to the era of human rights." No longer would

King confine himself to concerns of matters of due process (i.e., voting, equal protection, desegregation, etc.) that require little financial cost from the government and left the maldistribution of resources, imbalance of political power, and disparate material conditions of Americans unchanged. This new era required them to "raise certain basic questions about the whole society."[60]

With the Selma Campaign and the Voting Rights Act behind him, King led the Southern Christian Leadership Conference into "an era of revolution" where America would be challenged to live up to its professed democratic values.[61] "I am first a minister of the gospel," King declared.[62] King had come to see that "the evils of racism, economic exploitation, and militarism are all tied together, and you can't get rid of one without getting rid of the others."[63] King surveyed the world and judged that "the clouds of a third war are hovering mighty low." And if World War Three should happen, then, the American "government will have to take the chief responsibility for making this a reality."[64] America is the "greatest purveyor of violence in the world today," assailed King.

On the domestic scene, King held the American government accountable for the violence that engulfed depressed ghetto communities (for instance, Harlem in 1964 and Watts in 1965), because "Congress . . . running wild with racism"[65] refused to take the necessary steps to eliminate the economic conditions that made social strife more likely. The southern struggle had been about "Constitutional rights"; however, the northern campaign would be about "human rights" and the need for a radical redistribution of economic and political power. King biographer, David Garrow writes,

> Noting that Congress had cut back on urban poverty programs and had refused to pass other measures aimed at ghetto ills, King declared that "the suicidal and irrational acts which plague our streets daily are being sowed and watered by the irrational, irrelevant and equally suicidal debate and delay in Congress." The most important problem was the lack of jobs for tens of thousands of slum residents. "Let us do one simple, direct thing—let us end unemployment totally and immediately, he told Johnson. "I propose specifically the creation of a national agency that shall provide a job to every person who needs work." While I regret that my expression may be sharp . . . I believe that literally that the life of our nation is at stake here at home."[66]

When King spoke of "the government" he was thinking of the federal government, not local or state government. The distinction between the three branches of government, although he clearly understood their various powers, was not the point. However, King placed the greater weight of responsibility for securing order and social stability with the executive branch. This tendency toward favoring a centralized government with a designated leader may reflect King's familiarity with the hierarchical structure of the back Baptist church where the local pastor tends to have considerable authority. This explains why King frequently urged President Johnson personally to tour America's ghettos. "The tour by the President—seeing poverty conditions for himself—should be followed by a massive economic program, a program to give the people in the ghetto a stake in society."[67] Also, the conspiratorial relationship between some local governments and white supremacist groups often rendered appeals to city authorities dangerous.

On the international scene, King understood that the civil rights movement could not turn a blind eye towards international violence and racism. "Violence is as wrong in Hanoi as it is in Harlem," King continued, "we must disarm the whole world."[68] The government's position regarding Vietnam was wrong and "getting wronger every day." Equally wrong was the government's policy toward Rhodesia (present day Zimbabwe) and South Africa. King recommended that all contact with these racist states be severed and that an economic boycott be established posthaste. The government's position regarding Africa was wrong because it effectively meant that America was aiding and abetting governmental regimes bent on the perpetual exploitation and degradation of fellow human beings.

King's procedural grounds for objecting to the Vietnam War reflected the fact that the burden of executing the war was not equally shared among American citizens; black and brown Americans were dying in numbers in excess of their percentage of the population. "One of the incongruities of this situation is the fact that such a large number of the soldiers in the armed forces in Vietnam—especially the front-line soldiers who are actually doing the fighting—are Negroes," wrote King.[69]

The war in Vietnam also produced negative consequences because it limited the resources available for restructuring the social and economic orders so that poverty could be eliminated, joblessness ended, and educational opportunities expanded and improved. For King, the war was "immoral" because it took billions of dollars away from the "forty million poor."[70] Additionally, the war was wrong on moral considerations because the government had not done enough to try to negotiate for peace. But there was yet still a greater moral consideration that made the war objectionable; it was killing the democratic soul of America. King preached, "I had my own vacillations and I asked questions whether on the one hand I should do it or whether I shouldn't," he continued. "I picked up an article entitled 'The Children of Vietnam,' and I read it, and after reading that article I said to myself, 'Never again, will I be silent on an issue that is destroying the soul of our nation and destroying thousands and thousands of little children in Vietnam."[71]

A democratic government is evaluated, in part, by its ability to establish and maintain democratic procedures for ensuring that citizens are able to participate in the process of determining who will govern. Moreover, a government should be held accountable for the consequences of its actions.[72] Lastly, a democratic government must be evaluated in terms of its willingness to expand democracy and to eliminate any restriction on democracy due to arbitrary considerations of race, gender, class, or region. For King, these three evaluative features of government are interconnected and, as such, are a useful tool for assessing a democratic government.

The right to criticize government is itself a democratic value. "I am more than a civil rights leader," explains King. And as for the war in Vietnam, "I feel that it is necessary for me to continue to speak on it."[73] King's role as a minister of the Christian gospel leaned heavily toward the prophetic Christian tradition (e.g., Jeremiah, Amos, and of course Jesus). Following those who represent the best of the prophetic Christian tradition, King felt compelled to bear witness to the government and to the world, through means of "creative dissent," that "war is obsolete."[74] Furthermore, the best weapon we have against violence of all forms is love expressed through means of nonviolent resistance.

The right to resist and the right to protest are two of the most treasured deliberative features of democratic government. "We're at a terrible stage when we confuse dissent with disloyalty and we view every protester as a traitor," argues King. "I cannot stand idly by and see war continually escalated without speaking out against it."[75] King continues, "We in the civil rights movement must come all out now and make it clear that America is a hypocritical nation and that America must set her own house in order."[76]

King's political and religious life was principally consumed with advancing an optimistic human psychology and that, to this end, he used the African American experience, Judeo-Christian writings, and America's "sacred scriptures,"[77] to articulate his philosophy of nonviolence and ethic of love. His emphasis on a Christian love ethic makes love of one's neighbor a requirement of justice. The implications of such a requirement of justice are read against the Socratic notion of justice found in the *Republic*. King's evaluation of governments as reflected in his critique of the U.S. government's involvement in the Vietnam War. For King, the right of citizens to assess the domestic and foreign policies of the state is central to democracy.

NOTES

1. Martin Luther King Jr. *Why We Can't Wait* (New York: Penguin Books USA, 1963, 1964), 32–33.

2. King, *Why We Can't Wait*, 131. King is referring to the language in the Thomas Jefferson lead committee's first draft, "A Declaration by the Representatives of the United States of America, in General Congress Assembled," submitted to Congress on June 28, 1776. On July 4, after intense discussions and amendments, the document was

unanimously approved as "The Unanimous Declaration of the 13 United States of America." In the earlier version, however, Jefferson had charged the king with waging "a cruel war against human nature" by "captivating and carrying" a "distant people" into slavery on "another hemisphere." As a compromise with the southern states, most notably South Carolina, the reference to slavery was stricken from the document. See Carl Lotus Becker, *The Declaration of Independence: A Study of Political Ideas* (1922); Garry Wills, *Inventing America: Jefferson's Declaration of Independence* (1978); and Richard L. Bushman, "Declaration of Independence," in *The Reader's Companion to American History*, edited by Eric Foner and John A. Garraty (Boston: Houghton Mifflin Company, 1991), 271–72.

3. "MIA Mass Meeting at Holt Street Baptist Church," in *The Papers of Martin Luther King, Jr.: Birth of a New Age December 1955–1956*(vol. 3), edited by Clayborne Carson, Steward Burns, Susan Carson, et al. (Berkeley: University of California Press, 1997), 71.

4. "MIA Mass Meeting at Holt Street Baptist Church," 72–73.

5. Martin Luther King Jr., *Stride toward Freedom* (New York: Harper & Row Publishers, 1958), 173.

6. Charles W. Mills argues that "person" and "personhood" are highly contested notions in the modern world. See *The Racial Contract* (Ithaca: Cornell University Press, 1997).

7. King, *Why We Can't Wait*, 129.

8. King, *Stride*, 174.

9. King, *Why We Can't Wait*, 21.

10. Martin Luther King Jr. "I Have a Dream," in *A Testament of Hope: The Essential Writings and Speeches of Martin Luther King, Jr.*, edited by James Washington (New York: HarperCollins Publisher, 1986), 218.

11. Ibid.

12. Ibid., 83. King biographers have related the influence of Bayard Rustin on King's mature appreciation of nonviolent philosophy and its application to the civil rights movement. Rustin worked for the Fellowship Of Reconciliation (A. J. Muste's organization), served prison time as a conscientious objector, and traveled to India to study with Mahatma Gandhi. However, it was his Quaker background that drew him to pacifism. His relationship with King began in the early days of the bus protest in Montgomery, Alabama, and lasted until King's death. Clayborne Carson writes, "King recognized the advantages of Rustin's knowledge, contacts, and organizational abilities, and invited him to continue, albeit behind the scenes. . . . Between 1955 and 1960, Rustin influenced King's growing commitment to nonviolence." See "Rustin, Bayard (1910–1987)," in *The Martin Luther King, Jr. Encyclopedia* (Westport, CT: Greenwood, 2008).

13. King, *Why We Can't Wait*, 38.

14. Ibid., 79–80.

15. This position assumes, of course, that we think of enslaved persons as having an inherent moral advantage over their enslavers.

16. King, *Why We Can't Wait*, 93–94. This is the lesson of the Albany Movement where Chief Laurie Pritchett refused to use violence to suppress the marches.

17. Ibid., 36–37.

18. Ibid., 40.

19. Ibid., 152.

20. Ibid., 88.

21. Martin Luther King Jr., "Letter from Birmingham Jail," in *Why We Can't Wait*, 87–88.

22. King, *Why We Can't Wait*, 38–39.

23. Ibid., 39.

24. Ibid., 80.

25. Ibid., 20.

26. King, *Where Do We Go*, 43.

27. King, *Stride,* 167.

28. Ibid., 47.

29. "MIA Mass meeting at Holt Street Baptist Church." [12/5/55]. Montgomery, Ala. (At) 45 min. (I sound cassette: analog.) MLKJrP-GAMK: Box 107, 551205-004, in *The Papers of Martin Luther King, Jr.: Birth of a New Age December 1955–1956* (vol. 3), edited by Clayborne Carson, Steward Burns, Susan Carson, et al. (Berkeley: University of California Press 1997), 71–79.

30. King, *Why We Can't Wait,* 68.

31. Martin Luther King Jr., "A Time to Break Silence," in *A Testament of Hope: The Essential Writings and Speeches of Martin Luther King, Jr.,* edited by James Washington (New York: HarperCollins Publisher 1986), 233.

32. Ibid., 152.

33. King, "Loving Your Enemies," 46.

34. Ibid. Socrates states in the *Phaedrus,* "Let us then liken the soul to the natural union of a team of winged horses and their charioteer. The gods have horses and charioteers that are themselves all good and come from good stock besides, while everyone else has a mixture. To begin with, our driver is in charge of a pair of horses; second, one of his horses is beautiful and good and from stock of the same sort, while the other is the opposite and has the opposite sort of bloodline. This means that chariot-driving in our case is inevitably a painfully difficult business" (246b 1–5 and 248a 5–7). See Plato's *Phaedrus,* in *Plato: Complete Works,* edited by John M. Cooper and D. S. Hutchinson (Indiana: Hackett Publishing Company, Inc, 1997).

35. King, "Unfulfilled Dreams," in *A Knock,* 194–95. This is remarkably close to Plato's notion that justice is a kind of harmony within the soul or city. Socrates makes this clear when he states, "Action that destroys this harmony is unjust" (443e6–7). For King, however, the virtue of justice lies in the trying—the attempt to do what "conscious calls" and to work "towards the beloved community."

36. See the exchange between Socrates and Polemarchus in the *Republic* 335d4–14.

37. King, "Loving Your Enemies," in *A Knock,* 52.

38. This differs from Polemarchus's and Cephalus's position that justice is paying one's debts (*Republic* 331b1–5 and 331e3) and in that King is indiscriminating and universal. Moreover, it differs from Plato's position because it includes the emotive aspects of the human personality. So, justice requires that we both act and desire to act in ways that prompt the greater good for all.

39. In this sense, Socrates is correct when he states that we form cities because we need others to become our true selves.

40. Martin Luther King Jr., "Love in Action," in *Strength to Love,* 40.

41. Ibid.

42. Ibid., 48.

43. Quoted in Taylor Branch's *Parting the Waters,* 86.

44. King, "MIA Mass Meeting at Holt Street," 74–75.

45. Martin Luther King Jr. *Stride toward Freedom: The Montgomery Story* (New York: Harper & Row, 1958, 1964), 67.

46. Ibid., 86.

47. King, "Loving Your Enemies," *A Knock,* 59.

48. King, *The Autobiography ,* 19.

49. King, "Loving Your Enemies," 42.

50. James Melvin Washington, ed., *A Testament of Hope: The Essential Writings and Speeches of Martin Luther King, Jr.* (New York: HarperCollins, 1986), 47–48.

51. Martin Luther King Jr., "The Drum Major Instinct," *A Knock,* 185.

52. Ibid., 163–64.

53. King, *The Autobiography,* 20.

54. See the exchange between Thrasymachus and Socrates in the *Republic* 349d1–7 and 350b13–c24.

55. King, "Three Dimensions of a Complete Life," in *A Knock at Midnight,* 132.

56. King, "The Drum Major Instinct," in *A Knock at Midnight,* 194.

57. Ibid.

58. Ibid., 188.

59. King, *Where Do We Go from Here*, 37.

60. Quotations from Garrow, *Bearing the Cross*, 563.

61. Ibid.

62. Ibid., 561.

63. Ibid., 564.

64. Ibid., 562.

65. The 1966 civil rights bill did not pass through the Senate.

66. King was reading a telegram that had been sent to President Johnson following the rioting in Newark, New Jersey, in 1966. Garrow, *Bearing the Cross*, 570.

67. Quotations from Garrow, *Bearing the Cross*, 443.

68. Quotations from Garrow, *Bearing the Cross*, 453.

69. Martin Luther King Jr., "A Testament of Hope," in *A Testament of Hope*, 326.

70. Ibid., 315.

71. Quotations from Garrow, *Bearing the Cross*, 564.

72. King was in favor of reparations and most likely would have been sympathetic to the current reparation movement. He said, "The awesome predicament confronting the Negro in our slums is directly related to economic exploitation. . . . The only way it can rectify sins of the past is through some form of compensatory action." See Garrow, *Bearing the Cross*, 569.

73. Quotations from Garrow, *Bearing the Cross*, 430.

74. Ibid., 443.

75. Ibid., 453.

76. West, *Values Conference*, 1998.

77. This was the original title for Pauline Maier's work on the Declaration of Independence. However, upon the advice of her publisher, she changed the title to *American Scripture: The Making of the Declaration of Independence* (New York: Knopf, 1997). Besides from presenting a revisionist account of the making of the document, Maier argues that the Declaration of Independence has come to serve more than its initial purpose. It has become enshrined as a sort of holy writ that contains our sacred past. The full corpus of America's *holy writ* would include the Constitution of the United States of America, the Bill of Rights, works of Henry David Thoreau, and the words of Abraham Lincoln.

3

King's Ethics of Nonviolence

NINE

King, Levinas, and the Praxis of Peace

Scott Davidson and Maria del Guadalupe Davidson

The thought of both Martin Luther King Jr. and Emmanuel Levinas emerges in response to the "ascendancy of war" and violence throughout the twentieth century and the clear sense that it has presented the world with a final ultimatum: either choose peace or risk total annihilation.[1] Importantly, both thinkers suffered the direct consequences of violence in their personal lives. For King, this involved enduring the lasting effects of the Holocaust of black enslavement,[2] continued racial violence against blacks, as well as repeated personal attacks leading up to his assassination, while for Levinas this included the devastating experience of World War II in which he was detained in a prisoner of war camp and lost his entire Lithuanian family.[3] Thus both, in their own ways, could rightly be called post-Holocaust thinkers. That is to say that the central question in their thought is both political and deeply personal: it concerns how individuals and institutions can be transformed to avoid the total threat of violence and establish a just peace in its place. Given this significant convergence point in their thought, it is somewhat surprising that their work has never been put into direct contact, and one important objective of this chapter is simply to demonstrate some of the rich potential for further engagement between these two thinkers.

In the pursuit of this initial dialogue between King and Levinas, we will also issue a word of caution for peace scholars who might be eager to apply Levinasian ethics to concrete political contexts and concerns.[4] Some peace scholars, with good reason, might enthusiastically welcome Levinas's philosophy as an important new contribution to the study of peace, insofar as his most influential work, *Totality and Infinity* (1961), presents itself as the defense of an "eschatology of messianic peace" in face of the "ascendancy of war."[5] Moreover, a number of Levinasian notions developed there and elsewhere—for instance, the ethical resistance of the face, the inviolability of the other person, the redemptive power of suffering and love, and positive peace as proximity with the other—resonate with central concepts in peace studies. To be clear, it is not our intention to deny the potential importance and value of Levinas's thought for peace studies; however, our comparison of the ethical and political frameworks of King and Levinas will suggest that it proves to be much more difficult for a Levinasian ethics, than a Kingian one, to implement a politics and praxis of peace.[6]

FROM VIOLENCE TO THE ETHICS OF PEACE

At the outset of *Totality and Infinity*, Levinas asks whether we are not "duped by morality."[7] This indeed would be the case, if one were to follow political rationality that, as Levinas contends, is fundamentally guided by Heraclitus's dictum that "war is the father of all and the king of all."[8] Political rationality is only concerned with the "art of foreseeing war and winning it by all means" and thus war becomes all-pervasive within its calculations.[9] It gives rise to a condition of "total war" that leaves nothing outside or untouched by its calculations.[10] When this rationality governs all aspects of human life, then ethics (construed in terms of features like benevolence, altruism, and care) becomes a naïveté that can only dupe one into losing the war of all against all. Every display of altruism or disinterestedness would only count as an irrational move in the realm of political rationality, unless it resulted from "calculation, mediation, and politics."[11] As Levinas puts it, "The peace of empires issued from war rests on war."[12] That is to say that, within political rationality, peace can only serve as yet another instrument of war, to be used as a pawn within the broader politics of war. Peace might signify, for instance, a compromise made for the sake of winning political advantages or a teleological goal used for the sake of justifying the present reign of warfare.[13] In response to the political rationality that can only engender an unstable or negative peace,[14] Levinas calls for a positive peace that "goes beyond purely political thought."[15]

Positive peace, according to Levinas, must be peace rooted in ethics, where ethics no longer signifies a "branch of philosophy, but first philosophy."[16] This formula suggests that ethics, instead of being defined by political rationality, establishes a layer of meaning that precedes every historical, social, or political context of struggle. To say that ethics is "first philosophy," then, is to suggest that a genuine peace precedes every strategic or violent move occurring in the realm of politics. "War," as Levinas claims, "presupposes peace, the antecedent and non-allergic presence of the other; it does not represent the first event of the encounter."[17] Consequently, politics comes into play only "after" ethics.[18] This suggests that whereas political rationality conceives peace against the permanent backdrop of war, Levinas situates violence and war against the primordial peace with the other.[19] The distinctive nature of Levinas's understanding of ethics and this primordial peace calls for further examination.

The primary sense of ethics, according to Levinas, is discovered in the face-to-face relation between the self and the other. In his characterization of this encounter as an encounter with the face of the other person, it may seem as if Levinas were referring to some empirical feature of the racial physiognomy or the cultural adornments in which faces might appear. But, it is important to note that the face is distinct from objects of ordinary perception, on Levinas's view. Whereas objects are given to consciousness through the mediation of concepts and images, the manifestation of the face is unmediated. This presentation of the face by itself occurs concretely, for example, when the face speaks. In speech, the individuality of the other's discourse breaks through every social context or history and speaks directly to me as an individual.[20] Still, even if this provides a clear enough indication that the speech of the other establishes an interpersonal relationship, it is not immediately clear that such a relation has anything to do with ethics.

The ethical significance of this relation can emerge from further consideration of what the speech of the other can do. The speech of the other—or what Levinas calls the face—presents an ethical resistance that cannot be measured on the scale of physical resistance. Things—such as rocks or trees—can resist the physical power of my body, but their resistance can always in principle be overcome, say, by the greater force of a tool that is used to move them or break them. By contrast, over and beyond every physical force, the ethical resistance of the other "resists possession, resists my powers" and even resists "the power of power."[21] Even if, like a thing, another person can be overcome or seized through the use of physical force, the ethical resistance of the other always escapes power through the ability to say "yes" or "no." This type of resistance, unlike physical power, has an ethical significance for Levinas, because it establishes the possibility of a nonantagonistic relation between oneself and the other and thus opens the possibility for a genuine peace. "Peace," Levinas explains, "is produced as this aptitude for speech."[22]

Far from simply assuming an idyllic relationship to the other, however, Levinasian ethics recognizes that violence remains a permanent temptation in interpersonal relations. "The other person," Levinas observes, "is the sole being I can wish to kill."[23] The face-to-face encounter thus harbors an inescapable ambiguity within itself. On the one hand, the first word in every discourse on behalf of the other person, according to Levinas, implicitly contains an ethical resistance, associated with the prohibition on violence: "you shall not commit murder."[24] Yet, on the other hand, the other person presents the "infinity of the temptation of murder," insofar as violence and war "can be produced only where discourse was possible."[25] At once prohibiting and enabling violence, the face-to-face relation presents the permanent temptation of violence. Having established the temptation of violence, we can now glimpse the meaning of violence for Levinas.

It bears noting that violence is construed more broadly in Levinas's philosophy than in the ordinary understanding of this term. Violence, on Levinas's view, is connected to the notion of possession. Possession refers to the ego's attempt to appropriate, master, or control something other than itself. In so doing, something that is other than oneself is taken hold of and assimilated into oneself. By taking possession of something else, its otherness is reduced or destroyed. The use of violence against other people follows along roughly the same lines. In exercising violence against another person, I seize or take control of the other person in some manner, and in so doing, I try to reduce the will of the other person to my own will. But, even if violence against the other remains a permanent possibility in the life of the ego, the key point is that it can only remain a temptation, not an unalterable fact. Violence is only a temptation because it ultimately does not succeed. Violence fails due to the fact that it seeks to deny the undeniable: my relation to the other person. It is an attempt to turn away from the other person by nullifying the other's difference from me, for instance, by using the other as a tool to accomplish my own objectives.

Murder represents the most extreme case of violence against the other, inasmuch as it seeks a "total negation" of the other. The problem with murder, as Levinas suggests, is that it can never achieve its intended goal. To be sure, I can wish to kill the other, and I can even succeed in doing so. Although the murderer may overcome the physical resistance of the other, the murderer cannot overcome what Levinas calls the "ethical resistance" of the other. This ethical resistance is rooted in the alterity of the other, and it is something that cannot be possessed or mastered. Hence, the project of murder fails, because it attempts to assert power over something that escapes the power and mastery of the self.[26]

Although King does not provide anything like Levinas's ethics of the face, he would certainly agree with Levinas that peace signifies more than just the suspension of war or the cessation of violence. And, like Levinas, he seeks to establish a positive peace to overcome the antagonistic relationship between the self and the other, the oppressor and the oppressed. For King, however, the problem of violence is concretized in the context of his own specific place and time, namely, the "crisis in race relations."[27] In agreement with Du Bois who earlier observed that the "problem of the twentieth century is the problem of the color-line," the central problem for King was to overcome the antagonistic relation between whites who oppressed blacks and blacks who sought to retaliate against their white oppressors. Even after the momentous Brown case of 1954, King and his supporters were confronted with the unwillingness of white society to relinquish its hold over industry and the nation's socio-political institutions. This rejection of social change, as is well known, manifested itself in terms of continued violence against blacks, including acts of lynching, denials of the right to vote, and limitations on education-al opportunity, to name a few. On the side of the black community, these acts of violence, in turn, stirred a deep-seated sense of outrage and anger that waited for the right moment to be unleashed.[28] The problem, then, for King was to establish an alternative—a third way—to the antagonistic alternatives of either "white power" (the continued oppression of blacks by a white-dominated society) or "black power" (the retaliatory-violence of blacks against whites).

The cycle of white violence and black counterviolence easily could have been exacerbated, for example, when King's house was fire-bombed with his children inside. Crowds flooded to King's home that night armed with weapons and prepared to exact revenge on the white popula-tion. Concerning that night, King wrote: "Many men wanted to retaliate, to place an armed guard on my home. But the issue there was not my life, but whether Negroes would achieve first-class treatment on the buses. Had we become distracted by the question of my safety we would have lost the moral offensive and sunk to the level of our oppressors."[29] It was only King's commitment to peace as a way of life that successfully de-fused the threat of further violence that night. He called on the crowd not to retaliate with violence but to continue along the path of nonviolence with the same discipline as before. The crowd that night confronted the very same dilemma that faces all of the oppressed. King expresses this dilemma in the following terms: "How is the struggle against forces of injustice to be waged? There are two possible answers. One is to resort to the all too prevalent method of physical violence and corroding ha-tred. . . . The alternative to violence is nonviolent resistance."[30] Remind-ing his supporters of their broader mission, this example from King's own life, among countless others, demonstrates his refusal of violent struggle.

The underlying rationale for King's practice of nonviolence can be made explicit by analogy with Levinas's murder argument, which dem-onstrated the inability of murder to accomplish its objective of annihilat-ing the alterity of the other. King, likewise, believes that violence is a futile project, albeit for different reasons. For, his argument against vio-lence runs in precisely the opposite direction from Levinas's murder ar-gument: for King, violence seeks to annul the connectedness between the self and the other. We will demonstrate this point, in what follows, by calling on three core ethical principles underlying King's argument against violence.

The first of these principles is the sanctity of life—reflected spiritually in all of the world's religious traditions, morally in Kant's categorical imperative, and legally in the Declaration of Independence—establishing that all humans are creatures of God and that God loves all his children equally. What matters, then, about a human being is "not his specificity but his fundamentum, not the texture of his hair or the color of his skin but the quality of his soul."[31] On the basis of this principle, the physical differences between the races are insignificant in comparison to what all people share in common. The worth of persons is not conditioned by a person's belonging to a racial or national identity; instead, moral worth is intrinsic to all persons. On this point, King's thought resonates with Levinas's view that the other person, regardless of cultural or social context, "counts as such."

The second step in King's argument is a claim about the essential freedom of every human being. Influenced by his study of existentialism, King recognizes that all human beings have the desire and the right to be free. Since freedom is a defining feature of humanity, the denial of freedom is not just a limitation of an individual. It is tantamount to a denial of one's humanity. The desire for freedom, King observes, is what unites all oppressed people in a common struggle: "The determination of Negro Americans to win freedom from every form of oppression springs from the same profound longing for freedom that motivates oppressed people all over the world."[32] Yet, even if this struggle motivates all oppressed people, it need not pit them against their oppressors in a zero-sum game. For, all people are united in their striving for freedom, and thus a win-win outcome in which oppressor and oppressed find themselves to be liberated is available.

The final stage in King's argument is to show that the oppressor and the oppressed are implicated in a common fate.[33] Acts of violence and oppression desire to separate some human beings from the social body by either limiting their freedom or denying their shared humanity. These acts of violence fail, however, to accomplish their desired goal due to the interconnectedness of all persons. Acts of violence circulate throughout the human community; and just as an illness in one part of the body may adversely affect the functioning of the entire body, an act of violence in one part of the human community may cause harm to the entire social body. This applies equally to the violence used by the oppressor as well as to the counterviolence used against oppression. The addition of more poison cannot cure the body, and likewise counterviolence can never overcome violence—it can only beget more violence. Violence and counterviolence are thus equally doomed to fail in their effort to produce positive change, because the fate of every individual is interwoven with the fate of the entire social body.

Based on the above argument against violence, King concludes that the distinctive power of oppressed people does not reside in their brute strength but their moral force. This moral force, resting on the three principles outlined above, is asserted through the practice of nonviolent resistance. The effectiveness of nonviolence can be traced back to the fact that it does not seek to subdue the oppressor but to overcome the separation that exists between the oppressor and the oppressed. Nonviolence, in King's words, aims for a "redemption and reconciliation" of the self and the other, of the oppressor and the oppressed. To achieve this, King emphasizes that nonviolence exerts a spiritual force on the oppressor:

> The nonviolent resister is strongly opposed to the evil against which he protests as is the person who uses violence. His method is passive or non-aggressive in the sense that he is not physically aggressive toward his opponent. But his mind and emotions are always active, constantly seeking to persuade the opponent that he is mistaken. This method is passive physically but strongly active spiritually; it is non-aggressive physically but dynamically aggressive spiritually.[34]

The moral force involved in Kingian nonviolence bears a striking similarity to Levinas's notion of "ethical resistance." Both thinkers distinguish this type of resistance from all measures of physical strength and weakness. Nonviolent resistance, instead, operates on what might be called the level of spirit or will. Ethical resistance, as opposed to the negative peace established by physical force or the cessation of force, thus offers the promise of a true peace; it brings about "the presence of some positive force—justice, good will, and brotherhood."[35]

Both King and Levinas, as we have shown, agree that ethical or nonviolent resistance "springs forth from the needs of the other person" and thereby opens the door for a positive peace.[36] They disagree, however, with regard to the nature of this nonantagonistic relationship between the self and the other. For Levinas, the nonviolent relation is one that preserves the alterity of the other, while for King the alterity or separateness of the other is something to be overcome in order to promote "true brotherhood, true integration, true person-to-person relationships."[37] This difference concerning the nonantagonistic relationship with the other, as we will show, goes on to play a critical role in shaping their respective conceptions of political community and the praxis of peace.

FROM THE ETHICS OF PEACE TO THE POLITICS OF PEACE

Levinasian ethics, as Simon Critchley rightly notes, does not exist for its own sake, instead it is always connected to politics and ultimately aims to transform the nature of political society. As we noted above, Levinas is opposed to the view according to which all rationality would be political and all political rationality would pertain to the condition of war. As an antidote to this view, he points to a more fundamental type of rationality—described in the ethical relation to the other—which is supposed to inspire political rationality. But, in exploring the transition from ethics to politics in his thought, we will call peace scholars' attention to the way in which Levinasian ethics betrays its initial promise of peace.

Justice begins with the entrance of a third party. If there were only two of us, then the path to peace would be clear: I would act to satisfy the needs and demands of the other person. With the addition of a third person, however, the pursuit of peace becomes much more complicated. Here there is no longer a single other but multiple others. I cannot set aside my obligation to the other person, even while I have an added obligation to the other of the other and all of the other others. Between these obligations, it is necessary for me to choose. I must assemble the facts, compare them, and then weigh their importance; in short, I must do the work of justice, balancing their competing claims and giving to each what they are due. Inspired by the notion of a peace rooted in the ethical relation to the other, one might imagine that for Levinas the work of justice would extend the ethical relation and thus lead to the establishment of a peace shared between myself and all of the others. It is important to note, however, that Levinas's thinking of the political and justice does not in fact lead toward a universal peace.

Whereas Levinas understands the possibility of violence as a permanent temptation on the ethical plane, political violence becomes more than just a temptation—it becomes an inevitable reality.[38] Perhaps the most striking example of this recourse to political violence occurs in a discussion in which Levinas states that sometimes it is necessary to oppose the other for the sake of the third party:

> My resistance begins when the harm he does me is done to a third party who is also my neighbor. It is the third party who is the source of justice and thereby of justified repression; it is the violence suffered by the third party that justifies stopping the violence of the other with violence.[39]

In this passage, the notion of resistance undergoes two important displacements from its original meaning in the face-to-face relationship: it shifts from the other to the self and from the ethical to violent resistance. Due to this displacement, the ethical relation to the other, which was supposed to overcome violence, now becomes the sanction for violence. For, in cases where the other exerts a force against a third party, Levinas maintains that I can rightly use force against the other in order to prevent further harms to the third party. And, what is more, if it is the case that I am "always in relation with the third party," then violence would always seem to be an option, if not a necessary means, for solving conflicts between others. Since war always remains on the table as a strategic option for conflict resolution, it becomes difficult, if not impossible, to discern any meaningful difference between Levinas's politics and the politics of war that he sought to overcome.

Yet, one might bring more nuance to this account by adding that, while Levinas may condone the occasional use of violence in defense of the other, the ultimate purpose of his ethics is to call the use of force continually into question.[40] Ethics would wage, so to speak, a war on war, and Levinas himself frames this point in the following terms:

> The true problem for us Westerners is not so much to refuse violence as to question ourselves about a struggle against violence which, without blanching in non-resistance to evil, could avoid the institution of violence out of this very struggle. Does not war perpetuate that which it is called to make disappear, and consecrate war and its virile virtues in good conscience?[41]

Levinasian ethics, it might be said, thus provides an alternative to the options of either acquiescing to violence or retaliating violently against violence. Regardless of whether it is waged for or against one's own side, ethics continually challenges the establishment of "war in good conscience."[42] As such, the war against war would not be waged so much against the use of force as against having a good conscience about war. It would never allow us to feel good or self-assured about the wars that are fought, even if they are fought in the name of goodness or justice. But, if the role of the ethics of peace were simply critical, that is, if it only served to call into question our attitudes toward the use of force, then one might rightly question, as Derrida has, its ability to escape from the context of violence and warfare.[43] Doesn't Levinasian ethics remain entangled within the very same rationality—the logic of war—that it rejects? For, even if it continually calls war into question, it still does not provide a practical alternative to war. It merely prohibits anyone from feeling good about the wars that "must" be fought. Thus, in spite of its initial promise of a radically new ethics of peace, Levinasian ethics ultimately collapses into the same old politics as usual.

To be sure, King himself struggled with the question of the effectiveness of nonviolence in the face of great evil, and at one point in his journey on the way to nonviolence, he readily admits that he was not yet convinced that it would be possible to apply nonviolence to the level of political institutions.[44] At that time, King thought that war might serve as a "negative good," that is, as something that is not good in itself but yet the lesser of two evils. On this line of thought, for example, war could be accepted as a necessary evil, if it were fought in order to prevent the spread of a greater evil, such as totalitarianism. But, in his journey to nonviolence, King eventually arrives at the conclusion that war, especially in the age of weapons with the capacity to annihilate the world, cannot provide a genuinely practical solution to the world's problems.[45]

A number of King's contemporaries in the black community, however, did succumb to the view that violence is a necessary evil. One example of this viewpoint was expressed by a former president of the Monroe, North Carolina, chapter of the NAACP, Robert F. Williams (1925–1996). Williams's book *Negroes with Guns* had a significant impact on Huey Newton who founded the Black Panther movement.[46] Williams is famous for establishing the Black Guard, which protected the black community in Monroe from white-sponsored terrorist organizations like the KKK. After the acquittal of a white man who was accused of attempting to rape a black woman, Williams called for the use of violence:

> That there is no law here, there is no need to take the white attackers to court because they will go free and that the federal government is not coming to the aid of people who are oppressed, and it is time for Negro men to stand up and be men and if it is necessary for us to die we must be willing to die. If it is necessary for us to kill we must be willing to kill.

Clearly, Williams is not endorsing violence as a good in and of itself, instead his call for violence is situated in a context in which the rule of law is not enforced adequately by the state.[47] In the vacuum of legal protection and enforcement, it is clear that Williams's call for blacks to employ force to defend other blacks is issued as a last resort.[48] Inasmuch as Williams's rationale regarding the necessary recourse to violence in order to protect others against violence runs parallel to Levinas's acceptance of the need for political violence, it is particularly telling to examine King's rejection of those in the black community who, like Williams, called for the use of violence for the sake of protecting other blacks.

A good end such as empowerment, on King's view, could never justify the use of violent means, instead the "means must be as pure as the end, that in the long run of history, immoral destructive means cannot bring about moral and constructive ends."[49] This formula could all too easily be reduced to a paraphrase of Kantian ethics, which rejects the mean-ends calculations of utilitarian thinking. More profoundly, however, its roots can be traced back to King's understanding of community.[50] To explain, both violence and nonviolence share the same aims: they seek to bring about change in the community. But, violence accomplishes this goal at the expense of other members of the community. So, together with whatever positive changes that it might happen to realize, violence also leaves behind feelings of bitterness, resentment, and anger in its wake. These feelings can become the source of tension and future acts of violence in the community. Since violence keeps the same social antagonisms intact, it only reinforces the status quo. In response to advocates of political violence, then, King concludes that violence is an ineffective means for bringing about positive social change.[51]

The practice of nonviolence, by contrast, can realize change within the community, because it alone can overcome the antagonisms between self and other, oppressor and oppressed. This practice, which is rooted in the Christian understanding of love as agape, transforms our ordinary conception of love in which it is identified with "a resignation of power and power with a denial of love."[52] For King, love represents more than a sentimental feeling or an imaginary ideal; it is an active, creative power in the world.[53] This connection between power and love is what both Levinas's political rationality and the Black Power Movement fail to understand. King observes: "Power at its best is love implementing the demands of justice. Justice at its best is love correcting everything that stands against love."[54] Key to the practice of nonviolence is agapeic love, because it only can overcome hatred and the various antagonisms that tear communities apart. Nonviolence succeeds precisely because it, unlike violence, does not sidestep morality but fosters it. Its aim is to create and preserve community.[55]

Underlying Kingian nonviolence, we thus find a very different understanding of political community—which King refers to as the agapeic or beloved community—from what is found in traditional liberal theory.[56] Going beyond individual merit and past history, it recognizes the unconditional value of the person. And, in this respect, it is consistent with traditional liberal theory, which also affirms the absolute worth and inherent dignity of the individual. King's agapeic community, however, goes beyond the liberal emphasis on the separateness and dignity of persons by regarding the individual, at the same time, as a member of the human community. Within the agapeic community, each individual is interconnected with all other members of the community. This interconnectedness integrates all individuals into a single community with a single good but yet does not destroy the personality of the individual. It is precisely through community with others that the personality of the individual comes to its full fruition.[57]

Ultimately, this account of the agapeic community should help peace scholars to understand how King's ethics is able to transition much more smoothly into a politics and praxis of peace than Levinasian ethics does. Since individuals are all indissolubly connected to one another in King's agapeic community, the individual's well-being cannot be separated from collective well-being. This means that I cannot have peace or justice without peace and justice for the other and the other others. The violence exerted by one individual against another does not only destroy the other person; its effects circulate through the entire community and eventually do harm to all the others, even those whom violence seeks to protect. Within this community, agapeic love must provide both the measure and the means of political action. In contrast with King's emphasis on integration and inclusion in the community, Levinas's philosophy places an extreme emphasis on alterity and difference. This conception of community, to be sure, can provide a valuable corrective to some of the assimilationist tendencies in King's thought;[58] however, it is not without its own dangers. It all too easily leads, as we have seen, to a separation between the means and the measures of political action. Without a common good, the pursuit of peace and justice for some others can be justified at the expense of peace and justice for other others. For this reason, peace scholars who might otherwise welcome Levinas's critique of violence should be wary of its ability to generate a politics and praxis of peace. To borrow a familiar slogan, it yields no justice, no peace.

NOTES

1. While one could, to be sure, follow Gene Sharp in arguing that nonviolent movements had an equal, if not greater, impact on twentieth-century politics and thus that peace ascends over war, the underlying assumption shared by both King and Levinas seems to be that the latter half of the twentieth century, especially after the development of nuclear threats, is qualitatively different from any violence faced before inasmuch as it poses the threat of total global destruction. Regardless of which assumption is empirically true, this is really a conceptual question having to do with showing that there really is a concept of peace that can be thought about separately from war. Sharp's view is developed in his classic, *The Politics of Nonviolent Action* (Boston: Porter Sargent, 1973).

2. The use of the term Holocaust to describe black enslavement in the United States might be controversial to some. We borrow this expression, however, from Maulana Karenga, one of the pioneers in the field of Black Studies. Karenga justifies the use of the term Holocaust to describe black enslavement for the following reasons. First, he argues that millions of Africans died during the forced journey to the West. The Atlantic was more than an important shipping route; it was (is) also a graveyard. An incalculable number of Africans lost their lives on the way to the Americas. Second, to describe enslavement as a Holocaust emphasizes the moral dimension of enslavement. This is important since the enslavement of Africans oftentimes is reduced to economic trade (i.e., the Trans-Atlantic Slave Trade). But, Africans were not commodities but people whose lives were destroyed by enslavement. Thus, for Karenga, black enslavement has the status of a crime against humanity. See Maulana Karenga, *Introduction to Black Studies*, Second Edition (Los Angeles: University of Sankore Press, 1993).

3. A detailed biographical account of this period of Levinas's life is provided by Salomon Malka, *Emmanuel Levinas: His Life and Legacy*, trans. Michael Kigel and Sonja Embree (Pittsburgh: Duquesne University Press, 2006), 64–82. As is well known, *Otherwise than Being* is dedicated to "the memory of those who were closest among the six million assassinated by the National Socialists, and of the millions on millions of all confessions and all nations, victims of the same hatred of the other man, the same anti-Semitism." Emmanuel Levinas, *Otherwise than Being*, trans. Alphonso Lingis (Dordrecht: Nijhoff, 1974), i.

4. Here, in suggesting that Levinas's ethics cannot simply be applied straightforwardly to areas such as peace studies but is limited to inspiring a certain way of approaching issues, we follow the line of Levinas interpretation developed by Diane Perpich in *The Ethics of Emmanuel Levinas* (Stanford: Stanford University Press, 2008), where Perpich argues that Levinasian ethics cannot generate concrete norms but can only play a critical role in calling established norms into question.

5. Emmanuel Levinas, *Totality and Infinity*, trans. Alphonso Lingis (Pittsburgh: Duquesne University Press, 1969), 22.

6. Note, as an aside, the possible resources here for a Kingian response to Derrida's rejection of nonviolence. Derrida rejects the coherence of the concept of pure nonviolence: "We do not say pure nonviolence. Like pure violence, pure nonviolence is a contradictory concept. Contradictory beyond what Levinas calls 'formal logic.' Pure violence, a relationship between beings without a face, is not yet violence, is pure nonviolence. And inversely: pure nonviolence, the non-relation of the same to the other (in the sense understood by Levinas) is pure violence." In Jacques Derrida, *Writing and Difference*, trans. Alan Bass (Chicago: University of Chicago Press, 1978), 146–47.

7. Levinas, *Totality and Infinity*, 21.

8. Heraclitus, fragment 212.

9. Levinas, *Totality and Infinity*, 21, 300.

10. Here Levinas writes: "Not only modern war but every war employs arms that turn against those who wield them. It establishes an order from which no one can keep his distance; nothing henceforth is exterior" (*Totality and Infinity*, 21).

11. Levinas, *Otherwise than Being*, 4.

12. Levinas, *Totality and Infinity*, 22.

13. King, "Nonviolence and Racial Justice," 6. Henceforth, all citations of King will be cited by article name and all paginations will refer to: James M. Washington, ed., *A Testament of Hope: The Essential Writings and Speeches of Martin Luther King Jr.* (San Francisco: Harpers Collins, 1986).

14. Levinas writes: "Peace cannot be identified with the end of combats that cease for want of combatants, by the defeat of some and the victory of the others, that is, with cemeteries or future universal empires" (*Totality and Infinity*, 306).

15. Levinas, *Beyond the Verse*, 195.

16. Levinas, *Totality and Infinity*, 304. See also "Ethics as First Philosophy," in *The Levinas Reader*, edited by Sean Hand (New York: Routledge, 1989), 75–87.

17. Levinas, *Totality and Infinity*, 199.

18. This phrase "politics after" comes from the title of a 1982 radio interview; however, it can give rise to a misleading, which will be addressed later in this chapter, that would make it appear that the ethical relation would first exist and then the political relation would be introduced later. This misimpression of a narrative structure, as Bernasconi has argued, must be corrected by the realization that the Levinasian subject is always a political subject, and the role of the ethical is to interrupt the political and to call it into question. To support this point, one need only consider Levinas's own claim that "it is not that there would be a face, and then the being it manifests or expresses would concern himself with justice" (*Totality and Infinity*, 213). See Robert Bernasconi, "The Third Party: Levinas on the Intersection of the Ethical and the Political," *Journal of the British Society for Phenomenology* 30, no. 1 (January 1999): 76–87.

19. Derrida puts this point in the following way: "Allergy, the refusal or forgetting of the face, comes to inscribe its secondary negativity against a backdrop of peace, against the backdrop of a hospitality that does not belong to the order of the political, or at least not simply to a political space." Jacques Derrida, *Adieu to Emmanuel Levinas*, trans. Pascale-Anne Brault and Michael Naas (Stanford: Stanford University Press, 1999), 49.

20. This is one example, among others, of a key point of intersection between Levinas's philosophy and personalism that calls for further exploration, insofar as they all agree that interpersonal relations are fundamental to the meaning of human life. Given that King's thought is known to be influenced by personalism, such a study could deepen the possible connections between these two thinkers.

21. Levinas, *Totality and Infinity*, 197, 198.

22. Levinas, *Totality and Infinity*, 23.

23. Levinas, *Basic Philosophical Writings*, 9. See also *Totality and Infinity*, 198.

24. Levinas, *Totality and Infinity*, 199.

25. Levinas, *Totality and Infinity*, 199, 225.

26. Levinas, *Totality and Infinity*, 198.

27. King, "Nonviolence and Racial Justice," 5.

28. Although there have been a number of violent clashes between blacks and whites throughout the course of American history, such as the Atlanta Riots of 1906 and the Tulsa Race Riots of 1921, their frequency accelerated with the rise to prominence of groups like the Nation of Islam and the Black Panther Party for Self Defense in the 1950s. It is important to remember, then, that King was speaking within the context of a fertile ground for further violence such as would later be seen, for instance, in the 1965 Watts Race Riot and the 1967 Detroit Rebellion.

29. King, "Nonviolence and Racial Justice," 57.

30. King, "Nonviolence and Racial Justice," 7.

31. King, "Nonviolence and Racial Justice," 6.

32. King, "Nonviolence and Racial Justice," 7.

33. King, "An Experiment in Love," 20.

34. King, "Nonviolence and Racial Justice," 7.

35. King, "Nonviolence and Racial Justice," 6.

36. King, "An Experiment in Love," 19.

37. King, "Love, Law and Civil Disobedience," 51.

38. For example, in "Transcendence and Height," Levinas writes: "In order to suppress violence it is necessary to have recourse to violence." See Levinas, *Basic Philosophical Writings*, 15.

39. Levinas, *Of God Who Comes to Mind*, 83–84. Interestingly, Levinas goes on to add that "there are third parties and one cannot allow that third parties be persecuted!"

40. A good example of this view is Robert Bernasconi, "The Violence of the Face: Peace and Language in the Thought of Levinas," *Philosophy & Social Criticism* 20, no. 6: 81–93.

41. Levinas, *Otherwise than Being*, 177.

42. Levinas, *Otherwise than Being*, 160.

43. See Jacques Derrida, "Violence and Metaphysics," in *Writing and Difference*, trans. Alan Bass (Chicago: University of Chicago Press, 1978).

44. King, "Pilgrimage to Nonviolence," 39.

45. King, "Pilgrimage to Nonviolence," 38.

46. See Robert F. Williams, *Negroes with Guns* (Detroit: Wayne State University Press, 1998).

47. In a similar moment of rhetorical brilliance and clarity, Malcolm X pushes the dilemma further by questioning the coherence of the praxis of nonviolence in a country where blacks are drafted into the military:

"How are you going to be non-violent in Mississippi, as violent as you were in Korea? How can you justify being non-violent in Mississippi and Alabama, when your churches are bombed, and your little girls murdered and at the same time you are going to get violent with Hitler, and ToJo, and somebody else you don't even know. . . . If it is wrong to be violent defending black women and black children and black babies and black men, then it is wrong for America to draft us and make us violent in defense of her."

If it is permissible for America to call on blacks to go to war in defense of the rights of people in other countries, then clearly it should be permissible for individuals, black or otherwise, to practice violence in order to defend their own rights at home as well. King's reply would be to show that the solution to this apparent paradox is to realize that it is not just morally impermissible but also impractical to resort to violence in either case.

48. Williams explains his view in the following terms: "I advocated violent self-defense because I don't really think you can have a defense against violent racists and against terrorists unless you are prepared to meet violence with violence, and my policy was to meet violence with violence." See Robert F. Williams, *Negroes with Guns* (Detroit: Wayne State University Press, 1998).

49. King, "Love, Law, and Civil Disobedience," 45.

50. For a good account of King's sense of justice and community, see Greg Moses, *Revolution of Conscience* (New York: Guilford Press, 1997), especially chapter 5.

51. Within the specific context of calls on the black community to employ violence, King makes the following practical observations as to why these calls for violence will fail. First, blacks do not control the armed forces in the United States, and thus when black violence does break out, white society has the local police, national guard, and military to call on. Second, violent action by American blacks would gather little sympathy and support from the white majority. Finally, black violence does more harm to black communities than its intended targets. So, contrary to much public opinion, King concludes that violence does not offer an effective tool for social change in the black community.

52. King, *Where Do We Go from Here?*, 578.

53. King, "Love, Law and Civil Disobedience," 47.

54. King, *Where Do We Go from Here?*, 578.

55. King, "An Experiment in Love," 20.

56. We use the notions of the beloved community and the agapeic community interchangeably here, insofar as the beloved community for King is the embodiment of agapeic love. For a more detailed account of the roots of King's notion of the beloved community, see Gary Herstein, "The Roycean Roots of the Beloved Community," *The Pluralist* 4, no 2. (Summer 2009): 91–107.

57. Highlighting this connection between the individual and community, King writes: "If I meet hate with hate, I become depersonalized because creation is so designed that my personality can only be fulfilled in the context of community." King, "An Experiment in Love," 20.

58. Among a number of critics of King's assimilationist tendencies, see Harold Cruse, *Plural but Not Equal* (New York: Morrow, 1987) and bell hooks' chapter "Beloved Community: A World without Racism," in *Killing Rage: Ending Racism* (New York: Holt, 1995), 263–72.

TEN

Martin Luther King Jr. on Vietnam

King's Message Applied to the U.S. Occupation of Iraq and Afghanistan

Gail M. Presbey

INTRODUCTION

This chapter will explore King's position on Vietnam. While many know that he spoke about the war, his views are not always as well known, and they are not very well mainstreamed into widespread knowledge about King's philosophy and legacy. Perhaps it is because in his critique of the war, King criticized militarism in general and U.S. neocolonial foreign policy specifically. These are uncomfortable topics, and many Americans are in denial of U.S. neocolonial tendencies. But despite pressure to be silent on the issue, King held his duty to criticize the war with great conviction. For that reason we must explore his ideas.

The chapter begins with a survey of King's early years when he was reluctant to speak out on the war. We'll then explore the factors that led him to change his position and his strategy so that he became an outspoken critic. We'll look at insights from his February 1967 speech on the topic, and then at the more famous April 1967 speech, "Beyond Vietnam." We'll look at responses to his message among the American public. Then the chapter will explore two other topics at greater length. First, King's most important message to Americans was that there was a crisis of values, and that Americans had to rethink their values as well as their practices regarding war and militarism. Related to this is his challenge to Americans to get on the correct side of a worldwide revolution. Secondly, we'll explore the question of parallels between King's message to Americans during the Vietnam War, and the current context of the U.S. occupations of Iraq and Afghanistan. The wars are not identical, yet after carefully evaluating and delimiting the fruitfulness of an analogy, I will venture to say that King's earlier comments do have a relevant message to Americans today in the context of the Iraq and Afghanistan occupations.

Theologian James Cone had an interesting insight into the stages that Martin Luther King went through in his struggles for peace and justice. Cone argued that in the 1950s, the early King relied upon and emphasized the importance of love. At the time, he had white political allies and broad support within the black community as well. But as white allies began to withdraw as King emphasized the interconnections of poverty, racism, and war, and as black allies splintered off into other groups, King spoke less of love but became centered upon hope in a transcendent God. He said there was a "great benign power in the universe" that could "make a way out of no way."[1] This same emphasis on divine power was key to Gandhi's personal spirituality, and helped Gandhi to be confident of the power of nonviolence even when, in the short run, it seemed to be defeated.

King felt a duty to speak out against the Vietnam War, even if others remained silent so to not ruffle the feathers of the powerful, or so that they would continue to get their foundation grants. This compelling need to speak out is related, Cone argued, to the concept of preacher as prophet, which is alive in the black community.[2] In fact, we could trace the emphasis on prophecy back to African religious beliefs and practices. We often think of a prophet as a person who has somehow heard the voice of God conveying a message. A prophet can also be understood as a keen observer of trends who realizes that if things keep going the way they are going, there will be catastrophe down the road.[3] In his speeches on Vietnam, King showed himself to be a keen observer of trends, and a shrewd analyst of human nature. His advice, although not yet taken by those in powerful positions in America, is invaluable. King received the Nobel Peace Prize, and he has had a public holiday named after him in his home country. What remains is for Americans to embrace his message.

EARLY YEARS

People were not always satisfied with King's stand on the war. He was perceived, in the early years, as having too much faith in the possibility of direct negotiations with Presidents Kennedy and Johnson. King had a working relationship with President Johnson, which helped in passing the Civil Rights Act of 1964 and the Voting Rights Act of 1965. King himself, as well as others in the Civil Rights movement, did not want to jeopardize these good relations. King was seen to capitulate to presidential pressure to tone down criticism of the war. King explained that he did so out of hopes that negotiations out of the limelight would be more fruitful than angry public confrontations.[4] He stated that his motivation at all times was to do whatever he could to bring a speedy end to the war.[5]

Political activist David Dellinger admitted that King was so popular that he was inundated by people who wanted him to lend his endorsement to their cause, and so those who wanted him to focus on Vietnam had to join the throng that surrounded King. Dellinger was disappointed with the 1963 March on Washington, where King delivered his "I Have a Dream" speech, often hailed by many as one of the brightest points in American history. Kennedy used carrot-and-stick measures to control King. Kennedy put pressure on King to ensure that the March on Washington did not follow the original plans that would have involved massive civil resistance. Kennedy threatened to stop buses before they entered Washington, D.C., if the more radical plans were going to be followed. King accepted Kennedy's offer of money for SCLC (funds that were actually funneled through a CIA front, the Taconic Foundation), and in exchange, put pressure on John Lewis to cut certain parts of his speech that had been critical of Kennedy and his administration. One of the sentences cut said that "both the Democrats and the Republicans have betrayed the basic principles of the Declaration of Independence."[6]

Dellinger is convinced that part of the reason King was so conservative on Vietnam was because Hoover had threatened him with revealing tapes that Hoover had clandestinely collected on King, regarding his extramarital affairs. In December of 1964 Hoover publicly denounced King as a liar. According to Dellinger, King met personally with Hoover to ask for an apology. King went into the meeting "breathing fire and smoke and came out thoroughly cowed," because Hoover had threatened to reveal the tapes.[7]

In 1965 King announced that he would appeal directly to Ho Chi Minh, President Johnson, and the South Vietnamese, Chinese, and Russian governments to stop the war. But it was only a "public relations gesture," because, Dellinger explained, King never actually sent the letters. Dellinger thought that at the time, King was more conservative than other African American activist groups like SNCC and CORE. He thought that King's equal appeal to the various leaders of nations involved in the war obfuscated the particular responsibility that the United States had in ensuring that the war continued. Since black GIs were disproportionately bearing the burden of the war (being 23.5 percent of the casualties while only 11 percent of the troops in 1965), many black groups considered the war a race issue.[8]

Knowing all the pressures put on King to stay off the topic of Vietnam, it is all the more impressive that he finally decided to take a strong public stand. In January of 1966 King defended Julian Bond's right to oppose the war. In a May 1966 appearance on the television show *Face the Nation*, King implored U.S. leaders to stop the bombing of Vietnam.[9]

1967: KING'S POSITION ON VIETNAM EVOLVES

King described his own changes regarding his role in speaking out on Vietnam in early 1967. While in Jamaica in January 1967 he read an article called "The Children of Vietnam" and was very moved by it. He made a promise to himself, "Never again will I be silent on an issue that is destroying the soul of our nation and destroying thousands and thousands of little children in Vietnam."[10] He became convinced that his silence was a betrayal to suffering people. He felt a strong urging of conscience to speak out so that he could "erase my name from the bombs which fall over North or South Vietnam."[11]

In February of 1967 the U.S. government had spurned a peace offer conveyed by the North Vietnam government through the Soviet Union. King became convinced that the United States was not sincere in its assertions that it wanted peace. Instead, it wanted military victory. In Los Angeles in February of 1967 he delivered an important address, which prefigured the more famous sermon he would deliver a few months later. In this earlier speech entitled "The Casualties of the War in Vietnam,"[12] King outlined the extent of civilian casualties (over one million) with emphasis on women and children. But just as important was what he called "the casualties of principles and values." King charged that the United States had violated the Charter of the United Nations by attacking North Vietnam, whose political independence should have been respected. Rather than submitting the charge of North Vietnamese aggression against itself to the U.N. Security Council, the United States decided to attack. King said that the turmoil inside Vietnam was basically a civil war, and so the United States had no good grounds on which to intervene.

Another topic in this February speech was how U.S. actions in Vietnam served as a "new form of colonialism," insofar as they attempted to thwart Vietnamese desires for independence. King explained the history of the country, saying that in 1945, with Ho Chi Minh as their leader, Vietnam declared its independence. But President Truman decided to help France to reconquer its former colony, because Truman thought that Vietnam was not ready for its independence. Of course, Truman saw the decision about Vietnam in the context of an unfolding Cold War with the Soviet Union. Truman was concerned that Ho Chi Minh, the Vietnamese leader, was a communist. While France did the fighting, the U.S. government paid up to 80 percent of the bill for France's war. When France finally pulled out, the United States stepped in to continue the war, albeit as an "undeclared" war. This kind of war, against a people's own desire for self-determination, "seeks to turn the clock of history back and perpetuate white colonialism." At this point in his speech, King hinted about a theme that he would explore at greater length in his April speech: that the United States had betrayed its own heritage by becoming "anti-revolutionary."

By addressing the topic in this way, King let his audience know that he was in touch with the times. French troops that had been pulled out of Vietnam were reassigned to Algeria, where they engaged in counterinsurgency work that included torture of detainees. Algerians nevertheless continued to fight, and eventually won their independence from France. A popular film, *The Battle of Algiers* (1965) became famous and won a Golden Lion award in Europe in 1966. Advocates of Black Power in the United States watched this film. King was in an ideological struggle with advocates of Black Power, trying to convince them that they should not follow Fanon's philosophy, which justified Algerian uses of terrorism as part of a liberation movement. King was concerned that the example of violent revolution was swaying African Americans to choose violent expression in some of the recent riots in the United States.[13] While himself favoring Gandhi-style nonviolent revolutions, here, King nevertheless showed sympathy with people of other nations who turned to violence as self-defense against oppressive foreign forces. But his emphasis was on insisting that his own country's forces withdraw, making the violence of the oppressed unnecessary.

Related to the topic of colonialism is King's charge that Americans are arrogant in thinking that they have much to teach other countries but little to learn from them. The United States had appointed itself as World Policeman without asking other countries if it should take this role. Why should the president of the United States decide if another country is ready for its independence or not? Most likely the United States was worried that an independent but weak Vietnam would be easy prey for China, and the "domino theory" feared that communist countries wanted to expand their power. But who had decided that the United States should be the guardian of other countries? King pointed out that other dictatorships continued with U.S. help, such as white minority rule in South Africa and Rhodesia, all in the name of "fighting communism."

Other topics that King mentioned in this early speech and visited at greater length in April include the connection between ignoring domestic troubles of poverty and racism while lavishing funds and human resources on fighting the war in Vietnam. He considered it hypocritical for the United States to go to the far corners of the world to right wrongs there "while not setting out own house in order." In fact he made comments like this as early as March 1965, when he noted that the United States, while sending money and troops to Vietnam in concern for its security, could not protect African Americans from racist attacks while trying to practice their right to vote in Selma, Alabama.[14]

In the February speech King expressed how he had felt inhibited in speaking out against the war. People had argued that it was unpatriotic to criticize a war while it was going on. He noted that supporters of the war thought that criticism of the war would hurt the troops. But King said that Lincoln, Emerson, and Thoreau criticized the U.S. war with Mexico while it was going on. He thought the principle of dissent was an important part of our heritage. The lessons of history had shown that "wars are poor chisels for carving out peaceful tomorrows." He further clarified that it was only because he loved America so much that he found himself compelled to criticize its error in Vietnam. It was his high expectation for the country that had made his current disappointment so great. He challenged the country to re-evaluate its values, and realize that war, with its ever more dangerous weapons, was "obsolete."

This emphasis on re-evaluating our values coincides with the call by philosopher Alain Locke of Howard University, who insisted that new realities and contexts call for adapting values to a new context. Our norms must be constantly corrected so as to maintain our values. A wooden holding to the same practice or "age-old customs" in belief that only such rigidity can protect a value is faulty thinking.[15] Applying this insight to King's comments, we can see that the presence of nuclear weapons calls into question our old practice of engaging in war to protect the values of peace and security. We can still hold peace and security as values, but we must find new and better ways to act so as to safeguard those values.

THE APRIL 1967 SPEECH, "BEYOND VIETNAM"[16]

King soon had a chance to develop the ideas that he had begun to elucidate in his February speech in Los Angeles. King addressed a meeting of Clergy and Laity Concerned at Riverside Church in New York City. About three thousand people were gathered for the event, which also included Henry Steele Commanger, John Bennett, and Rabbi Abraham Joshua Heschel. King had drafted his speech with the help of Vincent Harding of Spelman College as well as John Maguire of Wesleyan University.[17]

King began his April speech musing on the topic of why he had chosen the topic. He explained that the "calling to speak is often a vocation of agony," suggesting that he did not find it easy to give voice to his views on Vietnam, but that he felt compelled to do so anyway. He clarified that he intended his speech for an American audience, and did not feel called to preach to the North Vietnamese or any other parties of the conflict. He explained why he cared about this topic by giving concrete examples about how his concern for race relations led him to be concerned about the war. He hoped that people would be brought out of poverty by programs that had not been enacted, because funds were going to the Vietnam War. He explained that African American men were losing their lives on the battlefield of Vietnam. He was also concerned that a violent government was a bad role model for angry youths who also thought that violence would solve their problems.

Next, he pondered how Americans could consider themselves liberators of other peoples, given the wars we were fighting. He recalled the early example of the U.S. Declaration of Independence, and explained that it had articulated the desires of peoples around the world to be free of their colonial oppressors. But when oppressed people fight for their liberty, and want to declare the Declaration of Independence as expressing their motivation for freedom (as did Ho Chi Minh in declaring Vietnam's independence from French colonists in 1945), the United States sometimes joined the forces trying to crush them. While Vietnamese may have had arguments among themselves about what was the best path for the country to take, now all sides had to turn against the occupier, the United States. While the United States said it would bring land reform and other good things, these had been empty promises. Instead, the United States tested its latest technological weapons on the Vietnamese, killing over one million of them, mostly civilians. U.S. forces had herded peasants into "fortified hamlets" that, King asserted, were little more than concentration camps. U.S. actions had been self-defeating since the United States had attacked the Buddhist church, which was a non-Communist organization that could have helped chart an alternative course for Vietnam. In this context, how could the United States rightly consider itself to be Vietnam's liberators? How could Americans expect Vietnamese peasants to consider Americans as liberators?

While Americans declared that they were in favor of democracy, they helped to squash elections in 1954 that would have most probably united Vietnam under Ho Chi Minh. King also said that the United States covered up North Vietnamese offers of peace so that military advisors could present to the American public the idea that North Vietnam had been an aggressor and so, a legitimate target in the war. The fact that so many lies were at the basis of the war led King to remark that U.S. soldiers were not only being brutalized while fighting the war—"We are adding cynicism to the process of death, for they must know after a short period there that none of the things we claim to be fighting for are really involved."

King also quoted Buddhist leaders of Vietnam who clearly distinguished the possibility of military victory (due to superior forces and armaments) from political victory, which King said would not be possible. Repeating his charge that U.S. involvement in Vietnam was a colonialist enterprise, he explained that practically speaking, the first thing that Americans must do is "admit that we have been wrong from the beginning of our adventure in Vietnam, that we have been detrimental to the life of the Vietnamese people." He said that Americans should sharply turn to a new direction in their foreign policy toward Vietnam, to "extricate ourselves from this nightmarish conflict." He asked for an immediate halt to the bombing, and for a date set for withdrawal of troops. On this latter point he noted that the Geneva Agreement of 1954 already asked for a date to be set. King went further to say that Americans should pledge funds for the rehabilitation of the country and also to grant asylum to Vietnamese who feared persecution under a new government. He also suggested that young people should be educated about the war and encouraged to apply for conscientious objector status. He reported with pride that seventy students from his alma mater, Morehouse College, had done so.

From these specific steps toward disengagement, King then pulled back to ask the bigger questions underlying the technical details of a withdrawal. He said that we couldn't keep focused only on Vietnam, for the war there is just "a symptom of a far deeper malady within the American spirit." Without attending to this deeper malady, the United States would continue to have Vietnam-like wars, and the peace community would have to organize against them one by one. The deeper cause of the conflicts was that the United States had taken the side of the wealthy. Its number one concern had been to protect investments abroad. The United States therefore sought stability where its money had been invested, even to the point of propping up dictators, and on the other hand it wanted to topple those who were seen as threatening U.S. corporate interests. King himself didn't go as far as to charge that such a change in the U.S. role had been done purposefully. He allowed that it may have happened accidentally. But however it happened, he argued, the United States must get back onto the right side of a world revolution.

King argued that the only way to newly prioritize our relations with other nations was to shift from a materialist, consumer-oriented culture to a person-centered community. We couldn't continue with our smug rich lifestyle while a majority of the world's population was barely surviving. If we wanted to show the world that we were a truly compassionate country, we couldn't just donate to charity relief. As King put it, our challenge was not just to fling a coin to a beggar; instead, we must realize that "an edifice which produces beggars needs restructuring." The fact that the annual U.S. government budget spent much more on weapons than on "programs of social uplift" was a sign, for King, that the nation was "approaching spiritual death." While the government said it had to arm itself against encroaching communism, King asserted that the best defense against communism was to practice justice and true democracy. Our concern for justice should not be limited to national boundaries. We should care for all peoples in this world.

Certainly King was not advocating a quietism or isolationism. However, an America that says it cares about justice should show the world it does so by first practicing it at home. If the United States were to eradicate or greatly reduce racism and poverty at home, and send a new message to its corporations about the limits to what the U.S. military will or will not do in order to protect investments abroad (that is, limits within moral guidelines), the need to fight wars abroad would greatly diminish.

AFTERMATH OF THE SPEECH

As soon as he spoke at Riverside Church in New York City on April 4, 1967, the press was filled with accounts of various religious and civil rights groups, including the NAACP, that denounced his stand. A review in *Time Magazine* said that King's speech sounded like "a script for Radio Hanoi," and the *Washington Post* said King had "diminished his usefulness to his cause, his country, and his people."[18] Many key SCLC financial backers threatened to cut off their funds to the organization if King dared to appear at a demonstration against the war on April 15, 1967. Dellinger said that he heard that Harry Wachtel told King he had a check for $20,000 in his pocket but he would not be able to give it to King if he marched. But King marched. In addition to financial threats, the New York Police Department had come to Dellinger's office before the march to warn them that there were people who were trying to kill King and they might do it during the march. But by then, King insisted on marching whatever the dangers might be. About 300,000 marched that day, and Dellinger and others surrounded King at all times, and placed the speakers' podium far back so that chances of being shot would be lessened.[19]

Despite these criticisms, King continued to address the problem of the Vietnam War in a series of speeches and sermons. Another related topic that King often addressed was how much more dangerous the world had become because of the creation and continued testing and development of nuclear weapons, and the ensuing arms race. In June of 1967 he delivered a speech, "A Knock at Midnight,"[20] in which he aimed his criticism, not directly at the U.S. government, but at church leaders who, by their silence and complicity or by their direct support, became "lackeys" of the State in disregard of their moral duty to denounce injustice. King said that it was "midnight" within the social order. Nuclear weapons threatened to destroy the world. People had become dishonest, subtly changing Darwin's maxim to "survival of the slickest." In such a situation, people knocked at the door of the church asking for guidance and help in seeking peace and economic justice, but too often they were disappointed. The church had shown itself to be irrelevant. Too often it had endorsed war and imperialist expansion. To become relevant again, the church had to free itself from the grip of the status quo.

In February of 1968 King delivered a sermon called "The Drum Major Instinct."[21] There he accused the United States of wanting to be first among nations, and to dominate other countries. But if all nations desired supremacy, the outcome would be suicidal for all. Again, he referred to nuclear weapons and how our world was now precarious. Referring to the U.S. role in Vietnam, he asserted: "God didn't call America to do what she's doing in the world now. God didn't call America to engage in a senseless, unjust war as the war in Vietnam. And we are criminals in that war. We've committed more war crimes almost than any nation in the world, and I'm going to continue to say it. And we won't stop it because of our pride and our arrogance as a nation." These were harsh words for his own nation that he loved.

But in the same speech King went on to clarify that wanting to be first was not in itself a bad thing. When James and John asked Jesus if they could sit at his right hand, he didn't tell them to be humble. But he clarified that being "first" meant being first in love, in generosity, and in willingness to sacrifice. King applied the same lesson to the United States. If we really wanted to be great, we should use our energies to serve others, to be great in helping others. Certainly, this is a major desire of Americans. We are a generous nation and have responded, for example during the tsunami disaster of December 2004, with charity. Imagine the generosity that America could practice were it to reduce its huge military budget.

PARALLELS TO CURRENT TIMES

All these years later, the criticism that the United States has become anti-revolutionary is still appropriate. It may be that for many Americans, the idea that the United States is supposed to be revolutionary, that is, siding with the downtrodden against the oppressors, is not a well-known aspect of our country's heritage. In the decades since King's death in 1968, worker membership in unions has plummeted, and the average American may think they have more to profit by being friendly to the rich (that is, by giving the rich big tax breaks) than by organizing in solidarity to get concessions from the rich (as the recent congressional vote to extend Bush's tax breaks for the rich has shown). Our recent and ongoing wars and occupations in Afghanistan and Iraq have been for the most part presented to the American people as a necessity for security reasons. A bold few may say with daring that Americans have every right to do whatever they want to keep up their "lifestyle" of gas-guzzling, but most don't have to go that far to justify extensive military occupations costing lives and billions of dollars. Only critics of the war point to it as examples of an ongoing colonialism by our country.

Currently, under the Obama Administration, both of our ongoing wars in Afghanistan and Iraq have been subsumed under the category of "Overseas Contingency Operations" (OCO), the new term that has taken the place of the Global War on Terror. Commenting on the new OCO terminology, Ira Chernus noted, "As early as 1937, Secretary of State Cordell Hull said publicly: 'There can be no serious hostilities anywhere in the world which will not one way or another affect interests or rights or obligations of this country.' Since the late 1940s, U.S. policymakers have assumed that there were no serious 'contingencies' of any kind, anywhere on the planet, that did not affect this country's interests." Due to such entrenched attitudes, Chernus thought that the new OCO terminology actually admits that "we're not at war, we're at empire."[22] This approach places no limits on U.S. intervention—such as sending drones into Pakistan where they strike targets and inevitably kill civilians. From January 2009 to October 2010 there have been 139 drone strikes, which have been terrorizing the people of North and South Waziristan.[23]

It is not a surprise that many authors have commented upon the parallels between Vietnam and the U.S.-led coalition forces' military actions in Iraq. Echoing King's earlier insights, commentators have noticed that our interest in that area of the Middle East seems to be another example of neocolonialism. In the 1980s we propped up Saddam Hussein in his fight against Iran, and our government seemed to tolerate, back then, Hussein's use of terrible weapons against his enemies. Hussein fell out of favor when he invaded Kuwait, a U.S. ally and major source of oil, in 1990. Back in 1991, before the U.S. invasion, George Katsiaficas commented upon parallels between George Bush Sr.'s proposed war in the Gulf and Vietnam. Katsiaficas quoted Sen. Kerry (who had served in Vietnam) who pointed out that in both cases, leaders Saddam Hussein and Ho Chi Minh were treated as the "incarnation of evil" and compared to Hitler. He thought the uses of such hyperbole were "gross exaggerations that inhibited clear thought."[24] Katsiaficas found other parallels. The United States would again be fighting an old civilization that most Americans know nothing about (Vietnamese society was four thousand years old), and fighting in a complicated political context where most Americans did not know the details of what led to the tensions.

In both cases the American public was told that there was an aggressive invader. In Vietnam, the North invaded the South; but Americans didn't know the history of how the line was drawn between North and South in the first place. The recent colonial history of the French played a large role in drawing the line. Likewise, British colonial history was involved in drawing the lines separating Iraq from Kuwait. Katsiaficas charged that the United States was involved in helping prop up the Kuwaiti government, which was nothing more than a corrupt puppet that kept Arabs at the mercy of Western powers. Likewise, the United States began its intervention in Vietnam propping up Ngo Dinh Diem and his family's rule in South Vietnam. Another parallel that Katsiaficas outlined in 1991 was "our arrogant underestimation of the enemy and overconfidence in our technological superiority."[25]

Closer to our own time, noted Middle East analysts like Juan Cole, American culture commentators like Tom Englehardt, and others have written and spoken on parallels between the Iraq war of 2003 and the Vietnam War. In fact, Bush supporter and ethics professor Jean Bethke Elshtain complained that critics of the Iraq war were stuck in a "time warp" and did nothing more than "dust off" their old rhetoric about the Vietnam war and recycle them as insights into the Iraq war.[26] Comments like this suggest that Iraq war critics have been lazy or uncareful. I intend to survey their claims and evaluate their appropriateness. In this section of the chapter we'll look at their estimations of the parallels between the two cases to ask whether the United States has been making similar mistakes in the Iraq war as were made in Vietnam. We'll then ask if Dr. King's advice for ending U.S. fighting in Vietnam could work for the current Iraq war.

Daniel Ellsberg, the former Marine and State Department official who leaked the Pentagon Papers to the press in 1969, summed up in June of 2006 what he thought to be the important parallels between Vietnam and Iraq. He called both a "reckless war of choice" in which the United States fought against "a country that has not attacked us."[27] He noted that the continued occupation and fighting by U.S. troops in Iraq, as in Vietnam, went against the wishes of most of the inhabitants of that country. Ellsberg said he released the Pentagon Papers during Vietnam when he finally realized that the Pentagon and State Department reflexively lie at every level. They misled the American public about the origins and purposes of the Vietnam War, and they had done the same for Iraq. The trail of lies created and later uncovered about the Iraq War is extensive.[28] In fact the King quote from "Beyond Vietnam" mentioned earlier, "We are adding cynicism to the process of death, for they must know after a short period there that none of the things we claim to be fighting for are really involved," was quite true of Iraq as well, and since the lies began to be known while the occupation was still going on, it did lead to the despair and demoralization of many in the U.S. armed services who were still deployed. A *New York Times*/CBS News poll in May 2007 showed that less than half of U.S. military and their immediate family believed that the United States did the right thing in invading Iraq.[29]

Author Stephen Pizzo noticed that certain themes, intended to raise the level of support for both wars among a skeptical public, were found in speeches of Richard Nixon and Lyndon Johnson in the 1960s, and repeated in Bush speeches about Iraq. Common themes include American self-sacrifice to give others the "gift of freedom," the emphasis on the threat to America, that the enemy has an animal nature, that we must listen to military experts, that we are making substantial progress, that local people are being trained to take over so that American troops will be able to leave, that Americans must not lose their nerve now, and that America must win.[30] King similarly appealed to human aspirations for self-sacrifice. He suggested that Americans lead by serving others, as Jesus told James and John. But in Bush speeches, the self-sacrifice necessarily came in a military mold, and the self-interest of politics and corporations was papered over with expressions of self-sacrifice.

This emphasis on American selfless doing-good by policing the world, ensuring that freedom and justice "prevail" wherever the United States decides its troops should go, was exposed and parodied during the Vietnam War by folk singer Phil Ochs in his song "Cops of the World." Many of the song's lyrics ring true for U.S. contemporary OCOs. Far from the "professional" image of the armed forces, the song is an unkind exposé of attitudes of "do-gooders" who presume the right to decide the affairs of other countries. After listing actions of U.S. troops including breaking down doors in the middle of the night, and killing the sons of those they come to "liberate," the "soldiers" in the song explain:

We own half the world, oh say can you see

And the name for our profits is democracy

So, like it or not, you will have to be free

'Cause we're the Cops of the World, boys, We're the Cops of the World.[31]

Jonathan Schell, author of *The Unconquerable World*, said he thought he had shown in his book that the era of imperialism was over. Anti-imperial movements had triumphed almost everywhere. Given that, Schell was puzzled by the U.S. invasion of Iraq, noting that it looked like a neo-imperial move. Schell said, "The most remarkable 'intelligence failure' in Iraq was not to see weapons of mass destruction where there were none; it was to blind ourselves to the struggle of national resistance that history told us would have to follow American invasion and occupation."[32] For Schell, the importance of the parallel with Vietnam was "not because the Vietnamese nation resembles the Iraqi nation but because Vietnam was America's very own, protracted, anguished experience of the almost universal story of imperial defeat at the hands of local peoples determined to run their own countries." Schell was frustrated that so many Americans were in denial of their own country's imperial and world-dominating aspirations. As a democracy we citizens have a duty to ensure that our country does not continue on an imperial path, a path that would, according to Schell, necessarily lead to defeat.

Political science professor and statistician John Mueller studied the parallels between U.S. public opinion about the Vietnam and Iraq wars. In both cases, there was broad support for the war in the beginning, with support dwindling as casualties went up. But in the case of Iraq, support for the war dropped much more precipitously. For example, in early 2005, over half of Americans polled said that the Iraq war was a mistake. But at the time there were only fifteen hundred U.S. casualties. In comparison, the Vietnam War only reached that position in public polls in 1968 after the Tet Offensive, when U.S. casualties had already reached twenty thousand. Mueller thought that the discrepancy between the two cases was due to the fact that Americans thought that the threats in Iraq were less than the earlier threats in Vietnam. After all, with no weapons of mass destruction discovered in Iraq, and links to international terrorism tenuous at best, Americans now saw Iraq as a humanitarian venture not worth the high cost in lives and funds.[33]

But is this estimation of the various levels of security threat accurate, and is it at the heart of the change in U.S. public opinion? Elshtain argued that communism did pose a real threat, so the Vietnam War had to be fought.[34] George W. Bush has likewise argued (sidestepping for the moment the issue of whether Iraq would have been a danger if the United States had not invaded) that a pullout from Iraq would leave Americans open to danger. We'll look at Bush's argument in the next section.

BUSH'S ANALOGY BETWEEN VIETNAM AND IRAQ

Back in 1991, George Bush Sr. repeatedly reassured the American public that there would not be a long, drawn out war as was the case in Vietnam. He seemed to be arguing that those who worried about parallels between Iraq and Vietnam had nothing to worry about.[35] In fact, George Bush Sr. said the reason he did not pursue Saddam Hussein into Iraq back in 1991 was that if he had done so, "we would have been forced to occupy Baghdad and, in effect, rule Iraq."[36] Now, George W. Bush joined with others in mentioning parallels between Iraq and Vietnam wars. While his speech to the Veterans of Foreign Wars in August 2007[37] included lessons learned from the war with Japan during World War Two and the Korean War, I will focus on his comments about the lessons of Vietnam for the Iraq war. He began by cautiously suggesting that the Vietnam War was complex and that he was only going to visit one aspect of the war in his talk, regarding the question of pullout of troops. Bush said that the struggle in Iraq was an ideological struggle, just as were the earlier wars of World War Two, the Korean and Vietnam wars. In each case the United States faced enemies who, like today's terrorists, have a harsh political vision.

Bush argued that antiwar critics in 1972 suggested that it didn't matter what would happen to Indochina (here, Bush wanted to include Cambodia) after U.S. troops left, because basically nothing could be worse than the present war. But he said that these critics were wrong, because the Khmer Rouge came to power, leading to the deaths of hundreds of thousands of people. In Vietnam, tens of thousands of people, including those who had been loyal to the United States, died in prison camps. He also said there were hundreds of thousands of "boat people" who fled Vietnam, and many of them died at sea. Since he has made his comments, many historians and other political commentators have disagreed with the lessons he has drawn from the earlier wars.

But other commentators, including Michael Hirsch, Josh Marshall, and Robert Scheer, have argued that history has shown that the United States did not have to fight in Vietnam in order to protect the United States or even East Asia from the communist threat. Once the United States pulled out of Vietnam, Vietnam distanced itself from the Soviet Union. East Asia did not collapse to communism. While Vietnam is still communist, it is surrounded by capitalist countries. Scheer argued that in Vietnam, "our blundering military presence fueled the native nationalist militancy we supposedly sought to eradicate."[38] Hirsch thought that the United States "won" the Cold War due to a thriving economy, not due to its military incursions.[39]

Reporter David Kirkpatrick wondered if Bush's speech was "rhetorical jiu-jitsu, an attempt to throw back at his critics their favorite historical analogy—Vietnam—for the Iraq war."[40] He said that some historians see the United States as bringing about Cambodia's destabilization, so in a sense preparing the groundwork for the later Khmer Rouge's chance at power. If that was the case, Bush could hardly use the brutality of the Khmer Rouge as an argument in favor of continued U.S. presence in Indochina. While Kirkpatrick did not name the historians who hold this view, documentarian John Pilger explained that he had created a documentary called *Year Zero: The Silent Death of Cambodia* that showed how the United States shared responsibility for the Khmer Rouge coming to power. Pilger explained that American bombing had "provided the catalyst for the rise of Pol Pot," and that he had CIA documents to back up his argument.[41] However, his documentary was not distributed in the United States, although it played in sixty other countries. This means that people from other countries have a better sense of how U.S. actions led to atrocities in Indochina than Americans do. Certainly the point that Bush tried to make would not hold water in such circumstances. Bush's arguments thrive in the context of an uninformed public, who were never taught about the complexities and realities of Vietnam.

However, we could imagine someone arguing that even if U.S. presence led to the destabilization of Cambodia and Pol Pot, that would only be an argument for not going there in the first place, and not an argument for leaving once one's presence has already created the destabilization. Historian David C. Hendrickson agreed that "the Khmer Rouge would never have come to power in the absence of the war in Vietnam—this dark force rose out of the circumstances of the war, was in a deep sense created by the war," and yet Hendrickson noted that when the United States pulled out of Vietnam and Cambodia, that led to "catastrophic consequences."[42] About 1.7 million people died in Cambodia under Pol Pot, and about one and a half million Vietnamese refugees fled their country. In the Iraq context, one might reason that if U.S. mistakes have already led to a deterioration of security and civil war-like conditions, that doesn't mean that the United States should now leave. Those mistakes can't be erased, and now, according to what both Colin Powell and Thomas L. Friedman have called the "Pottery Barn rule," if the United States broke Iraq, the United States has an obligation to stay and fix Iraq.[43] But it's not clear that staying longer in Vietnam could have led to the United States "prevailing" there, or that a longer fighting presence would have made the situation better for the Vietnamese.

Reporter Dan Froomkin argued that even if one lesson of the Vietnam War is that we shouldn't have gone there in the first place, a second lesson is that staying longer makes things worse. Thom Shanker noted that while Bush said the U.S. withdrawal brought tragedy to the region, he couldn't outline how staying there would have made America victorious. Vietnamese who were contacted for comment were upset with Bush's analogy. A veteran of the communist fight against U.S. troops, Vu Huy Trieu of Hanoi, was quoted as responding, "Does he think the U.S. could have won if they had stayed longer? No way."[44] Foreign Ministry spokesperson for Vietnam Le Dung released a statement in response, skirting direct confrontation with the U.S. president, but saying, "With regard to the American war in Vietnam, everyone knows that we fought to defend our country and that this was a righteous war of the Vietnamese people."[45]

Andrew J. Bacevich, a former platoon leader in Vietnam who is now an International Relations professor at Boston University, said that the United States could learn from its mistakes in Vietnam, by providing for Iraqi refugees who had helped the United States and who would be in danger in case of U.S. withdrawal.[46]

In the same speech to the VFW, Bush escalated his rhetoric when he insinuated that Americans who protest U.S. wars are doing bin Ladin's bidding. Bush said that in an interview with bin Ladin in Pakistan after the 9/11 attacks, bin Ladin said that "The American people had risen against their government's war in Vietnam. They must do the same today."[47] Bush said that the point of his analogy was to show that U.S. credibility had been hurt by the pullout of Vietnam. Bush also referred to al-Qaeda leader Zawahiri saying that the United States still suffers from "the Vietnam specter." Bush therefore suggested that the United States could not today afford to pull out of Iraq, because it would send the wrong message to the country's enemies. Terrorists throughout the Middle East would rejoice at a U.S. troop pullout, and then they would come to the United States and attack Americans at home. At this point, I suggest that Bush must have left the Vietnam analogy behind, because Vietnamese and/or Cambodians did not come to the United States after the war's end to attack our nation.

CIVILIAN AND PRISONER ABUSE IN IRAQ AND AFGHANISTAN

Soldiers involved in killing and/or brutalization of people often regret their participation in such activities. One mother, Penny Prezler, whose son Skyler was an infantryman who was in 2007 still on his second tour of duty in Iraq, recalled that her son said on the phone that he wished he could be wounded in battle so that he could come home. He told her, "Mom, we killed women on the street today. We killed kids on bikes. We had no choice." She recounted his saying that he had been greatly disturbed and saddened when he had to pick up the blown up parts of his dead buddy's body. "Then he looked up and saw an Iraqi boy picking up what was left of his dead father."[48] This compassion based on a flash of insight into the reality of other people's suffering is what King allowed himself to experience, having read the story of suffering children in Vietnam.

Another particularly appropriate, and disturbing, analogy between Vietnam and the Iraq and Afghanistan wars has been the abuse and torture of prisoners. King said about Vietnam, "And we are criminals in that war." The scandals of prisoner abuses in Abu Ghraib, Bagram, and Guantanamo have been explored in the 2008 documentary by Alex Gibney, *Taxi to the Dark Side*. As our Justice Department narrows the definition of "torture," justifying harsh interrogation, soldiers in a chain of command are brutalized psychologically as they in turn must brutalize prisoners.

Stephen Rohde commented on the Vietnam-Iraq parallel of young soldiers dying in an immoral war. Chris Hedges also noted that both Iraq and Vietnam were "atrocity producing sites."[49] At these sites, our service personnel are being psychologically scarred by their exposure to, and commission of, acts of atrocity. We have to live with these scarred fellow Americans. Already we know that Veteran's services (like those offered at Walter Reed hospital) are inadequate for treating those with posttraumatic stress disorder.[50] While Bush in his August 2007 VFW speech pledged additional funds to ensure adequate health care for veterans, it would be better to avoid putting them in "atrocity producing" situations in the first place.

King emphasized encouraging youths of draft age to register as conscientious objectors. While we don't have a current draft, all young people have to register for the draft, and so they can also apply for CO status. However, the United States does not accept selective conscientious objection. That is, the United States will not accept a person who does not object to all war but only a specific war in which the United States is engaged. Related to this issue is enlistment. The United States has an all-volunteer army, although it can be argued that those who signed up for the National Guard did not realize they could be sent to wars in Iraq. Also, service personnel have been redeployed to Iraq and told they have no choice in the matter. Under these circumstances, the rate of armed forces recruitment among African Americans has declined. While prior to the Afghanistan and Iraq wars, African Americans were in the armed services at rates higher than their percentage of the population, recent years (since 2002, citing Pentagon statistics) have seen a steep decline in their enlistment, down 30 percent for all armed services and down 45 percent particularly for the army. Gregory Black, a retired Navy officer, said that in his experience, declining recruitment is due to young people's opposition to the Iraq war.[51] King might have been relieved to know that young people were educating themselves on the issues and declining enlistment.

And yet recruiting U.S. soldiers to continue this work of killing in a badly planned and badly understood war is becoming more desperate. Armed Forces recruiters are now enlisting people with criminal backgrounds (often under duress of serving jail time or time in the service). More high school dropouts are being accepted. In high schools, armed forces recruiters are given access to students, offering them larger cash bonuses for signing up. With employment opportunities for youths dwindling, they are being pushed to enlist. King's concern about eradicating poverty would show itself by insisting that youths should not be put into a context where they have to choose between unemployment and enlistment.

King had earlier, in his "Letter from Birmingham Jail," expressed his frustration with white Christian ministers who were silent on race issues.[52] Their silence meant complicity. In "Beyond Vietnam" he expressed his frustration with a church silent on the issue of Vietnam. King's frustration with the silence of church leaders about war seems right on target today. Many churches have been silent, and are not engaged in counseling their youths about conscientious objector status. Pope John Paul II and the current Catholic pope Benedict XVI (as Cardinal Ratzinger back then) spoke out before the U.S.-led incursion into Iraq in 2003, saying that such a war would be unjust.[53] The war plans never got approval from the United Nations Security Council. UN Secretary General Kofi Annan called the war illegal.[54] And yet these critical messages about the war were hardly ever mentioned from pulpits or in religious education of the Catholic Church. Benedict XVI has given sermons denouncing war. In his 2007 Easter message he said, "Nothing positive comes from Iraq, torn apart by continual slaughter," and about Afghanistan, he said, "Afghanistan is marked by growing unrest and instability."[55] However, he did not take the opportunity to address the issue of just war in his meeting with President Bush in June of 2007.[56] Also, he has not spoken directly to American Catholics and especially young recruits about their participation in war.

As anti-Vietnam War activist Philip Berrigan aptly noted, the frustrating thing about the Catholic Church is that its leaders are always speaking against war, but never against *this* war—that is, the war at hand, the war being waged by their country in the present tense.[57] Rev. Bill Wylie Kellerman, a Lutheran minister, noted how scripture had earlier been written as a "tale of liberation," the account of a people experiencing that "God acts for justice in a specific time and place." But over time, scripture about God shifted from the concrete to the abstract, and we then have a God who has general attributes such as justice, but particulars about justice are no longer mentioned. It is only a short jump from that to "a God who does not do anything." This God reduced to an abstraction is fit for a religion of "world maintenance"—that is, maintenance of the unjust status quo, not a God of liberation.[58] When our parish priests and ministers choose to sidestep the "hot" issue of the ongoing war, they do their parishioners a disservice.

If our Christian churches promote "peace" as abstractly as a Christmas card message, while they cooperate with world leaders in the ongoing deaths in an unjust war, what has happened to Jesus's compassion, and his liberating message? Ending these wars is a life and death issue for thousands of Americans and Iraqis and Afghanis, and an important moral issue facing our country. For these reasons and all those stated above, King's insights into the Vietnam War and his challenges to Americans and religious people everywhere are still appropriate and important for us today. Englehardt discussed a troubling aspect of a possible parallel between Iraq and Vietnam. He noticed that U.S. use of aerial bombing in Iraq doubled from 2006 to 2007. Air strikes in Vietnam were always first reported as simple successes. Later, in some cases with much probing from journalists, the story of civilian casualties (like those in My Lai) were finally uncovered. Likewise, in both Afghanistan and Iraq, Englehardt covered the cases of aerial bombings that were first reported as successes and then, only after repeated attempts at reporting and investigation, were admitted to have had civilian casualties. In the Vietnam case, Nixon's call for "Vietnamization," where local troops would take over the role of U.S. troops, didn't really mean the removal of American forces, but rather their redeployment. As the ground war shrank, the air war stepped up its pace. This resulted in higher civilian casualties. Englehardt cautioned us that the same should not happen in Iraq. He was worried that continuing stipulations that "combat troops" (rather than all troops) should be withdrawn sets the stage for continued U.S. military presence.[59] In fact, one can now find enlarged use of air attacks in Afghanistan and Pakistan.

PRESIDENT OBAMA AND ESCALATION OF FIGHTING IN AFGHANISTAN

Currently, the Obama Administration has reduced a military force in Iraq from 144,000 troops (as Obama took office) to 50,000 troops. The remaining troops are supposed to help Iraqi security forces in an "advisory capacity" under a military campaign called Operation New Dawn. These lingering forces are supposed to depart by the end of 2011. But observers seeing the huge U.S. investments in Baghdad's Green Zone, with the U.S. Embassy coming in over budget at around $736 million, are convinced that substantial U.S. presence and influence will continue.[60]

Relatedly, combat troops are being redeployed from Iraq to Afghanistan where that war has escalated dramatically during the Obama presidency, emphasizing therefore that the end of combat in Iraq does not mean a revaluation of American values, as the emphasis on military solutions shifts to other venues. While Obama has refused to use Bush's "War on terror" rhetoric, he still reinforces the claim that the current war in Afghanistan is a legitimate response to the 9/11 attacks. Jamie Rubin, a Columbia University professor known to be an advisor to both Hilary Clinton and President Obama, insisted on the distinction between Vietnam and Afghanistan, saying "The whole world is on our side in Afghanistan; the whole world was clearly not on our side in Vietnam."[61] But does the Afghanistan war have so much more legitimacy than Iraq? Is it really exempt from being a neocolonial war?

A recent documentary, *Rethink Afghanistan*, used a gripping metaphor to explain that justifications for the Afghanistan war were flawed. Just as it would not be sound strategy to occupy a hotel in order to ensure that a bad guest does not decide to stay there again, so also it is costly and inefficient to occupy all of Afghanistan just to deny al Qaeda a foothold. Karsten Struhl relatedly argues in a philosophical context that the U.S. war in Afghanistan does not uphold just war principles.[62] A group of family members of those who died on 9/11 call themselves "September Eleventh Families for Peaceful Tomorrows." The message they spread is that they do not want the losses they suffered compounded by the losses of Afghan families who also lose their family members in attacks—losses at the hands of the U.S. military who claim to be acting out the will of the American people. In 2002, members of this group traveled to Afghanistan, listening to the stories of families there who had lost loved ones, and trying to help rebuild war-torn Afghanistan.

American (and British) hubris also shows up in the increased use of Predator drones, now being used in Afghanistan, Pakistan, Yemen, and Somalia. There has been a surge in the use of drones since Obama took office in January 2009. Reuters commentator Sanjeev Miglani wonders how the U.S. military, and war reporters like Thomas Ricks, can defend drone use, considering it akin to "police work" rather than an act of war, despite ignoring the sovereignty of the nations in which they are used.[63] *Der Spiegel's* independently researched study of 92,000 Wikileaks documents shows that the U.S. military logged 185,000 drone flight hours in Iraq and Afghanistan during 2009, an amount that is three times that of 2006. And yet *Der Spiegel* reports that the U.S. Department of Defense itself admits that drone use is rife with "system failures, computer glitches, and human errors."[64] An account of human error was given in an in-depth article in the *Los Angeles Times* (April 10, 2011), when a two-person, pilot/cameraman Predator crew stationed remotely in Nevada decided to target two vehicles with over two dozen civilians, including women and children, none of whom were insurgents. U.S. figures admit that sixteen were killed and twelve wounded in the Predator attack. Ironically, the record of the crew's discussion shows that they considered the vehicle's passengers getting out to pray at 6:15 a.m. as a suspicious activity. The Army itself admitted that evidence that the convoy was not hostile was "ignored or downplayed by the Predator crew."[65] There have been protests in both Afghanistan and Pakistan regarding the ongoing use of drones.[66] Casualties from drones are a part of the civilian casualties of the ongoing Afghanistan war, with six thousand Afghan civilians killed in 2009. The number of internally displaced persons has doubled since Obama took office.[67]

Juan Cole, who earlier pointed out the parallels between the Vietnam and Iraq wars, thinks there are also important analogies between Vietnam and Afghanistan. As he explained, "We invoke Vietnam against long, costly Asian land wars, the objectives of which are murky and the medium-term and long-term success of which is in significant doubt. And by these criteria, Afghanistan has 'Vietnam' written all over it."[68] An ABC news poll taken on December 16, 2010, found that 60 percent of Americans said the war in Afghanistan has not been worth fighting.

Englehardt is a keen critic of American history and culture. Like King, he looks into the heart of the American psyche to find out why Vietnam-like situations recur. At the heart of the matter, he finds Americans convinced that their help is indispensable. While Americans are to be commended for caring and wanting to help, there is a definite colonial mentality in the idea that the world will go to hell if Americans are not there to fix things. He explained, "In any situation where American 'interests' are at stake, the United States can only be imagined as part of the solution, not part of the problem."[69] This is at the heart of the U.S. problem with withdrawal from Iraq. The quote also points to the problem of

Americans disguising their self-interest as concern with others. While Englehardt is encouraged by polls that show a majority of Americans opposed to continued U.S. presence in Iraq, he is disheartened by the lackluster showing at protests against the war. He wonders why Americans aren't channeling their outrage about reprehensible government performance into demonstrations as did folks in the earlier Vietnam era. He fears that Americans are retreating into their private lives.

Both Gandhi and King knew that people had to be galvanized to show up in the streets, to voice their opinions, and force their governments to pay attention. Englehardt thinks that Americans should take heart that in the Vietnam context (according to a book about Henry Kissinger by reporter Seymour Hersch), Richard Nixon backed down from his plans to escalate the Vietnam War because of the large showing of protestors in Washington, DC, on October 15, 1969. He felt he couldn't escalate with so much of the American public against his plans.[70]

CONCLUSION: OBAMA ON EGYPT AND KING'S MESSAGE APPLIED TODAY

When Americans elected Barack Obama as President of the United States, some supporters just considered him a welcome alternative to President Bush and the Republicans. Others saw his election as even more important, as a great gain for the Civil Rights movement that King and so many others had struggled for. The United States Embassy in India, as a public relations gesture, printed up and distributed photos of the new President Obama sitting at his desk in his old Senate office, surrounded by photos of Martin Luther King Jr. and Mohandas Gandhi.[71] But Obama was no King, and as many knew from the start, and others would come to realize, Obama clearly saw his role as President and not as a new Martin Luther King.

When Obama, like King before him, received the Nobel Peace Prize, he clarified that as President he would use the armed forces to protect the security of his nation. Obama then, predictably, as many others have done, lauded the nonviolent accomplishments of Gandhi and King while choosing not to follow in their footsteps. Obama stated in his speech, "As someone who stands here as a direct consequence of Dr. King's life's work, I am living testimony to the moral force of non-violence," and he also quoted King's own Nobel Peace Prize speech, "Violence never brings permanent peace. It solves no social problem: it merely creates new and more complicated ones." Obama confirmed the wisdom of this insight, and yet argued that good nations would have to continue using war due to the presence of evil forces in our world bent on destruction, and more specifically, he as Head of State of the United States would have to send more troops into Afghanistan. He followed up news of his escalation with justifications for the U.S. role as selfless global policeman. As he said, "So yes, the instruments of war do have a role to play in preserving the peace. . . . The non-violence practiced by men like Gandhi and King may not have been practical or possible in every circumstance, but the love that they preached — their faith in human progress — must always be the North Star that guides us on our journey."[72] In this way he hoped to give homage to the ideal while, in the meantime, devoting himself to the mundane policies and practicalities of war. This practice of putting the two leaders on a pedestal to be admired rather than emulated continues the narrow observances of "King Day" as a nod to history that seems to have no practical application to current contexts.

On February 11, 2011, while the people of Egypt were gathered to topple their ruler of thirty years, President Hosni Mubarak (now age eighty-two, who had been bolstered by U.S. military aid for decades), President Obama had these words to share on the topic:

> Egyptians have inspired us, and they've done so by putting the lie to the idea that justice is best gained through violence. For in Egypt, it was the moral force of nonviolence — not terrorism, not mindless kill-ing — but nonviolence, moral force that bent the arc of history toward justice once more. . . . As Martin Luther King said in celebrating the birth of a new nation in Ghana while trying to perfect his own, "There is something in the soul that cries out for freedom." Those were the cries that came from Tahrir Square, and the entire world has taken note.[73]

While these general praises for the Egyptian people were made, commentators of various stripes noticed what Obama was not doing. Those on the political "left" noticed that he was not clearly siding with the people in the street who demanded that Mubarak immediately step down. Those on the "right" noted that he was sending an ambivalent message to long-standing allies in Israel. Other reporters noted how U.S. military strategists lacked any contingency plans in the case of a popular uprising in Egypt. They were blindsided, presuming their propping up of Mubarak would be effective in the foreseeable future.[74]

How could our own government be blindsided about the effects of propping up an unpopular government for so long? The 2010 budget for military aid to Egypt was $1.5 billion, despite the fact that Mubarak had ruled Egypt under emergency powers since 1981. While under Bush, the U.S. government allotted $45 million for programs promoting just government and democracy in Egypt, the Obama Administration slashed those funds in half. In November 2010, Human Rights First called upon Obama to speak out against the Mubarak regime's tactics of harassing and arresting opposition party members, suppressing journalists, med-dling in television talk shows, and passing stiffer regulations on mobile phone companies regarding text messaging news services.[75] How could

Obama continue this loyalty to Mubarak without realizing its dire consequences when in his own Nobel Prize speech he said, "I believe that
peace is unstable where citizens are denied the right to speak freely. . . .
Pent up grievances fester. . . . No matter how callously defined, neither
America's interests—nor the world's—are served by the denial of human
aspirations"?[76] While Obama may have prided himself on saying on behalf of his country, "America has never fought a war against a democracy, and our closest friends are governments that protect the rights of their
citizens," this kind of statement is surely a denial of the United States'
neo-imperial moves in many countries over decades. How could this
statement cover the U.S. relationship with Egypt, one of the leading beneficiaries of U.S. foreign aid?

Once the people in the streets accomplished their removal of Mubarak, Obama praised their nonviolence, and drew comparisons between
their struggle and that of Dr. King. Why hadn't nonviolent approaches
been funded under his Administration, rather than the military? There is
a large disconnect between rhetoric and substance.

It is not the first time there has been this disconnect. In November
2010, President Obama toured India, ostensibly to sell India more military technology. He had with him a plan to sell India 126 fighter planes,
and some estimated that India would spend $45 billion on arms. He also
wanted to ensure continued support for U.S. military goals in Afghanistan. As one reporter put it, "That paradox was on vivid display . . . when
Mr. Obama arrived in Mumbai . . . celebrating Gandhi's legacy but also
selling military transport planes and bringing along 200 American business leaders."[77] But while there he toured Mani Bhavan, the house that
Gandhi lived in while in Mumbai, currently turned into a museum. In the
guest book Obama wrote of Gandhi, "He is a hero not just to India, but to
the world."[78] Museum guides showed him Dr. King's signature in the
museum's guest book, signed 1959.

A letter to President Obama by Mairead Corrigan Maguire, Nobel
Peace Laureate from Northern Ireland, sent to him on June 20, 2011,
challenged the U.S. President for overseeing U.S. attempts to assassinate
Libyan Head of State Moammer Gadaffi. An attack on Gadaffi on May 1,
2011, had killed one of his sons and three of his grandchildren. The following day, U.S. Navy Seals participated in an extrajudicial killing of
Osama bin Laden and a woman and two men who were with him. Maguire argues that such attacks are international war crimes. She challenges President Obama since he appeared on national television justifying these extrajudicial killings. She says, "Do you really believe we will
all remain silent whilst under your warrior leadership the US Government and its allies dismantle basic human rights and international
laws?"[79]

Things could be worse. The United States could have a president that
scoffs at the accomplishments of nonviolence under the leadership of

Gandhi and King. Perhaps to have a president that admires nonviolence while engaging in war is to be on the road to a more nonviolent future. But do these allusions to King waken us to the gap between ideal and practice, or do they lull the public asleep with assurances that all is well? Obama himself, in his Nobel Peace Prize address, insisted that there is a tension between ideal and practice, and he wanted us to feel the tension. Will Obama during his presidency have the chance to react to that tension by funding peace more and war less, and finding strategies outside of the military mold? King did not direct his message merely or primarily at U.S. presidents, but rather at American citizens. We get the president we deserve. Our current challenge is to delve deep into King's philosophy of nonviolence, learn from its insights, and find ways to apply it to our activities as a nation.

NOTES

1. James Cone, *Martin & Malcolm & America: A Dream or a Nightmare?* (Maryknoll, NY: Orbis, 1993), 236.

2. Ibid., 241–42.

3. Charles Ambler, "What Is the World Going to Come To?: Prophecy and Colonialism in Africa," in *Revealing Prophets: Prophecy in East African History*, eds. David M. Anderson and Douglas H. Johnson (Athens: Ohio University Press, 1995), 225–28.

4. David Dellinger, *From Yale to Jail: The Life Story of a Moral Dissenter* (New York: Pantheon Books, 1993), 265, 274.

5. Claybourne Carson, ed., *The Autobiography of Martin Luther King Jr.* (New York: Intellectual Properties Management and Warner Books, 1998), 334.

6. Dellinger, *From Yale to Jail*, 265–70.

7. Ibid., 276–77.

8. Ibid., 259–60.

9. Carson, *Autobiography*, 333.

10. Ibid., 335. See also Cone, *Martin & Malcolm & America*, 237.

11. Carson, *Autobiography*, 336.

12. Martin Luther King Jr., "The Casualties of the War in Vietnam" (speech, Los Angeles, CA February 25,1967), *Speeches of Martin Luther King, Jr.*, http://mlk-kpp01.stanford.edu/kingweb/publications/speeches/unpub/670225-001_The_Casualties_of_the_War_in_Vietnam.htm

13. King, "The State of the Movement" (speech, Southern Christian Leadership Conference staff retreat, November 28, 1967), Archives of the Martin Luther King Jr. Institute, Stanford University.

14. King, "Beyond Vietnam" (speech, New York City, April 4, 1967), *A Call to Conscience: The Landmark Speeches of Martin Luther King, Jr.*, http://mlk-kpp01.stanford.edu/kingweb/publications/speeches/Beyond_Vietnam.pdf   or: http://www.information clearinghouse.info/article2564.htm

15. Alain Locke, "A Functional View of Value Ultimates," in *The Philosophy of Alain Locke: Harlem Renaissance and Beyond*, ed. Leonard Harris (Philadelphia: Temple University Press, 1989), 81–93.

16. King, "Beyond Vietnam."

17. King, "Beyond Vietnam."

18. See http://www.informationclearinghouse.info/article2564.htm. Also see letters criticizing King, and his response:
http://www.stanford.edu/group/King/liberation_curriculum/pdfs/vietnamdocs.pdf

19. Dellinger, *From Yale to Jail*, 282–85.

20. King, "A Knock at Midnight" (sermon, June 25, 1967), http://mlk-kpp01.stanford.edu/index.php/kingpapers/article/a_knock_at_midnight/.

21. King, "The Drum Major Instinct" (sermon, February 4, 1968), http://mlk-kpp01.stanford.edu/index.php/kingpapers/article/the_drum_major_instinct/.

22. Ira Chernus, "Requiem for the War on Terror: Goodbye GWOT, Hello OCO," *TomDispatch*, April 9, 2009, http://www.tomdispatch.com/post/175057/ira_chernus_requiem_for_the_war_on_terror.

23. David Wildman, "It's Time to End the War in Afghanistan," *Fellowship* 76, nos. 1–3 (2010): 14–17; Gareth Porter, "Report Shows Drones Strikes Based on Scant Evidence," *Truthout*, October 18, 2010, http://www.truth-out.org/report-shows-drones-strikes-based-scant-evidence64292.

24. George Katsiaficas, "Vietnam and the Persian Gulf: Historical Parallels," *Z Magazine*, January 1991, 28–32.

25. Ibid., 31.

26. Jean Bethke Elshtain, *Just War against Terror: The Burden of American Power in a Violent World* (New York: Basic Books, 2003).

27. Daniel Ellsberg, "Iraq's Pentagon Papers," *Los Angeles Times*, June 11, 2006.

28. I catalog many of these lies in my article, "Arendt on Language and Lying in Politics: Her Insights Applied to the 'War on Terror' and the U.S. Occupation of Iraq," *Peace Studies Journal* 1, no. 1 (November 2008): 32–62, http://www.peacestudiesjournal.org/archive/Presbey.doc.

29. Ian Urbina, "Even in Families Sworn to Duty, Misgivings Arise as War Goes On," *New York Times*, July 15, 2007, A1,14. See also Juan Cole, "10 Things Martin Luther King Would Have Done about Iraq," *Truthout*, January 16, 2006. See http://www.juancole.com/2006/01/10-things-martin-luther-king-would.html .

30. Stephen Pizzo, "Bush's Big Gambit," *Alternet*, June 30, 2005, http://www.alternet.org/story/23254/

31. Phil Ochs, "Cops of the World," http://www.elyrics.net/read/p/phil-ochs-lyrics/cops-of-the-world-lyrics.html.

32. Jonathan Schell and Tom Englehardt, "Jonathan Schell on the Empire That Rose as It Fell," *TomDispatch*, August 20, 2004.

33. John Mueller, "The Iraq Syndrome," *Foreign Affairs*, November/December 2005, http://www.foreignaffairs.org/20051101faessay84605/john-mueller/the-iraq-syndrome.html.

34. Elshtain, *Just War against Terror*, 72.

35. Katsiaficas, "Vietnam and the Persian Gulf," 31.

36. George Gedda, "Bush's Father Foresaw Costs of Iraq War," Associated Press, August 25, 2004. See http://www.commondreams.org/cgi-bin/print.cgi?file=/head-lines04/0825-08.htm.

37. "President Bush Attends Veterans of Foreign Wars National Convention, Discusses War on Terror," news release, August 22, 2007, http://georgewbush-whitehouse.archives.gov/news/releases/2007/08/20070822-3.html.

38. Dan Froomkin, "The Analogy Quagmire," *Washington Post*, August 22, 2007.

39. Michael Hirsch, "Why America's Pullout from Vietnam Was a Success," *Newsweek*, August 23, 2007.

40. David D. Kirkpatrick, "This War Is Not Like the Others—or Is It?," *New York Times*, August 26, 2007, WK 1, 4.

41. John Pilger, *Year Zero: The Silent Death of Cambodia*, video documentary (Active Home Pictures, 1979). John Pilger interview in "Freedom Next Time: Filmmaker & Journalist John Pilger on Propaganda, the Press, Censorship and Resisting the American Empire," *Democracy Now*, August 7, 2007, http://www.democracynow.org/2007/8/7/freedom_next_time_filmmaker_journalist_john.

42. Thom Shanker, "Historians Question Bush's Reading of Lessons of Vietnam War for Iraq," *New York Times*, August 23, 2007.

43. *Wikipedia*, s.v. "Pottery Barn Rule," http://en.wikipedia.org/wiki/Pottery_Barn_rule

44. "War Analogy Strikes Nerve in Vietnam," Associated Press, August 23, 2007.

45. Ibid.

46. Thom Shanker, "Historians Question Bush's Reading."

47. "President Bush Attends Veterans of Foreign Wars National Convention, Discusses War on Terror," news release, August 22, 2007, http://georgewbush-whitehouse.archives.gov/news/releases/2007/08/20070822-3.html.

48. Ian Urbina, "Even in Families Sworn to Duty, Misgivings Arise as War Goes On," *New York Times*, July 15, 2007, A1, 14.

49. Chris Hedges, "The Death Mask of War," *Adbusters*, July 28, 2007; Stephen F. Rohde, "Silence Is Betrayal," *Truthout*, April 4, 2007.

50. Kimberly Hefling, "Finding Therapists Proves Hard for Troops," Associated Press, June 11, 2007.

51. Gregory Black, "Numbers of African Americans Volunteering for Military Service Drops Drastically," August 26, 2007, http://www.blacknews.com/pr/blackmilitaryworld201.html

52. Ibid.

53. Michael Griffin, "Pope Benedict a Strong Critic of War," *Houston Catholic Worker*, XXV, no. 4 (2005), http://www.cjd.org/paper/benedict.html.

54. Ewen MacAskill and Julian Borger, "Iraq War Was Illegal and Breached UN Charter, Says Annan," *The Guardian*, September 16, 2004, http://www.guardian.co.uk/Iraq/Story/0,2763,1305709,00.html.

55. "'Nothing positive' in Iraq War, Pope Says Noting the World's Deep Wounds," *Catholic Online*, April 8, 2007, http://www.catholic.org/international/international_story.php?id=23681.

56. "Bush Visits the Pope, Italian President," *NPR* , http://www.npr.org/templates/story/story.php?storyId=10905929.

57. Murray Polner and Jim O'Grady, *Disarmed and Dangerous* (New York: Basic Books, 1997), 167.

58. Bill Wylie Kellerman, *Seasons of Faith and Conscience* (Maryknoll, NY: Orbis Books, 1991), 10.

59. Tom Englehardt, "'Accidents of War': The Time Has Come for an Honest Discussion about Air Power," *TomDispatch*, July 9, 2007, http://www.tomdispatch.com/post/174817/carnage_from_the_air_and_the_washington_consensus.

60. Ernesto Londoño, "As Clock Strikes 12, U.S. Hands Iraq Control of Green Zone," *Washington Post*, January 1, 2009; "Last U.S. Combat Brigade Leaves Iraq," Al Jazeera, August 20, 2010, http://english.aljazeera.net/news/middleeast/2010/08/201081818840122963.html.

61. Juan Cole, "Is Afghanistan Vietnam or Iraq?: Arguing with Obama and Rubin," *Informed Comment*, September 17, 2009, http://www.juancole.com/2009/09/is-afghanistan-vietnam-or-iraq-arguing.html.

62. Karsten Struhl, "Is War a Morally Legitimate Response to Terrorism?," *Philosophical Forum* 36, no. 1 (2005).

63. Sanjeev Miglani, "Drone Strikes Are Police Work, Not an Act of War?," *Afghan Journal/Reuters*, July 5, 2011.

64. Matthias Gebauer et al., "Afghanistan War Logs Reveal Shortcomings of U.S. Drones," *Dear Spiegel*, July 27, 2010, http://www.spiegel.de/international/world/0,1518,708729,00.html.

65. David S. Cloud, "Anatomy of an Afghan War Tragedy," *Los Angeles Times*, April 10, 2011.

66. "Protestors in Pakistan demonstrate against US drone attacks," *CNTV* April 24, 2011; "Afghan Protestors denounce US drone strikes," *CNTV* April 25, 2011.

67. David Wildman, "It's Time to End the War in Afghanistan," *Fellowship* 76, nos. 1–3 (2010): 14–17.

68. Cole, "Is Afghanistan Vietnam or Iraq?"

69. Tom Engelhardt, "Demobilizing America: Outsourcing Action in an Imperial World," *TomDispatch*, March 25, 2007, http://www.truthout.org/docs_2006/032607H.shtml.

70. Englehardt, "'Accidents of War.'"

71. Jim Yardley, "Obama Invokes Gandhi, Whose Ideal Eludes India," *New York Times*, November 6, 2010, http://www.nytimes.com/2010/11/07/world/asia/07gandhi.html.

72. Barack Obama, Nobel Prize Speech in Oslo, December 10, 2009, http://www.msnbc.msn.com/id/34360743/.

73. President Obama's Remarks on the Egyptian Revolution, February 11, 2011, http://www.truth-out.org/president-obama-speaks-egyptian-revolution67677.

74. David E. Sanger, "As Mubarak Digs In, U.S. Policy in Egypt Is Complicated," *New York Times*, February 5, 2011, http://www.nytimes.com/2011/02/06/world/middleeast/06policy.html?_r=1; Niall Ferguson, "Wanted: A Grand Strategy for America," *Newsweek*, February 14, 2011, http://www.newsweek.com/2011/02/13/wanted-a-grand-strategy-for-america.html.

75. William Fisher, "Egypt Cracks Down as U.S. Stands By," *Inter Press Service*, http://ipsnews.net/news.asp?idnews=53481.

76. Obama, Nobel Peace Prize Speech.

77. Yardley, "Obama Invokes Gandhi."

78. Yardley, "Obama Invokes Gandhi."

79. Mairead Corrigan Maguire, "Letter to President Obama, June 20, 2011," in *The Catholic Radical* (August/September 2011), 3.

ELEVEN

Martin Luther King Jr. and Frantz Fanon

Reflections on the Politics and Ethics of Violence and Nonviolence

Kathryn T. Gines

In "Black Power" (the second chapter of *Where Do We Go from Here?*), Martin Luther King Jr. asserts, "Besides opposing violence on principle, I could imagine nothing more impractical and disastrous than for any of us, through misguided judgment, to precipitate a violent confrontation in Mississippi. We had neither the resources nor the techniques to win."[1] Here King distinguishes between opposing violence in principle (an ethical question) and opposing violence for its impracticality (a political question), but ultimately he rejects violence for both ethical and political reasons. Arguing against the use of violence to confront anti-black racism in the United States, King calls on the oppressed to use nonviolent resistance and to build interracial coalitions. He goes on to apply his nonviolent philosophy outside of the United States as a method for confronting colonialism and even totalitarianism. Frantz Fanon also notes the ethical and political dimensions of violence, but in contrast to King, Fanon takes the position that confronting the violent system of colonialism entails violent resistance. Decolonization is a violent phenomenon. And although Fanon emphasizes the violent anticolonial struggle in the Algerian context, he also acknowledges that other regions have been able to achieve similar results through political struggle rather than through violence.

In this chapter I offer a comparison between King's philosophy of nonviolence and Fanon's descriptive analysis of colonial and anticolonial violence. Taking into account their divergent perspectives, I argue that in spite of the very different theory (and praxis) that each figure articulates about violent resistance, there are a few points of agreement and unexpected overlaps between King's and Fanon's positions. I begin by comparing how they assess their situations (King on the situation of the Negro in America and Fanon on the colonial situations in Martinique and Algeria). Concerning their analyses of violence and nonviolence, I underscore King's appeal to nonviolence and Fanon's critique of nonviolence; their accounts of violent systems of oppression and the problem of intragroup violence; and finally, their positions on violent resistance and the shortcomings of this approach. I conclude with a discussion of King's call for a program and Fanon's push for politicization.

THE SITUATION: KING ON AMERICAN RACISM AND FANON ON COLONIAL RACISM

In "Nonviolence and Racial Justice" (1957) King offers background on some of the legal history that has shaped the situation of the Negro in the United States of America.[2] This speech was written during the early formation of the Southern Christian Leadership Conference (SCLC), and King is presenting his philosophy of nonviolence as a guiding principle for the organization. At this point in time, he had already presided over the Montgomery Improvement Association, which successfully used the strategy of nonviolence in the bus boycotts in Alabama. King begins by historically situating the arrival of Africans to the shores of North America against our will in 1619.[3] He asserts that the institution of slavery dehumanized and thingified the Negro, denying him personhood.[4] Put differently, the Negro was treated as a thing rather than a person, as an object rather than a subject. We are also reminded of the *Dred Scott* (1857) decision that, King explains, "said, in substance, that the Negro is not a citizen of the United States; he is merely property subject to the dictates of his owner."[5] After 1863, despite emancipation from slavery and the brief political power held during Reconstruction, the Negro continued to confront oppression and inequality.[6] For example, with the 1878 compromise, King states that the government "bargained away" full equality for blacks.[7] And then in the late nineteenth century, the separate but equal doctrine upheld by *Plessy v. Ferguson* (1896) ushered in "a new kind of slavery."[8]

According to King, each of these legal and sociopolitical precedents created the conditions for a "negative peace" between the black and white races where "the Negro was forced patiently to submit to insult, injustice and exploitation."[9] These oppressive conditions instilled an inferior self-image and a deficient self-worth. And yet King claims that there has been a "radical change in the Negro's evaluation of himself" resulting from traveling, migration from the rural South to urban industrial areas, improved economic conditions, education, and religion.[10] The change in perception of the self (and the group) is not only radical, but also revolutionary—motivating the fight against racial oppression and the "determination to struggle and sacrifice until the walls of segregation have been fully crushed."[11] This self-revaluation and determination to end segregation challenged the negative peace, creating a crisis and tension in race relations.[12] Racial tensions were also exacerbated by white segregationist resistance to the *Brown v. Board of Education* (1954) decision, a legal precedent viewed by many at the time as a challenge to the earlier *Dred Scott* and *Plessy* decisions.[13]

While King examines the racialized system of slavery and Jim Crow segregation in the United States, Fanon criticizes racialized colonial oppression coupled with the resulting inferiorization and thingification of colonized subjects in the Antilles and Algeria. Fanon's earlier analysis of colonialism in *Black Skin, White Masks* (1952) expands and evolves later in *The Wretched of the Earth* (1961). In *Black Skin, White Masks* Fanon is clear (like Aimé Césaire before him) that the negative contacts between the Negro and the white man are a direct consequence of the racial oppression and economic exploitation created and maintained by the colonial system.[14] Within this system, both "the Negro" and "the white man" have been *created*, and the two entities are intertwined, each defined in terms of his difference from the other. The interactions between the colonized and the colonizers are ordered by racism and set up a situation in which the Negro is constantly battling to prove his worth to the white man.[15] There is a clear correlation between the oppressive colonial system and what Fanon describes as the Negro's inferiority complex (as well as the white superiority complex). But he hopes to "help the black man to free himself of the arsenal of complexes that has been developed by the colonial environment."[16]

Continuing his analysis in *The Wretched of the Earth*, Fanon describes the colonial world as a "Manichean" world defined by dichotomy and segregated into two compartments.[17] Although the two zones are opposed to one another, they still "follow the principle of reciprocal exclusivity."[18] The settler's town is strongly built, brightly lit, and clean with a good infrastructure. The people there are well clothed and fed. In contrast, the town inhabited by the colonized is described as "the Negro village, the medina, the reservation."[19] Rather than having strong and sturdy houses, the colonized live in crowded huts. The inhabitants are barely clothed and suffer from hunger. Viewed as two distinct species, the colonizers and the colonized inhabit two distinct zones in the colonial world.

The colonized are expected to stay in their place and within their boundaries. They are always on alert and always presumed guilty. But Fanon assures readers that they do not accept this guilt and they admit no accusation. The colonized are able to see that these stereotypes are false. While treated as inferiors, they are not convinced of this inferiority.[20] The colonized recognize that they can only escape the immobilizing effects of colonization by ending it, and that they must be the agents to bring the history of the nation and the history of decolonization into existence.[21] This realization is not achieved through travel, migration, education, or religion (as King describes in the U.S. context), but rather through violent resistance to the colonial system.[22] Fanon explains that violence is a remedy to the feeling of inferiority, "It frees the native from his inferiority complex and from his despair and inaction; it makes him fearless and restores his self-respect."[23]

KING'S PHILOSOPHY OF NONVIOLENCE, FANON'S CRITIQUE OF NONVIOLENCE

Even given the racist and violent history that has shaped black American experiences, King calls for nonviolent resistance to racial oppression. His nonviolent philosophy is explicitly guided by a Christian ethic of love ("At the center of nonviolence stands the principle of love"), and also influenced by Mahatma Gandhi.[24] King acknowledges the dual influenc.es of Christianity and Gandhian pacifism in "An Experiment in Love" (1958) explaining, "I had come to see early that the Christian doctrine of love operating through the Gandhian method of nonviolence was one of the most potent weapons available to the Negro in his struggle for freedom."[25] He elaborates, "Nonviolent resistance had emerged as the technique of the movement, while love stood as the regulating ideal. In other words, Christ furnished the spirit and motivation, while Gandhi furnished the method."[26]

James M. Washington notes that King is also influenced by Swedish theologian Anders Nygren's analysis of the Christian concept of love in *Agape and Eros* (1953).[27] Identifying three words for love in the Greek language—*eros*: aesthetic, romantic love; *philia*: reciprocal love between friends; and *agape*: selfless love—King explains that agape love "means understanding, redeeming good will for all men, an overflowing love which seeks nothing in return."[28] He Christianizes this notion of agape love claiming, "You begin to love men not because they are likeable, not because they do things that attract us, but because God loves them and here we love the person who does the evil deed while hating the deed that the person does."[29] King asks us to love our friends as well as our enemies, imploring us to "have love for the enemy-neighbor from whom you can expect no good in return, but only hostility and persecution."[30]

This ethic of love, coupled with several guiding premises, is central to King's early writings and speeches on nonviolence.

In outlining and defending his philosophy, King asserts that nonviolence is not a method for cowards; it does resist.[31] He rejects the idea that nonviolence is a cowardly response to oppression because nonviolent resistance is, in fact, resistance. Although this method of resistance is physically passive, it is mentally, emotionally, and spiritually active. For the nonviolent resister, "his mind and emotions are always active, constantly seeking to persuade the opponent that he is mistaken."[32] The method itself is, "strongly active spiritually . . . dynamically aggressive spiritually."[33] King asserts emphatically that nonviolent resistance does not amount to doing nothing; this method requires more courage and discipline than violent methods of resistance.

In expounding his philosophy, King is clear that a goal of nonviolent resistance is gaining the friendship and understanding of the opponent rather than defeating or humiliating the opponent.[34] Put another way, "Our aim is not to defeat the white community, not to humiliate the white community, but to win the friendship of all the persons who had perpetrated this system in the past."[35] This aim presupposes the possibility of converting some of the racist segregationists of the past into potential integrationists of the future and turning former aggressors into potential advocates. King asserts, "The end is redemption and reconciliation. The aftermath of nonviolence is the creation of a beloved community."[36] With this goal in mind, King is clear that the targets of nonviolent resistance are the forces of evil (often identified as racism and segregation), not the persons caught in these forces.[37] King wants to separate the proverbial "sin" of racism and segregation from the "sinners"—those white supremacists perpetuating individual, systematic, and institutionalized forms of anti-black racism. Thus, "It is the evil we are seeking to defeat, not the persons victimized by evil."[38] And here the victims of the evil forces are not black persons subjected to racial oppression, but rather the perpetrators of racial oppression. He states, "We are out to defeat injustice and not the white persons who may happen to be unjust."[39]

King also posits that nonviolence, including "a willingness to accept suffering without retaliation, to accept blows from the opponent without striking back," avoids both external physical violence and internal spiritual violence.[40] Again, he connects nonviolence to the ethic of love, arguing that the oppressed have to have the "sense and morality" to stop the cycle of violence and hate, believing instead that justice will prevail. Accordingly, the philosophy of nonviolence is also based on "the conviction that the universe is on the side of justice."[41] It is this "deep faith in the future that causes the nonviolent resister to accept suffering without retaliation."[42] He concludes with the admonition, "May all who suffer oppression in this world reject the self-defeating method of retaliatory violence and choose the method that seeks to redeem. Through using this method wisely and courageously we will emerge from the bleak and desolate midnight of man's inhumanity to man into the bright daybreak of freedom and justice." [43]

In "My Trip to the Land of Gandhi" (1959) King continues to build on his nonviolent philosophy and his case against violent resistance. [44] The trip to India had a tremendous impact on King, leaving him "more convinced than ever before that nonviolent resistance is the most potent weapon available to oppressed people in their struggle for freedom." [45] He argues, "The way of acquiescence leads to moral and spiritual suicide. The way of violence leads to bitterness in the survivors and brutality in the destroyers. But the way of nonviolence leads to redemption and the creation of a beloved community." [46] King even goes as far as to claim that the outcome in Alabama represents the possibilities of nonviolent resistance in Western civilization, and furthermore, it "suggests that nonviolent resistance *when planned and positive in action* can work effectively even under totalitarian regimes." [47] The claim that nonviolence could be effective against totalitarianism was a point of contention with several African students studying in India. For the students from Africa "nonviolent resistance could only work in a situation where the resisters had a potential ally in the conscience of the opponent." [48] For King, the students were mistaken because they tended to "confuse passive resistance with nonresistance." [49] While he claims to understand why the oppressed turn to violence to attain freedom, King explains, "it is my firm belief that the crusade for independence and human dignity that is now reaching a climax in Africa will have more positive effect on the world, if it is waged along the lines that were first demonstrated in that continent by Gandhi himself." [50]

King intentionally relates the fight for justice against oppression in the United States to international colonial conditions. He declares, "The determination of Negro Americans to win freedom from every form of oppression springs from the same profound longing for freedom that motivates oppressed peoples all over the world." [51] Regarding colonial oppression in Africa and Asia, King observes, "The dynamic beat of deep discontent in Africa and Asia is at bottom a quest for freedom and human dignity on the part of people who have long been victims of colonialism." [52] He continues, "The struggle for freedom on the part of oppressed people in general and of the American Negro in particular has developed slowly and is not going to end suddenly." [53] Casting aside ideals, King is cognizant of the challenges of fighting for freedom and expects the beneficiaries of oppression to resist. He states, "Privileged groups rarely give up their privileges without strong resistance." [54] And yet, we are called upon to confront and overcome this resistance until freedom is gained: "When oppressed people rise up from oppression there is no stopping short of full freedom." [55] Desiring freedom for the American Negro and for all, King declares, "The struggle will continue until freedom is a reality for all oppressed peoples of the world."[56] Within this context of oppression in the United States, Asia, Africa, and across the globe, King poses the following question for the world's oppressed: "How is the struggle against the forces of injustice to be waged?"[57] There are two possible answers—violence or nonviolence.

Fanon's likely reply to this question would be that the violent forces of injustice require a violent struggle for justice. It is well known that Fanon did not endorse nonviolence, but he does not reject nonviolent resistance altogether. For example, Fanon acknowledges that peaceful work stoppages, mass demonstrations, and boycotts bring pressure on colonialism and are sometimes successful, if only symbolically more than substantively.[58] However, he questions the motives of those appealing to nonviolence—particularly the bourgeoisie of the colonialist country. Fanon explains that when the colonialist bourgeois introduce the concept of nonviolence, this signifies the mutual interest between the colonized intellectuals and elites on the one hand, and the colonialist bourgeoisie on the other.[59] Both the colonialist bourgeoisie and the colonized intellectuals view the indigenous population as an indistinct or blurred mass.[60] Both groups are trying to stop the masses from destroying everything.[61] Fanon describes nonviolence as "an attempt to settle the colonial problem around a green baize table, before any regrettable action has been performed or irreparable gesture made, before any blood has been shed."[62] And the issue here is not so much with the avoidance of bloodshed, but rather with the denial of seats for the masses around the table.

The colonizers see themselves as superior to the colonized intellectuals and the masses. The colonized intellectuals want to distinguish themselves from the colonized masses and thus have adopted the empty, abstract, universal values of colonizers.[63] The intellectuals and elites want to live in peace with (and like) the colonizers. Fanon suggests that they actually want to be, or take the place of the colonizers, dominating the masses. This is part of the reason why he claims that the colonized elites and intellectuals are not the revolutionary class; rather, the peasants and masses are the revolutionaries. The colonized intellectuals fail to understand that the colonizers are not interested in co-existing without the colonial order remaining in place.[64] Put another way, the colonizers do not want to live in a world in which they are not able to maintain a position of superiority over the colonized (including the colonized intellectuals and elites). King's emphasis on agape love coupled with his goals of winning the friendship and understanding of the opponent are not presented by Fanon as viable options in the colonial context. There is no call to love one's enemy, or to differentiate the system of oppression from those perpetuating the oppressive system. There is no image of a beloved community in which the colonized and the colonizers come together.

KING AND FANON ON INTRAGROUP VIOLENCE

Returning to King's question about using violence to confront forces of injustice, he argues that one of the dangers of resorting to violence and hatred is that these methods and emotions are futile. Violence and hatred not only fail to solve existing social problems, they also create new, more complex problems in the present and the future. In the U.S. context, King warns, "If the American Negro and other victims of oppression succumb to the temptation of using violence in the struggle for justice, unborn generations will live in a desolate night of bitterness, and their chief legacy will be an endless reign of chaos."[65] At stake, then (in the use of violent resistance) is this generation as well as future generations. Over time, this philosophy of nonviolence would be met with contention, particularly with the emergence of the black Power movement. For example, in "The Social Organization of Nonviolence" (1959) we see a slight shift in King's presentation of his philosophy as he attempts to make room for the ideals of Black Power. King does not want to reject Black Power altogether, but attempts to make room for and even justify it within the boundaries of the Civil Rights movement, which "has reached a stage of profound crisis."[66] He warns that these frustrations (over token integration and similar problems) may result in two reactions: either more social organization and resistance, or violent retaliation for wrongful suffering.

King endorses social organizing and continues to warn against violent retaliation. He is especially concerned about the riots in major cities where the majority of people injured or killed are black. He charges the police with "goad[ing] our people to riot" through their prejudice.[67] Attempting to assuage white fears while simultaneously calling for caution in the black community, he contends, "the Negro, even in his bitterest moments, is not intent on killing white men to be free."[68] Violence within the black community is usually directed against other blacks, "but there is seldom a white person who is the victim of Negro hostility."[69] King laments the consequences of intragroup violence in the black community and observes, "By turning his hostility and frustration with the larger society inward, the Negro often inflicts terrible acts of violence on his own black brother. . . . But I would not advise Negroes to solve the problem by turning these inner hostilities outward through the murdering of whites."[70]

King considers it ridiculous for the question of self-defense to be raised as it pertains to nonviolent resistance. For King, this question is somewhat empty when the situation of the black man in America is considered seriously. He remarks:

> It is always amusing to me when a Negro man says that he can't demonstrate with us because if someone hit him he would fight back. Here is a man whose children are being plagued by rats and roaches, whose

wife is robbed daily at overpriced ghetto food stores, who himself is working for about two-thirds the pay of a white person doing the same job and with similar skills, and in spite of this daily suffering it takes someone spitting on him or calling him a nigger to make him want to fight.[71]

To be sure, these conditions and daily insults necessitate aggressive resistance, but not through violence or mere self-defense. Again, for both political and ethical reasons, King calls for nonviolent resistance.

Fanon also examines the phenomenon of intragroup violence, the insults against the colonized, and the myriad ways that their humanity is denied. He explains that the violence of the colonizers against the colonized is internalized with the psychosomatic effects of muscular tension and cramping. The violence remains dormant in the colonized because they are so often restrained. The colonized do not initially exercise even self-defense against the violence of the colonizer. Consequently, the aggression and violence that the colonized man has learned from the colonizer is first unleashed against his own people. Fanon reveals, "This is the period when the niggers beat each other up, and the police and magistrates do not know which way to turn when faced with the astonishing waves of crime in North Africa."[72] Fanon is calling attention to the intragroup violence that results from the colonial system. The colonized are not permitted to exhibit any violence (or self-defense) toward the colonizers and their anger festers without an outlet. They find that the only outlet for this violence is "bloodthirsty explosions, tribal warfare, and quarrels with individuals."[73]

The colonized endure the violence inflicted by the colonizer and then project that violence back into the group in very self-destructive ways. This is a reality and a consequence of the violent, racist colonial system. Fanon explains, "The settler or the police strike and insult the native all day without getting a response, but the native will reach for his knife if another native even looks at him the wrong way."[74] Since the colonized are not yet able to see a way out of the colonial system, they display patterns of avoidance. Fanon states, "It is as if plunging into a fraternal bloodbath allowed them to ignore the obstacle, and to put off until later the choice, nevertheless inevitable, which opens up the question of armed resistance to colonialism."[75] But this period of self-destruction is not a total loss for the colonized. Their muscular tension is set free through this self-destructive fratricidal violence. And although the bloodbath against other colonized men allows them to prolong the inevitable choice of armed resistance to colonialism, it is also a catalyst for recognizing that armed resistance is the only choice. In this way self-destruction is only the first stage of violence, which is followed by a violence that organizes the colonized against the colonizers.

Whereas for King, violence (including intragroup violence and violent resistance to oppression) can only lead to chaos and destruction, for Fanon the question is how to turn intragroup violence into unified violence against the oppressive system of colonialism. King posits that unearned suffering can be a powerful force. Willingly accepting violence on oneself without retaliation and receiving suffering rather than inflicting it on others is redemptive, offering educational and transformational opportunities.[76] Fanon posits that the colonized must figure out how to turn the atmosphere of violence into something productive for decolonization, how to utilize and organize these forces to convert them into action.[77] Violence becomes a unifying agent for the colonized when they all take hold of that violence as a tool against their oppressors instead of one another. Decolonization alters beings, transforms spectators into actors, and creates new men—including a new generation, new language, and new humanity.[78]

HALLMARK OF WESTERN CIVILIZATION: VIOLENT RESISTANCE AND ITS SHORTCOMINGS

In "Love, Law, and Civil Disobedience" (1961), King argues that hatred and physical violence in Western civilization "has been the hallmark of its grandeur, and the indispensible twin of western materialism."[79] Later, in "Black Power" King describes the call to violence as a way of upholding this problematic value of the West. He asserts, "One of the greatest paradoxes of the Black Power movement is that it talks unceasingly about not imitating the values of white society, but in advocating violence it is imitating the worse, the most brutal and the most uncivilized value of American life."[80] It is not the Negro, but the white man that has committed mass murder, bombed churches, lynched and drowned other human beings.[81] King is clear that the victims of oppression are not the initiators of violence because the oppressive system is always already a system of state-sponsored and state-sanctioned violence. In this regard, he would agree with Fanon that the system of colonialism is a violent system of oppression supported by state-sanctioned violence. King is also well aware that "it is unfortunately true that however the Negro acts, his struggle will not be free of violence initiated by his enemies, and he will need ample courage and willingness to sacrifice to defeat this manifestation of violence."[82]

King warns that unbridled state-sanctioned violence is sure to follow any use of violence by the oppressed, and the expected result would be bitterness and chaos. The example of the Vietnam War is used to illustrate King's point. He asserts that a choice to respond to violence with violence has to assess "the possible casualties to a minority population confronting a well-armed, wealthy majority with a fanatical right wing that is capable of exterminating the entire black population and which would not hesitate such an attempt if the survival of white Western materialism were at stake."[83] Thus, for King, violent resistance is presented (again) as both impractical and immoral.[84] It is impractical because the state's violence is always already more overwhelming than any violent resistance possible by the oppressed. But the immorality of violence lies in the perpetuation of a vicious cycle of violence, bringing ongoing negativity in the world. Responding to hate with more hate would only "intensify the existence of evil in the universe" insofar as "[h]ate begets hate; violence begets violence; toughness begets more toughness."[85]

Fanon and King agree that the oppressors initiated violence, or as Fanon puts it, the colonized learned the violence from the colonizers. Fanon states, "The settlers said that the native only understands the language of force and the native decides to give utterance by force. The settler, through his violence, has shown the native that violence is the only way that he can be free."[86] Since the colonized are oppressed through violence, they come to understand that violence will be required to overcome colonialism and attain freedom. Fanon explains, "The argument the native chooses has been furnished by the settler, and by an ironic turning of the tables it is the native who now affirms that the colonist understands nothing but force."[87] In other words, while the colonizers previously argued that the colonized only understand force, the colonized are now using that very argument against the colonizers.

Fanon's description of decolonization is not adorned with fancy words. He articulates what he sees unfolding before his eyes: "The naked truth of decolonization evokes for us the searing bullets and bloodstained knives which emanate from it. For if the last shall be first, this will only come to pass after a murderous and decisive struggle between the two protagonists. The affirmed intention to place the last at the head of things . . . can only triumph if we use all means to turn the scale, including, of course, that of violence."[88] Again, this violence is learned from the colonizers. Fanon expounds on this point, "The native who decides to put the program [of decolonization] into practice, and to become its moving force, is ready for violence at all times. From birth it is clear to him that this narrow world, strewn with prohibitions, can only be called into question by absolute violence."[89] The violence that was once used to oppress is appropriated as a tool for liberation.

Fanon is adamant, "The uprising of the new nation and the breaking down of colonial structures are the result of one of two causes: either of a violent struggle of the people in their own right, or of action on the part of surrounding colonized peoples which acts as a brake on the colonial regime question."[90] And once the violent process of decolonization has begun, it is too late for peace talks, negotiations, and diplomats. The destruction of the colonial world is not to open lines of communication or for cohabitation because "the destruction of the colonial world is no more and no less [than] the abolition of one zone, its burial in the depths of the earth or its expulsion from the country."[91] The colonized come to realize that "colonialism only loosens its hold when the knife is at its throat" and they don't find these terms too violent.[92] Fanon posits that these terms of decolonization "only expressed what every Algerian felt in his heart: colonialism is not a thinking machine, nor a body endowed with reasoning faculties. It is violence in its natural state and it will only yield when confronted with greater violence."[93]

According to Fanon, "National liberation, national resistance, the restoration of nationhood to the people, commonwealth: whatever may be the headings used or the formulas introduced, decolonization is always a violent phenomenon."[94] Decolonization is the meeting of two opposed forces, the colonizer and the colonized. Fanon argues, "Their first encounter was marked by violence and their existence together—that is to say the exploitation of the native by the settler—was carried on by dint of a great array of bayonets and cannons."[95] And he adds, "The single combat between the settler and the native takes the form of an armed and open struggle."[96] The very existence of an armed struggle demonstrates "that the people have decided to trust violent methods only."[97] Again, he emphasizes the fact that violence was already at the center of the colonial system, in its foundation and its maintenance.

While Fanon's perspective is in clear opposition to King's, he would not negate King's warnings about state-sanctioned violence. Fanon notes that in an effort to discourage resistance among the colonized, the colonizers respond with greater violence, increasing the police and military presence. They arrest political leaders and organize military parades. But these measures do not force the natives to retreat; it only reinforces their aggression.[98] Fanon argues that the violence of the colonial regime and the counterviolence of the colonized balance each other and respond to each other in an extraordinary reciprocal homogeneity. However, the results of all of this violence are not equivalent. The financial and military strength of the colonizing country make it possible for them to inflict far more destruction on the colonized people. The colonizers have at their disposal machine guns, airplanes, and bombardments from the fleet, and the impact of these weapons "go far beyond in horror and in magnitude any answer the natives can make."[99] Everyone knows there is no turning back. The colonized are aware that since they have decided to respond to colonial violence with counterviolence, they must be willing and ready to take on the consequences of resorting to violence.[100] The consequences include massacres by the thousands, kidnapping, torture, rape, and murder of the colonized.[101] The colonized are confronted with the setbacks of using violent resistance against colonizers who are able to exert a higher magnitude of violence sanctioned by the state.

The colonized remain caught in an atmosphere permeated by violence, but they are not without hope. Fanon states, "Already we see that violence used in specific ways at the moment of the struggle for freedom does not magically disappear after the ceremony of trooping the national colors. It has all the less reason for disappearing since the reconstruction of the nation continues within the framework of cutthroat competition between capitalism and socialism."[102] But this does not render the situation hopeless. The magnitude of the oppressor's resources against those of the oppressed does not thwart the revolution. Fanon asserts, "[T]he violence of the native is only hopeless if we compare it in the abstract to the military machine of the oppressor. On the other hand, if we situate that violence in the dynamics of the international situation, we see at once that it constitutes a terrible menace for the oppressor."[103]

Of course, King rejects the idea that violence offers any real solutions to the problem of racial oppression in the United States or elsewhere. Noting Fanon's influence on youth in the Black Power movement, King explains, "realizing that they are a part of the vast company of the 'wretched of the earth,' these young American Negroes . . . often quote Fanon's belief that violence is the only thing that will bring about liberation."[104] King asserts that arguments calling for the oppressed people of color to rise up against white people throughout the world "are at least fifty years away from being relevant."[105] And, furthermore:

> Ghana, Zambia, Tanzania and Nigeria are fighting their own battles for survival against poverty, illiteracy and the subversive influence of neo-colonialism, so that they offer no hope to Angola, Southern Rhodesia and South Africa, and much less to the American Negro. The cold hard facts of racial life in the world today indicate that the hope of people of color in the world may well rest on the American Negro and his ability to reform the structures of racist imperialism from within and thereby turn the technology and wealth of the West to the task of liberating the world from want.[106]

Here we find King drawing distinctions between the Negro's struggle in America and the struggles for independence throughout Africa. In the United States, we must continue to live with our oppressors against whom we are now struggling.[107] He asserts, "In the struggle for national independence one can talk about liberation now and integration later, but in the struggle for racial justice in a multiracial society where the oppressor and the oppressed are both 'at home,' liberation must come through integration."[108] For King, if we pay attention to the violent and destructive modern weapons of war that exist in the world, then we would see "the choice today is no longer between violence and nonviolence. It is either nonviolence or nonexistence."[109]

KING'S CALL FOR A PROGRAM, FANON'S CALL
FOR POLITICIZATION

King and Fanon obviously disagree about the viability and morality of violent resistance to racial oppression. While King aims at integration and befriending racist segregationists—to "get in" rather than to "overthrow" [110]—Fanon aims at decolonization understood as the elimination of the colonizer, or at least his removal from the colonized country. However, the two agree about the goal of freedom. King emphasizes the need for ongoing organization of nonviolent marches, boycotts, and economic noncooperation as strategies for a more just distribution of jobs and wages. He elaborates on the details of his desired social justice program in "Showdown for Nonviolence," an article that was published after he was assassinated. King asks readers, black and white, to return to nonviolent protest aimed at both racial and economic issues. He outlines an economic bill of rights that would guarantee a job to those who want to and are able to work, income for those who could not work (because of age or disabilities), housing, and improvements in education. [111] He criticizes the Vietnam War and the riots, while underscoring the positive impact of peaceful demonstrations aimed at offering solutions to these complex problems. But King also recognizes, "As committed as I am to nonviolence, I have to face this fact: if we do not get a positive response in Washington, many more Negroes will begin to think and act in violent terms." [112]

Fanon emphasizes the violent aspects of decolonization, but he also moves beyond this phase of violence and calls for politicization. Fanon critiques national leaders and the national bourgeoisie for imitating the European bourgeoisie and failing to develop meaningful connections with the people after fighting for independence. [113] He notes that they do not understand the economy of the country and their knowledge is academically abstract. The national leaders exploit agricultural workers without offering modernization of agriculture, development plans, or initiatives. [114] They perpetuate the divisions and racisms of the colonial period and are harsh toward the masses. Fanon challenges political leaders to learn from and educate the people without claiming, as the colonizers did, that the people are too slow. [115] He demands that the people be educated politically, making the totality of the nation a reality to each citizen. [116] Unfortunately, King's critique of Fanon (when King claims, "the problem is that Fanon and those who quote his words are seeking to 'work out new concepts' and 'set afoot a new man' with a willingness to imitate old copies of violence") slights this positive aspect of Fanon's work. [117] Although Fanon explains that violence was an important part of achieving consciousness in Algeria, he also acknowledges that the similar results have been achieved elsewhere with methods like political struggles and information campaigns.[118]

Frantz Fanon and Martin Luther King Jr. emphatically disagree on the means and even the ends of resistance to racial oppression; however, they would agree that we have to be attentive to issues of racial oppression, economic oppression, the development and implementation of a sociopolitical program for change, and the politicization of the people as full citizens. In this way, there are surprising overlaps and points of agreement between the two divergent perspectives that each figure contributes in his writings on systems of oppression and methods of resistance.

ABBREVIATIONS

*Martin Luther King Jr.**

BP: Black Power
EL: An Experiment in Love
LLCD: Love, Laws, and Civil Disobedience
NRJ: Nonviolence and Racial Justice
NORF: Nonviolence: The Only Road to Freedom
PN: Pilgrimage to Nonviolence
SN: Showdown for Nonviolence
SON: The Social Organization of Nonviolence
TPN: The Power of Nonviolence

*All King references are from *A Testament of Hope: The Essential Writings and Speeches of Martin Luther King, Jr.*, edited by James Washington (San Francisco: HarperSanFrancisco, 1991).

Frantz Fanon

BSWM: *Black Skin, White Masks*, translated by Charles Lam Markmann (New York: Grove Press, 1967). Originally published *Peau noire, masques blancs* (Seuil: Éditions du Seuil, 1952).
WE: *The Wretched of the Earth*, translated by Constance Arrington (New York: Grove Press, 1963). Originally published *Les damnés de la terre* (Paris: Petite collection Maspero, 1961).

NOTES

1. BP, 571. King is responding to questions on the use of self-defense versus nonviolence in the 1966 Freedom Marches in Mississippi. For a more comprehensive analysis on King's nonviolent philosophy, see Greg Moses's *Revolution of Conscience:*

Martin Luther King, Jr. and the Philosophy of Nonviolence (New York: The Guilford Press, 1997).

2. I retain King's masculinist language that presents "the Negro" in masculine terms—that is, only the black man. I am less concerned here about the word Negro (versus "black" or "African American") and more concerned about the gender exclusivity that problematically ignores not only the oppressive conditions confronted by black women, but also the contributions that black women were making to the Civil Rights Movement. For more on the term masculinist, see Joy James's *Transcending the Talented Tenth*. For more on black women's activism in this context see *At the Dark End of the Street: Black Women, Rape, and Resistance—A New History of the Civil Rights Movement from Rosa Parks to the Rise of Black Power,* by Danielle L. McGuire (New York: Knopf: 2010); *Freedoms Daughters: The Unsung Heroines of the Civil Rights Movement from 1830-1970,* by Lynne Olson (New York: Simon and Schuster, 2001); and *The Montgomery Bus Boycott and the Women Who Started It: The Memoir of Jo Ann Gibson Robinson,* edited by David J. Garrow (Knoxville: The University of Tennessee Press, 1987).

3. NRJ, 5. Ivan Van Sertma's *They Came Before Columbus: The Ancient African Presence in Ancient America* (New York: Random House Trade Paperback Edition, 2003; first published 1976) dates an African presence in the Americas before 1619. See also Ben Vincent and Herb Kline, *African Slavery in Latin America and the Caribbean* (Oxford: Oxford University Press, 2007).

4. I am intentionally using the language of dehumanization and thingification to draw connections between King's language regarding racism in the United States and Fanon's language analyzing colonial conditions. King states, "Throughout the era of slavery the Negro was treated in inhumane fashion. He was considered a thing to be used, not a person to be respected" (NRJ, 5).

5. NRJ, 6.

6. NRJ, 6.

7. SON, 32.

8. NRJ, 6. Note King's assessment of "separate but equal" as not only a Supreme Court approved doctrine of racial segregation, but also as a form of slavery.

9. NRJ, 6. It is in this context of describing "negative peace" that King argues, "True peace is not merely the absence of some negative force—tension confusion or war; it is the presence of some positive force—justice, good will and brotherhood" (NRJ, 6). He also explains, "Living under these conditions, many Negros lost faith in themselves" (NJR, 6).

10. NRJ, 5.

11. NRJ, 6.

12. NRJ, 6. LLCD, 44.

13. King also describes this as the "determined resistance of the reactionary elements of the South to the Supreme Court's momentous decision outlawing segregation in the public schools" and notes the weakened impact of *Brown* based on the lack of implementation and/or enforcement (NRJ, 5). He asserts, "Federal action by the legislative and executive branches was half-hearted and inadequate" (SON, 31). But he also critiques "Negro forces" in some cases because they "lacked consistency and militancy sufficient to fill the void left by government default" (SON, 27).

14. See Aimé Césaire's *Discourse on Colonialism* (New York: Monthly Review Press 2000). Originally published *Discours sur le colonialisme* (Paris: Editions Réclame, 1950), and (Paris: Présence Africaine, 1955). As with King, I retain Fanon's gender exclusive and masculine language of "the Negro" as male.

15. BSWM, 10, 30, 34, 47, 51, 81, 228.

16. BSWM, 30. The Negro has been created and stereotyped as bad, cannibalistic, animalistic, unintelligent, illiterate, savage, brute, and ugly (BSWM, 112–13, 117).

17. The settlers are constantly distinguished from the natives and are thought to represent everything the colonized are not and can never be. The colonized are characterized as the quintessence of evil, as insensible to ethics, and as both the absence and

the negation of values. The colonized are perceived as ugly and immoral, they are the collection of wicked powers, and the instruments of blind forces.

18. WE, 39.

19. WE, 39. "The native town is a crouching village, a town on its knees, a town wallowing in the mire. It is a town of dirty niggers and dirty Arabs" (WE, 39).

20. WE, 53.

21. WE, 51.

22. It is worth noting that Fanon is critical of religion, especially the Christian church, as working in the interest of the colonial system (WE, 42, 44). He asserts, "The colonialist bourgeoisie is helped in its work of calming down the natives by the inevitable religion. All those saints who have turned the other check, who have forgiven trespasses against them, and who have been spat on and insulted without shrinking are studied and held up as examples" (WE, 67).

23. WE, 94

24. NRJ, 8. See also TPN, 13; EL, 19.

25. EL, 16. King reiterates this dual influence of Gandhi and the Christian doctrine of love in "Pilgrimage to Nonviolence" (38). He also notes that Gandhi's name became well known in Montgomery, Alabama, after a white woman (Juliette Morgan) compared the bus boycotts to the Gandhian movement in a letter to the editor of the *Montgomery Advisor* (EL, 16). According to King, Morgan died during the summer of 1957. King attributes her death to her being "sensitive and frail" and unable to "survive the rejection and condemnation of the white community" (EL, 17).

26. EL, 17.

27. See Washington's introduction to "An Experiment in Love," in *A Testament of Hope: The Essential Writings and Speeches of Martin Luther King, Jr*. Washington also adds that King "overlooks critical discussions of Nygren's interpretation, and actually misinterprets Nygren's view at a number of points" (16).

28. NRJ, 8; TPN, 13; EL, 19.

29. TPN, 13.

30. EL, 19; LLCD, 46–47. Additionally, Kings claims, "Since the white man's personality is greatly distorted by segregation, and his soul is greatly scarred, he needs the love of the Negro. The Negro must love the white man, because the white man needs his love to remove his tensions, insecurities, and fears" (EL, 19).

31. NRJ, 7; TPN, 12; EL, 17.

32. NRJ, 7; EL, 18.

33. NRJ, 7.

34. NRJ, 7; TPN, 12; EL, 18.

35. TPN, 12; EL, 17.

36. EL, 18.

37. NRJ, 8; TPN, 12; EL, 18.

38. NRJ, 8.

39. NRJ, 8. I find this claim that white supremacists are "persons who are caught in those forces" of evil troubling because there is no agency or responsibility accorded to the white supremacists. They have *chosen* to perpetuate systems of racial oppression. One might respond that King does give an account of agency insofar as he beliefs that the very persons caught in the forces of evil can choose to and/or be persuaded to make different choices. In fact, his hope that white supremacists might be persuaded to make different choices undergirds the efforts to win the friendship and understanding of the opponent.

40. NRJ, 8; TPN, 13; EL, 18.

41. NRJ, 8; EL, 20. King explains, "There is something unfolding in the universe whether one speaks of it as an unconscious process, or whether one speaks of it as some unmoved mover, or whether someone speaks of it as a personal God" working on the side of justice (TPN, 13–14).

42. NRJ, 8.

43. NRJ, 9. These guiding principles of nonviolence are adjusted over time, based on King's audience as well as the fluidity of the situation unfolding around the issue of racial oppression and violence in the United States. For example, in the later speech "Love, Law, and Civil Disobedience" (1961), King addresses white liberals who wanted blacks to slow down and give things more time. (King's reply to this call to slow down is also found in the "Letter from Birmingham Jail" and *Why We Can't Wait*.) He adds several points to the guiding premises of nonviolence already discussed, but shifts language from the principles of nonviolence to the principles of "the movement."

44. This essay is quite celebratory of the nonviolent resistance to British colonialism in India, and there are a few issues that should not go unnoticed. King opens the essay reflecting on an arguably "orientalist" image of India going back to his childhood—"Even as a child the entire Orient held a strange fascination for me—the elephants, the tigers, the temples, the snake charmers and all the other storybook characters" (TLG, 23). At times, King seems to over-romanticize the relations between the formerly colonized and the colonizers in India. For example, he asserts: "Today a mutual friendship based on complete equality exists between the Indian and British people within the commonwealth" (TLG, 25). This is not to say that King altogether ignores the social and economic problems in India, for example, in the areas of housing, unemployment, underemployment, and mass poverty (TLG, 27). Additionally, it is disappointing to see King relegate Coretta Scott King to the "woman question" on one occasion ("Coretta was particularly interested in the women of India" [TLG, 24]) and to singer on another ("Indian people love to listen to Negro spirituals. Therefore, Coretta ended up singing as much as I lectured" [TLG, 24–25]).

45. TLG, 25.

46. TLG, 25.

47. TLG, 26, emphasis original.

48. TLG, 26. The students' response to King suggests that such a conscience is absent in the colonial context—a point that King misses.

49. TLG, 26.

50. TLG, 26.

51. NRJ, 7; LLCD, 44.

52. NRJ, 7.

53. NRJ, 7.

54. NRJ, 7; LLCD, 44.

55. NRJ, 7; LLCD, 44.

56. NRJ, 7.

57. NRJ, 7.

58. WE, 66–67. This is more symbol than substance because even when some countries, like Gabon, have independence in name, "nothing has changed; everything goes on as before" (WE, 67).

59. WE, 61.

60. WE, 44.

61. WE, 62.

62. WE, 61.

63. WE, 45.

64. WE, 45.

65. NRJ, 7; LLCD, 44.

66. SON, 31–32.

67. NORF, 55.

68. NORF, 55.

69. NORF, 55.

70. BP, 595.

71. NORF, 57.

72. WE, 52.

73. WE, 54.

74. WE, 54.
75. WE, 54.
76. EL, 18; LLCD, 47.
77. WE, 70.
78. WE, 36–37.
79. LLCD, 44.
80. BP, 595.
81. BP, 595.
82. SON, 33.
83. NORF, 55.
84. NORF, 55; EL, 17.
85. EL, 17.
86. WE, 84.
87. WE, 84.
88. WE, 37.
89. WE, 37.
90. WE, 70. This dynamic also operated in the U.S. context. For example, King and his nonviolent philosophy became more appealing when juxtaposed with figures like Malcolm X or with the Black Panther Party.
91. WE, 41.
92. WE, 61. This is a phrase that appeared on a famous leaflet distributed by the FLN in 1956.
93. WE, 61.
94. WE, 35.
95. WE, 36.
96. WE, 83.
97. WE, 83.
98. WE, 70–71.
99. WE, 89. According to Fanon, "Terror, counter-terror, violence, counter-violence: that is what observers bitterly record when they describe the circle of hate, which is so tenacious and so evident in Algeria" (WE, 89). But in a footnote he explains in more detail the tenacity of the violence launched against the colonized rebels. While the UNO asks for a peaceful and democratic solution, Lacoste sets out to organize European militias in Algeria to "lighten" the load of the French military in Algeria. The army was given civil powers, and civilians were given military powers. Every European was armed and instructed to open fire on any person who seems suspect to him. Every Frenchmen was authorized and encouraged to use his weapons. When the UNO asked to stop the bloodshed, Lacoste replied that the best way to do this was to make sure there remains no blood to shed (WE, 90).
100. WE, 92.
101. Fanon notes that after seven years of crimes in Algeria during the anticolonial struggle not a single Frenchman had been indicted before a French court of justice for the murder of an Algerian (WE, 92).
102. WE, 75.
103. WE, 79.
104. BP, 589.
105. NORF, 55–56.
106. NORF, 56.
107. King assumes, wrongly, that all independence movements in Africa resulted in the expulsion of the former colonizers.
108. BP, 594.
109. PN, 39.
110. NORF, 58.
111. SN, 67.
112. SN, 70.
113. WE, 149–50.

114. WE, 154–55.
115. WE, 194.
116. WE, 200.
117. BP, 597.
118. WE, 193.

TWELVE

A Shocking Gap Made Visible

*King's Pacifist Materialism and the Method of
Nonviolent Social Change*

Greg Moses

When deciding between violence or nonviolence as means of social change, people cannot but think about ends. Malcolm X said people have rights to "any means necessary" when pursuing freedom, justice, equality, or respect as human beings.[1] This chapter affirms that such rights to violence are secured on Malcolm's terms, because only other humans can withhold freedom, justice, equality, or respect, and because violence is usually how they do it. So long as some continue to use violence to suppress liberation, then rights to violence must be granted against them.

Nevertheless, Martin Luther King Jr. renounces violence. But why? In the first place, King's nonviolence does not renounce the right to violence.[2] Yet in circumstances where rights to violence obtain, the method of nonviolent social change renounces violent practice.

Without renouncing rights to violence, there are two general justifications for renouncing the practice of violence for purposes of self-defense or liberation. The first category of renunciation derives from an absolute duty or end-in-itself, usually grounded in faith, and I shall call this approach pacifist idealism, although it might also technically be called pacifist deontology. Although King expressed a duty to this kind of nonviolence, we won't be spending much time on it in this chapter.[3]

The second approach to renouncing violence, which I will call pacifist materialism, is strategic and falsifiable, deploying nonviolence as a discipline that intends to bring a person or movement closer to some effective, worldly result. In more technical discussions, this might also be called pacifist consequentialism or pragmatism.

When King justified nonviolence from the strategic, materialist, or consequentialist point of view, he warned against cycles of violence that are made increasingly deadly by advancing technologies.[4] As tools of human conflict are capitalized into multibillion dollar investments, any struggle that engages violent means will need to consider the costs of capitalizing the means of struggle. These expenses in turn will be deducted from budgets that could be allocated toward health, education, or welfare. And when expenses for people's peaceful needs are cut back, then hopes also will be slashed that peaceful methods of social life will prevail. The cycle of violence intensifies. In order to counteract these foreseeable consequences, King encouraged the discipline of nonviolent social change, including the development of nonviolent leadership.

In his final monograph, *Where Do We Go from Here: Chaos or Community?*, King began to explore the systematic adjustments to knowledge and power that would be required to produce a nonviolent humanity. Within this schema, King cleared space for the concept that is most readily associated with pacifism, nonviolence, or civil disobedience: what he called "mass nonviolent action."[5]

Within the conceptual schema of direct action, there are special cases where movements deliberately plan and deploy their right to violence as an absence or shocking gap, whose presence is asserted through erasure. By refusing to exercise a right to violence in a situation where it is justified, the palpable renunciation of violence can become an effective technique of open struggle. Because of this shocking gap, a people's rights to violence may show through in striking ways, causing the humanity of the struggling group to emerge with arresting force.

The "invisible man" who was the object of violent repression becomes the shockingly visible subject of nonviolent liberation. When this gambit results in effective, worldly transformations, then the conceptual distance between justifications for nonviolence converges, and so-called absolutist, idealist, or deontological commitments to nonviolence are open to reappraisal as signs of material, consequential shrewdness.

When philosopher-activists such as King use two distinct concepts to justify nonviolence as both dutiful end-in-itself and as shrewd strategy of liberation, then strategic innovations of materialist nonviolence practically approach the conceptual satisfactions of nonviolent idealism. As a liberation movement struggles to create innovative and effective expressions of nonviolent discipline, peoples may wage increasingly dramatic campaigns for their human rights that will be consistent with and more likely guided by the intuitions of pacifist idealism.

Objections to the nonviolence method are well represented by a June 1964 telegram to King in which Malcolm X asserts that in St. Augustine, Florida, King's confrontations with segregation had exhausted nonviolent means, and that it was time to "organize self-defense units around our people, and the Ku Klux Klan will then receive a taste of its own medicine. The day of turning the other cheek to those brute beasts is over."[6]

The timing of Malcolm's telegram to King is significant, because here Malcolm speaks for himself after returning from Mecca, and his reference to the Ku Klux Klan takes a doubled meaning. On the one hand, Malcolm is explicitly concerned with deterring Klan-type violence against the St. Augustine protesters. But also, as will become clearer in the final months of Malcolm's life, he is publicly rejecting his prior complicity in back-room deals that yielded a "hands off" approach between the Nation of Islam and the Klan. In the St. Augustine telegram, Malcolm deploys a sound assertion. Wherever folks are violently assaulted during peaceful pursuit of liberation, they have rights to violence of self-defense and perhaps more extensive rights to revolution.

There is no dispute between Malcolm and Martin when it comes to a people's rights to violence in the practice of self-defense or liberation. Arguments that aim to refute King's pacifism by asserting rights to violence miss the point. In fact, the nonviolence waged by King was never absolute. Rather, the nonviolence that we associate with King served the purpose of undermining the legitimacy of sovereign violence so that the powers who were caught in the act of using violence weakened their sovereignty. But here is the overlooked point. The violence of sovereignty was never challenged absolutely by King. Did he not call for federal protections? And were these federal protections not rights to a sovereign violence of equal protection?

Therefore, when peaceful people are being assaulted, including women and children in St. Augustine, Florida, they may choose, in a deliberate act of nonviolence, to refuse to exercise their rights to self-defense for the purpose of demonstrating the righteousness of their cause in strict juxtaposition to the unjust violence thrown against them.

Such disciplined refusal to act upon rights to self-defense is what nonviolent activists are famous for doing. And precisely the shock expressed by Malcolm X is what nonviolence seeks to convey. One cannot help but notice that the humans engaged in the liberation movement at St. Augustine have more rights than they are exercising. But this paradoxically makes them appear precisely as subjects who are entitled to more rights than they have been accorded, whether civil, human, or moral.

In the face of King's overt commitments to pacifist idealism of the "turn-the-other-cheek" variety, disparaging criticisms made by Malcolm X do illustrate important practical considerations for nonviolent leadership. So-called "fools" who encourage men, women, or children to "turn the other cheek" risk winning respect for their personal principles at the cost of making themselves suspicious as leaders of practical, social change.

Of course, fellow pacifists, who share commitments to ends of faithful obedience, may follow pacifist leaders as examples of moral duty as such. But when whole peoples are evaluating leadership for ability to actually win goals of freedom, justice, equality, and respect for human beings, then justifications of pacifist idealism may signal a leadership's willingness to place others under too-dangerous risks. Nonviolence does risk a wreckage of human pain that may never be wholly healed.

King's materialist line of justification for nonviolence was attentive to his leadership responsibilities. Violence, King argued, could not be justified as a form for the actual struggle of people during the Civil Rights Movement, because nonviolent means had not been exhausted, violence would simply not work to achieve the ends of liberation, and the world was fast approaching capabilities of technological destruction that would soon require a global ethic of nonviolence to prevent global omnicide. Both for proximate ends and distant ones, King walked the line for nonviolent social change.

King argued that under certain conditions, the choice not to exercise rights to self-defense "by any means necessary" could generate a more effective power for liberation. As Nietzsche had argued, so-called Christian meekness does not renounce the will to power. By turning the other cheek to imperial authority, a kind of power may be asserted that throws imperial centurions off guard. Richard B. Gregg called it "moral jiu-jitsu."

Howard Thurman acknowledged the unsettling effects that nonviolence could render to armies of Caesar, but Thurman placed more emphasis upon the care that struggling peoples must take with themselves.[7] Oppression unleashes psychological "hounds of hell" that attack the core being of disinherited subjects. As a fellow minister, King carried Thurman's works into nonviolent battle as a sign of his pastoral commitment to the psychological well-being of the struggling community. Nonviolence empowered people to stand and fight, while emphasizing a commitment to their own human dignity.

This complex line of justification for nonviolence I have called pacifist materialism, distinguished from pacifist idealism, because we now refer to ends of advancing struggle, including techniques of confrontation that assert power precisely within the gap where violence is not exercised. In technical terms, this position is to be distinguished from just war theory, not only because it incorporates ends of liberation as articulated by Malcolm X, but because it also renounces the practice of violence as a leadership choice, even when violence would be justified by "rights" to liberation and self-defense.

As Malcolm X said (and as King never disputed) nonviolent demonstrators are entitled to a violence of self-defense as they are being assaulted or killed. And quite often, for the individual being assaulted, a dutiful commitment to "turn the other cheek" may contribute to motives for withholding a violent response. On commitment cards signed by Birmingham protesters were vows to "Meditate daily on the teachings and life of Jesus" and to "Refrain from the violence of fist, tongue, or heart."[8] This dutiful obedience to nonviolence, following the example of Jesus, suspends the practice of violence. And so far as the refusal to exercise a right to violence is motivated along such lines, we may classify it as pacifist idealism.

But the wisdom of the Civil Rights Movement is more fully appreciated if we see how motives of sacred obedience are deployed in order to secure other ends, too. Therefore, while Malcolm X may be correct when he warns that an unwavering faith to nonviolence might constrict a people's access to violent strategies of struggle, it is equally true that faithful commitment to nonviolent leadership can open up effective resources of social change that would otherwise be too lightly regarded.

Therefore, people may choose leadership from pacifist idealists whenever they sense that more strenuous exhaustion of nonviolent options is the wiser course of action. In other words, people would choose leadership from pacifist idealists in order to better serve ends of pacifist materialism. And I do think this is one of the practical benefits that pacifist idealists offer to concrete struggles for liberation, when and if people are ready to cut a nonviolent path.

In the black churches of the southern states, this was the shrewd wisdom that accompanied faithful commitment to the teachings of Jesus. In the black southern scholarship of the social gospel (see Thurman, Benjamin Mays, or J. Leonard Farmer[9]) the words of Jesus were understood as teachings of deep resistance to imperial oppression, so the words of Jesus were therefore taken as clues toward achieving freedom, justice, equality, and respect as human beings in this lifetime.

As King argued, and as many nonviolent protesters affirmed with their bodies, if people are willing under certain circumstances to forgo exercising their rights to self defense, they may advance a people's movement further forward than if they fight it out violently on the spot. Especially when a people's movement is faced with well-armed enforcers of a status quo, who not only hold weapons in front of them but come strapped to propaganda machines behind them, the movement toward freedom might be more wisely waged if people do not hand back to the status quo provocations that would legitimize escalations of violence and hype.

King made frequent reference to cycles of violence. Certainly one's refusal to feed a cycle of violence may be motivated by pacifist idealism with its "turn the other cheek" imperative. But on grounds of pacifist materialism, one absorbs violent provocations for the purpose of disabling further escalation of the cycle. When this works, then the people's movement asserts some control over the level of violence that will condition further struggle.

Had Malcolm X actually organized self-defense cadres in St. Augustine, consistent with the just war theory developed by that city's namesake, then we would have seen who was the bigger fool of a leader. King's pacifist materialism joined issue with ends that Malcolm X had in mind, but King argued in good faith (and correctly) that, for people seeking liberation in this life, nonviolent options can supply necessary means to liberation.

King's pacifist materialism looked for ways to expose the violence that always enforces injustice—the cost of this exposure being paid down by protesters willing to submit their bodies as "exhibits A." In wars of legitimization, the pain and death of protesters may be deployed to bring down pretences of law and order, the better to shake loose structural habits of oppression from their ideological affirmations. And in the end, it was not violence as such that was decisively challenged, but unequal protections of violence. Demonstrators are often taken to be "demonstrating against," but the term in English also signifies a revelation, "demonstrating that."

Kingian principles and methods are widely respected and applauded by those who point at other people's liberation movements. However, once the liberation movement in question becomes one's own, it is notable how often the praiseworthy necessity of nonviolence is pronounced at once absolutely unrealistic and absurd. After the manner of John F. Kennedy, we may ask not whether to insist on nonviolence for other people's struggles (whoever "they" are for you); rather, ask if nonviolence is the path that we will insist upon for ourselves.

King himself was not able to exhaust his commitment to nonviolence. Sometimes he was faced with nonviolent weapons so militant that he was not sure he could take responsibility for the consequences in this world. More than blackmail or assassination plots, this was the torment of his final days. He had been to the mountaintop of nonviolence and had discovered why he would not get to the promised land. In order for nonviolence to work in the United States, there was too much to be learned too quickly, and he knew he was at least partly responsible for the fact that when interest in nonviolence should have been moving toward crescendo, it was already, tragically, piping down.

When nonviolent leadership moved northward for the Chicago campaign, the tragedy was not that northern people were incapable of assimilating the strategy of nonviolence as such. The tragedy was that King called off the nonviolent movement just as it was about to mount its most defiant march into white enclaves. After that, it would be said that nonviolence had met its limit, when the truth was that nonviolence had voluntarily backed down, why? Because King feared that the constituency of the coming march would not be able to forfeit their human rights to self-defense. As a result of King's retreat, the possibility of social cohesion around his leadership was damaged. People said they were prepared to back his nonviolent leadership. He was the one who decided that the people were not ready.

As with the fatal conflicts of Memphis, the trouble with King's nonviolence in these later campaigns lay in weak social ties between leadership and constituency, weaknesses that did not show through in Birmingham or Selma, near the birth home of Coretta Scott. Could nonviolence have worked in Chicago, Memphis, or the ill-fated Poor People's Campaign? History has too quickly answered no, because history has a bias toward violence, too. But history may be telling us that nonviolence depends upon a relationship between people and leadership that requires patient development. King in fact was trying to tell us this when he added "long-term organization" to his conception of nonviolent struggle in his 1967 book, *Where Do We Go from Here?*

Popular bias against nonviolence has only gotten fatter since 1968, and has become so obese that we have recently heard a national (and very Christian) mob rise up and shout in unison, "But we must practice war, otherwise we do nothing!" Even a "just war" theory informed by Malcolm X's ends of freedom, justice, equality, and respect as human beings would recognize that between war and doing nothing stands a necessarily rigorous inquiry into the possibilities of nonviolence that responsible leadership (in politics, religion, or media) is obliged to explore.

So it would be some improvement in any warmongering cultural climate if popular opinion would incline at least toward the discipline of a just war theory modified to the ends that Malcolm X suggests. But in any nation where 70 percent of the people believe in the virgin birth of Jesus, we would be cynical to accept such a limited development for popular nonviolence. Even if outright pacifist idealism would be unrealistic to expect from most followers of Jesus, we might encourage consideration of pacifist materialism, where the right to self-defense is recognized but does not confer any necessary legitimization of violence.

In a global quest for freedom, therefore, it is possible that accepting the suffering and death of some people can serve the actual liberation of the many, if the acceptance holds down the level of violence that we share in struggle, if it furthers the development of nonviolent leadership, and if it pays respect to the obligation of choosing a nonviolent human future. For pacifist materialism, finally, the exhaustion of peaceful means includes the special case of shrewdly and deliberately not exercising rights to self-defense, precisely in the name of cutting a better path to liberation. Pacifist materialism freely creates this imperative of struggle in moments where rights to self-defense apply.

Malcolm X was not absolutely wrong in his famous quip that in the Kennedy assassination America's "chickens have come home to roost." Violence is the roosting place for America's chickens (in politics, religion, and media). So we lay no claims to disappointment whenever America's chickens flock to violence like a swarm of imprinted raptors. In fact, we argue with King, that this is the very conditioning we are seeking to break from when we consider freely suspending violence as necessary means.

Of course, an important difference between pacifist idealism and pacifist materialism lies in the fact that pacifist idealism appears to have no falsifiable conditions. For pacifist materialism, on the other hand, it is strategically possible that nonviolence can fail the test of providing a necessary means for the liberation of a people. Therefore, when pacifist materialism shows no promise for liberation, even a pacifist idealist should be honest about it, and I think King would have been honest about it.

There may be conditions under which analysis would present no credible reasons to believe that pacifist materialism could win a people's liberation. Under these conditions, the pacifist idealist would lose the materialist line of justification for nonviolence, and, in order to maintain a nonviolent posture, would have to fall back exclusively on a faith commitment. This King never did. In fact, I think one reason why King maintained credibility as a leader is that he always supplemented his idealism with materialist analysis and vice versa, helping to sustain a conviction that nonviolence was not only right for him but shrewd for the people; not only shrewd but right. Still, the materialist line of nonviolent defense (that it can be shrewd) requires an honest assessment where nonviolence as a method meets its falsifiable condition.

Pacifist materialism therefore is obliged to interrogate the necessity of violence wherever a right to violence has been provoked. And with respect to recent experiences with belligerent times, there are four applications to consider.

First, pacifist materialism can help us to review the arguments for violence that were asserted in the aftermath of the 9/11 massacres. Here, a tactical appeal to just war theory should have opened up questions of nonviolent alternatives, especially in mass media presentations. Into situations of terror, pacifist materialism could recenter Malcolm X's ends of freedom, justice, equality, and respect as human beings. These ends can work to deflate reactionary impulses for retaliation or symbolic violence. On this point Malcolm X is often underappreciated. His logic tended to bind a community to its needs in such a way as to not get carried away by temptations to lash out. Upon this ground, pacifist materialism could also recenter means developed by King, and counsel people to consider more carefully what "necessary means" may be exhausted nonviolently in the interests of the people.

But beyond this, had a model of pacifist materialism as such been operative in public debate, it would have been possible to consider withholding a violence of self-defense in the name of controlling the cycle of violence as a global condition of the ongoing struggle for freedom. In fact, pacifists did try to make these points at the time, but they got no hearing worth speaking about. Today, however, we can see how the cycle of violence has grown to a point where funerals for American troops are commonplace news, and estimates of indigenous casualties overseas have become horrific.

As a second example, we should not forget that nonviolence has applications for insurgents, too. Although I think the peace movement in the United States did admirable work attempting to interrogate the violence of state-sponsored aggression, and although many were quick to recognize "rights" to violence of self-defense provoked by the invasions of Afghanistan and Iraq, pacifist materialism would be more critical of automatically converting such rights into practices. Out of the resulting gap might come possibilities for global, nonviolent solidarity.

Especially given our historical knowledge of the way that spirals of violence work, where even justifiable acts of self-defense may be appropriated as pretexts for redoubled aggression, pacifist materialism could prepare a moment for analytical restraint. In this regard, do the terrible casualties among Iraqi civilians stand witness to the awful realities of a cycle of violence unleashed and fed in part by violent reflexes that, even among antiwar voices, too quickly legitimized the transformation of violence from rights into practices?

In truth, I don't have the alternative analysis that would prove there were nonviolent alternatives for the Afghan or Iraqi people. In time, the analysis may come. Meanwhile, we have credible statistics for actual death tolls, and they supply reason enough to encourage the value of pacifist materialism whenever violent provocations are being converted from rights to self-defense into new plateaus of violence.

A third application that I would like to propose for pacifist materialism is the possibility of expanding the scope of conscientious objection. Of course, a first line of argument from what we might call pacifist idealism already enjoys a kind of legal status. If on the basis of some transcendent commitment, one shows opposition to all wars, regardless of what the people may be trying to achieve, and regardless of which means are necessary, then one may be certified as a conscientious objector and released from legal obligations to fight as a combat soldier.

But along with Lt. Ehren Watada[10] and Staughton Lynd,[11] I would like for this theory of pacifist materialism to join issue with attempts to expand valid criteria for conscientious objection. If a particular war does not meet the criteria of a necessary means for a people to achieve Malcolm X's ends of freedom, equality, justice, and respect for human beings, then it's a bad war, immoral, and any laws enforcing conscription or combat killing would be no laws at all. This line of justification for conscientious objection respects a Kantian sense of rational autonomy that cannot be overruled, especially by war fever.

To those who would argue that these expanded criteria would stall the readiness of the armed forces, pacifist materialism replies just so. Especially when it comes to warmaking by the United States, we have come to a point where citizens have been conferred a historical right to question sovereign judgments. Precisely in the context of this state and its military-industrial complex, pacifist materialism digs in its heels deeper than ever before.

Where powers given to warmakers have reached an historical apex, so should powers given to war resisters. Or to put it more actively: where warmakers have seized powers unlike any known before, where constitutional processes are flaunted, and rights to free speech so sullenly exercised, so must war resisters rise up to remind a democracy where the people belong, that is, as the teamsters of their own active conscience, delivering burdens of proof directly to the doorstep of the state to show cause, not only to the satisfaction of the president, who always wins power by starting a war, nor only to the satisfaction of Congress, which always blows with the wind, nor even only to the satisfaction of the Supreme Court, which seems to have no moral compass anyway apart from the evolving conscience of the nation.

Finally, I would like to consider the conundrum of indefinite detentions flagrantly practiced as antidote to terror, where people are picked up, confined, and tortured, without respect for rights to due process or humane treatment. In order to draw people into such cages, let us not forget, escape must be equated with death. Every image of indefinite detention alludes to threat of sudden execution. Wouldn't it seem wrong to demand that such threats of death be held morally immune from "rights" to violent reciprocation? Hence the conundrum: as flagrant means of waging alleged wars on terror, indefinite detentions provide clear moral justifications for "rights" to violent means of liberation.

But it is just at this point, where provocations are openly displayed, and rights to violence are manifest, that pacifist materialism intervenes. Especially in the face of behemoth powers, such as those that flagrantly practice indefinite detentions (and wars of choice), pacifist materialism is skeptical of the claim that wherever a right to violence exists, one is better off exercising violence in fact. Obligations to nonviolent social change persist, even in these terrible times.

So far, a narrative of U.S. history might confirm Malcolm X's claims that violence serves the interests of freedom for U.S. citizens, if freedom is defined as the ability to carry out one's life goals without impediment. But on closer examination, we want to interrogate the claim that any of the violence was necessary. And we want to ask if violence in any way moved us closer to justice, equality, or respect as human beings? In fact, U.S.-led violence since 9/11 has been largely gratuitous, signifying cowardly preferences for security, deployed with decadent arrogance, and resulting in litanies of bloody mess.

Compared with the circumstances under which Malcolm X offered to organize "necessary means" of self-defense in St. Augustine, Florida, the U.S.-led invasions of Afghanistan and Iraq betray no resemblance of courage or discernment, certainly no disciplined quest for freedom, equality, justice, or respect as human beings "by any means necessary." In fact, the principle of violence has been perversely transposed from Malcolm X's ethic "by any means necessary" to "any end desirable," which is the heritage of Klan violence flown the coop, and which leaves us knowing without a doubt that Malcolm X would support a right to self-defense against that!

What we need are more hooks we can throw around the beasts of collective power and more tools of conscience to anchor them. Pacifist idealisms offer beautiful resources to draw upon, but until we connect our deliberations about violence and nonviolence to some falsifiable criteria defined by the goals of people's freedom, justice, equality and respect as human beings, we will never appreciate how much the pacifist idealists can help us to extend the reach of nonviolence and thereby to press the means of violence further back into the necessary corners where they lurk.

NOTES

1. "Malcolm X: By Any Means Necessary." Video. YouTube. Web. July 1, 2011.

2. King, Martin Luther Jr. *Where Do We Go from Here: Chaos or Community?* (Boston: Beacon Press, 1968), 55.

3. King. "Loving Your Enemies." *Strength to Love* (Philadelphia: Fortress Press, 1981), 49–57.

4. King. *Where Do We Go from Here*, 58, 184.

5. King. *Where Do We Go from Here*, 129.

6. X, Malcolm. "Telegram to Martin Luther King," June 30, 1964. Web. July 7, 2011. www.malcolm-x.org.

7. Thurman, Howard. *Jesus and the Disinherited* (Boston: Beacon, 1968).

8. King. *Why We Can't Wait* (New York: Signet Classics, 2000), 68.

9. Farmer, James Leonard. *John and Jesus in Their Day and Ours: Social Studies in the Gospels* (New York: Psycho-Medical Library, 1956).

10. Watada, Ehren. "Lt. Watada's Initial Statement of Conscience," June 7, 2006. Web. July 6, 2011. peacephilosophy.org.

11. Lynd, Staughton. "Should a Soldier Who Changes His Mind about War Have a Right to Status as a Conscientious Objector?," March 3, 2005. Web. July 6, 2011. lewrockwell.com.

THIRTEEN

Socrates, Thoreau, Gandhi, and the Philosopher/Activist Dr. King

Politics of Civil Disobedience and the Ethics of Nonviolent Action

Benjamin O. Arah

This chapter recognizes the illustrious life of leadership and service[1] that Dr. Martin Luther King Jr. (1929–1968) was committed to and died for; it is written in the spirit of celebration of his liberatory and civil rights legacy.[2] President Barack H. Obama (forty-fourth president of the United States) offered his celebratory remarks[3] noting that Dr. King, as God's noble servant with prophetic vision, pointed his people to the mountaintop[4] and challenged all Americans (their governments, the courts, political and religious leaders) to align themselves fully with the ideas and principles of the American founding fathers. Dr. King was a deeply committed dissident thinker and an activist nonviolent liberator who, by personal sacrifices and moral commitment to racial equality and social justice, earned for himself the historic high place (although, he paid dearly with his life) on the moral pedestal alongside prominent figures as Socrates (469–399 B.C.), Henry David Thoreau (1817–1862), Mohandas/Mahatma Karamchand Gandhi (1869–1948), Nelson Mandela[5] of South Africa (1918–), and other exemplary moral leaders like them.

We are attracted and indebted to Dr. King, and continue to find his moral appeal and exemplary leadership irresistible, not because he was a philosophical democrat and transformed nonconformist,[6] not because he was a perfect human being without human fallibilities, but because he was a true catalyst for social change and the unabashed "drum major for justice . . . peace . . . righteousness."[7] He counseled against moral indifference and noninvolvement in the face of palpable oppression and injustice, and argued forcefully that "injustice anywhere is a threat to justice everywhere" for "whatever affects one directly, affects all indirectly."[8] Dr. King lived his life (in the service of others) on the moral principle that "all men and women are created equal, endowed by their Creator with certain fundamental rights and among them are life, liberty and the pursuit of happiness."[9] It was on this basis that he challenged every American, then and now, to join hands in common humanity to fight and end segregation, oppression, and white racism.

This interpretive essay sets out to examine the relationship that connected Socrates, Thoreau, and Gandhi with Dr. King's civil disobedience and nonviolent direct action; and it explores the reason for Dr. King's inevitable choice of the "third way"[10] which, for him, was a calculated and most viable political strategy deployed in the moral fight to end entrenched racial segregation and inequality as well as other forms of social injustice in America. The chapter is divided into five main parts, and the goal is to highlight how the philosophy of nonviolent resistance is intertwined with and inseparable from Dr. King's ethico-intellectual and religious idealism serving as the foundational springboard for his choice of the "third way" and the politics of civil disobedience. The politics of civil disobedience is ancillary to his philosophy (ethics) of nonviolent resistance, and Dr. King hoped to use them as a moral tool and political strategy to end segregation, white oppression, social injustice that will culminate in building the desired Promised Land or a racially integrated "beloved community"[11] rooted in Christian love. The Kingian "beloved community," as a universal goal, was to be achieved using his radical politics of civil disobedience with its nonconformist nonviolent protest. And what that demonstrated was showing Dr. King not merely as an idle dreamer, but a man of both action and an agent of transformative change who happened to be a philosopher/social activist, practical idealist, radical reformer, and pragmatist engaged with concrete human conditions. He sacrificed his life in an attempt to find lasting solutions to complex social problems of the time.

Dr. King had a unique human personality and sharp-persuasive intellect, coupled with the ability to speak the bitter truth with love and moral force, but in all, he was able to connect with and confront as well as engage people with what appeared then as a radical revolutionary vision of a new and racially integrated America. He, unlike others before him, had this radical and transformative vision that was deeply grounded in ethical idealism, Christian love, and the moral commitment to nonviolent resistance as a creative way to achieve racial equality and justice. Dr. King explained his type of practical and nonviolent social activism based on a conviction that "only through an inner spiritual transformation do we gain the strength to fight vigorously the evils of the world in a humble and loving spirit."[12] He distinguished himself from any others as a radical reformer who vehemently rejects and consistently condemns violence as both immoral and impractical, because "it thrives on hatred rather than love" and also "wants to humiliate the opponent rather than to win his understanding."[13]

Dr. King, as a creature of and moral witness to his immediate social environment, lived through and personally experienced racial segregation from an early age. This left indelible marks in his mind. He described racial segregation as a close cousin of slavery that must be overcome, and was determined to challenge segregation laws through the courts by using the strategies of civil disobedience and nonviolent protests to resist and end that twin "evil system." His liberatory legacy, which Americans and the rest of the world appreciatively celebrate, was founded on the principle of nonviolent civil disobedience to unjust laws as a matter of moral duty and political obligation practiced in the tradition of moral dissent.

SOCRATES, THOREAU, GANDHI, AND DR. KING: ON STRATEGY AND TYPE OF CHANGE

> If I had been a Negro in the South, I hope I would have disobeyed the state and local laws denying to Negroes equal access to schools, to voting rights, and to public schools. If I had disobeyed those laws, I've . . . been arrested and tried and convicted. Until the Supreme Court ruled that these laws were unconstitutional, I would have been a law violator.[14]

Dr. King was intellectually broad-minded, systematic, and eclectic, with broad knowledge in the liberal arts tradition, particularly in the disciplines of philosophy and theology. He understood the nature of race relations and the problem facing African Americans, since he too had some psychologically damaging and humiliating personal experiences of white racism,[15] despite his middle class family background and upbringing.

In Clayborne Carson (ed.), *Martin Luther King, Jr.: The Autobiography of Martin Luther King, Jr.* (1998), we were shocked about an incident of how Dr. King, as a young man of about eight years, was slapped by an unknown white woman at a store in Atlanta who for some reason accused him of stepping on her foot. And he grew up conscious of the color boundaries that created empty spaces and physical separation between white Americans and African Americans. Because of the doctrine of "separate but equal," white Americans and African Americans could neither use the same swimming pools nor eat together at public restaurants, and as school-age children could not attend the same schools and learn the same academic materials as white children. Dr. King narrated one of his racial experiences when the white bus driver ordered him and Mrs. Bradley to get up and surrender their bus seats to white passengers as they were returning from Dublin to Atlanta, Georgia, and he was probably about fourteen years old. At the urging of Mrs. Bradley, Dr. King had to obey the segregationist law and gave up his own seat for the white passenger, and they had to stand for more than ninety miles till they got to Atlanta, which was their destination. He complained that he felt terribly humiliated by that particular racial experience, and the incident made him very angry. Dr. King noted that such treatments certainly could adversely affect how a child thinks about oneself and looks at humanity, but some victims of white racism may lose their self-identity, dignity, self-esteem or self-worth or "somebodiness."[16]

In all of these racial experiences, Dr. King learned and was worried about the prevailing economic condition and its impact on race relations, and he believed that racial injustice and economic injustice are inseparable twins that must be replaced with a new sense of beloved community rooted in Christian love and the abnegation of violence. By being a moral witness to social injustice inherent in the Black Codes and Jim Crow Laws, Dr. King became increasingly disdainful of segregation and other "oppressive and barbarous acts that grew out of it" to the point of getting "perilously close to resenting all white people."[17]

Dr. King was deeply troubled by what he saw and had experienced, particularly the living condition of African Americans under legally safeguarded racial segregation and its unfounded white supremacy. After critically analyzing the situation, he became more determined about the urgent need for a radical social change and to end the system that fostered segregationists' ideology that created the condition for white racism to flourish. He needed a "systematic" method that would enable him to vigorously engage both white Americans and African Americans (who were at the receiving end), to boldly confront white racism, and aggressively combat segregation (as an evil system in need of a panacea) in all of its ramifications. Dr. King realized the difficulties involved in dealing with white Americans and African Americans, after so many years of segregation and white oppression, that "we must admit that the ultimate solution to the race problem lies in the willingness of men to obey the unenforceable" and came to the conclusion that the struggle must be waged from three possible fronts: public (courts, laws through legislation, and police enforcement of the laws to achieve order), private or personal (by creating open and honest people-to-people relationships between the races through education and the use of persistent nonviolent tactics), and to uplift peoples' spiritual consciousness. In his "Letter from Birmingham Jail" (1963), Dr. King demonstrated an acute awareness of the critical role that Courts and legislation had to play in the fight to desegregate the South and dismantle the artificial structures that people put up to sustain white racism and economic injustice. In addition to the Courts, legislative actions, and nonviolent direct resistance, education also had to play an important role if the choice of nonviolent strategy was to be effective. Dr. King acknowledged that in the struggle, efforts must be made to subtly break down all the legal barriers erected with the Black Codes and Jim Crow Laws of many years so as to help in bringing all Americans together under one umbrella on the common table of brotherhood, yet education was the one powerful tool that would be used creatively to "touch the hearts and souls of men so that they will come together spiritually because it is natural and right."[18]

Dr. King welcomed the new and activist role of the United States highest court, with its 1954 unanimous decision in the *Brown v. Board of Education* case that helped to bring an end to segregated public facilities and marked the turning point in the effort to desegregate American society. The fight in the public domain was to deal with peoples' fears, ignorance, self-pride, prejudices, and other such emotions that may force them, at times, to act in strange and irrational ways against those who may be different from them. Some of these emotions could lead people to such unwarranted and unhealthy racial tension that, in the long run, may constitute the racial structures and barriers to a truly integrated human society. So fighting white racism, on many possible fronts (public, private, and spiritual) would be necessary and most strategic to help in removing all the negative emotions, attitudes, and legal structures that people have developed for many years, to enable them clean their minds and hearts, and to create the necessary condition for people to be willing to start anew by cultivating the right and healthy "conviction that all men are brothers and that love is mankind's most potent weapon for personal and social transformation."[19]

Karl Marx, in his Eleventh Thesis on Ludwig Feuerbach (1845), stated categorically that "philosophers had hitherto only interpreted the world in various ways; the point is to change it." And, for Karl Marx, "change" was tantamount to a violent revolution to turn the existing social system upside down and on its head, since the masses had nothing at stake except their economic and political chains. But Dr. King approached change in a different way: the type of change that must be essentially nonviolent, gradual, and equally transformative. Dr. King, as a practical idealist in the tradition of President Lincoln, was keen on ushering in a radical social change designed to reform and transform the racial and economic realities for Americans based on the founding principles of "life, rights, equality of opportunity, and the pursuit of property or happiness for all." This was the aspect of his radical change that made him more of a practical idealist and pragmatist in the context of race relations. The question for Dr. King, as a young radical reformer and social activist, eager to confront segregation and usher in a transformative social change, was how or by what method to accomplish this ambitious moral agenda? Here was a man who was "deeply conscious of the varieties of injustice in our society" and "my concern for racial and economic justice was already substantial."[20] Dr. King had carefully analyzed and critically interpreted his American world in various ways, but as Karl Marx asserted, what was left was how best to confront and engage the brutal and oppressive white racism in order to change and transform it for good.

To attempt to change the segregated South and transform America would not be an easy battle, and Dr. King was cognizant of that material fact. But he had no choice other than to become morally committed to the politics of mass civil disobedience and adopt nonviolent resistance or protest as the most veritable strategy for social change and racial justice in the tradition of Thoreau and Gandhi. For Dr. King, all those individuals who had to resort to the strategy of nonviolent civil disobedience for social change and justice were soldiers whom he described as trained "brigades of ambulance drivers who have to ignore the red lights of the present system until the emergency is solved."[21] Dr. King insisted that civil disobedience, as a more symbolic public act of defiance in deliberate violation of the perceived unjust law and practice or tradition, was in the case of African Americans the only practical and moral road for them to gain their freedom and justice as Americans. In the case of Dr. King and the civil rights movement, radical change to end segregation and eliminate it as a "social evil" was a unique "revolution of conscience." Moses (1997) saw this as transformative and the kind that was necessary and "possible through the aegis of nonviolent direct action."[22] It was during a very agonizing personal moment and search for intellectual guidance, looking for direction and strategy to bring about real and transformative change, that Dr. King, by sheer accident or luck as he would suggest, at Morehouse College, in 1944 (at the age of fifteen), came into contact with Henry David Thoreau's moving *Essay on Civil Disobedience* (1848), or simply "Civil Disobedience."[23] As he said, he personally found nonviolent disobedience and noncooperative engagement powerfully compelling and interesting, thus was "fascinated by the idea of refusing to cooperate with an evil system."[24] But, before he discovered Henry David Thoreau's "Civil Disobedience," there was Socrates (a Greek philosopher) in the small city-state of Athens who can be duly credited for being the foundation and intellectual source of the modern nonviolent civil disobedience, and his rich philosophical experiences were reflected and dramatized in Plato's three sequel dialogues: *Apology, Crito,* and the *Phaedo.*

There is no doubt that Socrates (469–399 B.C.), a Greek "public intellectual" and the embodiment of a philosopher in the true sense of that term, influenced Dr. King. In many of his important speeches and writings, Dr. King made key references to Socrates in personable ways to suggest intellectual relationship and affinity, particularly in his "Letter from Birmingham Jail" (1963), where the name of Socrates appeared in three key places. It could be inferred that Socrates seemed to have provided the solid intellectual framework for civil disobedience, and Dr. King's style of writing reflected that aspect of Socratic moral foundation. John Ansbro remarked that Dr. King appealed to the actions of Socrates in his effort to provide a powerful defense and justification for "the moral legitimacy of his civil disobedience."[25] It was interesting to take into account that Dr. King made direct references to Socrates by way of explaining the strategic importance of having creative tensions through nonviolent direct action as a condition for dialogue and conflict management. He pointed out that "as Socrates felt that it was necessary to create a tension in the mind so that individuals could rise from the bondage of myths and half-truths to the unfettered realm of creative analysis and objective appraisal, so must we see the need for nonviolent gadflies to create the kind of tension in society that will help men rise . . . to the majestic heights of understanding and brotherhood."[26] Dr. King demonstrated a good grasp of the Socratic philosophical endeavor as a student of philosophy, but he was more of a philosopher of social action (praxis and pragmatist) in his tireless quest for racial integration and social justice in America.

In Plato's *Apology*, Socrates (a philosopher) and philosophy (an academic discipline or vocation of the mind) were on trial. Socrates made a robust defense for his life of philosophy, a philosophic life of simplicity and serving as a moral "gadfly" to the city of Athens. By a "gadfly," Socrates meant that he was a special gift from God (although with its "nuisance value") to pester and intellectually stimulate, ethically sting, and force the people to wake up from their deep moral slumber with serious social ramifications. The goal of the gadfly analogy was to liberate people and enable them to pursue the morally good life both privately (as individuals) and publicly (as members of a given political community). At the trial, Socrates was found guilty of impiety and corrupting the minds of the Athenian youths. But the jury was eager to set him free rather than put him to death on the condition that he agreed to stop philosophizing, stop being a philosopher and gadfly, so as to desist from philosophically teaching or reminding them that "the unexamined life was not worth living" and at the same time that the examined life was the most difficult human experience.

Socrates boldly rejected the offer of "not philosophizing" on the grounds that he would rather follow his conscience rather than listen to the ignorant public and morally err, for "I owe a greater obedience to God than to you, and so long as I draw breath. . . . I shall never stop practicing philosophy and exhorting you and elucidating the truth."[27] Although Socrates intentionally would not engage in acts of political or civil disobedience, he had to on the premise that he had to obey the dictates of a higher law that transcends human laws based on his inner voice or conscience to honor the gods and as service to humanity. Engaging in civil disobedience to challenge an unjust law would be the right course of action for Socrates to do, and doing so was in his nature and as a matter of both intellectual and moral consistency. Socratic ethics informs us that to know the good is to do the good or what is right, since a just and moral individual cannot act unwisely. Within the social context and the prevailing circumstance as depicted by Plato, Socrates was right and justified in his acts of defiance and disobedience, when human laws came in conflict with the divine edict. When situations left him no moral choice other than to follow his conscience, Socrates felt the need to disregard the human law and resist tradition for the divine since "this . . . is what my God commands, and it is my belief that no greater good has ever befallen you in this city than my service to my God."[28] Gregory Vlastos (1995) made a powerful point arguing that Socrates's obedience of the human command in the *Apology* would have resulted in disobeying his God and thereby giving up his philosophic quest as ordained by and in service to God. And "so his dialectic, which teased and mocked and bullied and bludgeoned his interlocutors into self-examination, opened up to them the possibility of a life worth living by man."[29] For Socrates not to have disobeyed the city and its unjust laws, at that time, Gregory Vlastos reasoned would have cost him "his moral identity" and that would have been an evidence that he lived a life of intellectual and moral inconsistency in which he could "have committed moral self-destruction."[30]

Dr. King read Thoreau's essay and became enamored with the theory that power and political governance reside with the will of the people from which the state or government can obtain and retain its authority and stewardship. For Henry David Thoreau, engaging in acts of civil disobedience to resist or protect forms of political injustice was a moral responsibility, and he was openly critical and objected to the United States government's practices and activities. He opposed slavery of African Americans and saw slavery as an evil institution that ought to be abolished. He was also against the U.S.-Mexican War. In his essay, Thoreau provided moral arguments in justification of noncooperative and nonviolent resistance to taxation without meaningful representation, and expressed willful contempt in the form of a "conscientious objection" to what he considered a tyrannical and unjustly constituted government with civil authorities. Henry David Thoreau's brand of civil disobedience was with or without violent resistance, as a calculated political strategy and moral obligation, but he was neither calling for radical revolution nor the abolition of government. Violence was a useful option, but it was a spirited agitation to improve society via "better government" that would end the ill-treatment of Indians, abolish the immoral enslavement of African Americans, and discontinue the illegal U.S.-Mexican War for economic reasons. He denied being an anarchist, but was a man of "conscience" and a citizen who was interested in using his limited political means, through civil disobedience, to bring about a better and more efficient government for an effective administration of justice. He was different from other people, especially "those who call themselves no-government men, I ask for, not at once no government, but at once a better government."[31] Henry David Thoreau refused to pay his taxes to the American government, and his refusal to pay such taxes to a government that was grossly inefficient by imprisoning citizens "unjustly" and serving as "the slave's government" was his quiet civil disobedience and noncooperative resistance under his self-proclaimed "war with the State" in his quest of a real social and moral reform. Obviously, Dr. King was influenced by Henry David Thoreau's philosophy of civil disobedience and noncooperative resistance, and he applied its principles to the Montgomery Bus Boycott (in 1955) in order not to cooperate with that racist "evil system" with the intention not to "put the bus company out of business, but to put justice in business."[32]

Dr. King found close affinity with Henry David Thoreau's noncooperative civil disobedience, for the bus boycott was a form of active resistance and deliberate refusal to cooperate with the oppressors for the sake of freedom and justice. In demonstrating the influence of Thoreau on Dr. King, and their close connection, despite the minor differences, Dr. King reminisced that "I became convinced that noncooperation with evil is as much a moral obligation as is cooperation with good . . . as a result of his writings and personal witness, we are the heirs of a legacy of creative protest" and "the teachings of Thoreau came alive in our civil rights movement . . . expressed in a sit-in at lunch counters, a freedom ride into Mississippi, a peaceful protest in Albany, Georgia, a bus boycott in Montgomery, Alabama, these are outgrowths of Thoreau's insistence that evil must be resisted and that no moral man can patiently adjust to injustice."[33]

Dr. King continued relentlessly with his search for an appropriate method as he studied some theological works and theories. He read several philosophical and theological works, including that of Reinhold Niebuhr; the existentialist philosophers (Kierkegaard, Nietzsche, Jaspers, Heidegger, and Sartre); the utilitarianism of Jeremy Bentham and John Stuart Mill; the social contract theories of Thomas Hobbes, John Locke, and Jean-Jacques Rousseau; Walter Rauschenbusch's *Christianity and the Social Crisis*; and other social theorists and moral philosophers that were readily available to him at that time. He studied other great philosophers, thinkers, writers, and theologians from Plato, Aristotle, and Georg W. Hegel to Martin Buber, and took special interest in Buber's doctrine of Personalism. It was almost six years after he first read and began studying Henry David Thoreau's essay that Dr. King attended and heard an informative lecture by the then Howard University President Mordecai Johnson. The lecture was centered on the life, social ethics and eclectic religious teachings of Mohandas/Mahatma Gandhi, but his focus was about his civil disobedience and nonviolent resistance.[34] President Johnson had recently returned from a brief visit to India, and his sermonized lecture on Gandhi and nonviolence philosophy was powerful and uplifting. The lecture had such a powerful and lasting impact on Dr. King's young mind that, in retrospect, he acknowledged "was so profound and electrifying that I left the meeting and bought half-dozen books on Gandhi's life and works."[35] Dr. King devoutly studied the Gandhian materials, and "as I read, I became deeply fascinated by his campaigns of nonviolent resistance. . . . The whole concept of 'Satyagraha' . . . was profoundly significant to me" and "as I delved deeper into the philosophy of Gandhi, my skepticism concerning the power of love gradually diminished and I came to see for the first time its potency in the area of social reform."[36]

Dr. King was overwhelmed by the new insight that he could glean from Gandhi's politics of civil disobedience and philosophy of nonviolence in relationship to the Christian ethics of love as espoused by Jesus Christ, and that immediately satisfied his intellectual thirst, searching for a viable and a more realistic strategy for racial integration and social justice. The influence of Gandhi was immediate with Dr. King, for

> [i]t was in this Gandhian emphasis on love and nonviolence that I discovered the method for social reform that I had been seeking for so many months, and more importantly the intellectual and moral satisfaction that I failed to gain from. . . . I found in the nonviolent resistance philosophy of Gandhi . . . the only morally and practically sound method open to oppressed people in their struggle for freedom.[37]

Also, in his "Pilgrimage to Nonviolence," which was a chapter in his *Stride toward Freedom* (1958), Dr. King acknowledged the connection how the exemplary activities of Mahatma Gandhi (an Indian gadfly in the Socratic tradition) informed his own personal evolution and ideological bent. His love-driven philosophy was based on the politics of civil disobedience and philosophy of nonviolent noncooperation with injustice. He spoke eloquently with excitement about his intellectual and spiritual journey to nonviolence, of his affinity with both Thoreau and Gandhi, and how "Gandhi convinced me that true pacifism is not nonresistance to evil, but nonviolent resistance to evil."[38] It was from Gandhi that he learned the power of "love" as a critical life force; L. D. Reddick upon reflection said that Dr. King's civil disobedience and nonviolence resistance strategy could be seen as a borne philosophy of love. L. D. Reddick concluded that the background to this unique philosophy of love can be fleshed out from "the teachings of the great three: Jesus, Thoreau, and Gandhi. . . . [I]t is not just a theory, it is an alternative to the conflict and killing that we usually associate with social progress."[39]

In his article "Nonviolence and Racial Justice" (1957), which was among his early developed essays to explain and justify his racial "nonconformist" philosophy, Dr. King used that forum to provide a sense of direction and the roadmap that guided the Montgomery Improvement Association and the Southern Christian Leadership Conference. In the article, he discussed nonviolent resistance in its relationship with civil disobedience, and argued that his civil disobedience and philosophy of nonviolent protest were creative forms for direct action in the strategic fight against white segregation and racial injustice. For no matter the situation, civil disobedience and nonviolent direct protests were the only viable alternative to white violence and entrenched segregation, because violence in all of its manifestations was both immoral and impractical with the inherent capacity to generate more violence and destroy the community. The civil rights movement, under his remarkable moral and political leadership, advocated total rejection of any use of violence in the struggle to end brutal white racism and achieve social justice. Dr. King rejected violence vehemently and consistently embraced the "third way," which he explained and discussed in his later work titled: *Where Do We Go from Here?*

In the struggle for radical change, Americans (both white Americans and African Americans) and their key institutions (particularly the churches, courts, etc.) have shared responsibilities and important activist roles. While the courts or churches, he insisted, "must face its historic obligation in this crisis . . . the problem of race is not a political but a moral issue."[40] But for the oppressed, he suggested, "there is much he himself can do about his plight," because as such a person created by God with moral sensibilities, that individual "has within his being the power to alter his fate" and "take direct action against injustice without waiting for the government to act or a majority to agree with him or a court to rule in his favor." He further explained that the one creative thing that an oppressed person can do has to do with how he approaches his state of oppression or condition, and the individual seemed to have three choices out of which to select the most fitting and appropriate: (1) acquiescence, (2) resort to physical violence that reflects hatred and the absence of love, and (3) the "third way" or the choice of nonviolent resistance.[41] The reason that Dr. King, as a civil rights leader, opted for the "third way" that required discipline and careful planning as well as coordination in complete repudiation and rejection of violence was that "violence solves no social problems; it merely creates new and more complicated ones. Through the vistas of time, a voice still cries to every potential Peter: 'Put up your sword.' . . . If the American Negro and other victims of oppression succumb to the temptation of using violence in the struggle for justice, unborn generations will live in a desolate night of bitterness, and their chief legacy will be an endless reign of chaos."[42]

POLITICS OF CIVIL DISOBEDIENCE AND THE ETHICS OF
NONVIOLENCE DIRECT ACTION

For civil disobedience to take place, in the tradition set out by Socrates, Henry David Thoreau, and Mohandas/Mahatma Gandhi, a citizen or group of citizens of any given society would have deliberately chosen to publicly and intentionally break the established rules, ordinances, and/or laws of that society in an organized mass protest or resistance with the full knowledge and willingness to bear and suffer the (legal and/or political consequences). All of these men, including Dr. King, went to jail and endured the humiliation and hardship that resulted from their various acts of nonviolent civil protest against injustice or social wrong inherent in the system. Normally, these acts of civil disobedience and nonviolent resistance could take the form of not paying taxes, deliberate violation of a court order, the Montgomery mass bus boycott, willfully refusing to sit in the designated areas for specific population or certain individuals, and/or mass public defiance and demonstrations. Howard Zinn defined civil disobedience in terms of knowing and deliberate violation of the law for vital social purpose[43] and which, in a democratic society, has to be both conscientious and nonviolent in submission to or acceptance of the existing political authority.[44] Dr. King played the politics of civil disobedience effectively with superb intellectual superiority and advantage, because he was able to articulate the racial struggle for justice in terms of both a universal right and moral duty of every citizen of a political community; and he included in such rights and duties that of dissent and protest against social injustice, exploitation, and oppression anywhere and everywhere. And with the ethics of his nonviolent direct protest, he was forceful and equally able "to arouse the conscience of the nation to return to the sublime principles proclaimed in the Declaration of Independence and to establish the conditions that would enable every citizen to develop a life consistent with the claims of universal justice and the sacredness of the human person."[45]

In April 1963, eight white clergymen from Alabama wrote and published a letter, "A Call to Unity." They charged Dr. King's civil disobedience and nonviolent protests in various places, particularly in Birmingham, as "unwise and untimely." Dr. King, while in the Birmingham jail at the time, decided to use the opportunity in lieu of idleness to fire back and provide a written response to their "criticism of my work and ideas." He felt that these privileged religious leaders were "men of genuine good will" and probably erred despite their outward best of intentions. Dr. King began his "open letter" by first explaining to the clerics (and the general public) why he came to Birmingham in the first instance — that he came there to engage in a carefully planned act of civil disobedience and nonviolent direct action against the city and its vested interest groups. He informed them about his current position as the leader (president) of the Southern Christian Leadership Conference (with many subsidiary organizations in the South), and that he was duly invited by the Alabama Christian Movement for Human Rights. He tried to dispel and debunk the charge that he was an "outsider coming in" to stir trouble and create "economic" havoc in the city, and Dr. King stated that his organizational ties and leadership responsibility were the moral grounds for participating in their organized nonviolent direct action. More importantly, Dr. King wrote that he was in the city of Birmingham and intended to stay as long as it would take to protest for social change and spread "the gospel of freedom," since "injustice is here" plaguing and destroying lives of people in the city. He preached that social injustice (racism, segregation, exploitation, police brutality, etc.) was like cancer and very contagious if left unchecked and untreated with dangerous consequences. Dr. King lectured the clergymen on the ethical implications of these maxims: that "injustice anywhere is a threat to justice everywhere," that "whatever affects one directly, affects all indirectly," and that "freedom is never voluntarily given by the oppressor, it must be demanded by the oppressed."[46]

Dr. King wondered why the eight privileged clergymen, as "men of good will," were quick to have issues with those nonviolent protesters for social justice and had to "deplore the demonstrations taking place in Birmingham," but would not forcefully express moral outrage and express "a similar concern for the conditions that brought about the demonstrations."[47] In their letter, "A Call for Unity," the clergymen were eager to "appeal for law, order and common sense in dealing with racial problems in Alabama" and "expressed understanding that honest convictions in racial matters could properly be pursued in the courts" with the hope that the courts' decisions regardless of their racial outcomes for the people "should in the meantime be peacefully obeyed."[48] Dr. King thought that their letter calling for action was hypocritical, and he lambasted them for being indifferent to the plights of African Americans who lived through the ugly Black Codes (1800–1866), the Jim Crow laws (1876–1965) and have continued to suffer the negative consequences of "separate but equal" doctrine enacted in *Plessy v. Ferguson* (1896) that created the "other America" for the nonwhites and all those without privileges, access to power, and opportunities. Dr. King found the actions of the religious clergymen to be as amusingly painful as their plea for continued patience in peacefully obeying courts' decisions. He reminded them that African Americans had endured and suffered, waited for more than 340 years to no avail for justice and equality as their "God-given rights" only to be told to "wait," which, in the long run, means "never." And the urgent reason why the victims of white racism and racial injustice, in America and anywhere else, cannot continue to wait any longer was that "justice too long delayed is justice denied."[49] Sarah Boyle (1962) thought that America, under its segregated laws (including the Black Codes and Jim Crow system) and with its "separate but equal" doctrine, was "un-Christian and undemocratic."[50] The danger in continuing to "wait" with outsiders counseling against civil disobedience and nonviolent protests to end segregation, as Dr. King argued, was because of their moral indifference to the plight of African Americans and the fear on the part of good Americans to confront, challenge and undermine the "un-Christian and undemocratic" system in the collective quest for racial integration, equality, and social justice.

In order for a nonviolent civil disobedience campaign to be successful, the civil rights movement (with Dr. King's visionary leadership) had to develop and articulate the four-step systematic strategy as outlined. The first step has to do with gathering the necessary factual information to ascertain if injustice exists as was the case with Birmingham, and Dr. King was able to indicate and certify that there was injustice evidenced in white segregation. The second stage involves bringing the issues or problems to the table for deliberation and negotiation with the key players in order to arrive at a lasting solution in the interest of all. The third step, beyond the good-faith negotiation and reconciliation for possible compromises and workable agreements, has to do with the appropriate education and training for all the potential participants for self-purification in preparation for the nonviolent direct action. The direct action in the form of protest or resistance has to be nonviolent, because Dr. King was consistent in his refusal and rejection of violence, and that was why he opted for the "third way." The final phase, if the negotiation happens to collapse with no other alternative course of action to end the existing social injustice, is then the real "nonviolent direct action" of organized civil disobedience. The direct action takes various forms as mass demonstration, picketing, boycotts (as with the Montgomery Bus Boycott), willful noncooperation with the constituted authorities, rides, strikes, breaking certain "unjust" laws, sit-ins, marches, blocking the streets and causing traffic jams, and so on.

In the case of the city of Birmingham with Mr. Eugene "Bull" Connor, the then Commissioner for Public Safety, good-faith negotiation for a win-win solution was not reached, resulting in and leaving one group feeling shafted or being the victims of a broken promise in the process. Deliberate and nonviolent civil disobedience via direct action, in any or a combination of its various forms, is used to morally compel the powers that be or leaders of the interested party to come to the table for constructive dialogue, good-faith negotiation, and sincere compromises in a manner of give-and-take based on rational discussion and persuasion.[51] Without such honest negotiation and compromises for the mutually desired political end, then people may resort to the use of violence. Dr. King rejected violence for nonviolent protest or resistance, and his approach was to undertake the direct nonviolence actions (as effective and expedient political strategy) that could bring about a crisis situation and create the needed tension for the whole community and its leadership to be forced to enter into continued good-faith negotiation to resolve problems in the public interest. This approach to generate "creative tension," within a democratic political experiment, could be considered healthy, necessary, and constructive in human relationships and for conflict management.

For Dr. King, civil disobedience or nonviolent resistance would not be the ultimate goal, but a necessary means or strategy in an effort to achieve worthy human goal beyond the individuals as participants. As a last resort, the nonviolent direct action was a calculated strategy to lead to further dialogue and negotiation to force the parties involved to make meaningful concessions with a vision and the hope for a transformative change. Dr. King abhorred violence, because it demonstrated complete abnegation of true love. But the unfortunate thing was that the white segregationists in the South and elsewhere wanted to cling to their privileges and advantages relative to the African Americans and others, and like those in positions of power for self-interest and personal gains would "seldom give up their privileges voluntarily."[52] The politics of it all, and also the rightness of civil disobedience and nonviolent action, can be measured in the context that "we have not made a single gain in civil rights without determined legal and nonviolent pressure."[53] Having tried nonviolent resistance in the Montgomery Bus boycott and in Birmingham City as well as in many other strategic places in the South, Dr. King was justified to conclude that "as the days unfolded, I came to see the power of nonviolence resistance more and more . . . nonviolence became more than a method to which I gave intellectual assent; it became a commitment to a way of life."[54]

The question is whether Dr. King was a reformer or revolutionary, or did he graduate "from reformer to revolutionary?"[55] Dr. King never set out to solve a universe of problems facing the United States and African Americans when he assumed the mantle of leadership for the Southern Christian Leadership Conference as part of the Southern Freedom Movement aimed at fighting and ending racial segregation. And obviously, everyone would agree with David Garrow that "so much had changed" in the South as well as in the United States and so many other parts of the world from the time that Mrs. Rosa Parks refused to give up her seat on the bus to Dr. King's death in 1968. Things have changed, lives transformed, and many people today enjoy the benefits of the civil rights legacy as a result of his transformational leadership and vision. Dr. King, from December 1955, set out to fight white racism, which was an uphill political and moral battle, because it was institutionalized and legalized in the Jim Crow laws and embedded in the Black Codes with devastating social, psychological, and economic ramifications for African Americans and other minorities. In fairness to his legal, political, and nonviolent

direct action coupled with his intellectual acumen and personable leadership skills, white racism was boldly confronted and undermined with
unprecedented results. But then Garrow charged that

> Martin King had grown from a naïve optimist who had told Montgom-
> ery's protesters that their passive withdrawal from the buses would
> persuade white southern of segregation's immorality to a sagacious,
> worn down realist who knew that the central injustice of American
> society lay not simply in its racial practices but in its entire economic
> structure. Toward the end of his journey, he began to see that only by
> confronting "class issues . . . the problem of the gulf between the haves
> and the have not," and only by openly advocating democratic social-
> ism, could . . . begin to combat the widespread economic injustice that
> underlay American racism, American militarism, and American mate-
> rialism.[56] (pp. 176–77)

There is a problem with such criticism, but the fact remains that Dr. King
with his "naïve optimism" and visionary leadership made a significant
difference that touched peoples' lives and changed the dynamics of race
relations in America, and he succeeded to effect such changes at a personal cost. The issue of whether he was a radical revolutionary or reformer
notwithstanding, because Dr. King's exemplary civil rights leadership
and philosophy of personalism played instrumental roles in the passage
and signing into law the Civil Rights Act of 1964 and the Voting Rights
Act of 1965, by President Lyndon Johnson. He was a reformer who believed that change was a gradual process, and focused on challenging
and dismantling the Jim Crow racist laws and divisive apparatus that
were put in place as "physical, spiritual, and psychological barriers that
hurt . . . kept African Americans politically disenfranchised and economically dependent."[57] It was not that Dr. King was a "naïve optimist" who
misinformed protesters that their passive withdrawal from using buses
would be a panacea to the problems that they faced, or whose refusal to
move toward democratic socialism was the evidence of his poverty of
political ideas and moral leadership. He had an economic agenda but,
like W. E. B. Du Bois, Dr. King was aware that the problem of the twentieth century was that of the color line (of double-consciousness) that had
to be addressed. He worked tirelessly to improve the human condition,
and he believed that change could easily be realized through legislation,
in the courts, and by way of useful education. He thought that these were
the necessary baby steps that must be dealt with in order to create the
condition for his "believed community" without resorting to violence.
Why education? Dr. King answered in one of his essays,

> Through education, we seek to change attitudes; through legislation
> and court orders, we seek to regulate behavior. Through education, we
> seek to change internal feelings (prejudice, hate, etc.); through legisla-
> tion and court orders, we seek to control the external effects of those

feelings. Through education, we seek to break down the spiritual bar-riers to integration; through legislation and court orders, we seek to break down the physical barriers to integration. . . . Anyone who starts out with the conviction that the road to racial justice is only one lane wide will inevitably create a traffic jam and make the journey infinitely longer.[58]

This was his reform strategy and leadership vision, and he invested time and energy for things to change and improve. Dr. King worked closely with other people and leaders to blend the goal of social integration with economic justice for Americans, and in subtle ways confronted these is-sues: alleviation of poverty, elimination of various forms of employment discrimination, fair employment opportunities and work programs, de-cent housing, and fully integrated education. Economic justice was a worthy and ambitious goal, but all of these challenges were equally worthy goals that needed to be tabled and realized through a radical restructuring and transformation of the American society based on his nonviolent civil and mass disobedience to the status quo. He was a radi-cal in the sense that he wanted to solve the human problems from their roots and, with a rich intellectual life committed to leadership and ser-vice, he offered a vision for a future "beloved community" based on Christian love and racial integration.

ACKNOWLEDGMENTS

The author thanks Dr. William B. Lewis and Dr. Mario Fenyo (his col-leagues at Bowie State University) for their encouragement and reading the initial drafts of this chapter, and he appreciates their comments and suggestions. This chapter was first read at the Marist College Conference on "Morality of War, Active Diplomacy, and Violence: The Paths for Nonviolence," on November 28, 2009. The conference was organized by The Society for Indian Philosophy & Religion in conjunction with the Departments of Politics and Praxis and Women's Studies at the Marist College, in New York.

NOTES

1. In "The Drum Major Instinct," Dr. King asked that he be remembered not for his money nor material gains but that people eulogize him as someone who simply fed the hungry and clothed the naked as well as "tried to give his life serving others" and also "tried to love and serve humanity" (1968). See James M. Washington (ed.), *I Have a Dream: Writings & Speeches That Changed the World* (New York: HarperOne, 1992), 191.

2. Charles S. Brown, "The Legacy of Martin Luther King, Jr. and the New Move-ment for Justice," in *Reflections of the Dream*, edited by Clarence G. Williams (Cam-

bridge, MA: MIT Press, 1996), 113–25. In the essay, Professor Brown wrote that "along with Rosa Parks . . . Martin Luther King, Jr. was a participant in this critical effort to make the promise and the dream of true democracy and freedom a reality in America. And in seeking to accomplish this end, he was committed to the dignity of every human being. . . . [H]e dared to take a stand for the dignity of the people at the bottom of the economic structure of our society" (122). Like Jesus Christ and Mahatma K. Gandhi, Dr. King wanted to radically transform his America and "liberate" the people, and then he died fighting for peace and justice (both racial and economic). Also look at Hubert E. Jones's "Martin Luther King, Jr.: What Does He Mean to Me?" (37–41); and John R. Bryant and Helen G. Edmonds's "The Legacy of Martin Luther King, Jr.: The Path to Human Dignity and Freedom" (147–61, particularly 157–61), both in *Reflections on the Dream*, edited by Clarence G. Williams (Cambridge, MA: MIT Press).

3. President Obama visited the Vermont Avenue Baptist Church in Washington, D.C., on January 17, 2010, where he delivered the speech. http://www.whitehouse.gov/thepress-office/remarks-president-remembered-dr-martin-1.

4. In reference to the political and economic gains made by African Americans and other minority groups due to many years of legal challenges and civil rights struggles (of 1896–1954, 1954–1969, and 1968 to the present), and the necessary social outcome and progress resulting from his nonviolent resistance and civil rights leadership gave impetus to the hope for a promised land that he called a "beloved community." It is to be a new America, a racially integrated moral community where, as he would have it, his four children would live (as Americans) and not be judged based on their skin color or texture but on the content of their character. The reference to "I've been to the mountaintop," by Dr. King, was contained in his very last paragraph to his last speech, at the Mason Temple/Church, on April 3, 1968, in support of the predominantly "poor" African American Sanitation Workers (asking for better wages and an improved working condition), in Memphis, Tennessee (a day before his assassination on the second floor at the Lorraine Motel, at the youthful age of thirty-nine).

5. His *Long Walk to Freedom: The Autobiographical of Nelson Mandela* (1995) is compelling, fascinating, and a must read manual for all those interested in pursuing the good life based on service and leadership as well as the practice of civil disobedience against racial oppression and social injustice.

6. Martin Luther King Jr., "Transformed Nonconformist" (1963), in *Strength to Love*, edited by Martin Luther King Jr. (New York: Harper & Rows Publishers,1963), 8–15.

7. Martin Luther King Jr., "The Drum Major Instinct" (1968), in *I Have a Dream: Writings and Speeches That Changed the World*, edited by in James M. Washington (New York: Harper San Francisco Publishers, 1992), 180–92.

8. Martin Luther King Jr., "Letter from Birmingham Jail" (1963), in *Why We Can't Wait*, edited by Martin Luther King Jr. (New York: Harper & Row Publishers, 1992), 76–95.

9. The concept of rights as "inalienable" and social contract theory as the foundation for any legitimate government or civil authority were advanced by John Locke (1632–1704), in *The Second Treatise of Civil Government* (1690); later by Thomas Jefferson, in the American Declaration of Independence (1776).

10. Dr. King noted clearly that the "oppressed people deal with their oppression in three characteristic ways," but he rejected the first two and chose the third way. The question was "Why"? See Dr. King's piece titled: "Where Do We Go from Here?" in his *Stride toward Freedom: The Montgomery Story-Birth of Successful Non-Violent Resistance* (New York: Harper & Row Publishers [Perennial Library], 1958), 166–201.

11. Both the concept and vision of "the beloved community," as Smith and Zepp (1998) would like to argue, remained "the capstone of King's thought . . . the organizing principle of all of King's thought and activity" (129). The notion of the "beloved community," of an America and the world as they "ought to be" and of a better nation and a world at peace, is his envisioned "promised land" where all of humanity (as

God's children) will have the creative capacity and sustainable "resources to achieve the ideals of brotherhood and harmonious living" (King, 1958, 166).

12. Martin Luther King Jr., "Letter from Birmingham Jail" (1963), in *Why We Can't Wait* edited by Martin Luther King Jr. (New York: Harper & Row Publishers,1992), 76–95.

13. John J. Ansbro, *Martin Luther King, Jr.: Nonviolent Strategies and Tactics for Social Change* (New York: Madison Books, 2000).

14. Abe Fortas, a former Associate Justice of the United States Supreme Court, believed that many African Americans were probably right and morally justified, by virtue of their rights as citizens, in disobeying what he described as "unjust laws." He would make a distinction between just and unjust laws; and, for him, "unjust laws" would be the unique kind that only the minority would be legally forced to obey or be subject to, but which would not be binding on the majority. In this situation, the minority would have the right to disobey such laws both openly and peacefully or through nonviolent direct action as recommended and practiced by Thoreau, Gandhi, and Dr. Martin Luther King. See his book *Concerning Dissent and Civil Disobedience* (New York: Signet Classics/Mentor Books, 1970).

15. He wrote, in his "Pilgrimage to Nonviolence" (1958), how he "had passed spots where Negroes had been savagely lynched, and had watched the Ku Klux Klan on its rides at night . . . seen police brutality with my own eyes, and watched Negroes receive the most tragic injustice in the courts" (72).

16. Clayborne Carson (ed.), *Martin Luther King, Jr.: The Autobiography of Martin Luther King, Jr.* (New York: Grand Central Publishing, 1998), 3–9.

17. Martin Luther King Jr., *Stride toward Freedom: Montgomery Story-Birth of Successful Non-Violent Resistance* (New York: Harper & Row Publishers [Perennial Library], 1958), 72.

18. Martin Luther King Jr., *Strength to Love* (New York: Harper & Row Publishers, 1963).

19. Ibid., 23.

20. Martin Luther King Jr., *Stride toward Freedom: Montgomery Story-Birth of Successful Non-Violent Resistance* (New York: Harper & Row Publishers [Perennial Library], 1958), 72–73.

21. Martin Luther King Jr., *The Trumpet of Conscience* (New York: Harper & Row Publishers, 1967), 53.

22. Greg Moses, *Revolution of Conscience: Martin Luther King, Jr. and the Philosophy of Nonviolence* (New York: The Guilford Press, 1997), vi.

23. In one of his most powerful dictums, Henry David Thoreau (1848), in his "Civil Disobedience," reasoned that "under a government which imprisons any unjustly, the true place for a just man is also a prison. . . . [T]he only house in a slave state in which a free man can abide with honor" (Krutch, 1982, 94).

24. Martin Luther King Jr., *Stride toward Freedom: Montgomery Story-Birth of Successful Non-Violent Resistance* (New York: Harper & Row Publishers [Perennial Library], 1958), 73.

25. John J. Ansbro, *Martin Luther King, Jr.: Nonviolent Strategies and Tactics for Social Change* (Lanham, MD: Madison Books, 2000), 114–15.

26. Martin Luther King Jr, "Letter from Birmingham Jail" (1963), in *Why We Can't Wait*, by Martin Luther King Jr. (New York: Harper & Row Publishers, 1992), 79–80.

27. Plato, *Apology* (28d–31b), in *The Collected Dialogues of Plato (including the Letters) with Introduction and Prefatory Notes*, edited by Edith Hamilton and Huntington Cairns (Princeton: Princeton University Press, 1989).

28. Plato, *Apology* (30a–38a).

29. Gregory Vlastos, "Socrates on Political Obedience and Disobedience," in *Studies in Greek Philosophy, Volume 2: Socrates, Plato and Their Tradition*, edited by Daniel W. Graham (Princeton: Princeton University Press, 1995), 41.

30. Ibid., 42.

31. Henry David Thoreau, "Civil Disobedience" (1848), in *Walden and Other Writings by Henry David Thoreau*, edited by Joseph Wood Krutch (New York: Bantam Books, 1982), 86.

32. Martin Luther King Jr., *Stride toward Freedom: Montgomery Story-Birth of Successful Non-Violent Resistance* (New York: Harper & Row Publishers [Perennial Library], 1958), 36–37.

33. Clayborne Carson (ed.), *Martin Luther King, Jr.: The Autobiography of Martin Luther King, Jr.* (New York: Warbner Books, 1998), 14.

34. Ibid., 23–24.

35. Martin Luther King Jr., *Stride toward Freedom: Montgomery Story-Birth of Successful Non-Violent Resistance* (New York: Harper & Row Publishers [Perennial Library], 1985), 78.

36. Ibid.

37. Ibid., 79.

38. Ibid., 80.

39. L. D. Reddick, *Crusader without Violence* (New York: Harper & Row Publishers, 1959).

40. Martin Luther King Jr., *Stride toward Freedom: Montgomery Story-Birth of Successful Non-Violent Resistance* (New York: Harper & Row Publishers [Perennial Library], 1958), 182.

41. Ibid., 188–89.

42. Martin Luther King Jr., "Nonviolence and Racial Justice" (1957), in *A Testament of Hope: The Essential Writings of Martin Luther King, Jr.*, edited by James Melvin Washington (New York: Harper & Row Publishers/San Francisco, 1986), 7.

43. Howard Zinn, *Disobedience and Democracy* (New York: Random House, 1968).

44. Carl Cohen, *Civil Disobedience* (New York: Columbia University Press, 1971).

45. John J. Ansbro, *Martin Luther King, Jr.: Nonviolent Strategies and Tactics of Social Change* (New York: Madison Books, 2000), xv.

46. Martin Luther King Jr., "Letter from Birmingham Jail" (1963), in *Why We Can't Wait*, by Martin Luther King Jr. (New York: Harper & Row Publishers,1993), 76–80.

47. Ibid., 77–78.

48. C. C. J. Carpenter et al., "A Call for Unity" (1963). It was this letter that prompted a response from Dr. King in what began to be known as his famous "Letter from Birmingham Jail" of 1963 (in *Why We Can't Wait*).

49. Martin Luther King Jr., "Letter from Birmingham Jail" (1963), in *Why We Can't Wait*, by Martin Luther King Jr. (New York: Harper & Row Publishers,1993), 80–81.

50. Sarah P. Boyle, *The Desegregated Heart: A Virginian's Stand in Time of Transition* (New York: William Morrow, 1962), xiii, 118.

51. Fairclough (1986) asked, somewhat rhetorically, "was nonviolent direct action a means of persuasion, or did it depend for its effectiveness upon pressure and coercion?" (2). The answer to the first part of the question is in the affirmative based on a careful reading of Dr. King's writings and speeches, particularly "Letter from Birmingham Jail" (1963) and *Stride toward Freedom* (1958). His education and other specialized training, one would argue, prepared him to be skillful in rhetoric and persuasion. And his adoption of nonviolent resistance fits in properly in the domain of negotiation and persuasion, and his obvious goal would be to make the white segregationists see the light of truth, be inspired by his choice of action, and abandon their racist tendencies as both will enter into a new kind of positive relationship in his new "beloved community" based on Christian love.

52. Martin Luther King Jr., "Letter from Birmingham Jail" (1963), in *Why We Can't Wait*, by Martin Luther King Jr. (New York: Harper & Row Publishers, 1993), 80.

53. Ibid., 80.

54. Martin Luther King Jr., *Stride toward Freedom: Montgomery Story-Birth of Successful Non-Violent Resistance* (New York: Harper & Row Publishers [Perennial Library], 1958).

55.   David J. Garrow, "From Reformer to Revolutionary," in *Martin Luther King, Jr. and the Civil Rights Movement,* edited by John A. Kirk (New York: Palgrave Macmillan, 2007), 176–83. Also see David Garrow (ed.), *Martin Luther King, Jr.: Civil Rights Leader, Theologian, Orator* (Vol. II) (New York: Carlson Publishing, Inc., 1989).

56.   Ibid., 176–77.

57.   Lewis V. Baldwin, Rufus Burrow Jr., Barbara A. Jones, and Susan Holmes Winfield (eds.), *The Legacy of Martin Luther King, Jr.: The Boundaries of Law, Politics, and Religion* (Notre Dame: University of Notre Dame Press, 2002), 15.

58.   Martin Luther King Jr., "Montgomery before the Protest," in his *Stride toward Freedom: Montgomery Story-Birth of Successful Non-Violent Resistance* (New York: Harper & Row Publishers [Perennial Library], 1958), 18–19.

4

Hope Resurgent or Dream Deferred: Perplexities of King's Philosophical Optimism

FOURTEEN

Hope and Disappointment in Martin Luther King Jr.'s Political Theology

Eclipse of the Liberal Spirit

Floyd W. Hayes III

In his important novel of ideas *The Outsider*, Richard Wright characterizes his protagonist's inner thoughts: "He sensed how Negroes had been made to live in but not of the land of their birth, how the injunctions of an alien Christianity and the strictures of white laws had evoked in them the very longings and desires that that religion and law had been designed to stifle."[1] I have begun this chapter with this quotation because it helps to orient my discussion of Martin Luther King Jr.'s political theology.[2] I employ the passage as a lens through which to scrutinize King's political theology specifically, and the existential situation of blacks generally, in relation to the American dream. Wright's ideas constitute the ingredients necessary for constructing a political philosophy of existence that says something meaningful about the complex and perplexing relationship between blacks and American political life. Wright's words give penetrating expression to the significance of being black in an anti-black American world. More than any black writer of his time, Wright possessed the intellectual power and courage needed to articulate a radical perspective about a changing and crisis-ridden oppressive modern society. Since the contemporary postmodern moment of disbelief marks the genuine insistence and persistence of thinking in the midst of global disaster, Wright's prescient insights constitute the guiding spirit of this chapter.

Knowing and seeing what is happening in the world today, I don't think that there is much of anything that one can do about it. But there is one little thing, it seems to me, that a man owes to himself. He can look bravely at this horrible totalitarian reptile and, while doing so, discipline his dread, his fear, and study it coolly, observe every slither and convolution of its sensuous movements and note down with calmness the pertinent facts. In the face of the totalitarian danger, these facts can help a man to save himself; and he may then be able to call the attention of others around him to the presence and meaning of this reptile and its multitudinous writhings.[3]

Since the origins and development of the American democratic republic, as the first new nation of the early modern era, the ideas that came to be known as the American dream have operated as a strategy of national cohesion and social pretense. Initially founded as a number of settler colonies by Western Europeans who were influenced by the religious thought of the Protestant Reformation and the political thought of the Enlightenment, early Euro-Americans fabricated a political theology that served to articulate the development of a common and exceptional white heritage [supposedly distinct from the old world of Europe] and to legitimate the oppression and exploitation of non-white peoples—early on, wars of annihilation against Native Americans and the trade and enslavement of captured Africans; later on, the exploitation of Asian labor and the confiscation of Hispanic land. Codified in such sacred political texts as the Declaration of Independence and the U.S. Constitution, lofty political values that comprised the so-called American dream—for example, freedom, justice, equality, individualism, the consent of the governed, and the pursuit of happiness—were never intended to apply to non-whites, most especially Native Americans and captured African slaves and their American descendants. Yet, by means of the structure of enslavement and the process of dehumanization, native blacks were coerced into believing in the very political system and social values originally designed to constrain black development. That is, the great multitude of black Americans came to embrace the so-called American dream, even as the evils of white supremacy and anti-black racism gnawed at their everyday existence.

This chapter proposes to undertake a critical interrogation of Martin Luther King Jr.'s political theology, focusing largely on his belief in the American dream. The architecture of his religious and political thought is anything but simple. Although often overlooked, dismissed, neglected, or forgotten, King's thinking about the American dream gradually changed. King's political theology sought to put idealism in the service of racial justice and economic equality, but his patient hope eventually turned into gnawing disappointment.[4] The point here is that King wrestled with his belief in the American dream and the capacity of the nation to move beyond anti-black racism and socioeconomic inequality. Although King generally is portrayed as eternally hopeful about the American dream, he was not always optimistic about this matter. A deeper interrogation of his thought demonstrates a growing frustration and disappointment in the lack of racial and economic progress during the few years before his murder. Therefore, this chapter provides an assessment of the trends and developments, contradictions and dilemmas, of King's political theology with respect to the American dream.

Initially, I comment on the genealogy of the American dream—its combination of Calvinist theology and modern political philosophy—and its meaning to black Americans, as an overriding context for understanding King's perspective about this phenomenon. Inspired by liberal Christian values, King began his career as a civil rights activist and political theologian optimistic about the realization of the American dream of freedom, justice, and equality, for the vast majority of blacks. He believed that the fundamental transformation of America's racist social order would be achieved by appealing to the conscience of white Americans. But the golden age of King's optimism passed by the mid-1960s, and he grew increasingly disappointed in America's willingness to overturn the system of racist injustice and economic inequality. I want to consider as the principle of organization of King's thought not a certain political-theological doctrine, such as his concept of agape, equality, racial integration, or justice. Rather, this chapter seeks to examine his response to a particular crisis, namely, the crisis of black American hopelessness and disbelief in the American dream—the descent into nihilism. For King saw the gathering Black Power movement and its ideology as forms of nihilism, which he thought should be resisted at all costs. At the same time, King viewed white supremacy as a form of societal degeneration, against which he called for a revolution of values. I will argue that although King's political theology changed from hope to disappointment—indeed, he wavered between these two opposing attitudes—King ultimately remained wedded to a hope in the liberal notion that America would be transformed even as a gathering storm of right-wing conservatism was replacing the liberal spirit.

MYTH OF THE AMERICAN DREAM: POLITICAL THEOLOGY AND THE MODERN ELECT STATE

For centuries, the myth of an American dream has dominated the consciousness of all Americans and want-to-be Americans—immigrants who continue to flow to this country. It is the illusion that by means of hard work any American can get rich, become successful, and thus reap all of the benefits and virtues of being successful. The myth of the American dream is buttressed by an equally mythical Creed: democracy; the essential dignity of the individual human being; the fundamental equality of all humans; certain inalienable rights to freedom, justice, fair opportunity; and the pursuit of happiness. Significantly, the dream was a myth because these universal principles have not applied to all of the people in America. Tied to those notions is the fundamental belief in American exceptionalism, that because of the Protestant Ethic and laissez-faire capitalism, which rested upon the foundation of Calvinist Puritan values of selective salvation (that some are born the elect of God while others are born outside God's salvation), America is special among modern nations and, thus, possesses a holy mission to spread its values throughout the world.[5] Hence, the fusion of Calvinist fanaticism (i.e., Calvin's doctrine of the interrelationship among predestination, providence, and election) with modern political thought, especially John Locke's, resulted in the rise of the modern American elect state. As Conrad Cherry writes in his book, *God's New Israel: Religious Interpretations of American Destiny*:

> Beheld from the angle of governing mythology, the history of the American civil religion is a history of the conviction that the American people are God's New Israel, his newly chosen people. The belief that America has been elected by God for a special destiny in the world has been the focus of American sacred ceremonies, the inaugural addresses of our presidents, the sacred scriptures of the civil religion. It has been so pervasive a motif in the national life that the word "belief" does not really capture the dynamic role that it has played for the American people, for it passed into the "realm of motivational myths."[6]

The American dream actually is a dream of hope. Americans want to believe in the American dream; they hope it will come true for them. Otherwise, there would be a culture of despair and disappointment. Yet, the so-called American dream is, and always has been, largely an illusion for the great majority of Americans. Moreover, this illusion has contributed to a *culture of pretense* in America in which Americans historically have sought to deny an assortment of guilty truths. As former slave and abolitionist Frederick Douglass declared over one hundred years ago: "America is false to the past, false to the present, and solemnly binds herself to be false to the future. . . . The existence of slavery in this country brands your republicanism as a sham, your humanity as a base pretense, and your Christianity as a lie."[7] The bad-faith dimension of the American collective psyche is visible in the current historical moment as white America continues to deny the existence of anti-black racism.[8]

Indeed, Americans have conceived of numerous mythic narratives that are designed to give meaning to the nation's experience.[9] For example, the original anticolonial war for American independence from England was not a revolutionary battle for democracy, as the story is told. Because of the 1772 *Sommersett* legal case[10] in England, which ruled that English law did not recognize slaveholding, thus freeing James Sommersett, a Jamaican slave brought to England—a fact pattern quite similar to the later *Dred Scott* case of 1857 in America that ruled differently—ruling white elites and slave-owning classes in America feared that England would abolish slavery in the colonies. Significantly, there was no American revolution; the war only separated England from its American colonies. However, the revolt against England did not result in a fundamental transformation of the political structure, class dynamics, social relations of power, system of values, ideology of domination, or the economic base of the American colonies. Indeed, the colonial structure of white domination, based upon the institution of chattel slavery and the exploitation of slave labor, remained in tact after the anti-colonial war! Therefore, the anticolonial rebellion against England was not a revolution fought over a lack of political representation, as the founding American myth suggests. Rather, colonial political elites and the slave-owning class initiated the war because they feared that England might terminate the profitable institution of chattel slavery in the American colonies.

America has called itself a democracy or a democratic republic; yet, *America never has been a democracy*! America sought to view itself as distinct from the Old World, but America was not a new beginning; indeed, European civilization found another lease on life in American colonies. Persecuted for their religious beliefs, European Puritans immigrated to American colonies and then employed their own religious values to oppress and exploit others. The original political architects of the American way were largely white supremacists who employed Calvinist political-theological doctrines to construct a pro-slavery constitution that guided and buttressed a white supremacist-capitalist-patriarchy[11] that became deeply imbedded in all aspects of American society—its ideology, politics, economics, culture, and social institutions.[12]

Professing lofty political values of liberty, justice, freedom, equality, consent of the governed, and the pursuit of happiness, early Euro-Americans also established a dehumanization process that denied to captured African slaves and their American descendants a sense of human dignity and personal worth; broke up the African families, communities, and societies; denied slaves literacy and quality education; developed rugged individualism and loyalty to the white master class by economically exploiting slaves and promoting get-rich-quick schemes; and enforced strict and violent discipline while denying slaves organization, free assemblies, and all political rights. A monumental hypocrisy to any concept of authentic democracy, chattel slavery was a total system of absolute power and radical evil built upon the practice of arbitrary terror, routine violence, savage brutality, and inhumane torture that controlled virtually all aspects of slaves' existence. It was by means of the dehumanization process, which was grounded fundamentally in a system of absolute power (e.g., political oppression, economic exploitation, cultural domination, religious fanaticism, anti-black hatred, and sexual sadism), that the identity and consciousness of captured African slaves and their American descendants were transformed, creating a new people.[13]

Hardly the land of the free and home of the brave, America asserted Calvinist Puritan values of hard work, thrift, individualism, and moral discipline, while violently and brutally exploiting slave labor. Puritanism emerged as the fanatical religion of the new commercial classes, as ruling class whites profited from the physical discipline and hard work of chattel slaves who actually built the foundation of the American capitalist leviathan.[14] Moreover, the American notion of exceptionalism, which had its origin in Calvinist Puritan political theology of selective salvation, served to legitimize American global hegemony from the nineteenth-century doctrine of Manifest Destiny to current imperialist delusions in the Middle East.

Hence, ruling white Americans historically have devalued the nation's highest political-theological values. White supremacy, enslavement of captured Africans, and annihilating wars against Native Americans made the claim of democracy a pretense. To the degree that modern American political thought secularized religious absolutist principles, the highest political-theological ideals lost their value and meaning in the realm of practice. Therefore, the origins and development of the American personality emerged in a cauldron of nihilism. As William Barrett argued in his book *Irrational Man*, American social life always has been deeply nihilistic.[15]

In the last analysis, the theological and political absolutism that comprised the modern doctrine of the American elect state embodied a veil of illusion that sought to give legitimacy to the so-called American dream. Paradoxically, it has been what Toni Morrison refers to as the "Africanist presence"[16] that has exposed the American way as a monument to hypocrisy—a culture of pretense. What is more, by means of an historic dehumanization process, captured African slaves and their American descendants were forced to live in America as outsiders—simultaneously both included in and excluded from the American way of life, in which the political manipulation and cultural coercion of Calvinist political theology and a white supremacist legal system deluded black Americans into embracing the same values and society designed to deny their existence as human beings. In his powerful novel of ideas *The Outsider*, Richard Wright articulates this perspective through one of his main characters:

> "I mean this," Houston hastened to explain. "Negroes, as they enter our culture, are going to inherit the problems we have, but with a difference. They are outsiders and they are going to *know* that they have these problems. They are going to be self-conscious; they are going to be gifted with a double vision, for, being Negroes, they are going to be both *inside* and *outside* of our culture at the same time. Every emotional and cultural convulsion that ever shook the heart and soul of

Western man will shake them. Negroes will develop unique and specially defined psychological types. They will become psychological men, like the Jews. . . . They will not only be Americans or Negroes; they will be centers of *knowing*, so to speak. . . . The political, social, and psychological consequences of this will be enormous."[17]

Therefore, the black situation in America has been complex, complicated, and often contradictory. The long historical nightmare—from enslavement to the present—created the crisis of black existence in America: the "psychic alienation"[18] of being black in an anti-black world. White supremacy historically has operated as a global system—of imperialism, colonialism, annihilating wars, enslavement, and racism.[19] This reality, and the resulting brutalized lived experience of black people, has constituted the occasion and catalyst for the emergence and articulation of Africana existential thought.[20] Because white Americans refused to treat blacks as fellow human beings, the consequential victimization produced a people whose existence and ideas have both challenged and embraced the American way. Through the pain, anguish, and desperation caused by the historic struggle to extricate themselves from what the revolutionary Caribbean psychiatrist Frantz Fanon referred to as the "zone of nonbeing,[21] Blacks have raised questions designed to give full expression to their desire for liberation. Consequently, black thought historically has taken place within the context of existential disaster.

By and large, blacks, to whom the so-called American dream was never meant to apply, have wanted to believe in this dominant myth. To be sure, there also has existed an often ignored pessimistic strain of black existential thought that has seen through the American dream's veil of illusion. Richard Wright once expressed this view eloquently:

We are a folk born of cultural devastation, slavery, physical suffering, unrequited longing, abrupt emancipation, migration, disillusionment, bewilderment, joblessness, and insecurity—all enacted within a *short* space of historical time! . . . There are some of us who feel our hurts so deeply that we find it impossible to work with whites; we feel that it is futile to hope or dream in terms of American life. Our distrust is so great that we form intensely racial and nationalistic organizations and advocate the establishment of a separate state, a forty-ninth state, in which we black folk would live. There are even today among us groups that forlornly plan a return to Africa.[22]

Against this cynical outlook, from the aftermath of enslavement to the present, great numbers of black Americans have inherited the theological politics of dreaming about a hoped-for America; they have invested much emotion, thinking, and activity in trying to transform the myth into reality. Foremost in this effort has been the impulse or attitude of hope. Confronted with the brutality and absurdity of white supremacy and anti-black racism, many misguided black Americans have hoped in vain for democracy, freedom, justice, equality, and the pursuit of happiness. No matter how desperate and humiliating the situation, many blacks continue to hold on tenaciously to the hope that America will become the nation it proclaims to be. Even as they dissented from white America's culture of pretense about freedom, justice, and equality, blacks hoped that their struggle against structures of racist injustice, economic inequality, and political oppression would fundamentally transform American society. This kind of optimism is a form of self-deception that has made life under the regime of white supremacy more tolerable but less genuine. Significantly, blacks never had a contract with America; they agreed to no covenant with hell. In the absence of power, people hope.

KING'S AMERICAN DREAM: OPTIMISM IN HIS POLITICAL THEOLOGY

No American represented hope in the so-called American dream more than Martin Luther King Jr., the major civil rights leader of the twentieth century. Yet, in view of the historical character of white supremacy in America discussed above—and the nightmare existence it caused black Americans—what did the so-called American dream mean to King? Initially, why was he optimistic about its realization? Was his expectation realistic? Was King's hope a product of blind faith and utopian belief in America that had no basis in fact? Does the abject failure of liberal democracy to alleviate the suffering and deprivation caused by racism, capitalism, and patriarchy point to the delusion of believing in the American dream? Did King fear that the masses of blacks were losing hope in the so-called American dream?

As the most well-known leader and political theologian of the modern civil rights movement, King constantly expressed his hope that America would live up to its self-representation as a liberal democracy that provided freedom, justice, and equality to all of its citizens, especially blacks. In the early years of the Civil Rights Movement (mid-1950s to the mid-1960s) King's vision of the so-called American dream rested upon religious and philosophical perspectives about the human condition. Even in the face of white America's historic belief in and practice of anti-black racism, he was convinced of the basic goodness of human beings and that universal Christian values should apply to all people. Nevertheless, he thought that increasing materialism and anti-black racism undermined civil society in America. The drive for unfettered materialism cunningly sidetracked an unconscious longing for a spiritual relationship into a voracious pursuit of money, which often accompanied growing, voguish religious ventures that offer banal pseudospiritual security and satisfaction. Racism destroyed the basis for social equality and racial integration.

Consequently, what was required, King believed, was a fundamental change in how Americans viewed themselves and the world.

In attempting this transformation, King wanted blacks to be the moral conscience of America. Embracing this role himself, he hoped to appeal to the hearts and minds of white Americans. This was a reason why he set forth his vision of the American dream and how to achieve it. Significantly, King generally embraced the universal democratic values of the dream—freedom, justice, equality, individualism—as articulated in the Declaration of Independence and the U.S. Constitution. Even so, King's political theology was shaped not only by modern religious and political thought, but also by his penetrating reading of the bible. For him, then, the American dream's democratic project was not necessarily about the pursuit of personal happiness, but about doing God's will. Importantly, King clearly recognized that whites refused to apply those democratic principles universally. Thus, King argued that white America suffered from a "schizophrenic personality."[23] Nevertheless, he believed in the essential goodness of white people.

Calling for change, King hoped in vain that white America was up to the task. But what was to be done to realize the American dream, according to King? As a dimension of his modern liberal social gospel, in counterdistinction to his more traditional political theology, he argued that if America was to survive, it had to develop a global perspective. Since modern scientific and technological advancements had minimized geographical time and distance among the world's peoples, Americans needed to see themselves as part of a world community; this meant that human beings were interdependent. In the face of modernity's secular impact on Western culture and civilization, King argued that moral and spiritual progress needed to keep pace with techno-scientific expansion. Further, in order to achieve the American dream, King called on whites finally and absolutely to destroy the regime of racism—the belief in superior and inferior races—and to terminate the practice of racist segregation. In short, King's liberal vision of the American dream required the achievement of an integrated society in which racial justice was paramount.[24]

King also called on black people to continue their struggle against racism. King admonished black Americans to overthrow the psychological effects of white supremacy and anti-black oppression by holding onto a sense of personal worth and human dignity. Racism should not become an excuse for black mediocrity and laziness, King said. Rejecting the crippling effects of racism on black social development, King used the examples of outstanding blacks in a variety of fields of endeavor, who overcame poverty-stricken circumstances in order to achieve greatness, to inspire blacks to continue the struggle for collective survival and salvation. Of particular importance, King argued that the struggle for racial justice should be based upon principles and practices of civil disobedient nonviolence. King thought this was the most practical and effective method of resistance because it would expose the viciousness and brutality of white supremacy and anti-black racism to America and to the world. Above all, King admonished the black church to play a leading role in the black freedom struggle—for collective survival, racial justice, political rights, and social development.[25]

Throughout the early years of the Civil Rights Movement, the objective reality and prevailing practice of white supremacy and anti-black racism proved to be problematic for King's political theology and social gospel. Yet, he held on to a belief in the basic goodness and moral courage of white Americans. He hoped in vain that they would overturn the evil system of white supremacy and anti-black racism. He believed that freedom, justice, and equality for black people could be achieved in America. In an era plagued increasingly by religious and political confusion in the Western world, King imagined that human society was moving toward a universal community and global peace. Yet, in the few years before his assassination, King's expectations were dashed in regard to America's will to overturn the system of racist injustice and economic inequality. As a result, he began to change his ideas about the so-called American dream. Hope gradually turned to disappointment.

KING AND THE CRISIS OF AMERICAN NIHILISM: ECLIPSE OF THE LIBERAL SPIRIT

By the mid-1960s, King began a gradual political-theological transformation that ultimately damaged, but did not totally destroy, his hope in the fulfillment of the American dream.[26] King was confronted with a set of objective circumstances that forced him to revise his image of America. King's hope turned to disappointment. At least three reasons accounted for this change: the 1965 Watts uprising in Los Angeles, the rise of the Black Power Movement, and the frailty of white liberalism.

In August 1965, shortly after the Watts revolt subsided, King went to Los Angeles and experienced there one of the major surprises of his life. He was astounded by the physical destruction of the area. King went to the Westminster Community Center, where he was confronted with blacks who had participated in the rebellion. There he learned about the seething anger, resentment, and cynicism among impoverished residents of Watts. King was surprised to learn that many young blacks were unfamiliar with him and had little respect for him; moreover, he was faced with blacks who repudiated nonviolence as a response to increasingly harsh impoverished socioeconomic conditions and police violence and murder. When King attempted to talk to the crowd and advocate nonviolence, a man shouted, "Get out of here Dr. King! We don't want you!"[27] This encounter forced King to see the real differences between black suffering in the south and in urban localities outside the south. Although the vicious and overt system of segregation, especially racially identified dual accommodations and the denial of political rights, plagued black southerners, blacks in inner cities outside the South experienced more subtle forms of disenfranchisement, such as economic deprivation, educational deterioration, and police brutality and murder. While the Civil Rights Act of 1964 and the Voting Rights Act of 1965 may have benefited the black middle class, and represented symbolic gains to many southern blacks, civil rights legislation hardly changed the nightmarish life experiences of impoverished urban blacks. Indeed, abject poverty gave rise to growing rage, vindictiveness, and pessimism among urban blacks. This was a reality that King no longer could ignore.

As a result of his visit to Los Angeles, King could not remain optimistic about America's will to overturn economic inequality. King's liberal thinking gradually shifted to the left, but he avoided classifying himself as a Marxist. As theologian James Cone observes: "But despite his caution, it is clear that a radical change was taking place in King's thinking about America, a transformation that was moving him along a revolutionary path that surprised many of his friends and supporters."[28] With his expectations increasingly blasted regarding the termination of economic inequality in America, King became more and more disappointed; in the process, his American dream turned into a nightmare. Indeed, the tone of King's speeches took on a more militant character, as he described America as a morally sick society in need of overall transformation. This included the expression of a more radical analysis of urban impoverishment, as was the case in 1966, when King took the Civil Rights Movement to Chicago. Cone writes:

> Martin began to speak of the ghetto as a "system of internal colonialism." "The purpose of the slum," he said in a speech at the Chicago Freedom Festival, "is to confine those who have no power and perpetuate their powerlessness. . . . The slum is little more than a domestic colony which leaves its inhabitants dominated politically, exploited economically, segregated and humiliated at every turn." The chief problem is economic, he concluded, and the solution is to restructure the whole society. The anticapitalist sentiments of his graduate school years had long been dormant, but the Watts and Chicago experience activated a cautious but serious examination of socialism as an alternative to the American political economy.[29]

Perhaps the rising significance of the Black Power Movement, with its demand for black solidarity and self-determination, constituted the most fundamental challenge to King's thinking about the so-called American dream. Significantly, King tried in vain to ignore Malcolm X and his Black Nationalist pronouncements. However, this was no longer the case as the emerging Black Power Movement forced King to engage the Black

Nationalist ideology that Malcolm X articulated. Importantly, the change in King's thinking moved him closer to Malcolm X's Black Nationalist position.[30]

In the summer of 1966, the radical Black Power Movement asserted itself on the national and international scenes. Black Power adherents were largely influenced by the dominating presence of Nation of Islam Minister Malcolm X, especially when he said:

> I'm one of the 22 million black people who are the victims of American-ism. One of the 22 million black people who are the victims of democ-racy, nothing but disguised hypocrisy. So, I'm not standing here speak-ing to you as an American, or a patriot, or a flag-saluter, or a flag-waiver—no, not I. I'm speaking as a victim of this American system. And I see America through the eyes of the victim. I don't see any American dream; I see an American nightmare.[31]

A new generation of black activists heeded the words of the revolution-ary Caribbean psychiatrist Frantz Fanon: "Each generation must, out of relative obscurity, discover its mission, fulfill it, or betray it."[32] Disillu-sioned by the continuation of anti-black racism and the failure of liberal integration, angry and resentful young blacks embraced various concep-tions of Black Nationalism, Marxism, Marxist-Leninism, and Pan-Africanism. Young radicals demanded black self-identity, unity, self-de-termination, community control, economic self-sufficiency, and self-de-fense. In their 1967 book *Black Power: The Politics of Liberation*, Kwame Ture (then Stokely Carmichael) and Charles Hamilton captured the senti-ment of this new black self-assertion:

> The adoption of the concept of black Power is one of the most legiti-mate and healthy developments in American politics and race relations in our time. . . . It is a call for black people in this country to unite, to recognize their heritage, to build a sense of community. It is a call for black people to begin to define their own goals, to lead their own organizations and to support those organizations. It is a call to reject the racist institutions and values of this society.[33]

Clearly, the Black Power Movement was a response to the obvious failure of the so-called American dream of liberal democracy to overturn the system of racist injustice and economic inequality. The anger, resentment, and desperation of the masses of impoverished and working-class urban blacks signaled a seismic shift in their attitude about white American sincerity. Indeed, the white pathology of anti-black hatred, especially in the form of continued white violence against blacks, constituted the ma-jor catalyst of the new movement. Like Stokely Carmichael (Kwame Ture), Kathleen Neal Cleaver, and James Forman, many Black Power warriors had worked in the Civil Rights Movement and had become radicalized as a result of the failures of nonviolent struggle for liberal integration.[34] The need for an alternative became paramount. Urban revolts set in motion the rise of an assortment of Black Power organizations that saw self-defense as the only reasonable response to white violence. As Fanon reasoned, the violence of the oppressor brought into existence the counterviolence of the oppressed.[35]

Significantly, mounting social anarchy brought on by urban revolts and the rise of Black Power forced King onto the horns of a dilemma. He was losing hope in the American dream, but he also was increasingly worried about the growing anger and resentment among blacks. The abject failure of liberal democracy to terminate anti-black racism and overcome economic inequality made him increasingly disappointed. Yet, in King's mind, the rising tide of Black Power represented a nihilist threat that needed to be forestalled.[36] Here was a major crisis for King—the real possibility that growing masses of blacks had become disillusioned about achieving the American dream and also had rejected nonviolent civil disobedience as a strategy for fighting against the violence of white supremacy and anti-black racism. Against the liberal Civil Rights Movement's petition for racial integration, the radical Black Power Movement called for black self-determination and demanded fundamental transformation of American society. King himself was severely disappointed in white America's unwillingness to overthrow the regime of racism. Wrestling with his feelings about the American dream, King often spoke of his growing disillusionment. Nowhere were King's words more cynical than during a 1967 talk in Atlanta. King declared:

> In 1963 . . . in Washington, D.C. . . . I tried to talk to the nation about a dream that I had had, and I must confess . . . that not long after talking about that dream I started seeing it turn into a nightmare . . . just a few weeks after I had talked about it. It was when four beautiful . . . Negro girls were murdered in a church in Birmingham, Alabama. I watched that dream turn into a nightmare as I moved through the ghettos of the nation and saw black brothers and sisters perishing on a lonely island of poverty in the midst of a vast ocean of material prosperity, and saw the nation doing nothing to grapple with the Negroes' problem of poverty. I saw that dream turn into a nightmare as I watched my black brothers and sisters in the midst of anger and understandable outrage, in the midst of their hurt, in the midst of their disappointment, turn to misguided riots to try to solve that problem. I saw the dream turn into a nightmare as I watched the war in Vietnam escalating. . . . Yes, I am personally the victim of deferred dreams, of blasted hopes.[37]

King began to speak less and less as an apostle of Christian love and more and more as a drum major for justice.[38] Increasingly, he spoke in prophetic terms not about an American dream, but about an American nightmare. He also dropped the term Negro, which Black Power adherents soundly rejected, and embraced the term Black Americans. Most significantly to his political theology, King gave up on the concept of Jesus Christ as a white man. Cone chronicles this development:

After Black Power, Martin's image of Jesus underwent a transformation. "Jesus," he said to a group of black ministers in Miami, "was not a
white man." Of course, Martin did not say that "Jesus was black," as
Malcolm often said. He gave no religious significance to Jesus' pigmen-
tation; Jesus' meaning transcended color. Now saying Jesus was not
white was Martin's way of denying the widespread assumption that
everything good and valuable came from Western society. "Christianity is not just a Western religion," Martin said. He urged black ministers to turn toward their own culture and history for the insight and
power to revolutionize the world. "We have the power," he told them,
"to change America, and give a kind of new vitality to the religion of
Jesus Christ." Although he remained a universalist in his views about
religion and politics, his thinking was deeply affected by his praxis,
causing him to affirm a concept of blackness that was in many respects
similar to Malcolm's and clearly absent from earlier speeches.

Yet, confronted with a new generational explosion, King wrestled with
the meaning and impact of Black Power, which he ultimately rejected. In
his last book *Where Do We Go from Here: Chaos or Community?*,[39] King
sought both to explicate and critique aspects of Black Power. Very much
like other Civil Rights leaders—except C.O.R.E. leader, Floyd McKissick,
who embraced the reactionary conception of Black Power as black capitalism—King feared the combination of the two words "black" and
"power" would be interpreted by whites not as black equality, but as
black superiority or Black domination or even anti-white hatred. King
suggested alternative terms, such as "black consciousness" or even
"black equality." King came to value black unity (economic, psychological, and political), but he viewed Black Power as a desperate cry of disappointment, hopelessness, despair, and resentment—these were attitudes
that he rejected as nihilist.

> Beneath all the satisfaction of a gratifying slogan, Black Power is a
> nihilistic philosophy born out of the conviction that the Negro can't
> win. It is, at bottom, the view that American society is so hopelessly
> corrupt and enmeshed in evil that there is no possibility of salvation
> from within. Although this thinking is understandable as a response to
> a white power structure that never completely committed itself to true
> equality for the Negro, and a die-hard mentality that sought to shut all
> windows and doors against the winds of change, it nonetheless carries
> the seeds of its own doom.[40]

It was this perceived nihilist threat that seemed to worry King the most.
Clearly, he understood devastating and cumulative impact of enslavement, segregation, and racism on the black psyche. He feared that the
Black Power revolution was grounded in a nihilist philosophy that rejected the meaning of America. In opposition to this possibility, King
called on black people to maintain their hope and faith in America. Even
with the continuation of vicious anti-black racism, King tried to admon-

ish blacks not to react with acrimony and pessimism. Although some white liberals might betray black people in the struggle against racial injustice and economic inequality, King held onto a faith in the alliance between blacks and liberal whites in the nonviolent struggle for racial integration and economic fairness in America. And King believed strongly that blacks could not win the battle for racial equality without white people.

> In the final analysis the weakness of Black Power is its failure to see that the black man needs the white man and the white man needs the black man. However much we may try to romanticize the slogan, there is no separate black path to power and fulfillment that does not inter-sect white paths, and there is no separate white path to power and fulfillment short of social disaster, that does not share power with black aspirations for freedom and human dignity. We are bound together in a single garment of destiny. The language, the cultural patterns, the music, the material prosperity and even the food of America are an amalgam of black and white.[41]

King interpreted Black Power's demand for self-defense as a call for black violence. He fiercely rejected violence. Black hatred and violence were futile; Black Power rhetoric about overthrowing the oppressive state, in King's view, was fantasy. In addition, King thought violence was immoral; it also made whites fearful of blacks. Therefore, he continued to maintain faith in the power of nonviolence as a method of social transformation. He continued to believe in the goodwill of liberal whites. Indeed, in the face of continued white violence and hatred of blacks, King went so far as to argue that blacks should forgive whites. At all costs, he argued, blacks needed not to threaten them, but to show whites that they had nothing to fear from blacks.

> The problem with hatred and violence is that they intensify the fears of the white majority, and leave them less ashamed of their prejudices toward Negroes. In the guilt and confusion confronting our society, violence only adds to the chaos. It deepens the brutality of the oppres-sor and increases the bitterness of the oppressed. Violence is the antith-esis of creativity and wholeness. It destroys community and makes brotherhood impossible.[42]

King was no revolutionary. More a modern liberal than a radical move-ment leader and political theologian, King never actually lost hope in the system that was originally designed to restrain black collective survival and social development. While he viewed some aspects of Black Power ideals as worthwhile, King generally considered those values extreme and philosophically and pragmatically indefensible. Because he expected more from the country of his birth, King often was frustrated with ongo-ing problems of achieving his beloved American community. Yet, he also wrestled with the dialectics of hope and disappointment. He wanted to believe that America could be compelled to live up to its stated ideals and respond to the genuine needs of its poorest citizens.

Ultimately, King's thoroughgoing hope in the American dream of freedom, justice, and equality outweighed his often troubling disenchantment. However, it is important to note that his political-theological optimism misread the objective facts of social life in America. His belief that America would eradicate white supremacy and anti-black racism proved untenable. His expectation about the viability of the American dream was unrealistic. In the abject failure of liberal democratic America to alleviate the anguish and dispossession of its teeming masses, King's ultimate faith in liberal integration and in comradeship with liberal whites proved to be illusory. Significantly, white liberals were becoming a dying breed. King's political-theological idealism clouded his vision of reality. On the eve of his assassination, King spoke in personal, prophetic, and apocalyptic terms about the black freedom struggle to a black congregation in Memphis, Tennessee. In a wide-ranging sermon that sought to inspire the continuing need for black freedom, but one that also recognized the impending difficulty in achieving it, King articulated hope against hope.

> Well, I don't know what will happen now. We've got some difficult days ahead. But it doesn't matter with me now. Because I've been to the mountaintop. And I don't mind. Like anybody, I would like to live a long life. Longevity has its place. But I'm not concerned about that now. I just want to do God's will. And He's allowed me to go to the mountain. And I've looked over. And I've seen the promised land. I may not get there with you. But I want you to know tonight, that we, as a people will get to the promised land. And I'm happy, tonight. I'm not worried about anything. I'm not fearing any man. Mine eyes have seen the glory of the coming of the Lord.[43]

King's ruthless assassination punctuated the declining significance of liberalism in the modern American polity. Liberalism proved to be a transitory stage; in the early years of the nation, not throughout its future, it may have been a hope but never a permanent achievement. The liberal spirit of American democracy represented romanticism, mystification, and pretense. However, with the white backlash and the advent of a conservative revival, together with the rise of the postindustrial-managerial state in the late 1960s, liberalism came to an end.[44] The collapse of the liberal spirit and the shift to a conservative reality exposed a general and growing cynical disillusionment in America and its so-called dream. That is to say, increasing decadence of the American social order has set in motion a generalized disbelief, beyond the anger and resentment of blacks, in the American way.[45]

Twenty-first-century American society is engulfed in a rising tide of cynicism and nihilism; it is a cancer of the spirit. Suspicion is increasing.

Trust is declining. There is a mounting sense of despair about the modern culture of progress that America was supposed to embody. A growing proportion of Americans seem skeptical about whether the institutions of progress are viable and beneficial: political leadership, religious organizations, public bureaucracies, business corporations, public schools, universities, political parties, the legal system, the mass media, and even the family. Popular discontent is becoming more comprehensive, penetrating, and corrosive.

This chapter represents not only a critique of King's political theology, but also an indictment of American hypocrisy—its historic culture of pretense. Now, as during King's life and work, the so-called American dream rings relatively hollow. Indeed, the growth and development of this concept proved to be nihilistic, as its underside gave expression to one of the most evil systems of oppression in modern history. And in the new millennium, evil continues to stalk the landscape of America, moving people's minds, ruling their actions, and producing in the current era the lies, avarice, pretense, and brutality that constitute the history of America.[46]

Thinking in the present moment of disaster and disbelief, it appears that America will not find the will to provide historically excluded, oppressed, and resentful Americans a sense of dignity, the formative modalities for social development, or genuine opportunities for democratic participation—the foundation for a people's society. Moreover, under the pretext of carrying out some ill-begotten mission from God, the political regime of George W. Bush represented the continued expression of the original Calvinist-elect notion of American exceptionalism in a delusional imperialist attempt to impose American democracy in the Middle East. Playing the cynical politics of God, an arrogant, ignorant, ruthless, reckless, and secretive Bush administration destroyed human lives in barbaric proportions without any sense of restraint or remorse. The global repercussions and consequences of America's rogue state behavior are unimaginable. In the last analysis, a spiritually bankrupt America seems doomed to continue its slide down the slippery slope of nihilism, decadence, hopelessness, chaos, and breakdown.[47]

ACKNOWLEDGMENTS

I want to thank the late Robert CheeMooke, my long-standing friend and philosophical interlocutor, Michael Hanchard, Samuel Hay, Judson Jeffries, and Katrina McDonald for much needed critical feedback on earlier versions of this chapter.

NOTES

1. Richard Wright, *The Outsider* (New York: Harper & Row Publishers, 1953), 140.

2. On the concept of political theology, the incorporation of the religious interest into the political interest, see Hans Blumenberg, *The Legitimacy of the Modern Age* (Cambridge: MIT Press, 1983).

3. Wright, *The Outsider*, 367.

4. For an informative interrogation of the impact of disappointment on the black sense of self, see Bill E. Lawson, "Social Disappointment and the Black Sense of Self," in *Existence in Black: An Anthology of Black Existential Philosophy*, edited by Lewis R. Gordon (New York: Routledge, 1997), 149–56.

5. There is a substantial and expansive literature on the trends, developments, and contradictions related to the construction and meaning of the so-called American dream. For example, see the following: Sacvan Bercovitch, *The Puritan Origins of the American Self* (New Haven: Yale University Press, 1975); Andrew Delbanco, *The Puritan Ordeal* (Cambridge: Harvard University Press, 1989); Jack P. Greene, *The Intellectual Construction of America: Exceptionalism and Identity from 1492 to 1800* (Chapel Hill: The University of North Carolina Press, 1993); Jennifer L. Hochschild, *Facing Up to the American Dream: Race, Class, and the Soul of the Nation* (Princeton: Princeton University Press, 1995); John Kane, *Between Virtue and Power: The Persistent Moral Dilemma of U.S. Foreign Policy* (New Haven: Yale University Press, 2008); Seymour Martin Lipset, *American Exceptionalism: A Double-Edged Sword* (New York: W. W. Norton & Company, 1996); Herbert McCloskey and John Zaller, *The American Ethos: Public Attitudes toward Capitalism and Democracy* (Cambridge: Harvard University Press, 1984); George McKenna, *The Puritan Origins of American Patriotism* (New Haven: Yale University Press, 2007); James A. Morone, *Hellfire Nation: The Politics of Sin in American History* (New Haven: Yale University Press, 2003); Gunnar Myrdal, *The American Dilemma: The Negro Problem and Modern Democracy* (New York: Harper & Brothers Publishers, 1942); Max Weber, *The Protestant Ethic and the Spirit of Capitalism* (Winchester: Allen & Unwin, Inc., 1976).

6. Conrad Cherry, ed., *God's New Israel: Religious Interpretations of American Destiny* (Chapel Hill: University of North Carolina Press, 1998), 19. See also Sacvan Bercovitch, *The American Jeremiad* (Madison: The University of Wisconsin Press, 1978); John Dunn, *The Political Thought of John Locke* (Cambridge: Cambridge University Press, 1982); Ralph C. Hancock, *Calvin and the Foundations of Modern Politics* (Ithaca: Cornell University Press, 1989); Sheldon S. Wolin, "Calvin: The Political Education of Protestantism," in *Politics and Vision: Continuity and Innovation in Western Political Thought*, exp. ed. (Princeton: Princeton University Press, 2004), 148–74.

7. Frederick Douglass, "What, to the Slave, Is the Fourth of July?" (1852), in *Negro Orators and Their Orations*, edited by Carter G. Woodson (New York: Russell & Russell, 1969), 207, 219.

8. See Lewis R. Gordon, *Bad Faith and Antiblack Racism* (Atlantic Highlands: Humanities Press International, Inc., 1995).

9. See Richard Hughes, *Myths America Lives By* (Champaign: University of Illinois Press, 2003).

10. See Alfred W. Blumrosen and Ruth G. Blumrosen, *Slave Nation: How Slavery United the Colonies & Sparked the American Revolution* (Naperville: Sourcebook, Inc., 2005); David B. Davis, *The Problem of Slavery in Western Culture* (Ithaca: Cornell University Press, 1996); A. Leon Higginbotham Jr., *In the Matter of Color: Race and the American Legal Process—the Colonial Period* (New York: Oxford University Press, 1978); Gary B. Nash, *The Unknown American Revolution: The Unruly Birth of Democracy and the Struggle to Create America* (New York: Viking, 2005).

11. This term comes from bell hooks, *Outlaw Culture: Resisting Representations* (New York: Routledge, 1994).

12. Forrest G. Wood, *The Arrogance of Faith: Christianity and Race in America from the Colonial Era to the Twentieth Century* (New York: Alfred A. Knopf, Inc., 1990).

13. See Ira Berlin, Marc Favreau, and Steven F. Miller, eds., *Remembering Slavery: African Americans Talk about Their Personal Experiences of Slavery and Emancipation* (Washington, DC: The New Press, 1998); John Blassingame, *Slave Community: Plantation Life in the Antebellum South* (New York: Oxford University Press, 1972); David B. Davis, *From Homicide to Slavery: Studies in American Culture* (New York: Oxford University Press, 1986); Steven Mintz and John Stauffer, eds., *The Problem of Evil: Slavery, Freedom, and the Ambiguities of American Reform* (Amherst: University of Massachusetts Press, 2007); Kenneth M. Stampp, *The Peculiar Institution: Slavery in the Ante-Bellum South* (New York: Vintage Books, 1956); Orlando Patterson, *Slavery and Social Death: A Comparative Study* (Cambridge: Harvard University Press, 1982).

It also needs to be acknowledged that dimensions of the dehumanization process and the total system of terror, violence, torture, and rape of black Americans by whites continued into the twentieth century and the period of the old Jim Crow south. See William Chafe, Raymond Gavins, and Robert Korstad, eds., *Remembering Jim Crow: African Americans Tell about Life in the Segregated South* (Washington, DC: The New Press, 2001); Philip Dray, *At the Hands of Persons Unknown: The Lynching of Black America* (New York: Random House, 2002); Leon F. Litwack, *Trouble in Mind: Black Southerners in the Age of Jim Crow* (New York: Alfred A. Knopf, Inc., 1998); Richard Wright, *Black Boy: A Record of Childhood and Youth* (New York: Harper & Brothers Publishers, 1945).

14. R. H. Tawney, *Religion and the Rise of Capitalism* (New York: Harcourt, Brace, and Company, Inc., 1926); Max Weber, *The Protestant Ethic and the Spirit of Capitalism*, op. cit. (1976).

15. William Barrett, *Irrational Man: A Study of Existential Philosophy* (New York: Anchor Book, 1958).

16. See Toni Morrison, *Playing in the Dark: Whiteness and the Literary Imagination* (Cambridge: Harvard University Press, 199).

17. Richard Wright, *The Outsider*, 129.

18. See Frantz Fanon, *Black Skin, White Masks* (New York: Grove Press, 1967).

19. Charles Mills, *The Racial Contract* (Ithaca: Cornell University Press, 1997).

20. See Lewis R. Gordon, "Introduction," in *Existence in Black: An Anthology of Black Existential Philosophy*, edited by Gordon (New York: Routledge, 1997); Gordon, *Existentia Africana: Understanding Africana Existential Thought* (New York: Routledge, 2000).

21. Fanon, *Black Skin, White Masks*. See also Lewis R. Gordon, "Through the Zone of Nonbeing: A Reading of *Black Skin, White Masks* in Celebration of Fanon's Eightieth Birthday," in *The C. L. R. James Journal* 11, no. 1 (Summer 2005): 1–43.

22. Richard Wright, *12 Million Black Voices* (New York: Thunder's Mouth Press, 1988), 142, 143.

23. Martin Luther King Jr., "The American Dream," in *A Testament of Hope: The Essential Writings of Martin Luther King, Jr.*, edited by James Melvin Washington (New York: Harper & Row Publishers, 1986), 217–20.

24. Ibid.

25. Ibid. King, "Nonviolence and Racial Justice"; "The Power of Nonviolence"; "Pilgrimage to Nonviolence"; "I Have a Dream," in *A Testament of Hope: The Essential Writings of Martin Luther King, Jr.*, edited by James Melvin Washington (New York: Harper & Row Publishers 1986).

26. James H. Cone, *Martin & Malcolm & America: A Dream or a Nightmare* (Maryknoll, NY: Orbis Books, 1991).

27. Ibid., 222; Taylor Branch, *At Canaan's Edge: America in the King Years 1965–68* (New York: Simon & Schuster, 2006), 296.

28. Cone, *Martin & Malcolm & America*, 224.

29. Ibid., 223.

30. Cone, *Martin & Malcolm & America*.

31. Malcolm X, "The Ballot or the Bullet," in *Malcolm X Speaks: Selected Speeches and Statements*, edited by George Breitman (New York: Grove Press, 1965), 26.

32. Frantz Fanon, *The Wretched of the Earth* (New York: Grove Press, 1963), 167.

33. Stokely Carmichael and Charles Hamilton, *Black Power: The Politics of Liberation* (New York: Random House, Inc., 1967), 44.

34. See Stokely Carmichael with Michael Thelwell, *Ready for Revolution: The Life and Struggles of Stokely Carmichael (Kwame Ture)* (New York: Scribner, 2003); Kathleen Neal Cleaver, "Women, Power, and Revolution," in *Liberation, Imagination, and the Black Panther Party,* edited by Kathleen Cleaver and George Katsiaficas (New York: Routledge, 2001), 122–27; James Forman, *The Making of Black Revolutionaries: A Personal Account* (New York: The Macmillan Company, 1972).

35. See Curtis J. Austin, *Up against the Wall: Violence in the Making and Unmaking of the Black Panther Party* (Fayetteville: University of Arkansas Press, 2006); Scot Brown, *Fighting for US: Maulana Karenga, the US Organization, and Black Cultural Nationalism* (New York: New York University Press, 2003); Judson L. Jeffries, ed., *Black Power in the Belly of the Beast* (Urbana: University of Illinois Press, 2006); Jeffries, ed., *Comrades: A Local History of the Black Panther Party* (Bloomington: Indiana University Press, 2007); Charles E. Jones, ed., *The Black Panther Party Reconsidered* (Baltimore: Black Classic Press, 1998); Peniel E. Joseph, ed., *The Black Power Movement: Rethinking the Civil Rights—Black Power Era* (New York: Routledge, 2006); Joseph, *Waiting 'Til the Midnight Hour: A Narrative History of Black Power in America* (New York: Henry Holt and Company, 2006); Jama Lazerow and Yohuru Williams, eds., *In Search of the Black Panther Party: New Perspectives on a Revolutionary Movement* (Durham: Duke University Press, 2006); Jeffrey O. G. Ogbar, *Black Power: Radical Politics and African American Identity* (Baltimore: Johns Hopkins University Press, 2004); Jane Rhodes, *Framing the Black Panthers: The Spectacular Rise of a Black Power Icon* (New York: The New Press, 2007).

It needs to be remembered that the Civil Rights movement did contain self-defense adherents. See Lance Hill, *The Deacons for Defense: Armed Resistance and the Civil Rights Movement* (Chapel Hill: University of North Carolina, 2004); Timothy E. Tyson, *Radio Free Dixie: Robert F. Williams and the Roots of Black Power* (Chapel Hill: University of North Carolina Press, 1999).

36. On the concept and implications of black American nihilism, see Cornel West, "Nihilism in Black America," in *Race Matters* (Boston: Beacon Press, 1993), 9–20; Floyd W. Hayes III, "Cornel West and Afro-Nihilism: A Reconsideration," in *Cornel West: A Critical Reader,* edited by George Yancy (Malden: Blackwell Publishers Inc., 2001), 245–60.

37. Quoted in James H. Cone, *Martin & Malcolm & America: A Dream or a Nightmare* (1991), 213.

38. Martin Luther King, Jr., "The Drum Major Instinct," in *A Testament of Hope: The Essential Writings of Martin Luther King Jr.,* edited by James Melvin Washington (New York: Harper & Row Publishers, 1986), 259–67.

39. King, *Where Do We Go from Here: Chaos or Community?* (Boston: Beacon Press, 1967).

40. Ibid., 44.

41. Ibid., 52–53.

42. Ibid., 61.

43. King, "I See the Promised Land," in *A Testament to Hope: The Essential Writings of Martin Luther King, Jr.,* edited by James Melvin Washington (New York: Harper & Row Publishers, 1986), 286.

44. Floyd W. Hayes III, "Government Retreat, the Dispossessed, and the Politics of African American Self-Reliant Development in the Age of Reaganism," in *African Americans and the New Policy Consensus: Retreat of the Liberal State?,* edited by Marilyn E. Lashley and Melanie Njeri Jackson (Westport, CT: Greenwood Press, 1994), 99–120.

45. For a philosophical discussion of decadence, see Lewis R. Gordon, "The Unacknowledged Fourth Tradition: An Essay on Nihilism, Decadence, and the Black Intellectual Tradition in the Existential Thought of Cornel West," in *Cornel West: A Critical Reader,* edited by George Yancy (Malden: Blackwell Publishers Inc., 2001), 38–58; Jacqueline Scott, "Nietzsche and Decadence: The Revaluation of Morality," in *Continental Philosophical Review* 31 (January 1998): 59–78.

46. Ali A. Allawi, *The Occupation of Iraq: Winning the War, Losing the Peace* (New Haven: Yale University Press, 2007); Wilber W. Caldwell, *Cynicism and the Evolution of the American Dream* (Washington, DC: Potomac Books, Inc., 2006); Claudia Card, *The Atrocity Paradigm: A Theory of Evil* (New York: Oxford University Press, 2002); Andrew Delbanco, *The Death of Satan: How Americans Have Lost the Sense of Evil* (New York: Farrar, Straus and Giroux, 1996); John Kekes, *The Roots of Evil* (Ithaca: Cornell University Press, 2005); Joseph Margulies, *Guantanamo and the Abuse of Presidential Power* (New York: Simon & Schuster, 2006); Adi Other, *The Ordeal of Evils: Toward An Ontology of Morals* (New York: Zone Books, 2005).

47. Today's so-called religious revival in America actually is the theological politics of evangelical fanaticism, which borders on fascism. A combination of right-wing political, neoconservative intellectual, and fundamentalist religious forces has resulted in a great amount of global death and destruction. On the harm and devastation of theological politics, see Richard Dawkins, *The God Delusion* (New York: Houghton Mifflin Company, 2006); Christopher Hitchens, *God Is Not Great: How Religion Poisons Everything* (New York: Twelve Hachette Book Group USA, 2007); Kevin Phillips, *American Theocracy: The Peril and Politics of Radical Religion, Oil, and Borrowed Money in the 21st Century* (New York: Viking, 2006).

FIFTEEN

The Aporia of Hope

King and Bell on the Ending of Racism

Bill E. Lawson

If you lose hope, somehow you lose the vitality that keeps life moving, you lose that courage to be, that quality that helps you go on in spite of it all. And so today I still have a dream.

—Martin Luther King Jr.

It appears that my worst fears have been realized: we have made progress in everything yet nothing has changed.

—Derrick Bell

The election of Barack Obama as the forty-fourth president of the United States came as a surprise to many Americans. Who could have imagined that the year 2008 would produce the first nonwhite male president of the United States? What does the election of Obama indicate about the current racial climate in the United States? In particular, what does it indicate about black and white race relations? Are we moving to a stage in American history were race plays less of a role in one's chance for a meaningful life? Does his election signal that racism is not permanent in the United States? While I will not try to answer all of these questions, I want to examine briefly the relationship of Obama's election to the positions of Derrick Bell and Martin Luther King on the permanence of racism and the hope that Obama's election should engender. Those persons who will look for some neat resolution to this examination will be disappointed. My only *hope* is to show that both Bell and King are leery of the ability of liberalism to end racial injustice in the United States. I contend that the election of Obama does not settle the question of the acceptance of blacks as full members of the state.

For many Americans, the election of Obama as president signifies the realization of King's dream and that the hope he expressed for racial harmony in the United States had not been in vain. Indeed, Ralph D. Abernathy notes that in the "I Have a Dream" speech,

> Instead of dwelling on the bitterness of the past or the severe problems of the present he gave the cheering crowd, as well as the millions who watched on television, the vision of a future no one else had defined and few black people could imagine. It wasn't that Martin disagreed with the grim messages the others had brought to the crowd and to the American people. The dream he envisioned acknowledged the truth of everything that had already been said. He simply looked beyond the injustice and hatred and division to see what America could become. It was a prophecy of pure hope at a time when black people and the nation as a whole needed hope more than anything else.[1]

Indeed, the election of President Obama seems to confirm the fulfilling or at least a move to the fulfilling of the hope that King had for America. What I want to focus on here is probably the most famous line from King's 1963 speech: "I have a dream that my four little children will one day live in a nation where they will not be judged by the color of their skin but by the content of their character."[2] Literary critic Eric Sundquist notes "those thirty-five spontaneous words have done more than any politician's polemic, any sociologist's theory, or any court's ruling to frame public discussion of affirmative action over the past four decades."[3] Politicians, social critics, political pundits, and common folks have referred to King's call for "character over color." It must be noted that it is unclear if King would have agreed with all of the uses of his words. Still, many take the election of Obama as a clear sign of selecting someone because of his character and not his color. As such his election seems rooted in both King's dream and his hope for America. What was the spiritual and intellectual basis for King's hope in America that anchored his dream?

Drawing on his reading of the Declaration of Independence and the U.S. Constitution, along with his religious convictions, King often remarked that the principles embodied in these documents establish the groundwork for the hope of a future that reflected the basic belief in human brotherhood. In 1962, King proclaimed:

> There is no graded scale of essential worth; there is no divine right of one race which differs from the divine right of another. Every human being has etched in his personality the indelible stamp of the Creator. This idea of the dignity and worth of human personality is expressed eloquently and unequivocally in the Declaration of Independence. "All men," it says, "are created equal. They are endowed by their Creator with certain inalienable rights, among these are life, liberty and the

pursuit of happiness." Never has a sociopolitical document proclaimed more profoundly and eloquently the sacredness of human personality.[4]

It was because these principles had not been adhered to that Martin Luther King's work for social justice became a benchmark event in the push for what can be called black or African American liberation. King, however, saw the liberation of black Americans deeply connected to the liberation of all Americans and eventually saw the struggle for civil rights in the United States connected to the worldwide struggle for social justice. He realized that the goal of universal brotherhood would come only after a long and difficult struggle. More importantly, he realized that he had to instill in persons of goodwill, both black and white, that to hope for such a future was not in vain. Racism in the United States is not permanent, and racial equality can be achieved.

While before his death King spoke of the American nightmare, he had no doubts that in the end, social justice would prevail. Persons of all racial complexions would live together as brothers and sisters. The evening before his assassination he again put forth his view that racial justice was coming to America, even if he would not be there to see its bounty.

> Well, I don't know what will happen now. We've got some difficult days ahead. But it doesn't matter with me now. Because I've been to the mountaintop. And I don't mind. Like anybody, I would like to live a long life. Longevity has its place. But I'm not concerned about that now. I just want to do God's will. And He's allowed me to go up to the mountain. And I've looked over. And I've seen the promised land. I may not get there with you. But I want you to know tonight, that we, as a people will get to the promised land. And I'm happy, tonight. I'm not worried about anything. I'm not fearing any man. Mine eyes have seen the glory of the coming of the Lord.[5]

Nonetheless, for all of King's faith in the hope of a future replete with the bonds of human brotherhood, there are some people who find little comfort in King's dream. Some scholars[6] like Derrick Bell, have argued that racism is a permanent aspect of life for persons living in the United States. This view of the future of race relations contrasts markedly from that of King. Bell thinks that King's dream and the hope it engenders is misleading because it is built on a false understanding of racism in the United States. Bell believes that racism will always be a staple of life in the United States. He wants blacks to reconsider their understanding of the struggle against racism. In a passage worth quoting at length, Bell writes:

> To initiate the reconsideration, I want to set forth this proposition, which will be easier to reject than refute: Black people will never gain full equality in this country. Even those Herculean efforts we hail as successful will produce no more than temporary "peaks of progress,"

short-lived victories that slide into irrelevance as racial patterns adapt in ways that maintain white dominance. This is a hard-to-accept fact that all history verifies. We must acknowledge it, not as a sign of submission, but as an act of ultimate defiance.

We identify with and hail as hero the man or woman willing to face even death without flinching. Why? Because, while no one escapes death, those who conquer their dread of it are freed to live more fully. In similar fashion, African Americans must confront and conquer the otherwise deadening reality of our permanent subordinate status. Only in this way can we prevent ourselves from being dragged down by society's racial hostility. Beyond survival lies the potential to perceive more clearly both a reason and the means for further struggle.[7]

In the epilogue of his book *Faces at the Bottom of the Well*, Bell acknowledges that there is a form of despair associated with the final narrative of his book *The Space Traders*. In this provocative tale, aliens from outer space finally come to earth and they are traders, who want to establish commercial relations with the citizens of the United States. The traders have a surprising trade offer for the citizens of the United States to consider. Bell describes the condition of trade:

> Those mammoth vessels carried within their holds treasure of which the United States was in most desperate need: gold, to bail out the almost bankrupt federal, state, and local governments; special chemicals capable of unpolluting the environment, which was becoming daily more toxic, and restoring it to the pristine state it had been before Western explorers set foot on it; and a totally safe nuclear engine and fuel, to relieve the nation's all-but-depleted supply of fossil fuel. In return, the visitors wanted only one thing-and that was to take back to their home star all the African Americans who lived in the United States.[8]

After some deliberation, there was a national referendum to vote on the trader's offer. The story evolves around the debate of accepting or rejecting the trade. Everyone knew that if the trade was accepted, it meant sending blacks away to some distant unknown land. In the end, the white majority vote to send blacks off with the traders. The vote was not even close. Bell ends this story with the following lines:

> 17 January. The last Martin Luther King holiday the nation would ever observe dawned on an extraordinary sight. In the night, the Space Traders had drawn their strange ships right up to the beaches and discharged their cargoes of gold, minerals, and machinery, leaving vast empty holds. Crowded on the beaches were inductees, some twenty million silent black men, women, and children, including babes in arms. As the sun rose, the Space Traders directed them, first, to strip off all but a single undergarment; then, to line up; and finally, to enter those holds which yawned in the morning light like Milton's "darkness visible." The inductees looked fearfully behind them. But, on the dunes

above the beaches, guns at the ready, stood U.S. guards. There was no escape, no alternative. Heads bowed, arms now linked by slender chains, black people left the New World as their forebears had arrived.[9]

Not only will blacks not be seen as full members of the state, but, if given the chance, whites would trade blacks for items that benefitted white interests. Black people will never gain full equality in this country. This view of race relations in the United States is, of course, in sharp contrast to King's visions of the future of race relations in the United States. Some readers may object at this point that Bell's position is just a polemic stance. It should not be taken seriously. Nonetheless, when I use this narrative in my classes, I am no longer surprised that many of the students both black and white agree that the white citizens of United States would make such a trade. These students argue that dislike of blacks is so strong that whites would gladly take the trade. Some have said that many whites would let the aliens take blacks if the United States got nothing in return. When I ask persons outside of the college setting if they think that racism is permanent in the United States, their answer, more often than not, is yes. I must admit that my survey is not a scientific one. But I think that Bell's position is shared by a number of Americans both black and white. [I hope I will be forgiven for using the racial binary of black and white.]

I believe that it can be stated without much contradiction that many persons of all racial stripes [races] believe that racism is a permanent condition for African Americans in the United States. The government can legislate that people not act in racist ways, but that will not change how they think about persons they deem members of another inferior race. In the United States the laws and social practices work in the interest of whites, and there is no reason for whites to push to change how these laws and practices advantage whites. According to Bell even those events, like Brown and, I would conjecture, the election of Obama, are merely symbolic acts that in the end will not aid in racial equality or the ending of racism. It is often claimed that it is natural for one group to oppress another group for money or wealth. Sometimes students claim that it is just human nature to discriminate against persons perceived to be different. If it is a fixed aspect of human nature to discriminate against members of other races, then Bell's claim about the permanence of racial is trivially true.

Bell, I think, believes that racism is permanent in a more significant and fundamental and philosophically interesting way. He argues that white interests, particularly economic ones, and not advancing morality or the imperatives of law set the social and political agenda. This view connects with Bell's theme of "Interest Convergence."[10] He has argued that the only time black concerns are given any weight is when these concerns align with the interest of white hegemony. Bell calls this view "racial realism." There are, at least, two ways to use the term racial realism. In the first account, races are real entities that have distinct social, mental, and biological traits that are relevant in how we treat members of these different races. Bell's view opposes this notion of racial realism and offers what he takes to be a more meaningful understanding of racial realism. It is a social and political philosophy that forces blacks to realize that neither the law nor the legal system will ever work to protect the interest of blacks and that material well-being of blacks will always be subverted to the interest of whites.[11]

> While implementing Racial Realism, we must simultaneously acknowledge that our actions are not likely to lead to transcendent change and, despite our best efforts, may be of more help to the system we despise than to those we are trying to help. Nevertheless, our realization, and the dedication based on that realization, can lead to policy positions and campaigns that are less likely to worsen conditions for those we are trying to help, and will be more likely to remind those in power that imaginative, unabashed risk-takers refuse to be trampled upon. Yet confrontation with our oppressors is not our sole reason for engaging in Racial Realism. Continued struggle can bring about unexpected benefits and gains that in themselves justify continued endeavor. The fight in itself has meaning and should give us hope for the future.[12]

Bell thinks that the struggle itself is enough to make black people continue to fight. Bell does not think that all whites are racist; rather that racism benefits all whites. It is this fact that makes racism impossible to eradicate. Obviously, he does not expect black people to be happy with this state of affairs. Nevertheless, once they accept the racial reality, their lives will be much better. Blacks will be better off once they accept this harsh truth and give up the hope to be viewed as equal to whites.

What does Bell mean by better off? Bell thinks that taking a realistic view of one's social and political condition makes one face the world with a better understanding of how to deal with racism. This "more" realistic view is psychologically healthier than believing in something that is not validated by our experiences. Once the healthy person realizes that some state of affairs will not materialize, they change their understanding of what is possible and how they should behave. Once blacks accept that whites will never see them as social equals, they can adjust their struggle for "rights" with a better understanding of what is possible. Importantly, blacks should not look or hope for the day that we have overcome.

Bell observes that in late 1950s and early 1960s King "lead a struggle toward a goal—racial equality—that seemed possible, if not quite feasible."[13] Reflecting on King's essay *A Testament of Hope*, Bell draws two provocative but insightful conclusions about King's mission. First, King understood the commitment of courageous struggle whatever the circumstances or odds. And secondly, a part of that struggle was the need to speak the truth as he viewed it even when that truth alienated rather than unified the speaker to general censure rather than acclaim.[14] Bell's pronouncement of the permanents of racism is his speaking the truth even if the truth makes some people uncomfortable. "The challenge throughout has been to tell what I view as the truth about racism without disabling despair. For some of us who bear the burdens of racial subordination, any truth—no matter how dire—is uplifting."

To one one's surprise, Bell's position has not been uplifting. The vision of America he proposes is not the one persons enamored with King's dream will find uplifting.

King's vision of the end of racism entails that racism or oppressive tendencies are not a fixed aspect of human nature. He must believe that humans as God's creatures can and will come to understand the brotherhood of men. King's hope for the future is based on his belief in God's goodness and the human desire for social betterment. Michael J. Nojeim, in his insightful book *Gandhi and King: The Power of Nonviolent Resistance*, remarks that,

> For King, the beloved community could only be achieved through a peaceful and harmonious integration of whites and blacks, poor and rich, Jews and gentiles, and so forth. The beloved community and the true peace that it would bring is not achieved simply by eliminating the presence of a negative evil force such as segregation. Rather, this must be accompanied by the presence of a positive force, one that would ensure justice, goodwill, and brotherhood. The key to creating this beloved community was integration, which was far more than merely ending segregation.[15]

For King integration means seeing the humanity of each individual and treating that person with the utmost respect. In this manner, we could achieve a nonracist society. I want to suggest that King has to believe at least one basic proposition in order to sustain his overall vision of a nonracist future: white Americans will come to respect the humanity of black Americans.

This belief grounds King's hope for a nonracist future. Let me be clear, I am not claiming that this belief is the only belief he has to hold to hope for a future free of racism and social strife. I am, however, assuming that this is a basic belief. I want to focus on this proposition—"White Americans will or can come to respect the humanity of black Americans." Why? The ending of systemic racism seems to turn on whites acknowledging and respecting the humanity of blacks. It is on this point that our understanding of hope for the future of race relations turns. King and Bell seem to differ on their belief in the truth of this proposition. It appears that for those persons committed to King's dream, it must be true. If one believes for whatever reasons white attitudes towards blacks are fixed unfavorably, then King's dream is a nightmare. Persons invested in King's dream are working to do something that cannot be done. They will not be able to get white people to respect the humanity of blacks. The basis of hope for the ending of racism in the future turns on a belief in the future behavior of whites. In what follows, I want to explore the differences between King and Bell on this point and discuss how it impacts on our understanding of hope for a future free of racism. First, we must examine how King and Bell both distrust liberalism as a means to end the suffering of blacks.

KING AND BELL AND THE FAILING OF LIBERALISM

In King's "Pilgrimage to Nonviolence," he writes that his

> early theological training did the same for me as the reading of [David] Hume did for [Immanuel] Kant: it knocked me out of my dogmatic slumber.
>
> At this stage of my development I was a thoroughgoing liberal. Liberalism provided me with an intellectual satisfaction that I could never find in fundamentalism. I became so enamored of the insights of liberalism that I almost fell into the trap of accepting uncritically everything that came under its name. I was absolutely convinced of the natural goodness of man and the natural power of human reason. [16]

The more King read and thought about liberal ideology, the more he came to question the liberal conception of the person. "It was mainly the liberal doctrine of man that I began to question. The more I observed the tragedies of history and man's shameful inclination to choose the low road, the more I came to see the depths and strength of sin." His reading of Reinhold Niebuhr made him aware of the complexity of human motives.

> Moreover, I came to recognize the complexity of man's social involvement and the glaring reality of collective evil. I came to feel that liberalism had been all too sentimental concerning human nature and that it leaned toward a false idealism.
>
> I also came to see that liberalism's superficial optimism concerning human nature caused it to overlook the fact that reason is darkened by sin. The more I thought about human nature the more I saw how our tragic inclination for sin causes us to use our minds to rationalize our actions. Liberalism failed to see that reason by itself is little more than an instrument to justify man's defensive ways of thinking. Reason, devoid of the purifying power of faith, can never free itself from distortions and rationalizations. [17]

King, while not totally rejecting liberalism, began to study existentialism. He thought that existentialism had grasped certain basic truths about man and his condition that could not be permanently overlooked.

> Its understanding of the "finite freedom" of man is one of existentialism's most lasting contributions, and its perception of the anxiety and conflict produced in man's personal and social life as a result of the perilous and ambiguous structure of existence is especially meaningful for our time. The common point in all existentialism, whether it is atheistic or theistic, is that man's existential situation is a state of estrangement from his essential nature. In their revolt against [Georg Wilhelm Friedrich] Hegel's essentialism, all existentialists contend that the world is fragmented. History is a series of unreconciled conflicts and man's existence is filled with anxiety and threatened with meaninglessness. While the ultimate Christian answer is not found in any of these existential assertions, there is much here that the theologian can use to describe the true state of man's existence. [18]

It was during this period, while studying systematic theology and philosophy, that King became more and more interested in social ethics. He was particularly interested in ending racial injustice. It was his reading of Rauschenbusch's *Christianity and the Social Crisis* that created the challenge of a program of social action. Rauschenbusch, King felt, had fallen to the "'cult of inevitable progress' which led him to an unwarranted optimism concerning human nature. Moreover, he came perilously close to identifying the kingdom of God with a particular social and economic system—a temptation which the church should never give in to."

King acknowledges Rauschenbusch's shortcoming but realizes that he gave American Protestantism a sense of social responsibility that it should never lose. For King, "The gospel at its best deals with the whole man, not only his soul but his body, not only his spiritual well-being, but his material well-being. Any religion that professes to be concerned about the souls of men and is not concerned about the slums that damn them, the economic conditions that strangle them and the social conditions that cripple them is a spiritually moribund religion awaiting burial."

This realization set King on a serious study of the social and ethical theories of the great philosophers. To his dismay their works did not provide what he took to be a realistic approach to solving social problems. It was, however, his reading of the life and teaching of Gandhi that gave him the inspiration and insight to use nonviolence as a method of social change. King's use of nonviolence as a method of social change came as a result of his active engagement with liberal ideology. He was still committed to "moral suasion" but felt that a more visceral approach was needed to move the individual and society toward the beloved community. This would be a community in which whites could and would respect the humanity of blacks.

Bell is also distrustful of the use of liberal ideology as a means to end racial injustice. Like King, Bell is dissatisfied with the manner in which progress is understood within the liberal ideological framework. The achievement of social justice and racial equality are admirable goals according to Bell. They are significant goals. There is however a very low probability that that they will be achieved in America. I have noted that Bell gives two important reasons for thinking that racism is permanent. Racial realism entails understanding that the social practices and legal system work to protect the interest of whites. What grounds Bell's thinking on these points is his belief that that racism is built into the ideological fabric of liberalism and this ideology excludes blacks from being full participants in the liberal state. Liberalism for all of its promise of social and moral inclusion is really a theory of exclusion. For whites to see themselves as enlightened, they needed a contrasting group. The groups used to point out the merits of white culture are the nonwhite groups. The ideological trick, Bell seems to think, is having blacks buy into this brand of liberalism with its supposed emphasis of equality. An ideology only keeps nonwhites in a position of lesser beings, socially and politically in the United States. Tommy Curry explains:

> Equality only serves as an imaginative allure—a fantasy, and this is the reality that must be conceptually disengaged. The demand for equality is a request to be recognized as rational, as individual, as ahistorical, and of course as un-Blackened by whites. The longing for equality forces Blacks to mistake humanity as an analytic truth, in which we mistakenly assume that our birth as human necessarily gives us our "humanity." But this is an errant basis to begin theorizations of Black resistance; genuine Black resistance is not based in the analytics of humanity; it is not a purely intellectual activity. Regardless of Black appeals to genetic similarity or to the theme that "God created all men equal," race will continue to reference our nonhumanity. Instead of trying to meet the criterion whites have placed on humanity, genuine Black resistance must be rooted in the right to develop and assert a new cultural world.[19]

It is because anti-black racism is an essential element of liberalism that to change the view white persons have of blacks as fully human would mean that they (whites) would have to reconceptualize what it means to be white in relation to blacks. Accordingly, blacks in the United States have been the marker for white identity and white progress. The social structure of the United States is set up to appease the white population by maintaining the power, prestige, and privilege of their whiteness. It is the deeper realization that the ideology that underpins the social institutions is embedded with racism. Bell thinks that whites will never see blacks as humans with ends. Instead, whites will always view blacks as partial or subhumans to be used merely as means. This understanding of human value is always at the core of social and political decisions. John Locke's

word in the Fundamental Constitution of Carolina set the basic understanding for the relationship of whites and blacks with the liberal state.
"Every freeman of Carolina shall have absolute power and authority over
his negro slaves, of what opinion or religion soever." Legal scholar Leon
Higginbotham after an extensive review of a thousand legal statutes and
cases found what he took to be ten precepts of American Slavery Jurisprudence, only two of which I will cite here—(1) inferiority: presume,
preserve, protect, and defend the superiority of whites and the inferiority
of blacks; and (2) property: define the slave as the master's property,
maximize the master's economic interest, disregard the humanity of the
slave except when it serves the master's interest, and deny slaves the
fruits of their labor.[20] Some might think that Higginbotham's work only
represents the history of race relations in the United States. It is argued
that times have changed and the legal system has been an aide in promoting social and political equality. Bell thinks this is a foolish assumption.
Unfortunately civil rights advocates continue to assume that legislations
and makeshift policies will result in racial justice. Indeed this was King's
view.

> Now the other myth that gets around is the idea that legislation cannot
> really solve the problem and that it has no great role to play in this
> period of social change because you've got to change the heart and you
> can't change the heart through legislation. You can't legislate morals.
> The job must be done through education and religion. Well, there's
> half-truth involved here. Certainly, if the problem is to be solved then
> in the final sense, hearts must be changed. Religion and education must
> play a great role in changing the heart. But we must go on to say that
> while it may be true that morality cannot be legislated, behavior can be
> regulated. It may be true that the law cannot change the heart but it can
> restrain the heartless. It may be true that the law cannot make a man
> love me but it can keep him from lynching me and I think that is pretty
> important, also. So there is a need for executive orders. There is a need
> for judicial decrees. There is a need for civil rights legislation on the
> local scale within states and on the national scale from the federal
> government.[21]

Bell's position is that the legal system still works to protect and preserve
the superiority status of whites over blacks. As a racial realist he sees the
laws and legal system as promoting black inferiority. Any protections the
laws accord blacks are always mediated in relation to their impact on the
interest of whites. The laws have worked this way since the founding of
the country. In this regard, there has been no linear progress in civil
rights or in the recognition of the humanity of blacks. The laws and
policies have not and will not change the social status of blacks. Racial
justice will never prevail. The lack of racial justice means that blacks will
always be at the low end of the social and economic ladder. The socioeconomic position of the majority of blacks will never change. It is this racial

reality that blacks must come to appreciate. In this regard, racial realism requires that blacks give up the hope for full equality in the United States. It does not mean that blacks give up the struggle for a meaningful quality of life. However, they must realize that it is the struggle that gives meaning to their lives, not white acceptance of them as humans. For Bell, the success of liberalism in the United States requires the exclusion of blacks as full members of the state and the human community. This means that racism is permanent in part because of it symbiosis with liberal ideology. Bell would contend that the arm of the moral universe bends toward whites in liberal theory and its social framing in the United States. Whites will never see blacks as their social and moral equals.

KING, HOPE, AND THE ENDING OF RACISM

Any discussion of the nature of hope has to address two sets of questions: those concerning the nature of hope (what hope *is*) and those concerning its characteristics (what it is *to* hope). There have been numerous attempts to answer this question. Darren Webb thinks that those scholars who have attempted to explain the nature of hope have all been partly right. He notes that often hope is thought to be an undifferentiated experience, which means with few exceptions hope theorists have regarded themselves as having identified the characteristic of hope. He wants to suggest that it seems reasonable to view hope as a socially mediated human capacity. "Understood in this way, different individuals and social classes, at different historical junctures, embedded in different social relations, enjoying different opportunities and facing different constraints, will experience hope in different ways."[22]

> The central claim being made here is that the various conceptualizations are all in some sense right, i.e. each captures something about what it is to hope. Human beings have concrete experiences like those described by Marcel and they would rightly call them hope. Human beings have concrete experiences like those described by Moltmann and Snyder and Rorty and, in each case, they would rightly call them hope. Taken as a whole, then, the theories examined here constitute a kind of phenomenology of hope. They capture something of the range of conscious experiences that could, and do, go by that name. More than simply a variable concept, hope is presented as a highly differentiated experience, the characteristics of which each of the various conceptualizations, in part, helps us to grasp. There are different modes of hoping and the article delineates a range of such modes.[23]

While there is a great deal to discuss in Webb's article, it is his distinction between open-ended hope and goal-directed hope that marks the difference between King and Bell and their understanding of the ending of racism and the chance of racial equality. King and Bell are assessing the future of racism from differing modes of hope. King, I contend, is drawing on what Webb calls "open-ended" hope.

> Sometimes we hope. Not for anything concrete, determinate or particular. We just hope. The experience of this "open-ended" hope tends to be emphasized and theorized by those subscribing to an ontology of not-yet-being. The notion that we as human beings are wayfarers who remain as yet undefined, have within us what we could become, and are travelling the path to ourselves, unites a wide range of writers. For each, hope is the human attribute which simultaneously reconciles us to our ontological status as a traveller and propels us along the path to ourselves. The precise manner in which it does this, however, is open to dispute. In extremely broad terms, theorists of open-ended hope would all agree that it is characterized by an openness of spirit with respect to the future and casts a positive glow on life. Nonetheless, there is a profound difference—in terms of the way in which this openness of spirit and positive glow are interpreted—between theorists of "patient" and "critical" hope.[24]

According to Webb, "patient" hope is hope directed toward an objective that is so open and generalized—in the end all shall be well, our status as wayfarers ultimately makes sense—as to defy any attempt to map. This sense of hope is a basic trust in the goodness of the world, which affords a sense of safety and security. This hope is other directed. To hope is to be patient and stand firm in the behavioral activity of another, and to await an unforeseen future.[25] On the other hand, "'critical' hope is directed toward the *ultimum novum* of a world without hunger, oppression and humiliation which defies the hypostasis of 'closed' or 'final' representation. This hope is a passionate suffering and restless longing for that which is missing. It is a hope of social criticism in which the forward pull of the *ultimum novum* is experienced as the compulsion to critically negate the conditions giving rise to present misery and the sense of unfulfilment."[26]

King's struggle for social justice can be seen as an expression of critical hope. He said that the arm of the moral universe is long and bends toward justice.[27] In 1957 he gave his justifications for his belief in nonviolence.

> I am quite aware of the fact that there are persons who believe firmly in nonviolence who do not believe in a personal God, but I think every person who believes in nonviolent resistance believes somehow that the universe in some form is on the side of justice. That there is something unfolding in the universe whether one speaks of it as a unconscious process, or whether one speaks of it as some unmoved mover, or whether someone speaks of it as a personal God. There is something in the universe that unfolds for justice and so in Montgomery we felt somehow that as we struggled we had cosmic companionship. And

this was one of the things that kept the people together, the belief that
the universe is on the side of justice.[28]

King held on to this position until his death. He saw the suffering to
bring about social justice in the United States connected to a larger cosmic
story. The suffering of blacks would transform them—they would be and
had become more aware of their humanity through the use of nonviolent
struggle. Their suffering was redemptive suffering. In his own case, he
notes,

> My personal trials have also taught me the value of unmerited suffer-
> ing. As my sufferings mounted I soon realized that there were two
> ways that I could respond to my situation: either to react with bitter-
> ness or seek to transform the suffering into a creative force. I decided to
> follow the latter course. Recognizing the necessity for suffering I have
> tried to make of it a virtue. If only to save myself from bitterness, I have
> attempted to see my personal ordeals as an opportunity to transform
> myself and heal the people involved in the tragic situation which now
> obtains. I have lived these last few years with the conviction that un-
> earned suffering is redemptive.[29]

The struggle is meant to bring about a world that unites people through
universal brotherhood. King thought up to his untimely death that racial
justice would prevail. His hope for the future was, of course, rooted in his
beliefs in the Goodness of God; God's plan for human happiness, and the
possibility of racial equality. King believed that white Americans would
come to respect the humanity of black Americans. It nonetheless would
be a difficult struggle.

> The American people are infected with racism—that is the peril. Para-
> doxically, they are also infected with democratic ideals—that is the
> hope. While doing wrong, they have the potential to do right.[30]

BELL, HOPE, AND THE ENDING OF RACISM

Webb's other metamode of hope is objective hope. He cites three modes
of objective hope: estimative hope, resolute hope, and Utopian hope.
Bell's view of the future of racism in the United Sates is situated in the
estimative hope mode. The objective of estimative hope is future-oriented
significant desire: hope directed toward an object of desire that is future-
oriented and deemed to be of significance to the hoper. The cognitive-
affective dimension of this hope: mental imaging + probability estimate:
hope is the belief that one's desired objective is possible of attainment
(probability $> 0 < 1$), founded on a careful study of the evidence. The
behavioral dimension of this form of hope, according to Webb, possible
goal-directed action in cases of more than a fair gamble: some hopes may

be worth the risk actively pursuing, but these hopes "because of" the evidence are unlikely to be personally and socially transformative.[31]

For Bell, to bet on the end of racism is the fool's bet. In this regard,

> While Bell does believe that history verifies that racial patterns adapt to maintain white dominance, a lesson he learned from Robert L. Carter, this fact in itself does not condemn Bell to the narrow logic of historical determinism. In fact Bell resists this interpretation explicitly, since "empiricism is a crucial aspect of racial realism." Instead of making universal or abstract judgments about racism, Bell follows the Legal Realists in focusing on the function of law rather than its promises. By looking to statistics and empirical evidence concerning the quality of life for blacks. Bell believes that continued Black oppression is confirmed. This revelation makes Black oppression a question of what is going on in the world and not the remedial instantiations of white emotionalism.[32]

According to Bell, the manner in which the laws continue to reinforce the subordinate status of blacks is rooted in the very ideology that liberals claim can liberate blacks. This is an empirical fact about black life in the United States. For Bell, Gunnar Myrdal and his followers were wrong in thinking that racism was just a holdover from slavery. Bell cites Jennifer Hochschild's work, *The New American Dilemma*, in which she calls Myrdal's view the "anomaly thesis" and concludes that the permanence of racism cannot be explained by that position:

> Rather the continued viability of racism demonstrates that "racism is not simply an excrescence on a fundamentally healthy liberal democratic body, but is part of what shapes and energizes the body." Under this view, "liberal democracy and racism in the United States are historically, even inherently, reinforcing; American society as we know it exists only because of its foundation in racially based slavery, and it thrives only because racial discrimination continues. The apparent anomaly is an actual symbiosis."[33]

The permanence of this "symbiosis" ensures that civil rights gains will be temporary and setbacks inevitable.[34] Bell notes that Fanon understood that racist structures were permanently embedded in the psychological, economy, society, and culture of the modern world. Even with this understanding of racism, persons of color must resist. This is why Bell can claim that racism is permanent and yet urge blacks to resist.

I would contend that Bell is not committed to the notion that black people give up all hope. They should give up the hope that whites will come to respect the humanity of blacks. Whites will never see blacks as beings with their own ends, but beings that can serve as means or mere means only. It is this understanding of the permanence of racism that is the heart of racial realism. In this regard, one can hope to have a decent job, good housing, and safe neighborhood. These remain viable hopes as long as they are in the interest of whites. This is in fact the moral of the story of the "Space Traders." The liberal model was in play when it came to blacks. There is a difference between respecting a being as human and respecting that being as a person with ends that have to be respected. Blacks are not seen as individuals with their own ends that should be respected. In the story of the space traders, they were seen, as blacks always have been seen, as means to better the lives of whites. There is one other major hope, however, blacks need to hold on to: they should hope that America's racial policy does not turn genocidal. But they should not hold for the "beloved community" because its foundations are not found in liberalism as practiced in the United States.

PRESIDENT OBAMA AND THE ENDING OF RACISM

If my reading of King and Bell is correct, it would appear that the election of President Obama gives us reason to pause in our understanding of the role of race and racism in the United States. His election took almost everyone by surprise. I say almost because there may have been that lone thinker that thought it was possible. In the vein, William Jelani Cobb, at a conference a few weeks after the historic event, asked

> a panel of political scientists, historians and sociologist, "What did we miss?" In response I received a moment of silence and a few skeletal theories. The fact is that the 2008 election was what Donald Rumsfeld once referred to as an "unknown unknown." And sometimes even hindsight gives you only a partial view. [35]

While I like the notion of an "unknown unknown," I would call the election of Obama, in the parlance of Nassim Nicholas Taleb, a Black Swan Event. The Black Swan Theory refers to high-impact and unexpected events.

> First, it is an *outlier*, as it lies outside the realm of regular expectations, because nothing in the past can convincingly point to its possibility. Second, it carries an extreme impact. Third, in spite of its outlier status, human nature makes us concoct explanations for its occurrence *after* the fact, making it explainable and predictable. [36]

The conventional wisdom was once that "all swans are white" and "all of the presidents of the United States are white." Both of these claims have been proven false. One could claim that regarding Obama we could only say that all U.S. presidents have been white and not make any prediction about the future race of U.S. presidents. Still no one expected Obama in 2008, maybe 2108. The election of Obama was indeed an outlier: a high impact and unexpected event. Obama's election gives followers of both King and Bell a chance to show how much or how little America has changed.

I will not attempt to show how King and Bell would deal with the election of Obama other than to note that King would probably see it as the arc of the Universe bending toward justice and that time when a person will be judged by his or her character rather than the color of their skin. Bell could acknowledge that the election was a highly important event, but it remains only symbolic. The United States, may, as Cobb notes, be willing to elect a Catholic president, a disabled president, and even a nonwhite president, but the country's overall attitude toward these groups still remains negative.

Gary Young, writing in *The Nation*, gives one account of the problem of looking at the election of Obama as a sign of hope for racial equality. One reason is the attitude of whites regarding Obama:[37]

> Half of white Americans in a Pew survey shared the birthers' doubt that Obama was born in this country. After the president produced his long-form birth certificate, Donald Trump demanded his college transcripts (claiming he was not smart enough to get into the Ivy League), and Newt Gingrich branded him the "food stamp president." In the face of such brazenly racist attacks, defending Obama's right to the office becomes easily blurred with defending his record.[38]

White attitudes toward Obama do not seem to support the position that he is seen as a full member of the moral community or the state. We have not overcome. If the racial climate is bad for Obama, the climate for the rest of the black community must be worse. Indeed, the situation is not that bright for the rest of the black community. The unemployment rate for blacks is much higher than that of whites. It does not appear that things will change any time soon, and it seems clear that programs that might help the situation of the masses of blacks are off the policy table. It is difficult to think that beyond that small group of blacks who have been highly successful (financially and socially mobile) in the past three decades there has been a lessening of racism toward blacks collectively. A few black faces in high places tell us nothing about the ending of racism in the United States or that character matters more than color.

Finally, as noted, both King and Bell were leery about the promise of liberal ideology to solve the race problem. This is why King chose to use nonviolence and "soul force" as a form of moral suasion. People can change, but they often need more than reasoned argument. Bell does not think moral suasion will work since it works against the interest of whites. Racism, for Bell, is embedded in the ideology of liberalism. This is why a change in the social institutions within *this* liberal framework will not end racism. The election of Obama does not give us an answer to the question of the permanence of racism. At best, his election, like the writings of King and Bell, urges us to consider the meaning and value of concepts such as "personhood," "liberalism," "agency," and "hope." In the end, when one thinks about the election of President Obama, reflecting on the merits of the arguments given by King and Bell may make it difficult to decide what his election tells us about the future of racism in the United States.

As I stated at the outset, there is no neat conclusion to this chapter, but after writing it, I am reminded of the following quote: "I had hopes once, but I gave them up."[39]

NOTES

1. Ralph Abernathy, *And the Walls Came Tumbling Down: An Autobiography* (New York: Harper & Row, 1989), 280.

2. Martin Luther King and James Melvin Washington, *A Testament of Hope: The Essential Writings of Martin Luther King, Jr.* (San Francisco: Harper & Row, 1986), 219.

3. Eric J. Sundquist, *King's Dream* (New Haven: Yale University Press, 2009), 194.

4. King and Washington, 119.

5. King and Washington, 203.

6. "Is Racism Permanent?" *A Symposium From Poverty & Race* 2, no. 6 and 3, no. 1, Poverty & Race Research Action Council, 1711 Connecticut Ave. NW, Suite 207, Washington, DC 20009, 202-387-9887. http://www.nysccc.org/T-Rarts/Articles/race-perm.htm.

7. Derrick A. Bell, *Faces at the Bottom of the Well: The Permanence of Racism* (New York: Basic Books, 1992), 12.

8. Bell, *Faces*, 194.

9. Bell, 194.

10. Bell, 2004, *Silent covenants: Brown v. Board of Education and the Unfulfilled Hopes for Racial Reform*, 230.

11. Derrick Bell, "Racial Realism," *Connecticut Law Review* 24, no. 2 (Winter 1992).

12. Bell et al., "Racial Realism," in *The Derrick Bell Reader*, 76.

13. Bell, *Faces*, xi.

14. Bell, *Faces*, xi.

15. Michael J. Nojeim, *Gandhi and King: The Power of Nonviolent Resistance* (Westport, CT: Praeger, 2004), 194.

16. http://mlk-kpp01.stanford.edu/index.php/encyclopedia/documentsentry/pilgrimage_to_nonviolence.

17. King and Washington, 36.

18. King and Washington, 37.

19. Tommy Curry, "Saved by the Bell: Derrick Bell's Racial Realism as Pedagogy," *Ohio Valley Philosophy of Education Society* 39 (2008): 42.

20. A. Leon Higginbotham, "The Ten Precepts of American Slavery Jurisprudence: Chief Justice Roger Taney's Defense and Justice Thurgood Marshall's Condemnation of the Precept of Black Inferiority," *Cardozo Law Review* 17 (May 1996).

21. http://thegospelcoalition.org/blogs/justintaylor/2008/09/20/martin-luther-king-response-to-you-cant/.

22. Darren Webb, "Modes of Hoping," in *History of the Human Sciences* 20, no. 3 (2007): 68.

23. Webb.

24. Webb.

25. Webb, 80.

26. Webb, 80.

27. King and Washington, 230.

28. King and Washington, 13–14.

29. King and Washington, 41.

30. King and Washington, 71.

31. Webb, 81.

32. Tommy Curry, *Cast Upon the Shadows: Essays Towards the Culturalogic Turn in Critical Race Theory* (Unpublished Manuscript), 74.

33. Derrick A. Bell, "The Difficulty of Doing Good: Civil Rights Activism as a Metaphor," in *The New Politics of Race: From Du Bois to the 21st Century*, edited by Marlese Durr (Westport, CT: Praeger, 2002), 181.

34. Bell, *Faces*, 10.

35. Cobb, *The Substance of Hope*, 140.

36. Nassim Taleb, *The Black Swan: The Impact of the Highly Improbable* (New York: Random House, 2007), xvii.

37. Also see Adia Harvey Wingfield and Joe R. Feagin, *Yes We Can?: White Racial Framing and the 2008 Presidential Campaign* (New York: Routledge, 2010).

38. http://www.thenation.com/article/160782/obama-and-black-americans-para-dox-hope.

39. Humphrey Bogart in *Key Largo*.

SIXTEEN

The Concept of Hope in the Thinking of Dr. Martin Luther King Jr.

Clanton C. W. Dawson Jr.

Much has been written about the concepts of love and justice in the thinking of the Rev. Dr. Martin Luther King Jr. Yet little has been written about the centrality of the concept of hope in the thought of Dr. King. Perhaps the lack of scholarly attention to and examination of the importance of hope in King's thought is due to an assumption that hope is a necessary condition for any serious postulation of love and justice. It takes hope, to argue as King did, if love is to be used as a tool for social transformation. The creation of a society where justice is an actuality and not just a conceptual possibility, or, the formation of a beloved community can be realized only if hope resides at the center. In each of these cases hope is logically prior to love, justice, and the beloved community. Hope is the necessary condition for all social and political desires.

On the flip side, some scholars may be reluctant to engage in the discussion of the relationship of hope and King's thought primarily because for them hope and wishful thinking are too often the twin mythical creatures that serve as vehicles for empty human fantasies and self-defeating aspirations. The skeptics among us charge that given the massive social, economic, and political problems that confront us globally and locally, thinking about Kingian hope may tantalize the mind, but in the end hoping wishfully is useless for any substantial, systemic change. Therefore, the skeptic muses, why bother with an analysis of hope at all? In the end, wishful thinking and hope are too similar to be distinguishable, and therefore to engage in a conceptual dialogue regarding hope is an example of sound and fury signifying nothing.

It must be acknowledged that wishful thinking can creatively imagine as does hope. Wishful thinking can conjure an idea of a just society, envision individuals transformed by love, and project utopian societies of multitudinous variety. Yet, in spite of the skeptic's critical reflection, this final chapter will examine the nature and function of hope in King's thinking. The project will operate from the position that hope serves as the principal concept of King's thought and action. Taking the skeptics' challenge seriously, I will distinguish between hope and wishful thinking suggesting that there is a fundamental difference between the two, and it was hope that inspired King and not mere wishful thinking. This project will posit that the centrality of hope for King is best demonstrated in three main areas: his concept of God, his commitment to the possibility of a just society, and his ideal of a Beloved Community. The conclusion of this chapter will examine the strength and weaknesses of King's hope and then conclude with an affirmation that in spite of the thought problems hope confronts us with, hope of the sort that King possessed is still worthy of maintaining in the twenty-first century.

What is hope in King's thought and how it different from wishful thinking? Hope, for King, is a rational belief based in the future possibility of (1) an action by an agent(s) being accomplished, or (2) in the creation of a tangible state of affairs not currently present. Hope, for King, is grounded in present and/or past concrete historical events that serve as justification for the rational hope belief, and yet is future oriented. As Charlotte Martin[1] rightly suggests, authentic, rational hope must have some indication of its own fulfillment. For King, the success of nonviolent direct action demonstrations, or the 1965 Voting Act, served as historical evidence justifying hope and providing the first fruits of the material conditions necessary for hope's fulfillment.

Wishful thinking, on the other hand, is a sort of yearning that raises the possibility of desirable action or state(s) of the world beyond what is warranted.[2] Wishful thinking needs no justification or indication of fulfillment to activate, it only needs a creative imagination of the subject. Thus it may occasionally find fulfillment, but such a result was more the product of random chance than rational reflection. Such wishful thinking was not the center of King's thought.

What is the function and nature of hope for King? Hope, in general and for King specifically, has a unique double value. It has an instrumental value and intrinsic value.[3] Luc Bovens, for example, suggests that the instrumental value of hope is that it counteracts risk aversion.[4] For Bovens's hope keeps rational agents from the fear of loss in less than fair gambles. Bovens's discussion regarding the concept of hope in decision theory is helpful when analyzing hope for King. Hope not only counteracts risk aversion as presented in decision theory, but hope also gives one the resolve to act when confronted by ontic/psychological threats such as anxiety, dread, fear, and meaninglessness. For King, hope allows one to act in the context of an unfair social condition that threatens harm, hurt, and/or death. King states,

> People are often surprised to learn that I am optimistic. They fail, how-ever, to perceive the sense of affirmation generated by the challenge of embracing struggle and surmounting obstacles. They have no compre-hension of the strength that comes from faith in God and man. It is possible for me to falter, but I am profoundly secure in my knowledge that God loves us; he has not worked a design for our failure.[5]

The instrumental value of hope for King is evident time and time again when one thinks of the countless occasions when he and his family were threatened with violence and yet he continued to act. What sustained his resolve? It was the instrumental value of hope.

Hope is of intrinsic value for King as well. Hope provides the neces-sary and sufficient conditions for envisioning a sociopolitical context where segregation is transformed into integration, and racism is replaced by a connected koinia.

> So I say to you, my friends, that even though we must face the difficul-ties of today and tomorrow, I still have a dream. It is a dream deeply rooted in the American dream that one day this nation will rise up and live out the true meaning of its creed—we hold these truths to be self-evident, that all men are created equal. This is our hope. With this faith we will be able to hew out of the mountain of despair a stone of hope. With this faith we will be able to transform the jangling discords of our nation into a beautiful symphony of brotherhood.[6]

The envisioning or what Bovens calls "mental imaging" has an overflow affect in that it "provides for the pleasures of anticipation [that are] . . . especially important in times of hardship."[7] The envisioning may even cause a restructuring of our hopes that imparts a fresh understanding of our selves and the agenda(s) we undertake. This "hope envisioning" pro-vides the framework for the anticipation of social/political pleasures, as well as a pragmatic understanding of self and purpose. It is this type of intrinsic value for selves in King's thinking. King states,

> But we must also say that the crisis has been precipitated on the other hand by the determination of hundreds and thousands and millions of Negro people to achieve freedom and human dignity. If the Negro stayed in his place and accepted discrimination and segregation there would be no crisis. But the Negro has a new sense of dignity, a new self-respect and a new determination. He has reevaluated his own in-trinsic worth. Now this sense of dignity on the part of the Negro grows out of the same longing [hoping] for freedom and human dignity on the part of the oppressed people all over the world.[8]

King understands how hope's intrinsic value motivates people in the midst of struggle. Hope empowers a people, immersed in the struggle for freedom, to reevaluate their selves as a people worthy of dignity and freedom. King knew that hope reminds an oppressed people that their worth is not determined by what they are called by the oppressor or treated by an oppressive system. Instead their worth was absolutely determined by what they called themselves and the hope for the fundamentally new social order that they envisioned.

Hope therefore had both instrumental and intrinsic value for King. It was central in his reflection and strategy creation. It was also central to black people who were facing an oppressive and racist American system. Now we turn our attention to three areas in which we may best observe the fundamental importance of hope for Dr. King.

THEO-PHILOSOPHICAL HOPE: THE PERSONAL GOD OF HUMAN HISTORY

To understand the power of hope in the thinking of Dr. Martin Luther King Jr., one must seriously engage King's conceptual understanding of God. God, for King, is an immanent and personal God who is active in human history and stands on the side of justice. God is, for King, the creator of the universe, and the universe God created is moral. The God of King is not the well-spring of being as with Tillich, nor the God of becoming who cannot intervene in human affairs viz. Whitehead, but instead the God who is personal, active in human affairs, who demands justice. God is omnipotent, omniscient, omnipresent, caring, and good. For King it is this God in whom we live, and move, and have our being.[9] Rufus Burrows writes,

> King's deepest faith was in a personal God of love and reason who is the creator and sustainer of all life. King perceived such a God to be infinitely loving, caring responsive, active, righteous, just, and on occasion, wrathful. . . . [T]his was unquestionably the stance of King, who was, after all, influenced by the ancient ethical prophets, most especially Amos, Isaiah, Jeremiah, and Micah. King was deeply influenced by this tradition.[10]

This concept of a personal God was undergirded by an African American preaching tradition that was the cradle of his theological framework. After all, King was a fourth generation preacher, reared in the South. He was not only surrounded by evidences of racism, but was also birthed in a caring and proud religious community whose generational history and hope was one that was entrenched in the belief that God would bring about social and political change in history. This same community sang 'soon I will be done with the troubles of this world' not because of a wish to flee to an "other world" experience, but because they believed that the God of history and justice would one day send a Moses who would strike Pharaoh down. In was in this kind of community that served Martin

Luther King Jr. his first milk of righteousness. Of course, King's theo-philosophical thinking was honed and polished as he received a formal education. But, his first training came in the black church and the black religious community in which he was reared. Too often this fact is either underplayed or dismissed by scholars.

King's hope in a God who was personal and active in the lives of human beings was not only eschatological in character but was, also, a belief that God acts in the phenomenological now. He believed in and hoped securely for a social reality, "where the wicked cease from troubling and the weary can be at rest."[11]

Observe King's remarks in the American Dream. He writes,

> God is not interested merely in the freedom of black men and brown men and yellow men. God is interested in the freedom of the whole human race and in the creation of a society where all men can live as brothers, where every man will respect the dignity and worth of human personality. That will be the day when all God's children, black men and white men, Jews and gentiles, Catholics and Protestants, will be able to join hands and sing in the words of the old Negro spiritual, "Free at last! Free at last! Thank God Almighty, we are free at last!"[12]

King's hope in a personal and active God is pivotal to King's work and thought as a whole. King's hope in the possibility of a just society and in the creation of a beloved community starts with the hope in a personal God. This God is a God of power who is active in human history.

Along with hope in the power of God, King's hope was bulwarked by two central religious principles: (1) that God is good and (2) that God wishes to be in fellowship with humans.[13] King's belief that God is good states for him that God wants the best possible moral state for humans. Goodness, in this conceptual framework, is not simply a moral characteristic for God, but a moral condition for human beings and their interrelated social state of affairs. To assert that this personal, powerful, good God wants to be in cooperative fellowship with humanity demands an understanding that the God of King is willing to elevate humanity to be cocreators with God joining with them in the enterprise of creating a new state of affairs. King writes,

> At the center of the Christian faith is the conviction that in the universe there is a God of power who is able to do exceedingly abundant things in nature and in history. Theologically, this affirmation is expressed in the doctrine of the omnipotence of God. The God we worship is not a weak and incompetent God. He is able to beat back gigantic ways of oppression and to bring low prodigious mountains of evil. The ringing testimony . . . is that God is able.[14]

Hope in such a personal God gave impetus for his social activity. Peter J. Paris insists that "freedom and liberation" are at the core of King's conceptualization of God. While eminent thinker Rufus Burrows points to "reason" as part of the essential nature of the God of Martin Luther King, Paris insists that freedom is the fundamental aspect for King's theology:

> In fact, King believed that the phrase "God is Spirit" means "God is freedom." Consequently, the nature of the imago dei in humanity means freedom, not reason, as so many have supposed. Thus, the struggle for freedom is the struggle for the restoration of true humanity, in other words, the imago dei in humanity. That struggle implies a partnership with God, who determined in creation both humanity's true nature and final end. [15]

It is the position of this project that the God of King was one of both reason and freedom. It would make no sense to King that the God in whom he invested absolute faith, hope, and trust would be a God of irrationality. Nor would it fit into King's theological framework to posit that God was not a God of freedom and liberation. After all King is clearly a product of the black church and a black religious community that affirmed that the God of hope is a God of wisdom and knowledge and who sets the captive free.

In no way am I attempting to minimize the significant contribution that people like Brightman, Tillich, and others made to King's theological and philosophical framework. To do so would be foolish. But on the other hand, contemporary scholarship on King and his thought has often elevated his formal training at the expense of his black church education. King's first thinking about hope, the relationship between God and humanity, and suffering started in midst of a people who confronted oppression on a daily basis and yet insisted that they were children of a God who cares and makes all things new.

One can easily see how a belief in such a God generates both instrumental and intrinsic hope. Hope served King instrumentally by creating the courage to stand against the segregation de jure as well as the very structures that produced them. Intrinsically hope provided King with a creative vision of what a personal God can do with a responsive humanity. It was a vision of the fundamentally new with a personal God who is involved in the human condition.

SOCIAL AND POLITICAL HOPE: FROM SEGREGATION TO INTEGRATION

In this section we examine the concept of hope as it influenced King's idea of moving toward a just society. Hope allowed King to envision a social order that would be fundamentally different from the one he and his ancestors had experienced. Born in an era of Jim Crow and brute segregation, King's hope allowed him to believe that a country that espoused 'liberty and justice for all' could actually live up to those ideals.

King's "I Have a Dream" speech is the most noted articulation of the role of hope in his conceptualization of a just society. However, there are many places that King spoke to his hope for the social order. King states in his commencement speech to Lincoln University,

> For in a real sense, America is essentially a dream, a dream yet unful-filled. It is a dream of a land where men of all races, of all nationalities and of all creeds can live together as brothers. The substance of the dream is expressed in the sublime words, words lifted to cosmic pro-portions: We hold these truths to be self-evident, that all men are creat-ed equal, that they are endowed by their Creator with certain unalien-able rights, that among these are life, liberty, and the pursuit of happi-ness." This is the dream.[16]

King's hope in a personal God is coupled with a belief in the "kinship of all people."[17] Due to the fact that King's primary religious education was in the cradle of black church tradition, King realized that God was con-demning all forms of racial oppression and segregation. Such is the char-acter of the black church at its best. However, the kinship was created by not only his theology, but also by his sociopolitical philosophy. For King, Americans hold a 'common kindred' not only because we are created by the same God, but also because we are citizens under the same constitu-tion. King stated in 1957, "If the executive and legislative branches of the government were as concerned about the protection of our citizenship rights as the federal courts have been, the transition from a segregated to an integrated society would be infinitely smoother."[18]

Three major historical events were paramount to the hope King had for an integrated society. The first was the Supreme Court of 1954, Brown versus the Topeka Board of Education. This landmark case resulted in the integration of public schools in the United States and gave rise to a hope that mentally imaged the construction of an integrated society. The think-ing was that if the public schools were integrated, it would not be long for the remainder of the social institutions and the social order as a whole to integrate as well. Thus, the move to integrate public education was taken as the commencement of the material conditions necessary for so-cial hope fulfillment.

King stated,

> The United States Supreme Court decision of 1954 was viewed by Ne-groes as the delivery of part of the promise of change. In unequivocal language the Court affirmed that "separate but equal" facilities are inherently unequal, and that to segregate a child on the basis of his race is to deny that child equal protection under the law. This decision brought hope to millions of disinherited Negroes who had formerly dared only to dream of freedom.[19]

King included himself in that group of "Negroes" who had formerly dared to dream of freedom." The Supreme Court decision of 1954 fundamentally fanned the flame of hope not only in the hearts of black citizens but the cognitive framework of King. He began to realize that change in the United States context would be a slow process, but change would happen. The Court decision was evidence that his hope in the change of social structure of this country could be realized.

The second major event that served as evidence for hope for King was the bus boycott in Montgomery, Alabama. The December 1, 1955, event began with a black woman of slim build and short in stature refusing to move to the back of a Montgomery bus after a hard day of work. That woman was Rosa Parks. Ms. Parks was subsequently arrested for her refusal to move from the seat she occupied and move to a seat in the "colored" section of the bus. Ms. Parks was not the first black person arrested for such a Jim Crow violation, but the fact that she was a former Montgomery NAACP Branch secretary and a young preacher by the name of Martin Luther King Jr. was the pastor of Dexter Ave. Baptist Church brought attention to the matter. A meeting was called at Dexter Ave. Church, and a huge crowd gathered for the meeting. A boycott was called by King and others. On the morning of December 5, 1955, a boycott against the Montgomery bus company was launched. The boycott of the bus company by black workers lasted 381 days amid threats and acts of terrorism. Finally on November 13, 1956, the Supreme Court ended the boycott and declared that Alabama's state and local laws demanding segregation on buses was illegal. The boycott was a complete success.

The Montgomery boycott demonstrated several important things that fortified his social and political hope. The boycott demonstrated that his beloved black community had the resolve to stand against oppression structures until a change was made. Of course there were people in the black community who thought that King was only making bad matters worse. But many more supporters than detractors turned out to answer the call for social change—perhaps even to the pleasant surprise of King. To boycott the Montgomery Transit Authority was more than a suffering of inconvenience. Those who participated in the boycott had to withstand insult, terrorist tactics, and for many, injury. But inspite of all they endured, still the black community rose up, and King had concrete evidence that black, Southern America was ready for change and was willing to participate in its own liberation from segregation.

One additional caveat must be noted. Not only did Dr. King witness a community ready to mobilize for action, he realized he had the right methodology for the movement in the moment: nonviolent direct action. King's knowledge of Jesus-centered Christian ethics and Gandhi's nonviolent protests formed the perfect methodology to employ in a Southern context. The strong revolutionary rhetoric of Elijah Muhammad or Marcus Garvey was not a voice Southern blacks could hear easily. But the message of "turn the other check" and "love is action" was a message familiar to not only the black community of the South, but to its white counterpart as well. King writes,

> I am convinced that if the Negro succumbs to the temptation of using violence in his struggle for freedom and justice, unborn generations will be the recipients of a long and desolate night of bitterness. . . . [T]here is another way, namely of nonviolent resistance. This method was popularized in our generation by a little man from India by the name of Mohandas K. Gandhi. This has been the method . . . used . . . in the South and all over the United States. They must consistently refuse to inflict injury upon another. But . . . they [also must] avoid internal injury of the spirit. This is why the love ethic stands so high. . . . When one rises to love on this level, he loves men not because he likes them, not because their ways appeal to him, but he loves every man because God loves him. I think this is what Jesus meant when he said "love your enemies." [20]

The methodology of nonviolent direct action grounded in love proved workable and successful first in Montgomery and then later as the Civil Rights movement continued. The attention nonviolent direct action drew to the issue of segregation proved helpful in making white America face how deeply rooted racism was in the Jim Crow structures in the South. Its success definitely gave rise to a hope that one day segregation would end and that an integrated society would emerge.

The boycott opened another window of hope in that it was the first experience of watching a movement in action. The television media allowed Americans to see the Movement unfold before their very eyes. The result was that King and the Civil Rights movement arrested the imagination of the American conscious. Television captured and presented the boycotts, the demonstrations, and the violence inflicted upon those who participated in nonviolent direct action. America was in shock. For many who watched the unleashing of violence against Americans by Americans, the question was asked "Can we really be this cruel?" [21] The answer was yes. Television captured the moments and etched them indelibly on the American psyche. Through the media of television King demonstrated the plight of a segregated black America to the world. The way in which the media captured the activity in Montgomery brought attention not only to Montgomery but to the Civil Rights movement in toto. An arrested and responsive American imagination fed King's hope for the establishment of an integrated America.

The third major evidence for hope was the 1965 Voting Rights Act. King had been very critical of the way in which the legislative and executive branches of the government had not followed swiftly the lead of the Supreme Court's 1954 decision to integrate public schools, or the 1956 decision to end Alabama's segregated transit ordinances. King had called for the right to vote as a final and necessary part of African American citizenship. King states,

> The denial of this sacred right [to vote] is a tragic betrayal of the highest mandates of our democratic traditions and it is democracy turned upside down. So long as I do not firmly and irrevocably possess the right to vote I do not possess myself. I cannot make up my mind—it is made up for me. I cannot live as a democratic citizen, observing the laws I have helped to enact—I can only submit to the edict of others. So our most urgent request to the president of the United States and every member of Congress is to give us the right to vote.[22]

With all of the seeds of hope the Voting Rights brought, the preliminary days of garnering the right to vote were some of the darkest in the time of King and the movement. Medger Evers had been killed in Mississippi in 1963. The assault on marchers crossing the Pettus Bridge by the Alabama State Troopers in 1965 and the subsequent March on Selma, Alabama, brought world attention to the inability of African Americans to vote and live meaningful lives. The cameras caught not only the terror that black Southern Americans were facing, but also the presence of young, white students from the North predominantly who were filling the ranks of protestors against segregation. After the spotlight was focused so brightly on the injustices occurring in the South, President Lyndon B. Johnson signed into law the 1965 Voting Rights Act.

The signing of the Voting Rights Act rekindled King's hope that the movement toward an integrated society would actually materialize. The movement had employed the right weapon—nonviolence. The movement was becoming more interracial, intergenerational, and had captured the conscience of America. Even the president of the United States had to sign the Voting Rights Act giving all Americans the right to vote. Hope was being realized in a powerful way.

ULTIMATE HOPE: THE CREATION OF THE BELOVED COMMUNITY

> The logic of King's struggle for racial justice would lead him to extend that concern to other forms of human oppression.
> —Martin Luther King Jr., *A Testament of Hope*[23]

In this third section we examine King's notion of hope and its relationship to his yearning for the establishment of the beloved community. In the later years of his quest for racial equality in the American context, King began to articulate a more universal idea of freedom that included the end of oppression for citizens of the world community and not just African Americans in the United States. I suggest two factors lead to his thinking in this manner.

The first factor that contributed to King's hope for the beloved community was his commitment to the Christian concept of the kingdom of God rooted in the theology of the black church. Unlike its white counterpart, black church theology insisted that a change in the world order would become a reality. This concept was no "other world" wishing but instead a sustained belief that God with humans would establish the kingdom on earth as it was in heaven. For King the kingdom of God was the beloved community. King wrote,

> The Kingdom of God will be a society in which men and women live as children of God should live. It will be a kingdom controlled by the law of love. Although the world seems to be in bad shape today we must never lose faith in the power of God to achieve his purpose.[24]

As a black Christian preacher King could not escape an envisioning of a world community where injustice would be eradicated and justice would roll like an ever-flowing stream. Steeped in the black church tradition, it was not strange for King to hope for a beloved community that mirrored the notion of the kingdom of God that he had known of from his youth. King had been nurtured by black preaching that insisted one day all God's children would finally live in peace. The voices of great black thinkers like Mordecai Johnson and Benjamin E. Mays had forged the conceptual context for his hope for the beloved community.

Some scholars have insisted that the lack of King's referencing of black thinkers demonstrates that his theological framework was not influenced by black theology. Such thinking is erroneous. King was an integrationist. The type of integration that was operative with King demanded deferring to white Western European thinkers, though one's acquaintance with the concepts were first introduced by black intellectual mentors. We must remember that King lived in a time when to have intellectual credibility, one had to reference white thinkers in order to be accepted. I suggest that his omission of mentioning the influence of black thinkers was a response to his social context and not a dishonoring of his primary intellectual origin. Before King knew anything about Josiah Royce or Paul Tillich, he was familiar with Richard Allen, Nannie Burroughs, and Howard Thurman.

The second factor that provided justification for his hope of a beloved community was the growing unrest and calls for liberation around the world. Vietnam, Cuba, and South Africa were examples of the growing awareness for universal understanding of the beloved community. The world community was demanding freedom in the same way the black person in America was calling for freedom and justice. No longer could the plight of the oppressed and disenfranchised of the world be overlooked by King. King was aware that injustice anywhere is injustice everywhere.

> Yes, as nations and individuals, we are interdependent. We must be concerned about . . . the sacredness of all human life. Every man is somebody because he is a child of God. One day somebody should remind us that, even though there may be political and ideological

differences between us, the Vietnamese are our brothers, the Russians are our brothers, the Chinese are our brothers; and one day we've got to sit down at the table of brotherhood. . . . [W]hen we truly believe in the sacredness of human personality, we won't exploit people, we won't trample over people with the iron fee of oppression, we won't kill anybody.[25]

This call for an affirmation of the sacredness for all human life King believed was the foundation on which the beloved community could be erected. Such an affirmation demanded (a) a declaration of nonviolence by the nations of the world and (b) a continual recognition of the interdependency of the world community. In the same manner in which the world watched the Civil Rights movement in the United States overcome seemingly unmovable obstacles, so King believed that the same would transpire in the rest of the world. The result would be the establishment of the first fruits of a beloved community.

IS TWENTY-FIRST CENTURY KINGIAN HOPE POSSIBLE? AN EPILOGUE

Now hope that is seen is not hope.

—Saul of Tarsus

When one reflects on the hope that Dr. King maintained, the simple yet complex question that emerges is this: is it possible to hold the same kind of hope belief in God, America, and the beloved community in the twenty-first century that King held in his day? Clearly some things have changed in this country since the Civil Rights Era. Overt statutes of segregation no longer exist today as they did in the past. There exist no overt statutes of segregation in the United States today. Bull Connor is dead. If one has money, she can employ public transportation with relative ease. On the surface, it seems that access to privilege and power is available to all Americans equally. The Civil Rights movement was a success. Things have changed.

But as things change, some things remain the same. The huge economic and social disparity that prevails between the elite and the underclass in this country causes one to wonder have we really come very far. The middle class barely exists, if at all, anymore. The emergence of "dope economy" and the prevalence of drugs in the black and brown communities, the existence of the three strike rule, and the privatization of prisons has caused many people to believe that the penitentiary is the new slavery in America. Yes, the president of the United States of America is an African American, but the contention about his birth, the rancor and disrespect white Americans display in the words of Marvin Gaye, "make me want to holler, throw up both my hands."[26]

One would be hard pressed to embrace the classical integration model that was operative for King. The integration model King operated under was one that believed that if black Americans could prove they were worthy of moral, social, and intellectual consideration to the wider white culture, the white community would accept black people as equals. Such is the classical integration model. There exist numerous variations of this model but the bottom line, according to this model, is that for integration to take place, integration can only come about by the terms established by the dominant white culture or there can be no integration. It is obvious that such a model is offensive and demeaning not only to black Americans but to all Americans of color who possess some sense of culture identity and pride. The problem is what model of social interaction should one espouse for sociopolitical hope to be viable in the contemporary setting? On the surface the prevalence of biracials on the American scene might entice some to think that integration is becoming a reality. Yet the disparity in access to privilege and power between white and black America is as much of a reality as ever before. The idea of social integration would be laughable if it was not so painful. Sadly, it seems that the only time we act as if we are, "one nation . . . indivisible, with liberty and justice for all" is when we are confronted by a natural disaster or foreign enemy (real or imagined), and then the sentiment is short lived.

It is difficult for the best theist, of any rational repute, to believe in the God of King's personalism given the astronomical amount of evil in the world. Belief in the "omniGod" while proclaimed by many is no longer rationally justifiable.[27] The internal contradictions that follow from the omniGod position cause many to claim that belief in God is a matter of irrational faith. Since faith is unjustifiable, therefore all beliefs, including hope, that are theologically attached to faith in God are irrational. If hope in God is unjustifiable, then the hope of King is an example of wishful thinking and not hope in the true sense of the word. For instance, if God is good and personal as King thinks, then why the massive sufferings in places like Haiti, Darfur, or Japan? Unless my religiosity is as shallow as the "prosperity" ministry egomaniacs, belief in a God who is good, wills the good for all human beings, and has created a universe that bends toward justice seems impossible to believe given the amount of evil in the world.

These things and more serve as antagonists to hope: hope in a God of history, hope in the full integration of this society, hope for a beloved community. But perhaps such is the nature of hope. Because hope is futuristic, the present ontic realities always appear brighter and larger than the fleeting images of hope. We know that in the day of King, the obstacles he and the movement faced seemed insurmountable, and yet Jim Crow and segregation de jure was legally defeated. Change of human hearts and minds take much longer.

What will assist our hope in the present for the future? More time and space is needed to go in depth. However, as a philosophical prolegomena I suggest that we should consider the following in order to speak meaningfully about hope in our time. First, theists and atheists are going to have to be more honest and open in our critical reflections about God. Both theists and atheists seem reluctant to let go of the OmniGod concept in theo-philosophical discourse. Theists worry that we will not be able to sustain an alternative God concept worthy of religious worship. Atheists latch on to the OmniGod concept because their anti-God arguments fit so neatly into a narrow conceptual framework. An alternative concept of God can help both sides do some meaningful work. After all, the God concept that King maintained in his day for many people in the black church was strange and unusual. Yet King's God concept helped demonstrate hope in concrete ways. Perhaps that is a contribution King has made that most overlook—he dared to think and speak about God differently than the rhetoric of the status quo. Many atheistic philosophers contend that a concept of hope connected to God is by definition irrational. But given the lack of consensus in defining rationality, to purport a belief, like hope, as irrational because it has theological foundations is a form of begging the question. To purport a belief as warranted simply because it is grounded in faith is ridiculous. We need each other. A new theo-philosophical dialogue needs to take place. Perhaps instead of trying to maintain old Western European metaphysical concepts of being, we need to investigate "becoming" and the myriad of possibilities such a concept can hold for the human enterprise. Maybe Heraclitus, Whitehead, Thurman, and John Cobb have more to say to us about God, the world, and hope than Aristotle, Thomas Aquinas, and Tillich.

Second, maybe hope is best served when we acknowledge that the social-political-economic system under which we operate needs an absolute structural transformation. We may not want to support King's integration model, but King's thirst for a new way of being human and a citizen we must support wholeheartedly. The materialistic capitalism we as Americans attempt to maintain will never bring about the kind of just society we all need and deserve. King saw that this is true. We know it to be true as well. We realize that what has caused much of the unrest in other places in the world is in fact due to American greed, militarism, and an inordinate thirst for materialistic acquisition. A systemic and not a cosmetic change is necessary. I can change the color of the person in the White House, but unless the system is changed, all we have done is placed much emphasis on symptoms and ignored the cause. We cannot put new wine in old wineskins. Here is a hopeful idea: how about taking the challenge of being jazz musicians of the mind and thinking about social formations that go beyond traditional socialism, capitalism, and communism models? Of course to do so is to dare to hope in the fundamentally new.

Third, hope demands that we understand that no real change happens without change of the human heart. The beloved community makes sense while the transformation of the human person is accomplished. King was right that the law can only keep a person from killing me, not make them love me. For some that is enough. For many of us what is important is more than a prohibition against X. Hope envisions a time and space where human beings respect and affirm one another simply because they recognize each other as "kindred and kind." Most people talk in terms of me, myself, and I. Change of the heart insists that our conversation can bespeak our resolution: we, us, our. I grew up with the adage, "Self-preservation is the first law of nature." A changed heart states *our* preservation is the new law of nature. One thing is clear: given the challenges of the world economy, environmental concerns, religious fanaticism, and more, if we do not strive toward the construction of a beloved world community where humanity lives together, we will surely die together. Pogo is right—we have seen the enemy and it is us! Unless a change of heart takes place—or at least is aspired to—we will be eternally recorded as the creators of our own doom.

This project still affirms, believes, and hopes in the possibility of creating the fundamentally new. In spite of the many assassins of hope that loom all around us, hope will prevail. For without hope, a people perish; with hope a people prosper.

NOTES

1. Charlotte Martin, *Dynamics of Hope*.
2. Luc Bovens, "The Value of Hope," in *Philosophy and Phenomenological Research* 59, no. 3 (September 1999).
3. Bovens, "The Value of Hope," 1999.
4. Bovens, 670.
5. Martin Luther King Jr., "A Testament of Hope," in *A Testament to Hope: The Essential Writings and Speeches of Martin Luther King, Jr.*, edited by James Washington (New York: HarperCollins Publishers, 1986).
6. Martin Luther King Jr., "I Have a Dream," delivered August 28, 1963, Washington, DC.
7. Bovens, 676.
8. King, "Love, Law, and Civil Disobedience," in *Testament of Hope*, edited by James M. Washington (San Francisco: Harper Collins Publishing, 1986), 44.
9. Acts 17:28.
10. Rufus Burrow Jr., *God and Human Dignity: The Personalism, Theology, and Ethics of Martin Luther King, Jr.* (Notre Dame: University of Notre Dame Press. 2006), 102.
11. Burrows, *God and Human Dignity*, 102. The quotation, however, is a familiar statement to those who were in the black church experience.
12. Martin Luther King Jr., "The American Dream," in *The Negro History Bulletin* 31 (May 1968): 14.
13. Burrows, *God and Human Dignity*, 107.
14. Martin Luther King Jr., "Our God Is Able," in *Strength to Love*, found in *Testament of Hope*, edited by James M. Washington (New York: Harper Collins Publisher, 1986).

15.　Peter J. Paris, "The Theology and Ethics of Martin Luther King, Jr.: Contributions to Christian Thought and Practice," in *Princeton Theological Review* XI, no. 1.

16.　King, "American Dream," in *A Testament of Hope*, 208.

17.　Paris, "The Theology and Ethics of Martin Luther King Jr.," 7.

18.　King, "Give Us the Ballot-We Will Transform the South," in *A Testament of Hope*, 198.

19.　King, "The Burning Truth in the South," in *A Testament of Hope*, 95.

20.　King, "Law, Love, and Civil Disobedience," 44–47.

21.　Many of my colleagues are probably quaking unbelievably that I would suggest that some white Americans did not realize the cruelty segregation brought. What many of us forget is that these were the last days of America's sleepwalking days, the world according to *Leave It to Beaver*. In that world all were white, right, and happy. It was the demonstrations captured by television that made America at least momentarily wake from its slumber.

22.　King, "Give Us the Ballot—We Will Transform the South," in *A Testament of Hope*, 197.

23.　Ibid., 5.

24.　Martin Luther King Jr., "A Christian View of the World," in *God and Human Dignity*, 167.

25.　King, "A Christmas Sermon on Peace," in *A Testament of Hope*, 254, 255.

26.　Marvin Gaye, from "Inner City Blues," in *What's Going On* (1971).

27.　I get this term from John Bishop in "Can There Be Alternative Concepts of God?" *Nous* 32, no. 2 (January 1998): 174–88. I would argue that personalism is a concept grounded in the omniGod conceptual framework.

Selected Bibliography

Abernathy, Ralph. *And the Walls Came Tumbling Down*. New York: HarperPerennial, 1990.

Adler, Mortimer J. "The Idea of Dialectic." Pp. 154–77 in *The Great Ideas Today*, edited by Mortimer Adler. Chicago: Encyclopedia Britannica, Inc., 1986

Albert, Peter J., and Ronald Hoffman, eds. *We Shall Overcome: Martin Luther King, Jr. and the Black Freedom Struggle*. New York: Da Capo Press, 1993.

Ansbro, John J. *Martin Luther King, Jr.: Nonviolent Strategies and Tactics for Social Change*. New York: Madison Books, 2000.

———. *Martin Luther King, Jr.: The Making of a Mind*. Maryknoll, NY: Orbis Books, 1992.

Azbell, Joe. "At Holt Street Baptist Church." Pp. 51–53 in *Eyes on the Prize Civil Rights Reader: Documents, Speeches and Firsthand Accounts from the Black Freedom Struggle*, edited by Clayborne Carson et al. New York: Penguin, 1991.

Baldwin, Lewis V. *There Is a Balm in Gilead: The Cultural Roots of Martin Luther King, Jr.* Minneapolis: Fortress Press, 1991.

Baldwin, Lewis V., Rufus Burrow Jr., Barbara A. Jones, and Susan Holmes Winfield, eds. *The Legacy of Martin Luther King, Jr.: The Boundaries of Law, Politics, and Religion*. Notre Dame: University of Notre Dame Press, 2002.

Beifuss, Joan. *At the River I Stand: Memphis, the 1968 Strike, and Martin Luther King (Martin Luther King, Jr. and the Civil Rights Movement, vol. 12)*. Brooklyn: Carlson Publishers, 1989.

Bell, Daniel. *The End of Ideology: On the Exhaustion of Political Ideas in the Fifties*. New York: Free Press, 1966.

Bell, Derrick A. *Confronting Authority: Reflections of an Ardent Protester*. Boston: Beacon, 1994.

———. *Ethical Ambition: Living a Life of Meaning and Worth*. New York: Bloomsbury, 2002.

———. "Racial Realism." *Connecticut Law Review* 24, no. 2 (1992): 363–79.

———. *Silent Covenants: Brown v. Board of Education and the Unfulfilled Hopes for Racial Reform*. Oxford: Oxford University Press, 2004.

Bell, Derrick A., Richard Delgado, and Jean Stefancic. *The Derrick Bell Reader*. New York: New York University Press, 2005.

Bhaskar, Roy. *Freedom: The Pulse of Freedom*. London: Verso, 1996

Birt, Robert E. "Of the Quest for Freedom as Community." Pp. 87–104 in *The Quest for Community and Identity: Critical Essays in Africana Social Philosophy*, edited by Robert E. Birt. Lanham, MD: Rowman & Littlefield, 2002.

Bottomore, T. B. *Critics of Society: Radical Thought in North America*. New York: Pantheon Books, 1968.

Boyle, Sarah P. *The Desegregated Heart: A Virginia's Stand in Time of Transition*. New York: William Morrow, 1962.

Boxill, Bernard. "Bell on Brown." Unpublished paper presented at Pacific APA. Vancouver, BC, April 2009.

Branch, Taylor. *Parting the Waters: America in the King Years, 1954–1963*. New York: Simon & Schuster, 1989.

Brightman, Edgar S. *Personalism in Theology*. Boston: University of Boston Press, 1943.

Brown, Charles S. "The Legacy of Martin Luther King, Jr. and the New Movement for Justice." Pp. 113–25 in *Reflections on the Dream*, edited by Clarence G. Williams. Cambridge, MA: MIT Press, 1996.

Bruns, Roger. *Martin Luther King, Jr.: A Biography*. Westport, CT: Greenwood Press, 2006.

Bryant, John R., and Helen G. Edmonds. "The Legacy of Martin Luther King, Jr.: The Path to Human Dignity and Freedom." Pp. 147–61 in *Reflections on the Dream*, edited by Clarence G. Williams. Cambridge, MA: MIT Press, 1996.

Brym, Robert J. *Intellectuals and Politics*. London: George Allen & Unwin, 1980.

Buber, Martin. *Paths in Utopia*. Syracuse: Syracuse University Press, 1996.

Burks, Mary Fair. "Trailblazers: Women in the Montgomery Bus Boycott." Pp. 71–83 in *Women in the Civil Rights Movement: Trailblazers and Torchbearers 1941–1965*, edited by Vicki L. Crawford, Jacqueline A. Rouse, and Barbara Woods. Bloomington: Indiana University Press, 1993.

Burrow, Rufus, Jr. *God and Human Dignity: The Personalism, Theology and Ethics of Martin Luther King, Jr.* Notre Dame: University of Notre Dame Press, 2006.

Carpenter, C. C. J. et al. "A Call for Unity." In *Why We Can't Wait*. New York: Signet Books, 1963.

Clayborne Carson, ed. *Martin Luther King, Jr.: The Autobiography of Martin Luther King, Jr.* New York: Warner Books, 1998.

Carson, Clayborne, and Kris Shepard, eds. *A Call to Conscience: The Landmark Speeches of Dr. Martin Luther King, Jr.* New York: Warner Books, 2001.

Carson, Clayborne, and Peter Holloran, eds. *A Knock at Midnight: Inspiration from the Great Sermons of Reverend Martin Luther King, Jr.* New York: Intellectual Properties Management in Association with Warner, 1998.

Cobb, William Jelani. *The Substance of Hope: Barack Obama and the Paradox of Progress*. New York: Walker & Company, 2010.

Cohen, Carl. *Civil Disobedience*. New York: Columbia University Press, 1971

Cone, James. *A Black Theology of Liberation*. New York: J. B. Lippincott Company, 1970.

———. *God of the Oppressed*. Maryknoll, NY: Orbis Books, 1975.

———. *Martin & Malcolm & America: A Dream or a Nightmare*. Maryknoll, NY: Orbis Books, 1992.

Coser, Lewis. *Men of Ideas: A Sociologist's View*. New York: Free Press, 1965/1997.

Couch, Carl J. "Collective Behavior: An Examination of Some Stereotypes." Pp. 105–19 in *Readings in Collective Behavior*, edited by Robert E. Evans. Chicago: Rand McNally, 1969.

Curry, Tommy. *Cast Upon the Shadows: Essays Towards the Culturalogic Turn in Critical Race Theory*. Unpublished manuscript.

———. "Saved by the Bell: Derrick Bell's Racial Realism as Pedagogy." *Ohio Valley Philosophy of Education Society* 39 (2008): 35–46.

Dyson, Michael E. *I May Not Get There with You: The True Martin Luther King, Jr.* New York: Free Press, 2000

Eisenstadt, S. N. "Intellectuals and Tradition." *Daedalus* (Spring 1972): 1–16.

Ellison, Ralph. *Invisible Man*. New York: Vintage Books, 1952.

Erskine, Noel Leo. *King Among the Theologians*. Cleveland: The Pilgrim Press, 1994.

Eyerman, Ron. *Between Culture and Politics: Intellectuals in Modern Society*. Cambridge: Polity Press, 1994.

Eyerman, Ron, and Andrew Jamison. *Social Movements: A Cognitive Approach*. University Park: The Pennsylvania State University Press, 1991.

Fairclough, Adam. "Was Martin Luther King a Marxist?" *History Workshop* 15 (Spring 1983): 117–25.

———. "Martin Luther King, Jr. and the Quest for Nonviolent Social Change." Pp. 1–15 in *Martin Luther King, Jr.: Civil Rights Leader, Theologian, Orator* (vol. 2), edited by David J. Garrow. New York: Carlson Publishing, Inc., 1986.

———. "Martin Luther King, Jr. and the War in Vietnam." *Phylon* 45, no. 1 (1984): 19–39.

Fanon, Frantz. *Black Skins, White Masks*. New York: Grove Press, 1967.

———. *The Wretched of the Earth*. New York: Grove Press, 1968.

Ferree, Myra M. "The Political Context of Rationality: Rational Choice Theory and Resource Mobilization." Pp. 29–52 in *Frontiers in Social Movement Theory*, edited by Aldon D. Morris and Carol M. Mueller. New Haven, CT: Yale University Press, 1992.

Feuer, Lewis. "What Is an Intellectual?" Pp. 47–58 in *The Intelligentsia and the Intellectuals*, edited by Aleksander Gella. Beverly Hills: Sage, 1976.

Flacks, Dick. "Making History and Making Theory: Notes on How Intellectuals Seek Relevance." Pp 3-19 in *Intellectuals and Politics: Social Theory in a Changing World*, edited by Charles Lemert. Newbury Park, CA: Sage, 1991.

Fortas, Abe. *Concerning Dissent and Civil Disobedience*. New York: Signet Special Broadside from New American Library, 1971.

Franklin, Robert M. "An Ethic of Hope: The Moral Thought of Martin Luther King, Jr." *Union Seminary Quarterly* 40 (1968): 41–51.

———. "In Pursuit of a Just Society: Martin Luther King, Jr. and John Rawls." *Journal of Religious Ethics* 18, no. 2 (1990): 57–77.

Garrow, David J. *Bearing the Cross: Martin Luther King Jr. and the Southern Christian Leadership Conference*. New York: Vintage, 1988.

———. "From Reformer to Revolutionary." Pp. 176–83 in *Martin Luther King, Jr. and the Civil Rights Movement*, edited by John A. Kirk. New York: Palgrave Macmillan, 2007.

———. "The Intellectual Development of Martin Luther King, Jr.: Influences and Commentaries." *Union Seminary Quarterly Review* 40, no. 1 (1986): 5–20.

———. "The Origins of the Montgomery Bus Boycott." *Southern Changes* 7 (October–December 1985): 21–27.

Garrow, David, ed. *Martin Luther King, Jr.: Civil Rights Leader, Theologian, Orator* (vol. 2). Brooklyn: Carlson Publishing, Inc., 1989.

Gella, Aleksander, ed. *The Intelligentsia and the Intellectuals*. Beverly Hills: Sage, 1976.

Giddings, Paula J. *Ida: A Sword among Lions*. New York: Harper Amistad, 2009.

———. *Where and When I Enter: The Impact of Black Women on Race and Sex in America*. New York: Bantam, 1988.

Goffman, Erving. *Stigma: Notes on the Management of Spoiled Identity*. New York: Simon & Schuster, 1963/1986.

Goldfarb, Jeffrey C. *Civility and Subversion: The Intellectual in Democratic Society*. Cambridge: Cambridge University Press, 1998.

Gooding-Williams, Robert. "Evading Narrative Myth, Evading Prophetic Pragmatism: Cornel West's The American Evasion of Philosophy." *The Massachusetts Review* (Winter 1991–1992): 517–42.

Goulbourne, Harry. "The Institutional Contribution of the University of the West Indies to the Intellectual Life of the Anglophone Caribbean." Pp. 21–49 in *Intellectuals in the Twentieth-Century Caribbean (Spectre of the New Class: The Commonwealth Caribbean*, vol. 1), edited by Alistair Hennessy. London/Basingstoke: Macmillan, 1992.

Gouldner, Alvin W. *The Dialectic of Ideology and Technology: The Origins, Grammar, and Future of Ideology*. New York: Seabury Press, 1976.

———. *The Future of Intellectuals and the Rise of a New Class*. New York: Seabury Press, 1979.

Gramsci, Antonio. *Selections from the Prison Notebooks*, edited by Quintin Hoare and Geoffrey Smith. New York: International Publishers, 1999.

Grant, Jacqueline. "Civil Rights Women: A Source for Doing Womanist Theology." Pp. 39–50 in *Women in the Civil Rights Movement: Trailblazers and Torchbearers 1941–1965*, edited by Vicki L. Crawford, Jacqueline A. Rouse, and Barbara Woods. Bloomington: Indiana University Press, 1993.

Grant, Joanne, ed. *Black Protest: 350 Years of History, Documents, and Analyses*. New York: Fawcett Columbine, 1968

Greenfield, Eloise. *Rosa Parks*. New York: HarperCollins, 1995.

Habermas, Jürgen. *The Structural Transformation of the Public Sphere: An Inquiry into a Category of Bourgeois Society*. Cambridge, MA: MIT Press, 1991.

Harding, Sandra. *The Science Question in Feminism*. Ithaca: Cornell University Press, 1986.

Hegel, G. W. F. *Hegel's Logic*, edited by William Wallace. Oxford: Clarendon Press, 1975.

———. *Phenomenology of Spirit*. New York: Oxford University Press, 1977.

———. *The Philosophy of History*, translated by J. Sibree. New York: Dover Publications, 1956.

———. *Science of Logic*. New York: Humanities Press, 1969.

Heidegger, Martin. *The Phenomenology of Religious Life*, translated by Matthais Fritsch and Jennifer Anna Gosetti-Ferencei. Bloomington: Indiana University Press, 2004.

Higginbotham, A. Leon. "The Ten Precepts of American Slavery Jurisprudence: Chief Justice Roger Taney's Defense and Justice Thurgood Marshall's Condemnation of the Precept of Black Inferiority." *Cardozo Law Review* 17 (1996).

Hoffer, Eric. *The True Believer: Thoughts on the Nature of Social Movements*. New York: HarperCollins, 1951.

Holsaert, Faith et al., eds. *Hands on the Freedom Plough: Personal Accounts by Women in the SNCC*. Urbana: University of Illinois Press, 2010.

Hughley, Michael W. "Civil Rights and Affirmative Action: Hope or Despair." *International Journal of Politics, Culture, and Society* 7, no. 2 (1993): 287–95.

Ilyenkov, Evald. *Dialectical Logic: Essays on Its History and Theory*. Moscow: Progress Publishers, 1977.

Jackson, Thomas F. *From Civil Rights to Human Rights: Martin Luther King, Jr. and the Struggle for Economic Justice*. Philadelphia: University of Pennsylvania Press, 2007.

Johnson, Paul E., ed. *African-American Christianity: Essays in History*. Berkeley: University of California Press, 1994.

Jones, Hubert E. "Martin Luther King, Jr.: What Does He Mean to Me?" Pp. 37–41 in *Reflections on the Dream*, edited by Clarence G. Williams. Cambridge, MA: MIT Press, 1996.

Jones, William R. "Liberation Struggles in Black Theology: Mao, Martin or Malcolm?" Pp. 229–41 in *Philosophy Born of Struggle*, edited by Leonard Harris. Dubuque, IA: Kendall/Hunt Publishing Co., 1983.

Kaufmann, Walter. *Existentialism from Dostoevsky to Sartre*. New York: Meridian Press, 1975.

Key Largo, directed by John Huston. Warner Bros. Pictures, 1948.

King, Coretta Scott. "Foreword." Pp. vii–viii in *Martin Luther King, Jr.-I Have a Dream: Writings and Speeches that Changed the World*, edited by James M. Washington. New York: Harper San Francisco Publishers, 1992.

King, Martin Luther, Jr. *The Autobiography of Martin Luther King, Jr.*, edited by Clayborne Carson. New York: Warner Books, 1998.

———. "The Drum Major Instinct." Pp. 180–92 in *Martin Luther King, Jr.-I Have a Dream: Writings and Speeches that Changed the World*, edited by James M. Washington. New York: Harper San Francisco Publishers, 1992.

———. *The Essential Writings and Speeches of Martin Luther King, Jr.*, edited by James M. Washington. New York: HarperCollins, 1991.

———. "An Exposition of the First Triad of Categories of the Hegelian Logic—Being, Non-Being, Becoming." In *The Papers of Martin Luther King, Jr.: Rediscovering Precious Values, 1951–1955* (vol. 2), edited by Clayborne Carson. Los Angeles: University of California Press, 1994.

———. "Facing the Challenge of a New Age." Speech delivered to Institute for Nonviolence and Social Change, December 3, 1956.

———. "Letter from Birmingham Jail." Pp. 76–95 in *Why We Can't Wait*, by Martin Luther King Jr. New York: Harper & Row Publishers, 1963.

———. "Nonviolence and Racial Justice." Pp. 5–9 in *A Testament of Hope: The Essential Writings of Martin Luther King, Jr.*, edited by James M. Washington. New York: Harper & Row Publishers/San Francisco, 1986.

———. "Nonviolence: The Only Road to Freedom." Pp. 125–34 in *Martin Luther King, Jr.-I Have a Dream: Writings and Speeches that Changed the World*, edited by James M. Washington. New York: Harper San Francisco Publishers, 1992.

———. *Papers of Martin Luther King, Jr.: Called to Serve, 1929–1951* (vol. 1), edited by Clayborne Carson, Ralph E. Luker, and Penny A. Russell. Berkeley/Los Angeles: University of California Press, 1992.

———. *Papers of Martin Luther King, Jr.: Rediscovering Precious Values, 1951–1955* (vol. 2). Berkeley/Los Angeles: University of California Press, 1994.

———. *Papers of Martin Luther King, Jr.: Birth of a New Age, 1955–1956* (vol. 3). Berkeley/Los Angeles: University of California Press, 1997.

———. *Papers of Martin Luther King, Jr.: Symbol of the Movement, 1957–1958* (vol. 4). Berkeley/Los Angeles: University of California Press, 2000.

———. "The Reemerging Revolutionary Consciousness of the Reverend Dr. Martin Luther King, Jr., 1965–1968." *The Journal of Negro History* 71, no. 1 (Winter/Autumn 1986): 1–22.

———. *Strength to Love*. New York: Walker and Company, 1981.

———. *Stride toward Freedom: The Montgomery Story*. San Francisco: HarperCollins, 1986.

———. *A Testament of Hope: Essential Writings and Speeches of Martin Luther King, Jr.*, edited by James M. Washington. San Francisco: HarperCollins, 1986.

———. *The Trumpet of Conscience*. New York: Harper & Row Publishers, Inc., 1968.

———. *Where Do We Go from Here: Chaos or Community?* Boston: Beacon Press, 1967.

———. *Why We Can't Wait*. New York: Signet Books, 1963/2000.

———. *The Words of Martin Luther King, Jr.* New York: Newmarket Press, 1958/1987.

King, Martin Luther, Sr., and Clayton Riley. *Daddy King: An Autobiography*. New York: William Morrow, 1980.

King, Richard H. "Martin Luther King, Jr. and the Meaning of Freedom: A Political Interpretation." Pp. 130–52 in *We Shall Overcome: Martin LutherKing, Jr. and the Black Freedom Struggle*, edited by Peter J. Albert and Ronald Hoffman. New York: Da Capo Press, 1993.

King, William M. Lenin. *Philosophical Notebooks* in *Collected Works* (vol. 38). Moscow: Progress Publishers, 1961.

Lasch, Christopher. *The New Radicalism in America 1889–1963: The Intellectual as a Social Type*. New York: Norton, 1965.

Lawson, Bill E. *The Underclass Question*. Philadelphia: Temple University Press, 1992.

Lazarus, R. S. "Hope: An Emotion and a Vital Coping Resource Against Despair." *Social Research* 66, no. 2 (1999): 653–78.

LeBon, Gustave. *The Crowd*. New York: Viking, 1895/1985.

Lee, Chana Kai. "Anger, Memory and Personal Power: Fannie Lou Hamer and the Civil Rights Leadership." Pp. 130–70 in *Sisters in the Struggle: African American Women in the Civil Rights-Black Power Movement*, edited by Bettye Collier-Thomas and V. P. Franklin. New York: New York University Press, 2001.

Levinas, Emmanuel. *Otherwise than Being*. Dordrecht: Nijhoff, 1974.

———. *Totality and Infinity*. Pittsburgh: Duquesne University Press, 1969.

Lewis, David Levering. *King: A Critical Biography*. Urbana/Champaign: University of Illinois Press, 1978.

Lipset, Seymour M., and Asoke Basu. "The Roles of the Intellectual and Political Roles." Pp. 111–50 in *The Intelligentsia and the Intellectuals*, edited by Aleksander Gella. London: Sage, 1976.

Lipset, Seymour M., and Richard Dobson. "The Intellectual as Critic and Rebel: With Special Reference to the United States and the Soviet Union." Pp. 137–98 in *Intellectuals and Tradition*, edited by S. N. Eisenstadt and S. R. Graubard. New York: Humanities Press, 1973.

Lischer, Richard. *The Preacher King: Martin Luther King, Jr. and the Word That Moved America.* New York: Oxford University Press, 1995.

Lyght, Ernest Shaw. *The Religious and Philosophical Foundations in the Thought of Martin Luther King, Jr.* New York: Vantage Press, 1972.

Mannheim, Karl. *Ideology and Utopia.* New York: Harvest Books, 1936.

Marable, Manning. *Black Leadership: Four Great American Leaders and the Struggle for Civil Rights.* New York: Penguin, 1999.

Marx, Karl. *Writings of the Young Marx on Philosophy and Society,* edited by Loyd D. Easton and Kurt Guddat. Indianapolis: Hacket Publishing Company, 1997.

McAdam, Doug. *Political Process and the Development of Black Insurgency, 1930–1970.* Chicago: The University of Chicago Press, 1999.

McCarthy, John D., and Mayer N. Zald. "Resource Mobilization and Social Movements: A Partial Theory." *American Journal of Sociology* 82, no. 6 (May 1977): 1212–41.

McGuire, Danielle L. *At the Dark End of the Street: Black Women, Rape and Resistance—A New History of the Civil Rights Movement From Rosa Parks to the Rise of Black Power.* New York: Knopf, 2010.

McKeon, Richard. "Dialectic and Political Thought and Action." *Ethics* 65, no. 1 (October 1954): 1–33.

McLaughlin, Wayman B. *The Relation Between Hegel and Kierkegaard.* Boston University, PhD dissertation, 1958.

Meueller, Gustav E. "The Hegel Legend of 'Thesis-Antithesis-Synthesis.'" *Journal of the History of Ideas* 19, no. 3 (June 1958).

Mill, John Stuart. *On Liberty and Other Writings,* edited by Stefan Collini. Cambridge: Cambridge University Press, 2005.

Minnis, Jack. "The Mississippi Freedom Democratic Party A New Declaration of Independence." *Freedomways* 5, no. 2 (Spring 1965): 264–79.

Morris, Aldon D. "A Man Prepared for the Times: A Sociological Analysis of the Leadership of Martin Luther King, Jr." Pp. 35–58 in *We Shall Overcome: Martin Luther King Jr. and the Black Freedom Struggle,* edited by Peter J. Albert and Ronald Hoffman. New York: Da Capo Press, 1993.

———. *The Origins of the Civil Rights Movement: Black Communities Organizing for Change.* New York: Free Press, 1984.

———. "Reflections on Social Movement Theory: Criticisms and Proposals." *Contemporary Sociology* 29, no. 6 (2000): 445–54.

Moses, Greg. *Revolution of Conscience: Martin Luther King, Jr. and the Philosophy of Nonviolence.* New York: Guilford, 1997.

Mueller, Carol. "Ella Baker and the Origins of 'Participatory Democracy.'" Pp. 51–70 in *Women in the Civil Rights Movement: Trailblazers and Torchbearers 1941–1965,* edited by Vicki L. Crawford, Jacqueline Anne Rouse, and Barbara Woods. Bloomington: Indiana University Press, 1993.

Nojeim, Michael J. *Gandhi and King: The Power of Nonviolent Resistance.* Westport, CT: Praeger, 2004.

Oberschall, Anthony. "Protracted Conflict." Pp. 45–70 in *The Dynamics of Social Movements: Resource Mobilization, Social Control, and Tactics,* edited by Mayer N. Zald and John D. McCarthy. Cambridge, MA: Winthrop, 1979.

———. *Social Conflict and Social Movements.* Englewood Cliffs, NJ: Prentice-Hall, 1974.

O'Brien, Michael. "Old Myths/New Insights: History and Dr. King." *The History Teacher* 22, no. 1 (November 1988): 49–65.

Olson, Lynne. *Freedom's Daughters: The Unsung Heroines of the Civil Rights Movement from 1830 to 1970.* New York: Scribner, 2001.

Parks, Rosa (with Jim Haskins). *Rosa Parks: My Story.* New York: Puffin Books, 1992.

———. "'Tired of Giving In': The Launching of the Montgomery Bus Boycott." Pp. 61–74 in *Sisters in the Struggle: African American Women in the Civil Rights-Black Power Movement,* edited by Bettye Collier-Thomas and V. P. Franklin. New York: New York University Press, 2001.

Pinn, Anthony B. *Moral Evil and Redemptive Suffering: A History of Theodicy in African-American Religious Thought*. Gainesville: University of Florida, 2002.

———. *Why, Lord?: Suffering and Evil in Black Theology*. New York: Continuum, 1995.

Plato, *Apology* (28d-31b), edited by Edith Hamilton and Huntington Cairns. In *The Collected Dialogues of Plato (including the Letters) with Introduction and Prefatory Notes*. Princeton, NJ: Princeton University Press, 1989.

Ransby, Barbara. *Ella Baker and the Black Freedom Movement: A Radical Democratic Vision*. Chapel Hill: The University of North Carolina Press, 2003.

Reddick, L. D. *Crusader without Violence*. New York: Harper & Row, 1959.

Robinson, Jo Ann Gibson. *The Montgomery Bus Boycott and the Women Who Started It: The Memoir of Jo Ann Gibson Robinson*. Knoxville: The University of Tennessee Press, 1987.

Robnett, Belinda. *How Long? How Long?: African-American Women in the Struggle for Civil Rights*. New York: Oxford University Press, 1997.

Rouse, Jacqueline A. "'We Seek to Know . . . in Order to Speak the Truth': Nurturing the Seeds of Discontent—Septima P. Clark and Participatory Leadership." Pp. 95–120 in *Sisters in the Struggle: African American Women in the Civil Rights-Black Power Movement*, edited by Bettye Collier-Thomas and V. P. Franklin. New York: New York University Press, 2001.

Shils, Edward. "The Intellectuals and the Powers: Some Perspectives for Comparative Analysis." Pp. 27–53 in *On Intellectuals: Theoretical Studies/Case Studies*, edited by Philip Rieff. New York: Anchor Books, 1970.

Smelser, Neil. *Collective Behavior*. New York: Free Press, 1965.

———. "Theoretical Issues of Scope and Problems." Pp. 89–94 in *Readings in Collective Behavior*, edited by Robert E. Evans. Chicago: Rand McNally, 1969.

Smith, D. H. "An Exegesis of Martin Luther King, Jr.'s Social Philosophy." *Phylon: A Review of Race and Culture* 31 (1970): 89–97.

Smith, Kenneth L., and Ira G. Zepp. *Searching for the Beloved Community: The Thinking of Martin Luther King, Jr.* Lanham, MD: University Press of America, 1986.

Soper, Kate. *Humanism and Anti-Humanism*. Lasalle, IL: Open Court Press, 1986.

Stace, W. T. *The Philosophy of Hegel*. New York: Dover, 1955.

Sturm, Douglas. "Martin Luther King, Jr., As Democratic Socialist." *The Journal of Religious Ethics* 18, no. 2 (1990): 79–105.

Sundquist, Eric J. *King's Dream*. New Haven, CT: Yale University Press, 2009.

Taleb, Nassim. *The Black Swan: The Impact of the Highly Improbable*. New York: Random House, 2007.

Tarrow, Sidney. *Power in Movement: Social Movements, Collective Action, and Politics*. Cambridge: Cambridge University Press, 1994.

Thoreau, Henry David. "Civil Disobedience" (1848). Pp. 85–104 in *Walden and Other Writings by Henry David Thoreau*, edited by Joseph Wood Krutch. New York: Bantam Books, 1982.

———. *Civil Disobedience and Other Essays*. New York: Dover Publications, 1993

Tunstall, Dwayne A. *Yes, But Not Quite: Encountering Josiah Royce's Ethico-Religious Insight*. New York: Fordham University Press, 2009.

Vlastos, Gregory. "Socrates on Political Obedience and Disobedience." Pp. 30–42 in *Studies in Greek Philosophy: Socrates, Plato and their Tradition* (vol. 2), by Gregory Vlastos, edited by Daniel W. Graham. Princeton, NJ: Princeton University Press, 1995.

Walton, Hanes. *The Political Philosophy of Martin Luther King, Jr.* Westport, CT: Greenwood Press, 1971.

Washington, James M. *Martin Luther King, Jr.-I Have a Dream: Writings and Speeches that Changed the World*. New York: Harper San Francisco Publishers, 1992.

Washington, James M., ed. *A Testament of Hope: The Essential Writings and Speeches of Martin Luther King, Jr.* New York: HarperCollins, 1991.

Washington, Joseph R. "Black Hope." Pp. 252–72 in *Moral Evil and Redemptive Suffering: A History of Theodicy in African-American Religious Thought*. Gainesville: University of Florida, 2002.

Webb, Darren. "Modes of Hoping." *History of the Human Sciences* 20, no. 3 (2007): 65–83.

West, Cornel. *The American Evasion of Philosophy: A Genealogy of Pragmatism*. Madison: University of Wisconsin Press, 1989.

———. *The Cornel West Reader*. New York: Basic Books, 1999.

———. "The Religious Foundation of the Thought of Martin Luther King, Jr." Pp. 113–29 in *We Shall Overcome: Martin Luther King Jr. and the Black Freedom Struggle*, edited by Peter J. Albert and Ronald Hoffman. New York: Da Capo Press, 1993.

Willet, Cynthia. "The Master-Slave Dialectic: Hegel vs. Douglass." In *Subjugation and Bondage: Critical Essays on Slavery and Social Philosophy*, edited by Tommy L. Lott. New York: Rowman & Littlefield Publishers, 1998.

———. *Maternal Ethics and Other Slave Moralities*. New York: Routledge, 1995.

Williams, John Alfred. *The King God Didn't Save: Reflections on the Life and Death of Martin Luther King, Jr*. New York: Pocket, 1971.

Wingfield, Adia Harvey, and Joe R. Feagin. *Yes We Can?: White Racial Framing and the 2008 Presidential Campaign*. New York: Routledge, 2010.

Younge, Gary. "Obama and Black Americans: The Paradox of Hope." *The Nation*.

Zepp, Ira G. *The Social Vision of Martin Luther King, Jr*. Brooklyn: Carlson, 1977.

Zinn, Howard. *Disobedience and Democracy*. New York: Random House, 1968.

Index

About the Contributors

Benjamin O. Arah is assistant professor of philosophy and government at Bowie State University. He received his PhD in political science (political philosophy, 2001), and his Master of Distance Education from the University of Maryland in 2008. He teaches courses in political science, philosophy, and women's studies. Dr. Arah is currently working on a logic textbook with Kendall-Hunt Publisher.

Robert E. Birt is assistant professor of philosophy at Bowie State University, holding a PhD in philosophy from Vanderbilt University. He is contributor/editor of *The Quest for Community and Identity: Critical Essays in Africana Social Philosophy* (Rowman & Littlefield, 2002). His research interests include Africana philosophy, existentialism, phenomenology, critical theory, and philosophical anthropology. His articles have appeared in *International Philosophical Quarterly, Social Science Information, Philosophy East and West, Philosophy and Social Criticism, Quest: Journal of African Philosophy, Man and World, Continental Philosophy Review, APA Newsletter on Philosophy and the Black Experience, Radical Philosophy Review,* and in a number of anthologies.

Scott Davidson is associate professor and chair of the philosophy department of Oklahoma City University. He has written on a range of issues in contemporary French philosophy, and more recently, is coeditor of *Totality and Infinity at 50* (Duquesne University Press). He also serves as the editor for the *Journal of French and Francophone Philosophy*.

Maria del Guadalupe Davidson is assistant professor of African and African American studies at the University of Oklahoma. She does research in the area of black feminism. She is a coeditor of *Convergences: Black Feminism and Continental Philosophy* (SUNY Press, 2010). Her current project looks at the role of agency in the lives of young black women.

Clanton C. W. Dawson Jr. is associate professor of philosophy at Bethune-Cookman University in Daytona Beach, Florida. Dawson earned his Master of Divinity from Princeton University, and his MA and PhD in philosophy from the University of Missouri. He is author of several articles, the most recent being "Race as an Existential and Phenomenological Choice," in the *Bethune-Cookman Research Journal* (September 2011), and

"God, Hope and Suffering: An African-American Perspective," in *Testamentum Imperium* (Winter 2011–Spring 2012). Dr. Dawson is also coeditor of *An Introduction to Ethics*, published by Kendall-Hunt Publishers (2011).

Stephen C. Ferguson II is asssociate professor in liberal studies at North Carolina A&T University. His areas of expertise include Africana philosophy, Marxist philosophy, social-political philosophy, and philosophy of sports. He coedited the *Oxford Handbook on World Philosophy* (2011) and is coauthor of *Beyond the White Shadow: Philosophy, Sports and the African-American Experience* (forthcoming). Ferguson has also published articles in journals such as *Socialism and Democracy* and *Cultural Logic*.

Kathryn T. Gines, PhD, is assistant professor of philosophy at the Pennsylvania State University and founding director of the Collegium of Black Women Philosophers. Her primary research and teaching interests lie in continental philosophy, Africana philosophy, black feminist philosophy, and critical philosophy of race. Major figures in her scholarship include Hannah Arendt, Simone de Beauvoir, Jean-Paul Sartre, Frantz Fanon, Richard Wright, and Anna Julia Cooper. Gines has published articles on race and racism, postracialism, assimilation, gender, sexuality, black feminism, intersectionality, violence, and existentialism. Her publications have appeared in the *Journal of Social Philosophy*, *Hypatia*, *Philosophia Africana*, *Sartre Studies International*, and *Signs*. She is also coeditor of an anthology titled *Convergences: Black Feminism and Continental Philosophy* (SUNY Press, 2010).

James B. Haile III is McAnulty College Scholar-in-Residence at Duquesne University. He received his MA degree in philosophy from University of Memphis. His research interests are in African American philosophy, philosophy and literature, and twentieth-century continental philosophy. Haile has also published articles in these areas. He has recently edited a collection on Richard Wright and philosophy.

Floyd W. Hayes III is senior lecturer in the Department of Political Science and coordinator of Programs and Undergraduate Studies in the Center for Africana Studies at Johns Hopkins University. He is author of numerous scholarly articles and book chapters in areas of Africana political philosophy, politics, and public policy. Presently, Hayes is working on a book titled *Domination and Ressentiment: The Desperate Vision of Richard Wright*.

Richard A. Jones is author of *African-American Sociopolitical Philosophy: Imagining Black Communities* (2004). He has published articles in *Teaching Philosophy*, *Wagadu*, *Journal of Black Studies*, and *Radical Philosophy Review*. Jones has taught philosophy at Howard University since 2001. His research interests include racial dialectics, critical race theory, and twentieth-century analytic philosophy. He is former cocoordinator of the Radical Philosophy Association.

Tim Lake completed his PhD at Bowling Green State University (Ohio) in American culture studies with a concentration in political philosophy. He is currently an associate professor at Wabash College in Indiana. He recently published "Speaking of Africa and Singing of Home: The Trope of Africa in African-American Historiography," in *Africana Cultures and Policy Studies: Scholarship and the Transformation of Public Policy*, edited by Zachary Williams (Palgrave Macmillan, 2009). Lake's book *Love and Democracy: The Political Philosophies of Martin Luther King, Jr. and Cornel West* is currently under review with the University of Notre Dame Press. Lake is a former fellow with the King Papers Project at Stanford University.

Bill E. Lawson is distinguished professor of philosophy at the University of Memphis, where he teaches courses in areas of African American philosophy and social and political philosophy. He has published articles on Frederick Douglass, the urban underclass, environmental ethics, and jazz. He also testified before a Congressional subcommittee on the issue of welfare reform. He was 2011–2012 University of Liverpool Fulbright Fellow at the University of Liverpool, UK.

John H. McClendon III is professor in the Department of Philosophy at Michigan State University. He holds a Bachelor's degree in black studies and political science from Central State University (Ohio), and an MA and PhD in philosophy from the University of Kansas. McClendon previously published an article on Dr. King titled "A Time to Break Silence on Dr. King's Final Mission and Message: A Conspectus on Dr. King, Du Bois, and West." He is also author of *C. L. R. James' Notes on Dialectics: Left Hegelianism or Marxism-Leninism?* (Lexington Books, 2005). McClendon is also working on a manuscript, *Conversations with My Christian Friends*, which focuses on African American religious beliefs from the standpoint of philosophy of religion.

Greg Moses is author of *Revolution of Conscience: Martin Luther King, Jr. and the Philosophy of Nonviolence* (Guilford, 1997). He lives in Austin, Texas, where he teaches courses in philosophy and general education. His professional publications include work on King's philosophy, race and racism, and studies in the work of Alain L. Locke. Dr. Moses is currently exploring the work of J. L Farmer as an historical framework for the philosophical legacy of nonviolence during the Civil Rights era. He is also editor of the *Concerned Philosophers for Peace Newsletter*.

Gail M. Presbey is professor of philosophy at University of Detroit Mercy. Her areas of expertise are social and political philosophy as well as philosophy of nonviolence and African philosophy. Presbey has done research in Kenya, South Africa, Ghana, and India. She was J. William Fulbright Senior Scholar at University of Nairobi, Kenya, from 1998 to 2000. In 2005 Presbey went to India for six months for a research project sponsored by Fulbright on *ahisma* (nonviolence) from Gandhi's perspective. She has coedited a textbook, *The Philosophical Quest: A Cross-Cultural Reader*, an anthology, *Thought and Practice in African Philosophy*, and edited *Philosophical Perspectives on the "War on Terrorism."* Presbey has over forty articles and book chapters published. Her articles appear in *International Philosophical Quarterly*, *Journal of Value Inquiry*, *Human Studies*, *Constellations*, *Research in African Literatures*, and *Philosophy and Social Criticism*. She also has a long-standing involvement in peace and justice studies. Presbey has been executive director (five years) and president (two years) of Concerned Philosophers for Peace.

Maurice St. Pierre is professor and chair of the Department of Sociology and Anthropology at Morgan State University. His current research interests concern social epistemology, especially the manner in which collective actions such as social movements tend to produce "new" knowledge. Among his various publications is the book *Anatomy of Resistance: Anti-Colonialism in Guyana 1823–1966*, a study of the political independence struggle in that country.

George Yancy, associate professor in the Department of Philosophy at Duquesne University, received his PhD in philosophy from Duquesne University, and his MA degree in philosophy from Yale University. He received his second MA degree from New York University in Africana studies. He is author of *Black Bodies, White Gazes: The Continuing Significance of Race* (Rowman & Littlefield, 2008), which received an Honorable Mention from the Gustavus Myers Center for the Study of Bigotry and Human Rights. He has also authored *Look, a White! Philosophical Essays on Whiteness* (Temple University Press, 2012). Yancy has also edited twelve influential books, three of which have received *Choice* awards. He is currently working on several edited books and an authored book exploring a panoply of cultural themes.